TUBBY NUGGET'S
TEARABLE BOOK

THIS PAGE INTENTIONALLY NOT LEFT BLANK; OTHERWISE, THIS SENTENCE WOULDN'T BE HERE.

TUBBY NUGGET'S TEARABLE BOOK

COMICS, COMPLIMENTS, AND CHEER TO TEAR AND SHARE WITH YOUR LOVED ONES

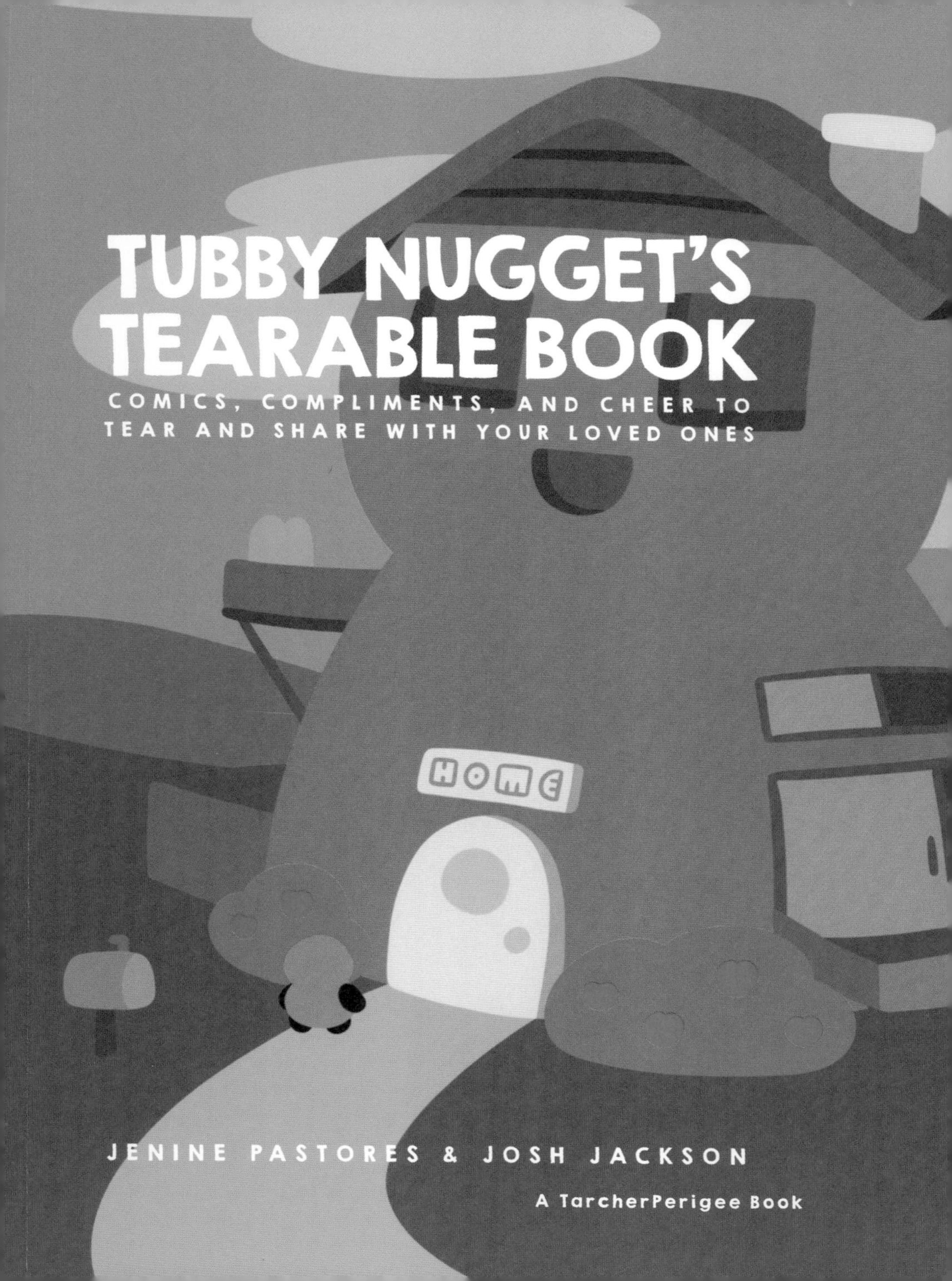
HOME

JENINE PASTORES & JOSH JACKSON

A TarcherPerigee Book

tarcherperigee

an imprint of Penguin Random House LLC
penguinrandomhouse.com

TarcherPerigee with tp colophon is a registered trademark of Penguin Random House LLC

Most TarcherPerigee books are available at special quantity discounts for bulk pur-
chase for sales promotions, premiums, fundraising, and educational needs. Special
books or book excerpts also can be created to fit specific needs. For details, write:
SpecialMarkets@penguinrandomhouse.com.

Trade Paperback ISBN: 9780593716922
Library of Congress Control Number: 2023949978

Printed in China
1 3 5 7 9 10 8 6 4 2

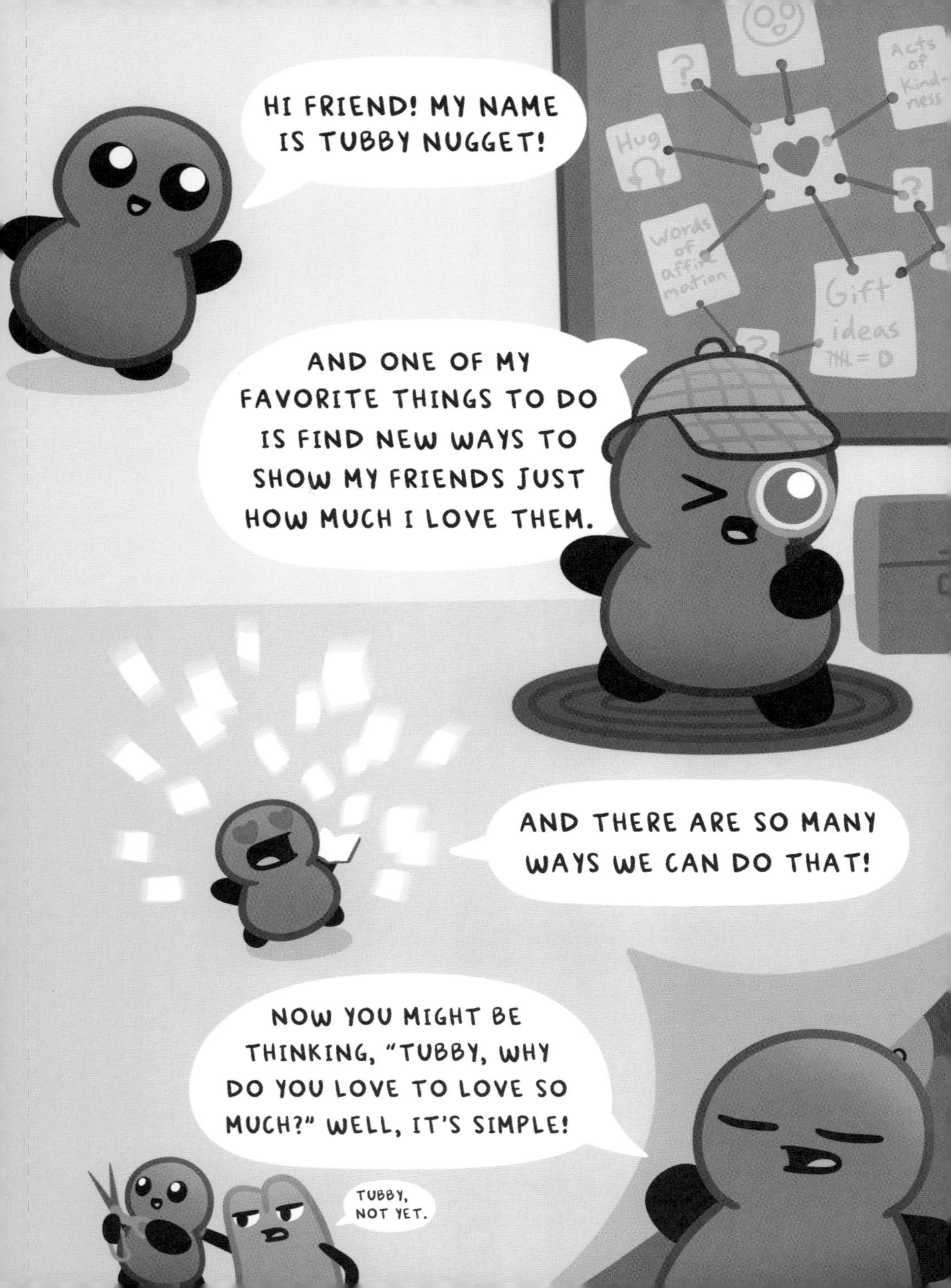

HI FRIEND! MY NAME IS TUBBY NUGGET!
Acts of Kind-ness
Hug
Gift ideas
AND ONE OF MY FAVORITE THINGS TO DO IS FIND NEW WAYS TO SHOW MY FRIENDS JUST HOW MUCH I LOVE THEM.
AND THERE ARE SO MANY WAYS WE CAN DO THAT!
NOW YOU MIGHT BE THINKING, "TUBBY, WHY DO YOU LOVE TO LOVE SO MUCH?" WELL, IT'S SIMPLE!
TUBBY, NOT YET.

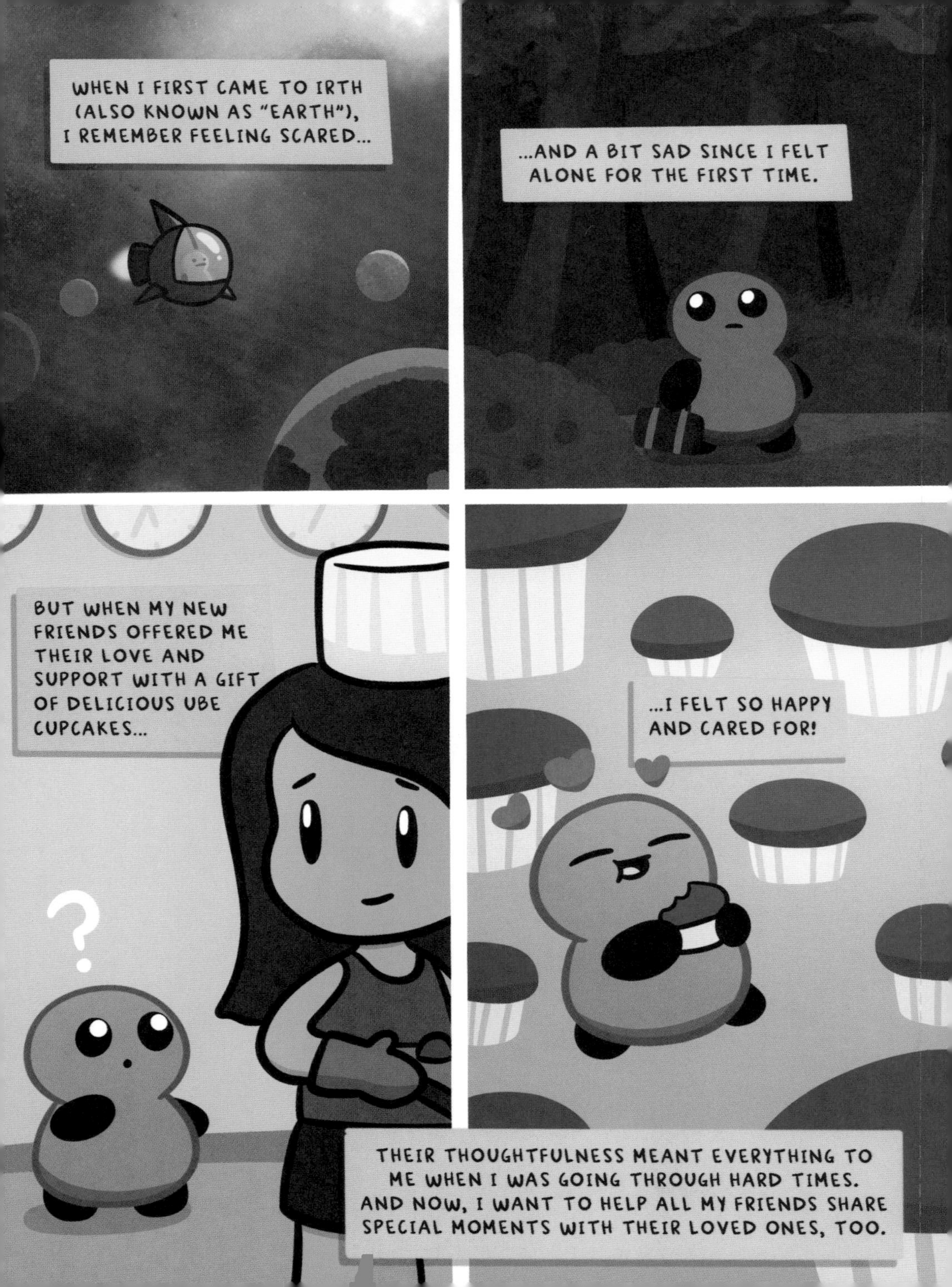
WHEN I FIRST CAME TO IRTH (ALSO KNOWN AS "EARTH"), I REMEMBER FEELING SCARED...
...AND A BIT SAD SINCE I FELT ALONE FOR THE FIRST TIME.
BUT WHEN MY NEW FRIENDS OFFERED ME THEIR LOVE AND SUPPORT WITH A GIFT OF DELICIOUS UBE CUPCAKES...
?
...I FELT SO HAPPY AND CARED FOR!
THEIR THOUGHTFULNESS MEANT EVERYTHING TO ME WHEN I WAS GOING THROUGH HARD TIMES. AND NOW, I WANT TO HELP ALL MY FRIENDS SHARE SPECIAL MOMENTS WITH THEIR LOVED ONES, TOO.

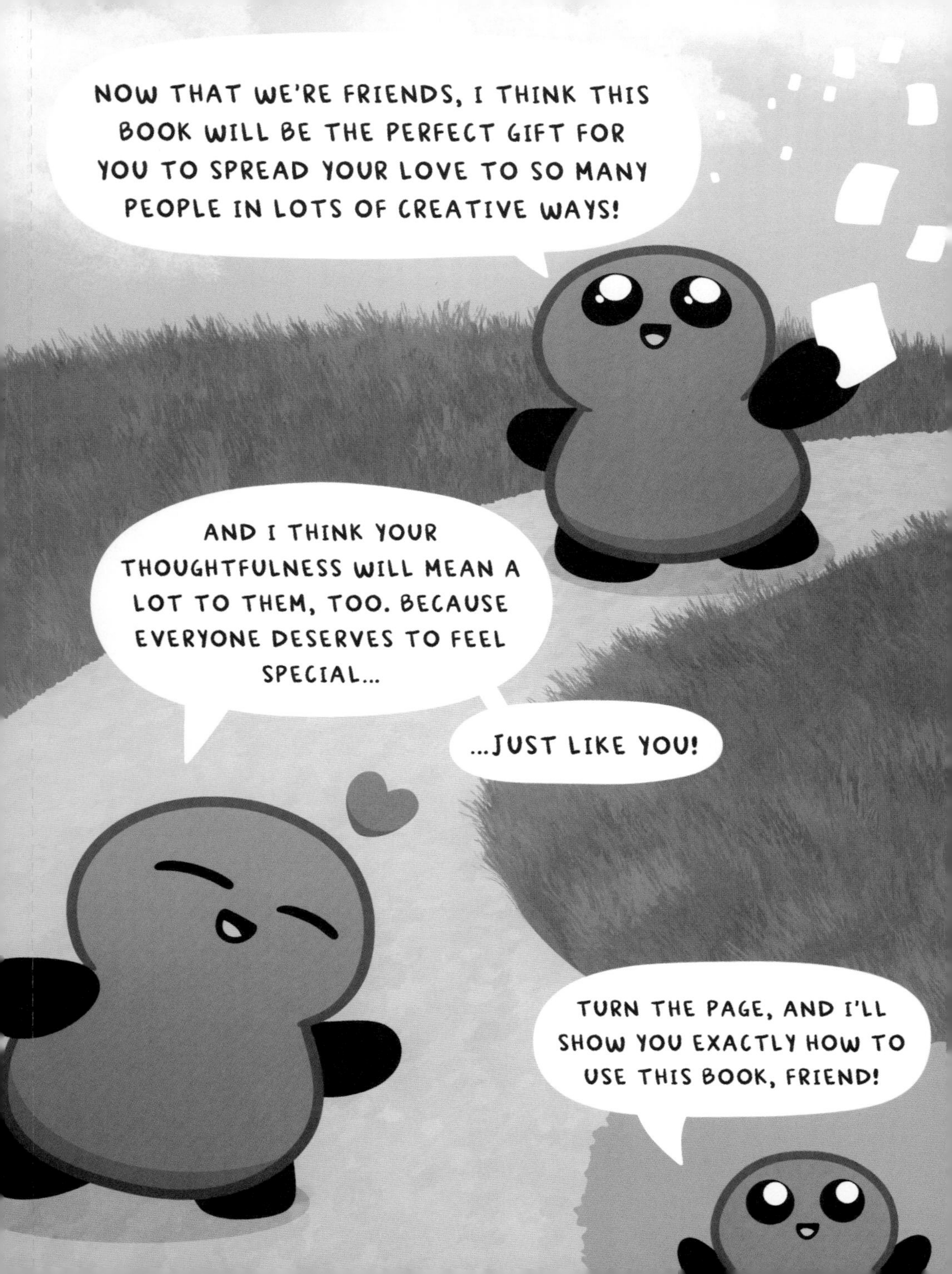
NOW THAT WE'RE FRIENDS, I THINK THIS BOOK WILL BE THE PERFECT GIFT FOR YOU TO SPREAD YOUR LOVE TO SO MANY PEOPLE IN LOTS OF CREATIVE WAYS!
AND I THINK YOUR THOUGHTFULNESS WILL MEAN A LOT TO THEM, TOO. BECAUSE EVERYONE DESERVES TO FEEL SPECIAL...
...JUST LIKE YOU!
TURN THE PAGE, AND I'LL SHOW YOU EXACTLY HOW TO USE THIS BOOK, FRIEND!

Here's what makes this special book even **MORE** special —

every page of it can be torn out and given to someone you love!

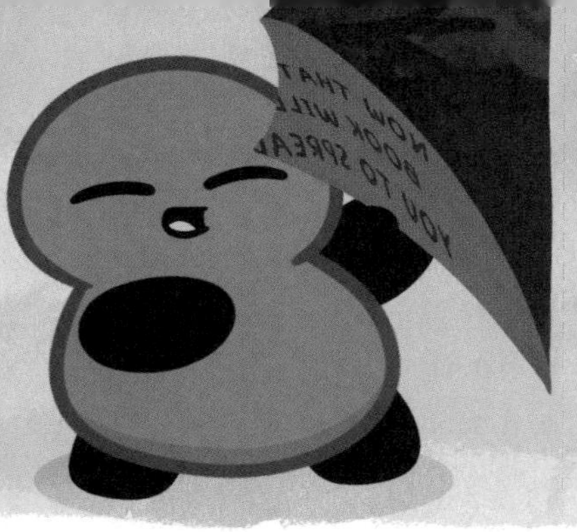

...well, most of the pages. Maybe not these next couple pages. These are instruction pages. Probably not something you'd wanna give away, but, hey. To each their own!

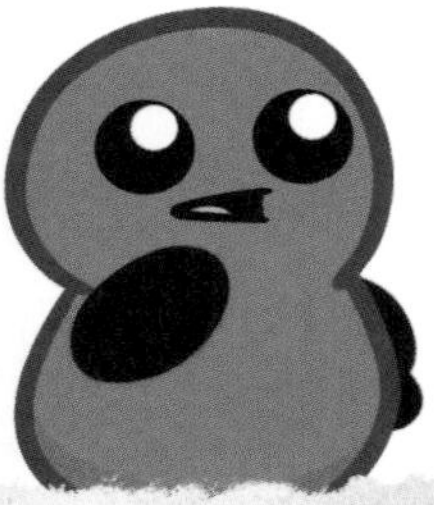

I've actually made it so some of the pages can be folded in special ways before you pass them off to your loved one!

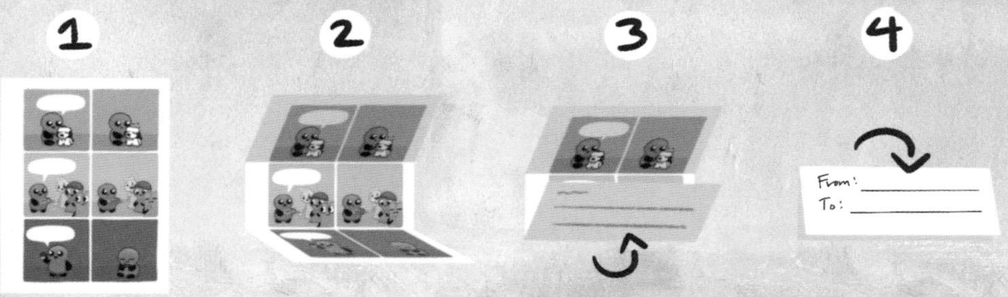
1
2
3
4
From:
To:

See here? This page has an area where you can write a personal message!

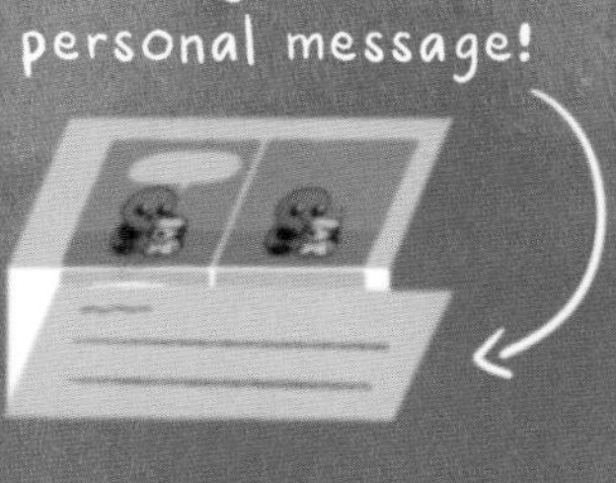

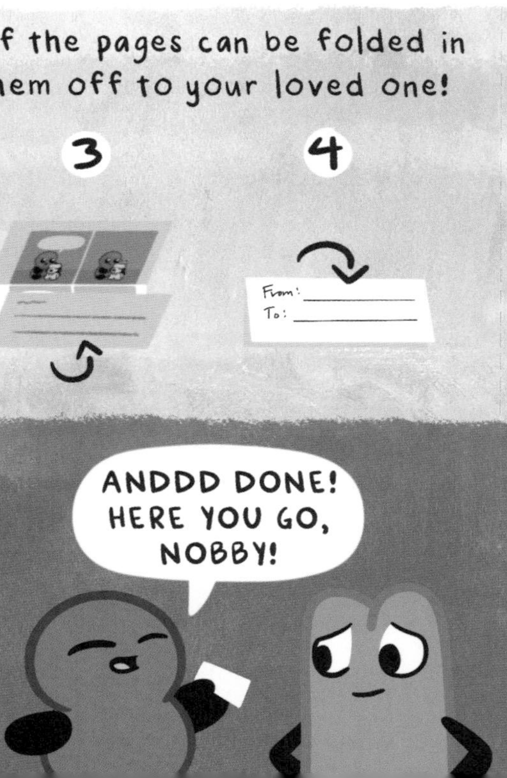
ANDDD DONE! HERE YOU GO, NOBBY!

Here are a couple of helpful icons you'll also see while perusing this book!

FOLD — this icon will be accompanied with a line and indicates where you should fold the page! If there are multiple fold icons, you can check the number on the icon to see what order each fold should be made in.

CUT — this icon will be accompanied with a dotted line. Simply grab a pair of scissors, and cut along the line!

Looks like our nugget friends left some secret symbols on certain pages of this book, too! Can you find them all? They might come in handy later!

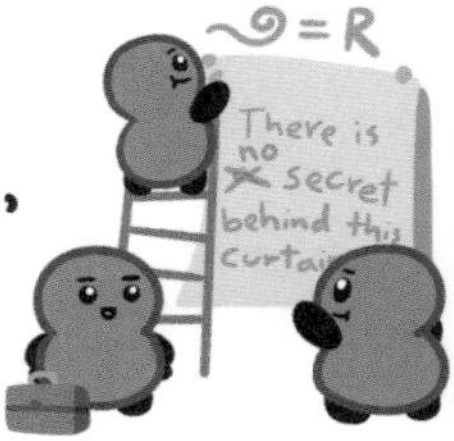
There is
no
secret
behind this

If you need more help, or even more detailed instructions, I've made some nifty tutorials right here for you, friend!

Go to tubbynuggetbook.com for more help (and a silly message from me)!

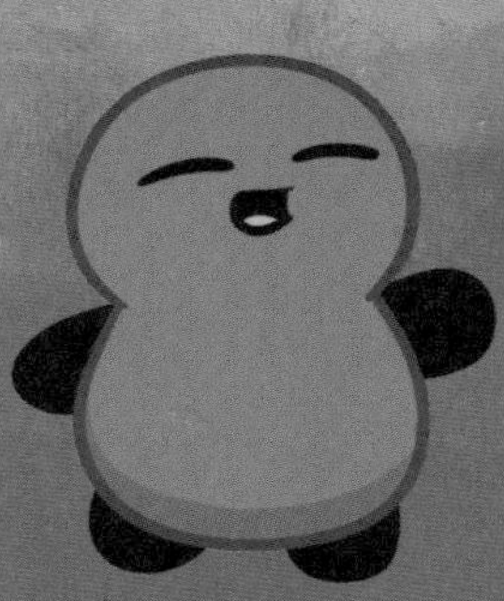

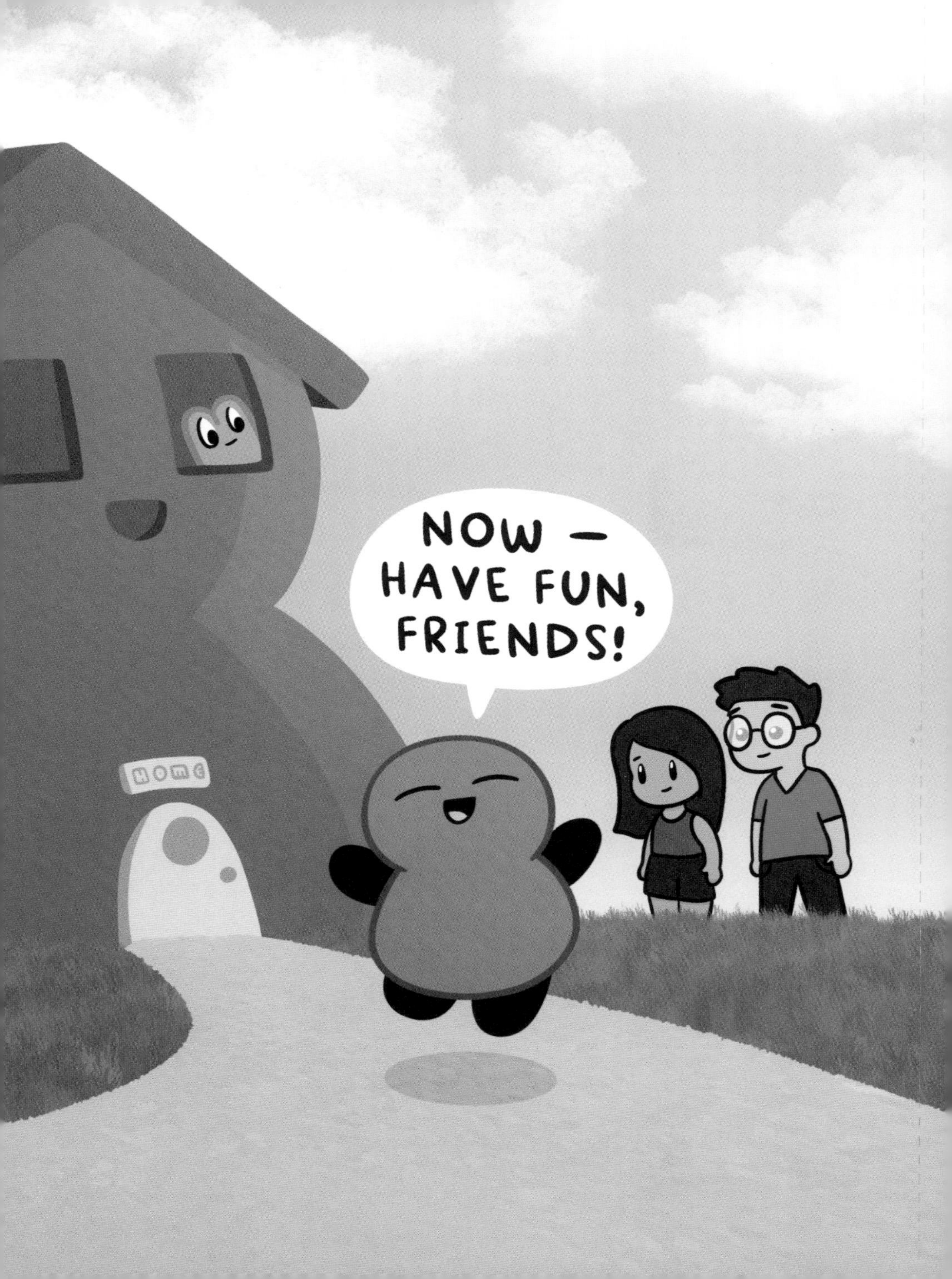
NOW — HAVE FUN, FRIENDS!
HOME

TUBBY-MADE PAGES

Sometimes, we don't always have
the words to tell someone exactly
how we feel. And if that's the
case — Tubby's got your back!

I made you lots of
pages that are already filled with
some of my favorite things.
Things that I think your friends and
family would love to see, too!

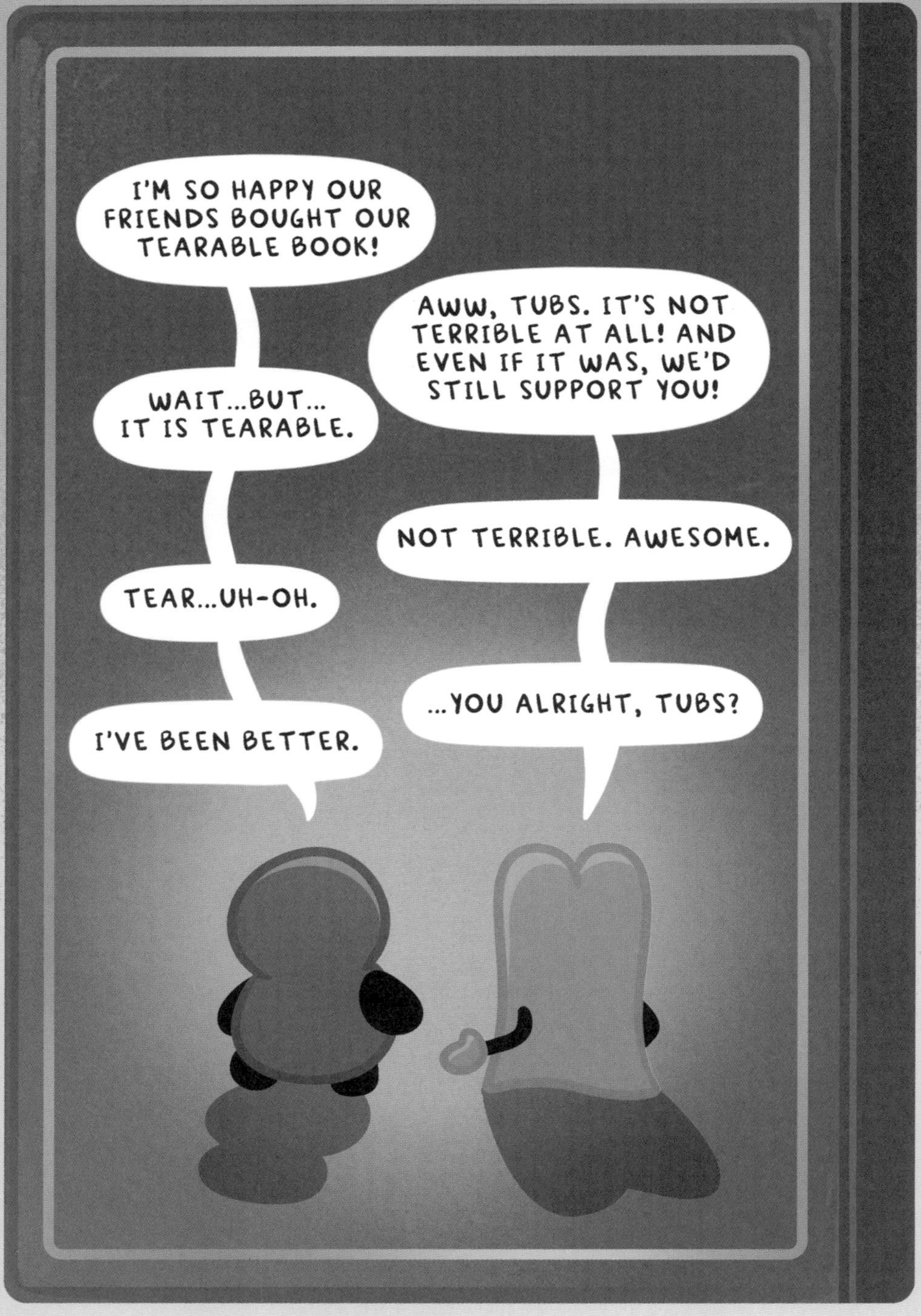
I'M SO HAPPY OUR FRIENDS BOUGHT OUR TEARABLE BOOK!
AWW, TUBS. IT'S NOT TERRIBLE AT ALL! AND EVEN IF IT WAS, WE'D STILL SUPPORT YOU!
WAIT...BUT... IT IS TEARABLE.
NOT TERRIBLE. AWESOME.
TEAR...UH-OH.
...YOU ALRIGHT, TUBS?
I'VE BEEN BETTER.

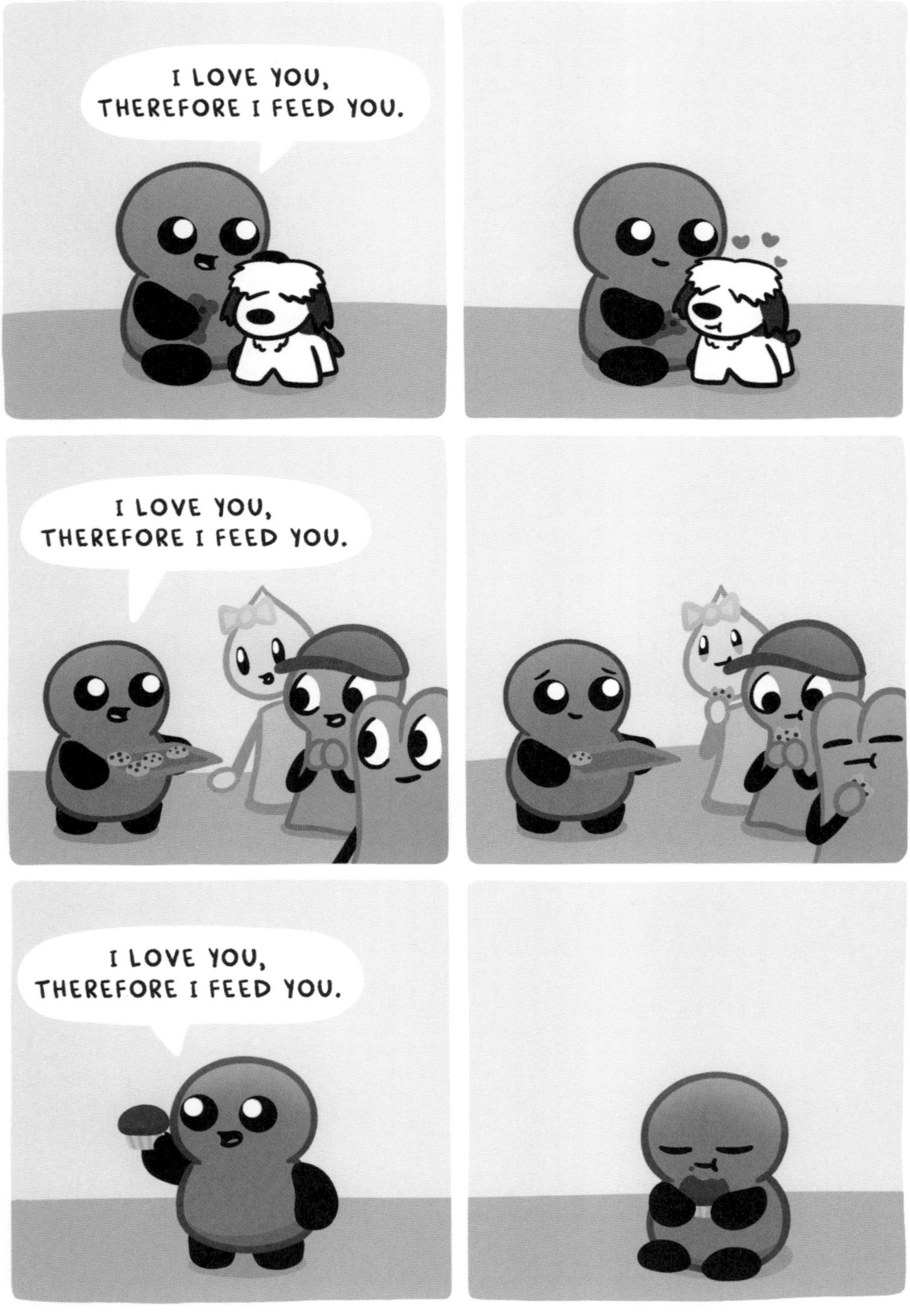
I LOVE YOU, THEREFORE I FEED YOU.
I LOVE YOU, THEREFORE I FEED YOU.
I LOVE YOU, THEREFORE I FEED YOU.

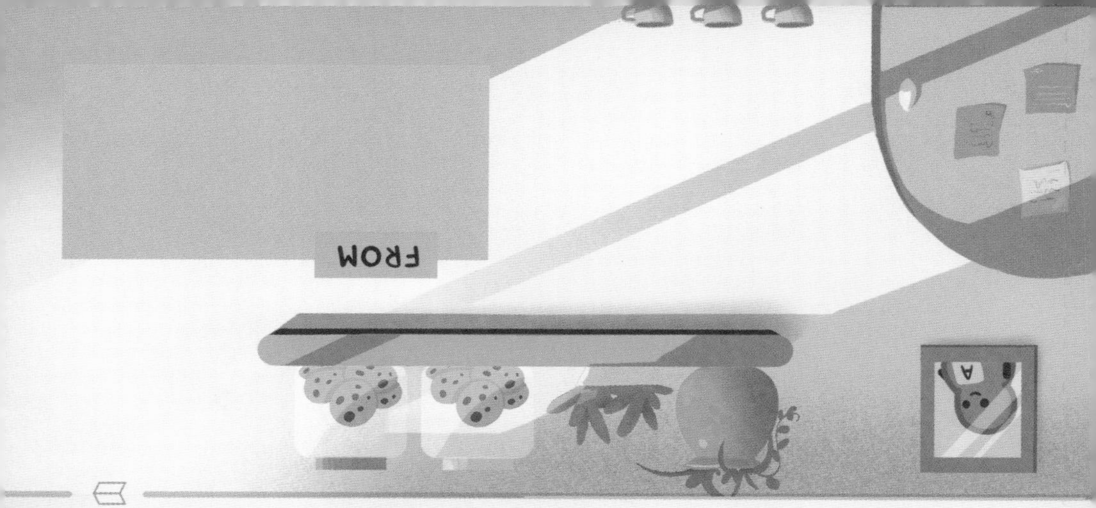
FROM

I LOVE YOU, THEREFORE

I FEED YOU!

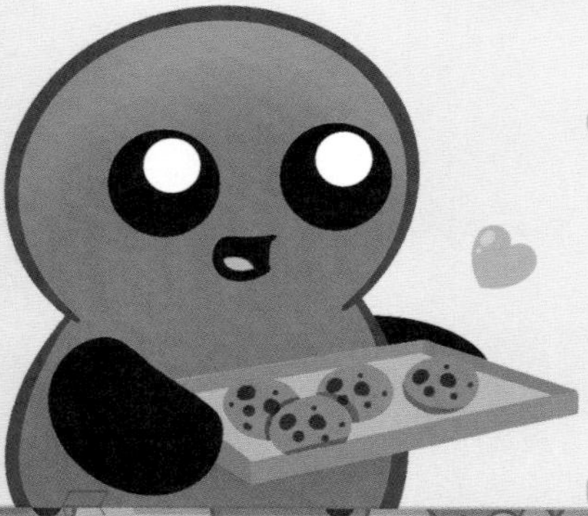

TO

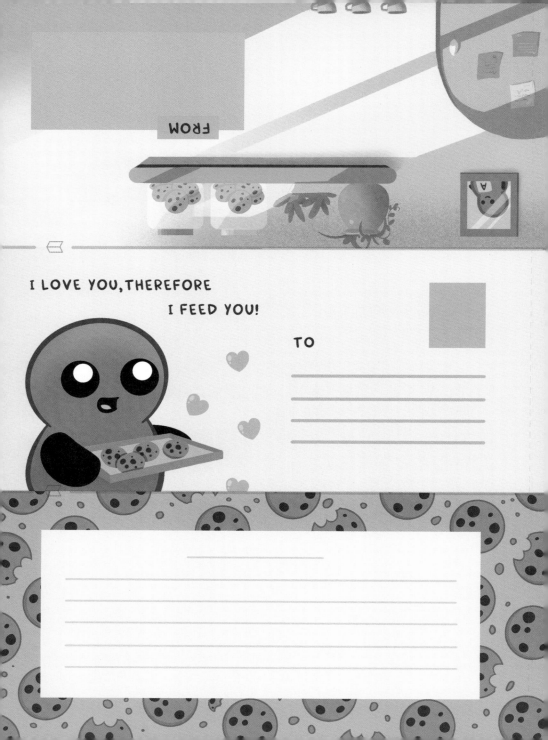

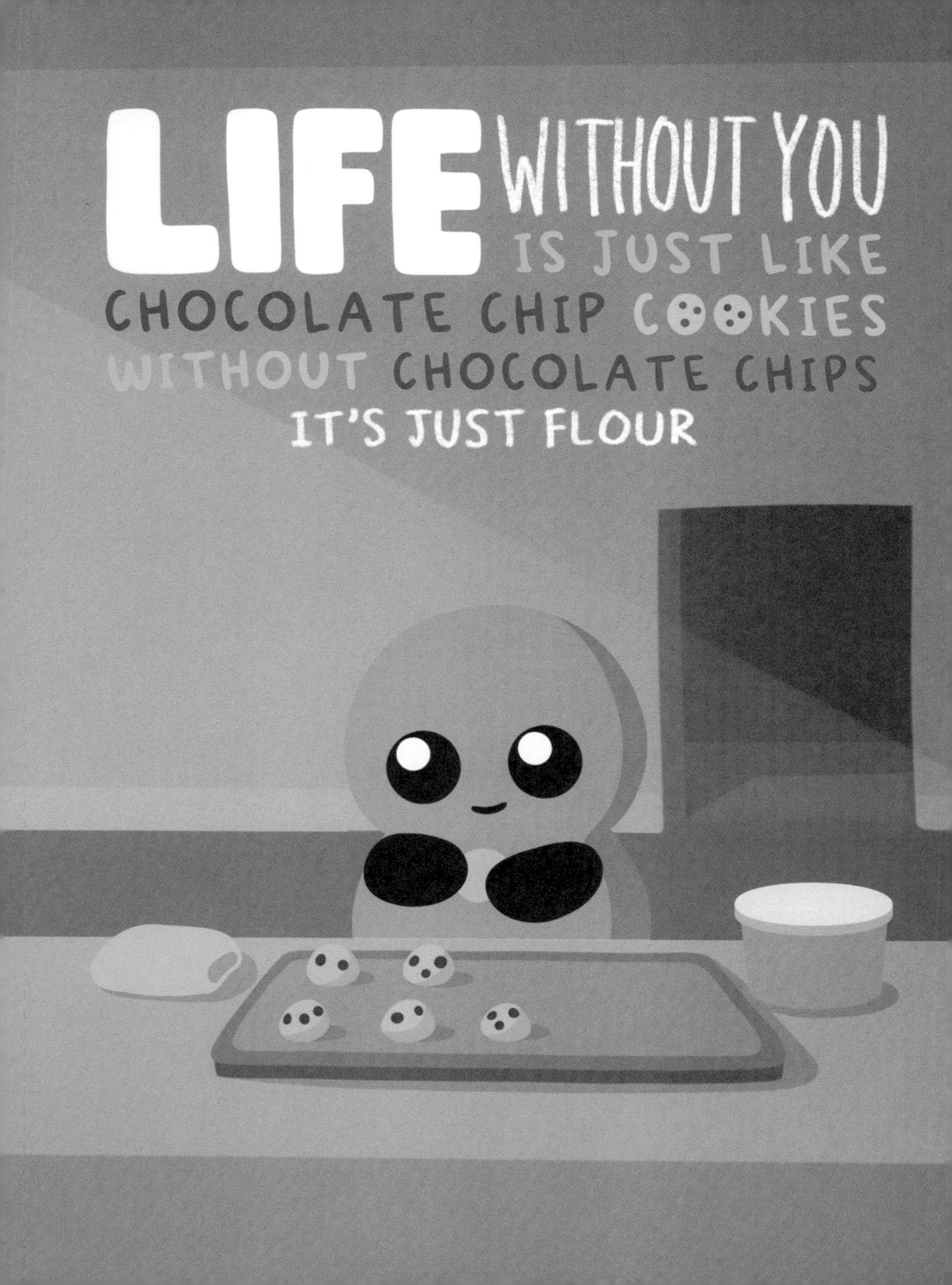
LIFE WITHOUT YOU
IS JUST LIKE
CHOCOLATE CHIP COOKIES
WITHOUT CHOCOLATE CHIPS
IT'S JUST FLOUR

LIFE WITHOUT YOU IS JUST LIKE...

________ WITHOUT ________

________ WITHOUT ________

________ WITHOUT ________

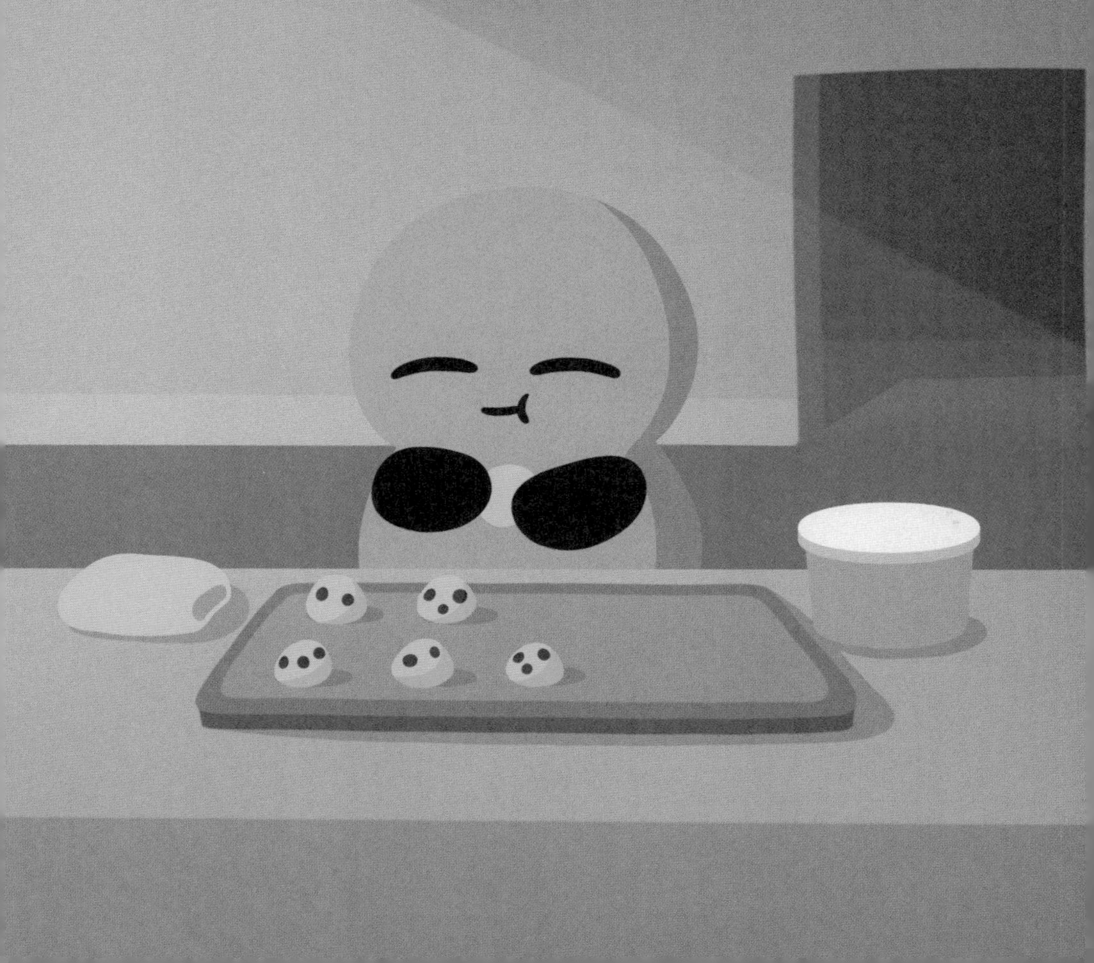

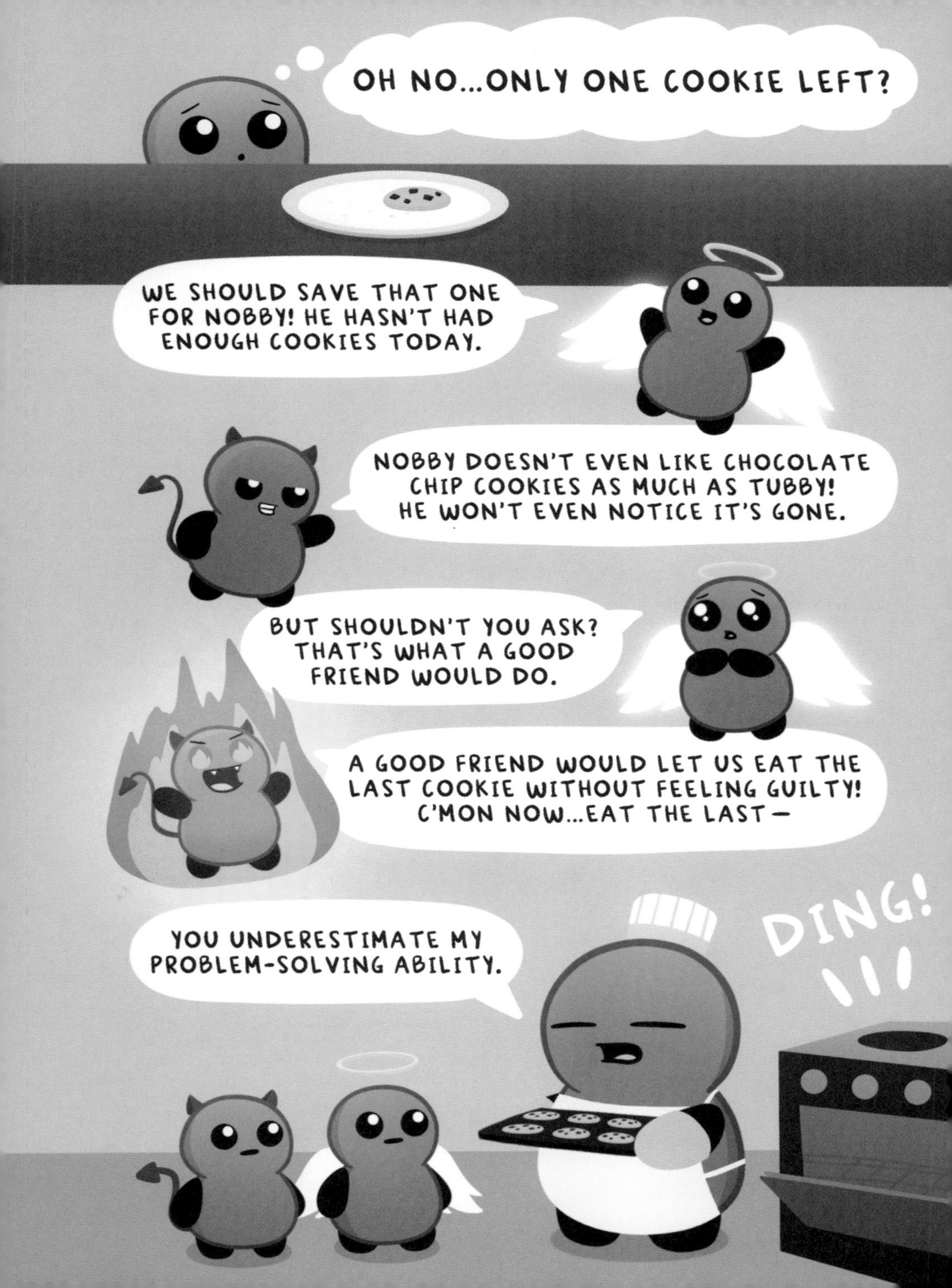
OH NO...ONLY ONE COOKIE LEFT?
WE SHOULD SAVE THAT ONE FOR NOBBY! HE HASN'T HAD ENOUGH COOKIES TODAY.
NOBBY DOESN'T EVEN LIKE CHOCOLATE CHIP COOKIES AS MUCH AS TUBBY! HE WON'T EVEN NOTICE IT'S GONE.
BUT SHOULDN'T YOU ASK? THAT'S WHAT A GOOD FRIEND WOULD DO.
A GOOD FRIEND WOULD LET US EAT THE LAST COOKIE WITHOUT FEELING GUILTY! C'MON NOW...EAT THE LAST—
YOU UNDERESTIMATE MY PROBLEM-SOLVING ABILITY.
DING!

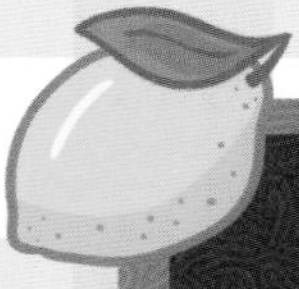

GRANDPA BO'S LEMON CREAM COOKIES!

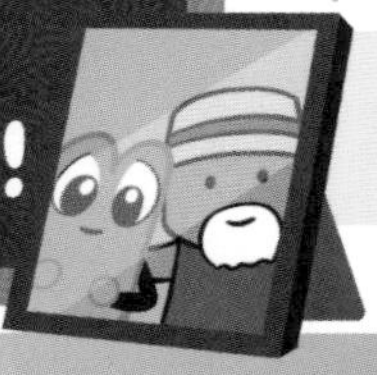

NOBBY'S GRANDPA BO USED TO MAKE HIM THESE DELICIOUS LEMON CREAM COOKIES WHENEVER HE WAS FEELING SAD. SO, WE WANTED TO SHARE THAT RECIPE WITH YOU TO ENJOY NOW, TOO!

INGREDIENTS:

2 CUPS OF ALL-PURPOSE FLOUR
1 TSP OF BAKING POWDER
8 TBSP OF SOFTENED BUTTER
1/2 BLOCK (4 OUNCES) OF CREAM CHEESE
1 CUP OF GRANULATED SUGAR
ZEST AND JUICE OF 2 LEMONS
1 EGG
1 TBSP OF PURE LEMON EXTRACT
1 TBSP OF VANILLA EXTRACT
1 CUP OF CONFECTIONERS' SUGAR

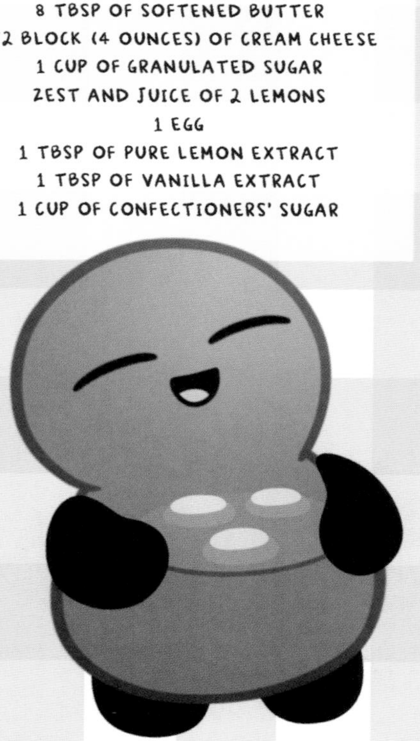

DIRECTIONS:

1. SIFT THE FLOUR AND BAKING POWDER INTO A BOWL.
2. IN A SEPARATE BOWL, CREAM THE BUTTER USING A SPATULA OR WHISK.
3. ONCE THE BUTTER IS CREAMED, MIX IN THE CREAM CHEESE.
4. ADD THE GRANULATED SUGAR AND STIR WELL.
5. WHEN THE MIXTURE IS SMOOTH, ADD 1 TBSP OF THE LEMON ZEST AND YOUR EGG, AND STIR TO COMBINE.
6. COMBINE THE FLOUR AND BAKING POWDER WITH THE BUTTERY MIXTURE.
7. ADD 2 TBSP OF THE LEMON JUICE, THE LEMON EXTRACT, AND THE VANILLA TO THE BOWL, THEN MIX UNTIL YOU HAVE A CREAMY TEXTURE. POP THE BATTER INTO THE FRIDGE FOR 20–60 MINUTES.
8. PREHEAT THE OVEN TO 350 DEGREES FAHRENHEIT.
9. REMOVE THE DOUGH FROM THE FRIDGE. COVER YOUR HANDS IN FLOUR, AND ROLL THE DOUGH INTO LITTLE BALLS.
10. POUR THE CONFECTIONERS' SUGAR INTO A BOWL, AND DIP THE BOTTOM OF A WET GLASS INTO THE SUGAR. USE THE GLASS TO FLATTEN THE BALLS OF DOUGH INTO COOKIES, AND PLACE THEM ON A TRAY LINED WITH OVEN-SAFE PARCHMENT PAPER.
11. BAKE FOR 10–12 MINUTES. REMOVE FROM THE OVEN AND ALLOW TO COOL ON A WIRE RACK BEFORE ICING.
12. FOR THE ICING: POUR THE REMAINING 3 TBSP FRESH LEMON JUICE AND 2 TBSP LEMON ZEST INTO THE BOWL OF CONFECTIONERS' SUGAR, AND STIR.
13. DRIZZLE 1 TSP OF ICING OVER EACH COOKIE, AND ENJOY!

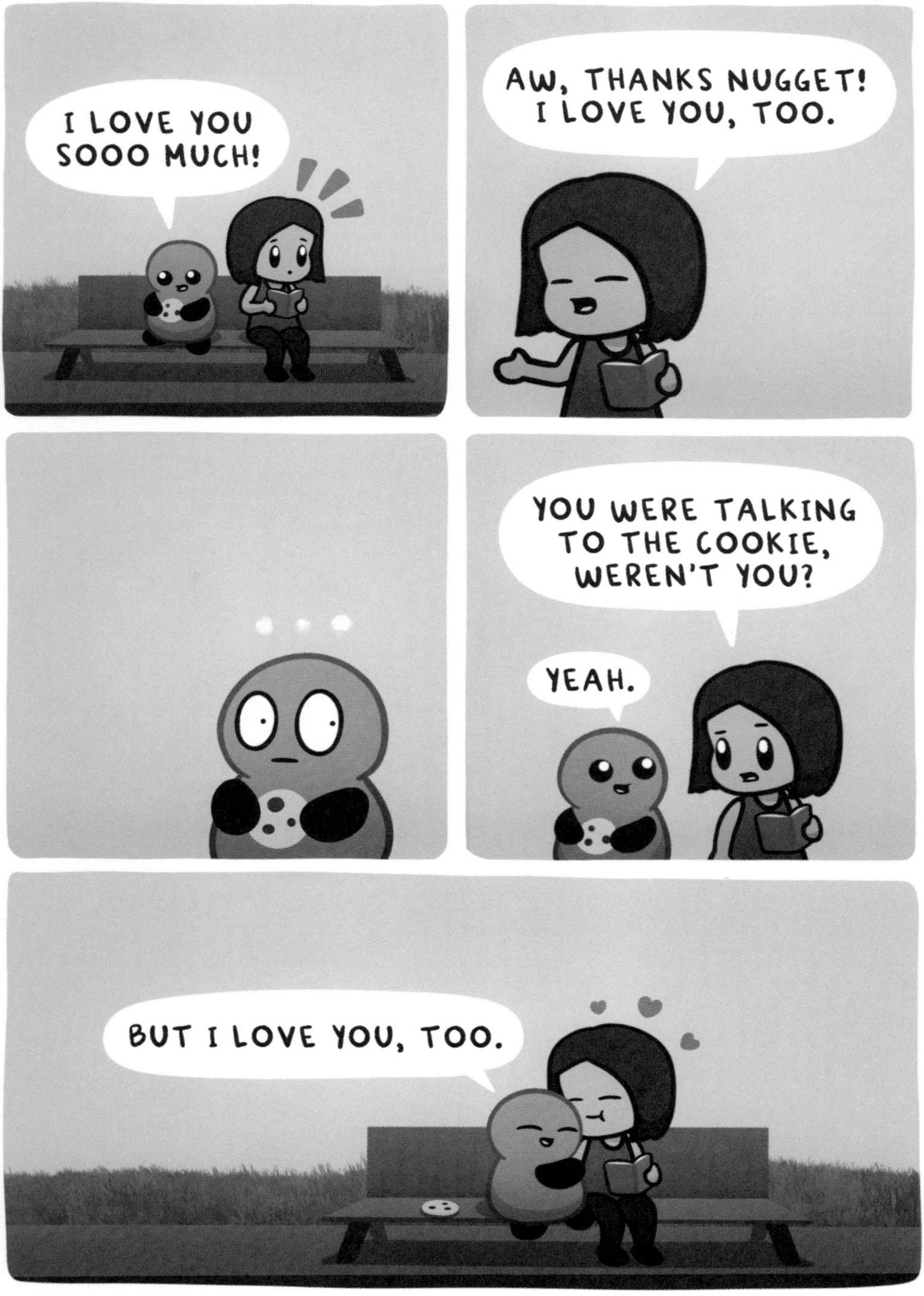
I LOVE YOU SOOO MUCH!
AW, THANKS NUGGET! I LOVE YOU, TOO.
YOU WERE TALKING TO THE COOKIE, WEREN'T YOU?
YEAH.
BUT I LOVE YOU, TOO.

TO

FROM

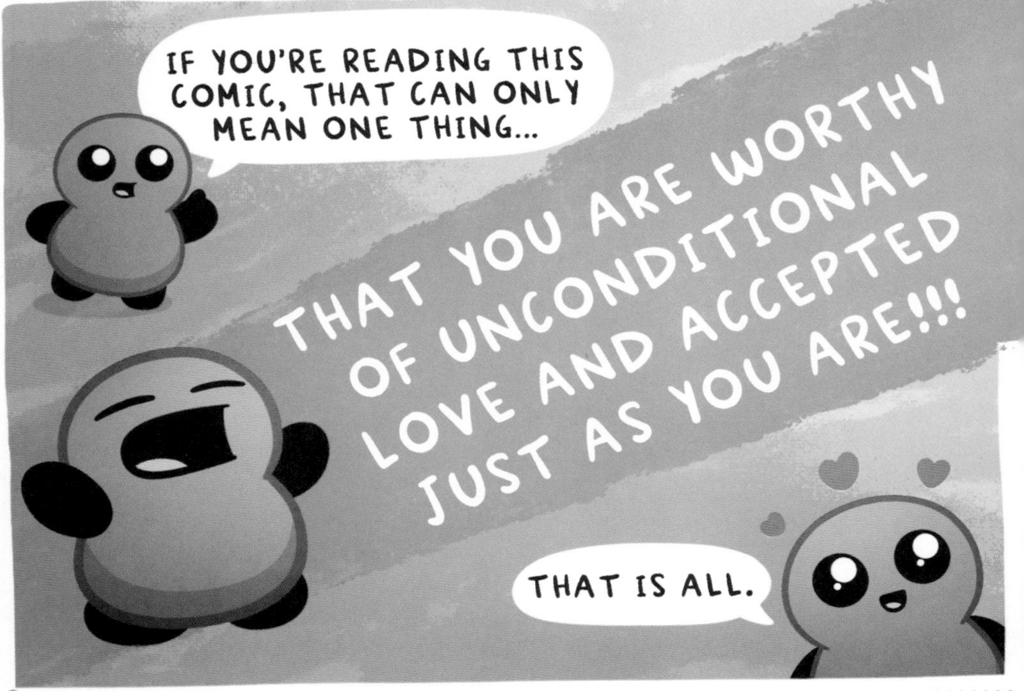
IF YOU'RE READING THIS COMIC, THAT CAN ONLY MEAN ONE THING...
THAT YOU ARE WORTHY OF UNCONDITIONAL LOVE AND ACCEPTED JUST AS YOU ARE!!!
THAT IS ALL.

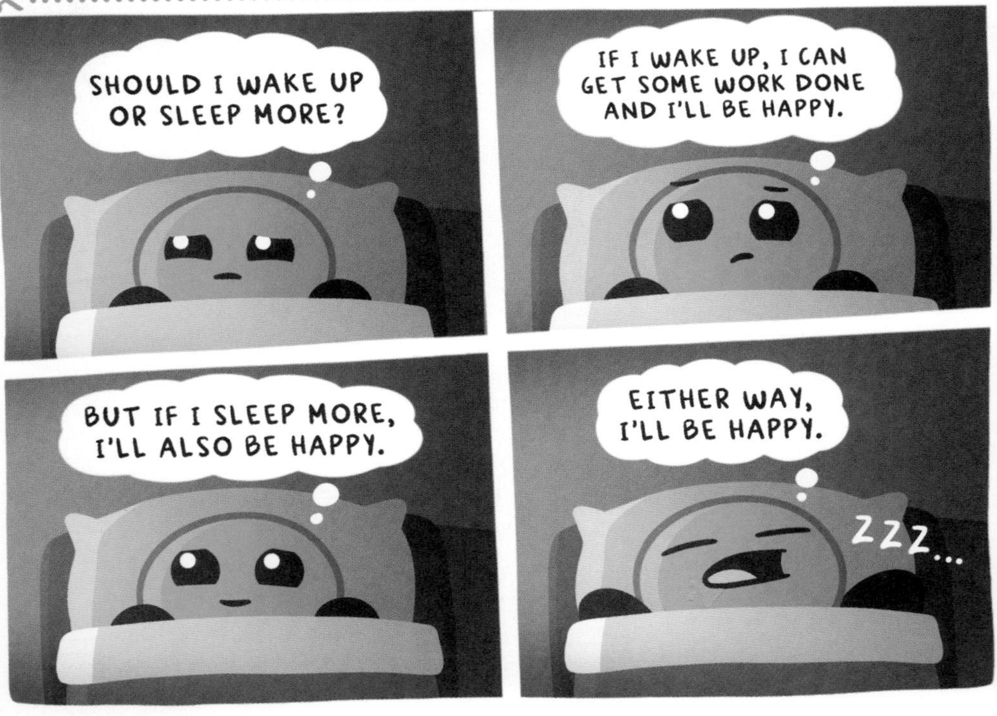
SHOULD I WAKE UP OR SLEEP MORE?
IF I WAKE UP, I CAN GET SOME WORK DONE AND I'LL BE HAPPY.
BUT IF I SLEEP MORE, I'LL ALSO BE HAPPY.
EITHER WAY, I'LL BE HAPPY.
ZZZ...

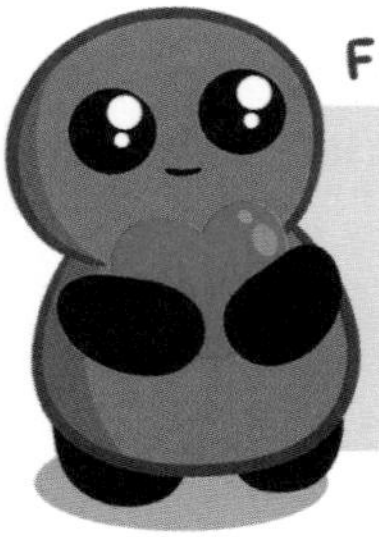

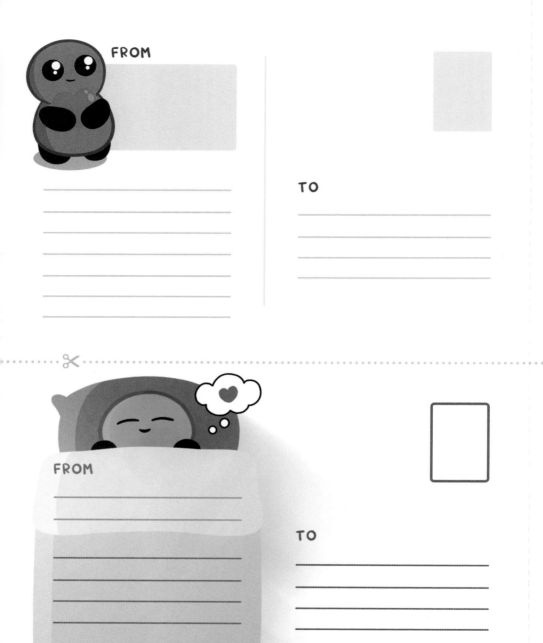

FROM

TO

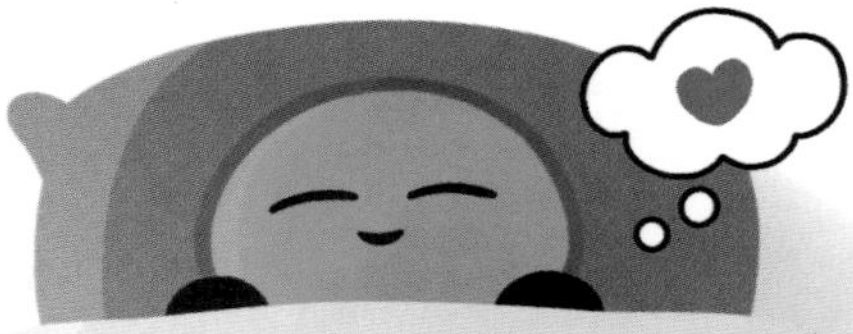

FROM

TO

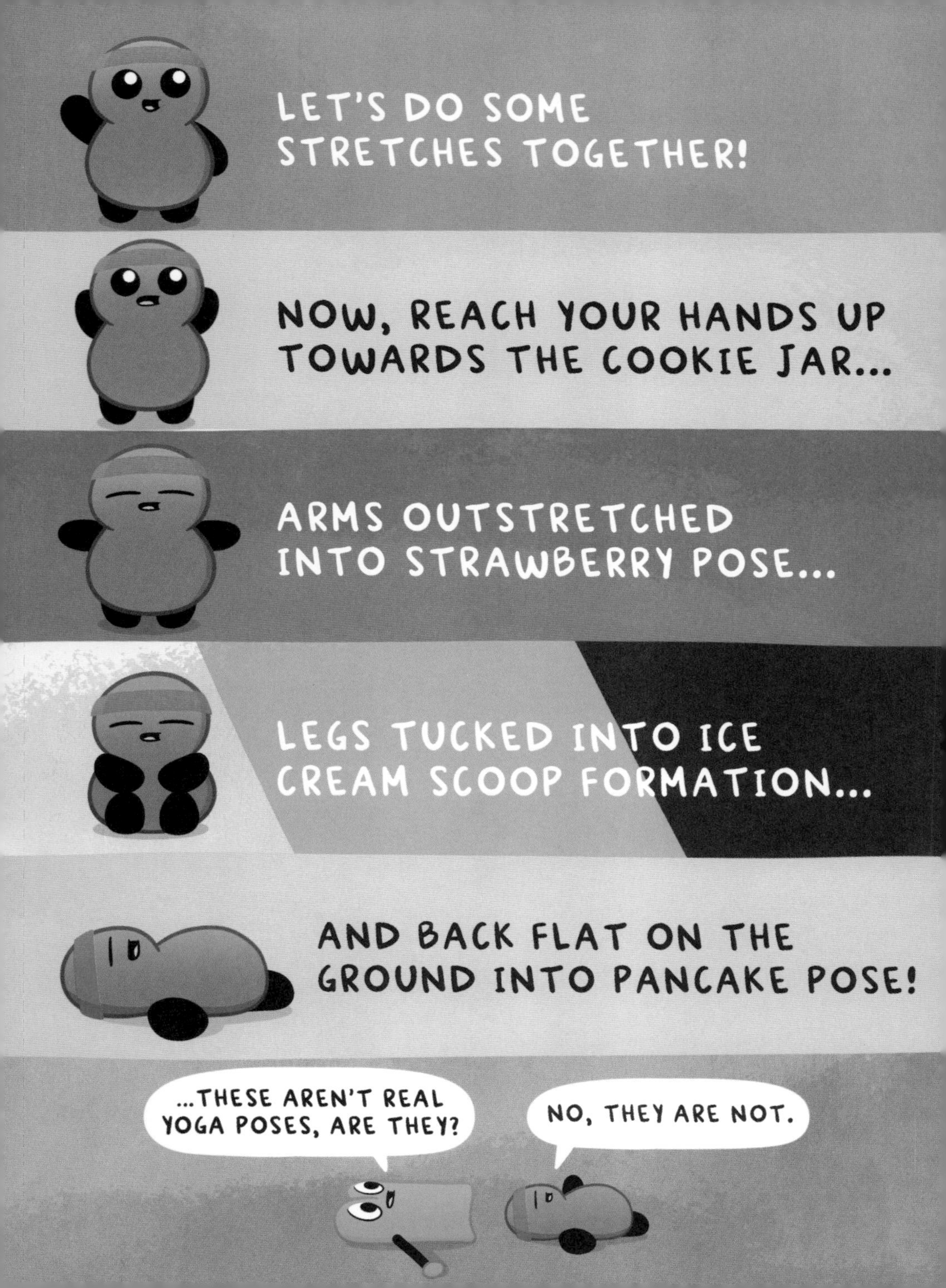
LET'S DO SOME STRETCHES TOGETHER!
NOW, REACH YOUR HANDS UP TOWARDS THE COOKIE JAR...
ARMS OUTSTRETCHED INTO STRAWBERRY POSE...
LEGS TUCKED INTO ICE CREAM SCOOP FORMATION...
AND BACK FLAT ON THE GROUND INTO PANCAKE POSE!
...THESE AREN'T REAL YOGA POSES, ARE THEY?
NO, THEY ARE NOT.

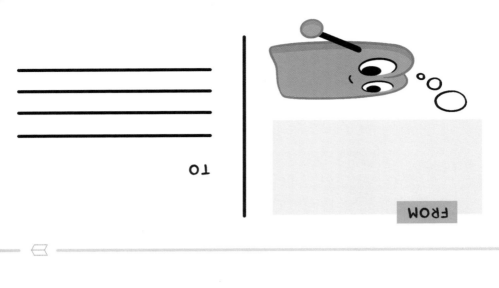

TO

FROM

REMEMBER TO STRETCH
AND HYDRATE!

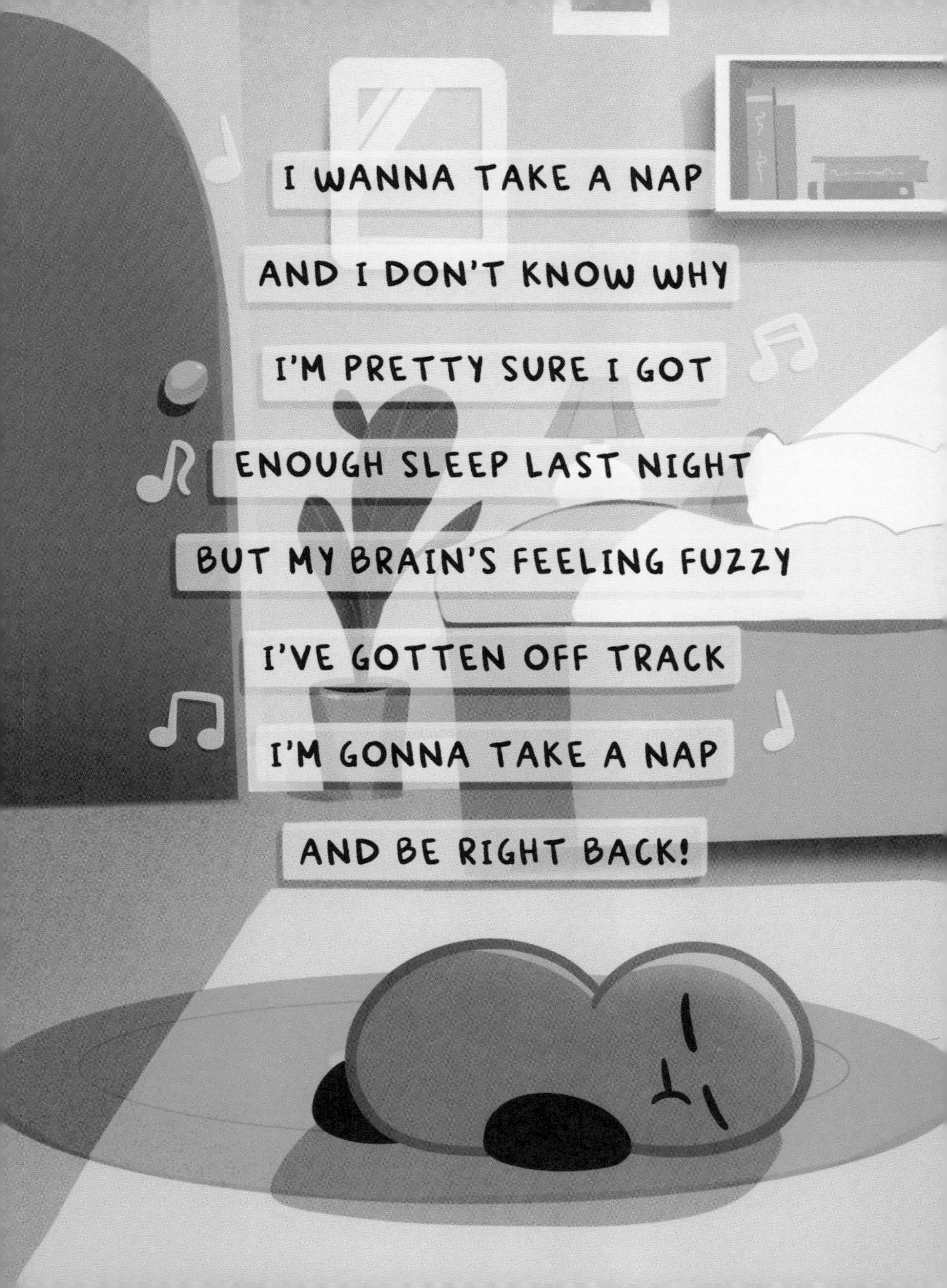

I WANNA TAKE A NAP
AND I DON'T KNOW WHY
I'M PRETTY SURE I GOT
ENOUGH SLEEP LAST NIGHT
BUT MY BRAIN'S FEELING FUZZY
I'VE GOTTEN OFF TRACK
I'M GONNA TAKE A NAP
AND BE RIGHT BACK!

CERTIFICATE OF ACHIEVEMENT FOR THE NUMBER ONE NAPPER

This certificate is presented to

_____

for being the <u>best</u> napper I know!

In fact - now that you have this certificate,
I think you should celebrate with a nap!!

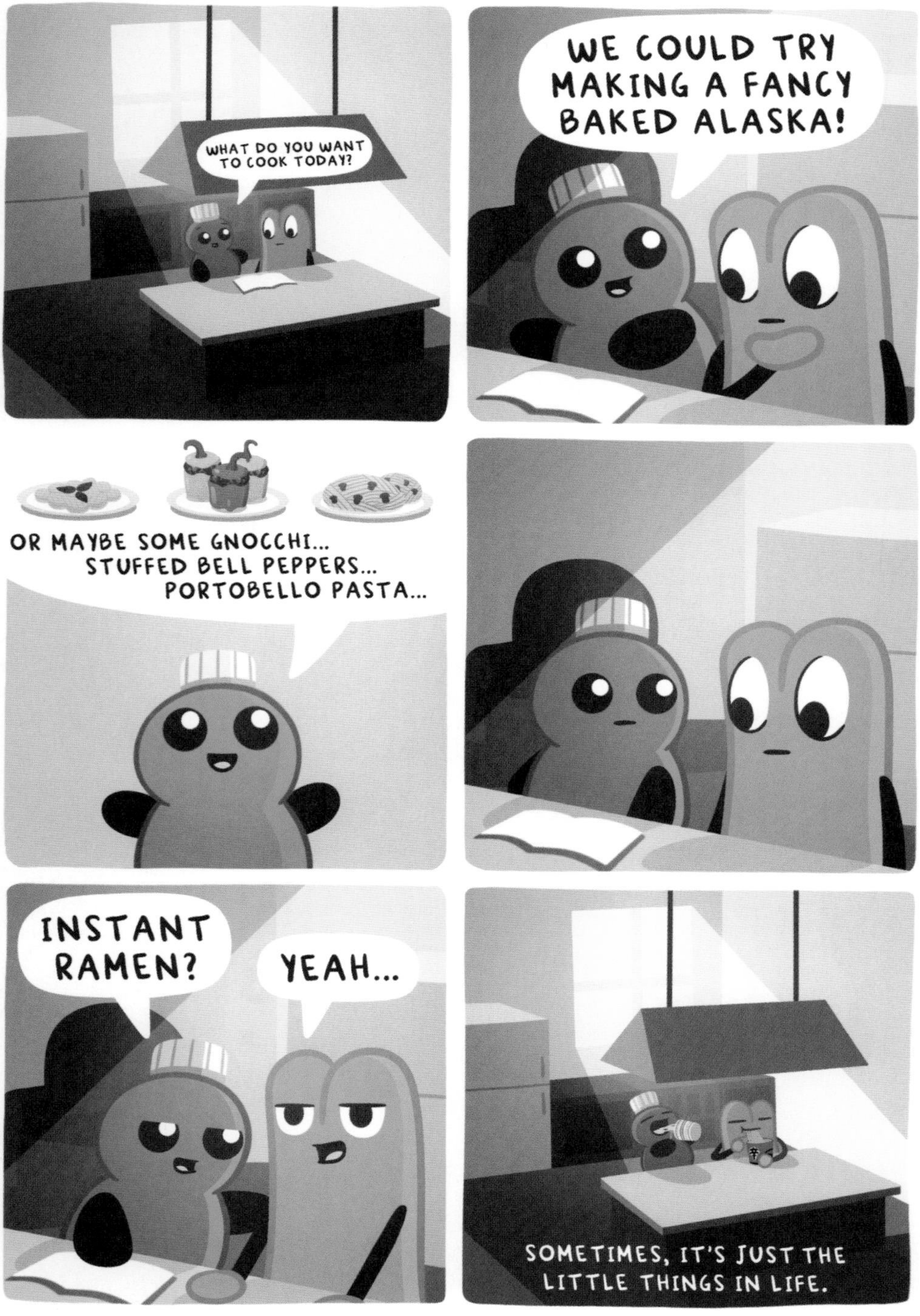
WHAT DO YOU WANT TO COOK TODAY?
WE COULD TRY MAKING A FANCY BAKED ALASKA!
OR MAYBE SOME GNOCCHI... STUFFED BELL PEPPERS... PORTOBELLO PASTA...
INSTANT RAMEN?
YEAH...
SOMETIMES, IT'S JUST THE LITTLE THINGS IN LIFE.

HOW TO SPRUCE UP YOUR INSTANT RAMEN!

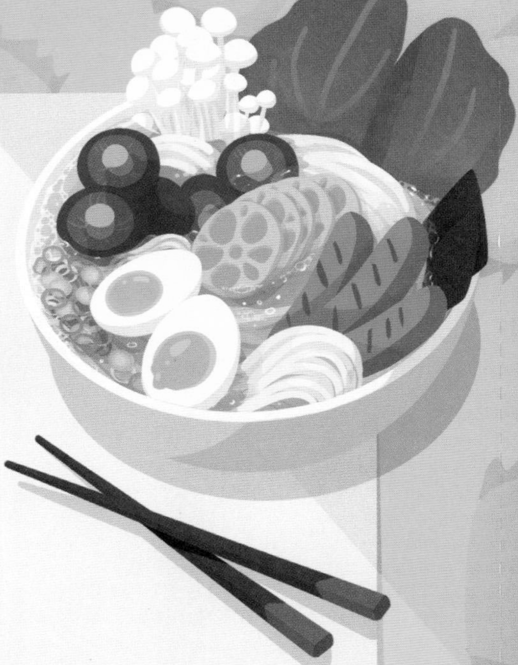

Here are some of Tubby's and Nobby's favorite things to add to their ramen!

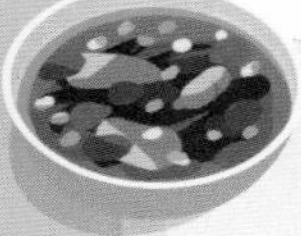

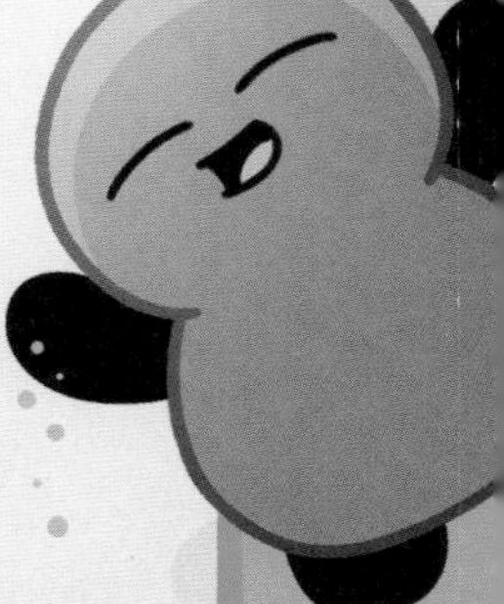

- A scoop of miso paste
- A tablespoon of your favorite chili oil, or a teaspoon of sesame oil
- A slice of your favorite melty cheese
- Fresh veggies, like spinach, bok choy, and bean sprouts
- Kimchi (if you like some spice!)
- Chopped scallions

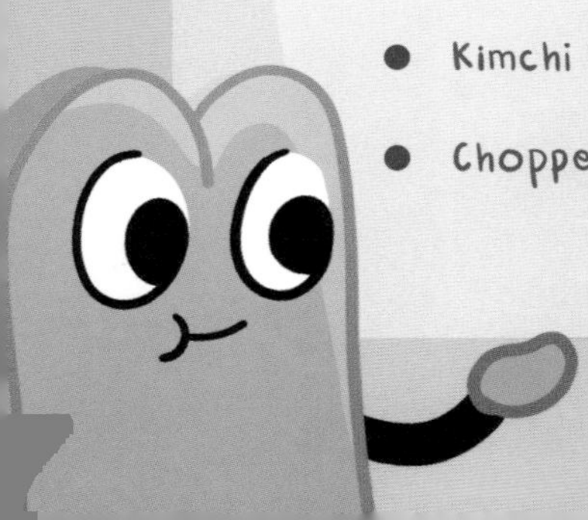

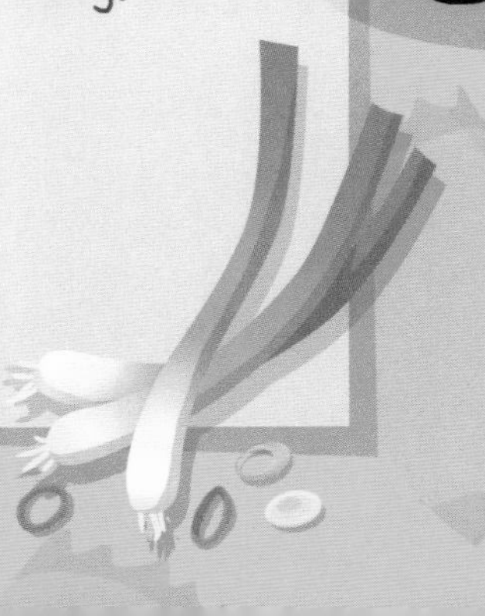

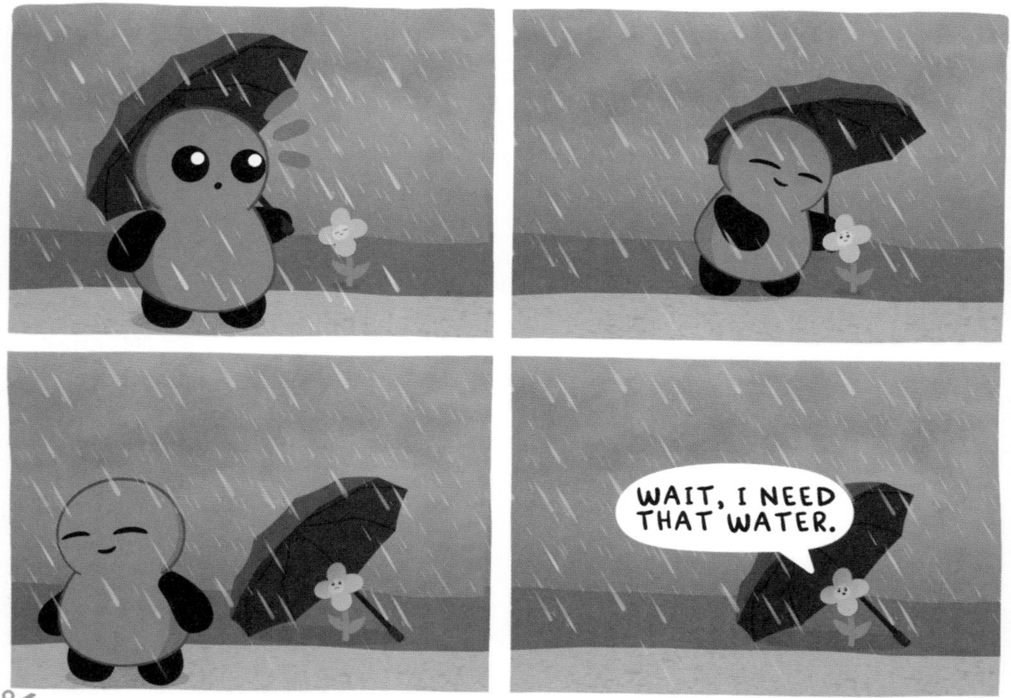
WAIT, I NEED THAT WATER.

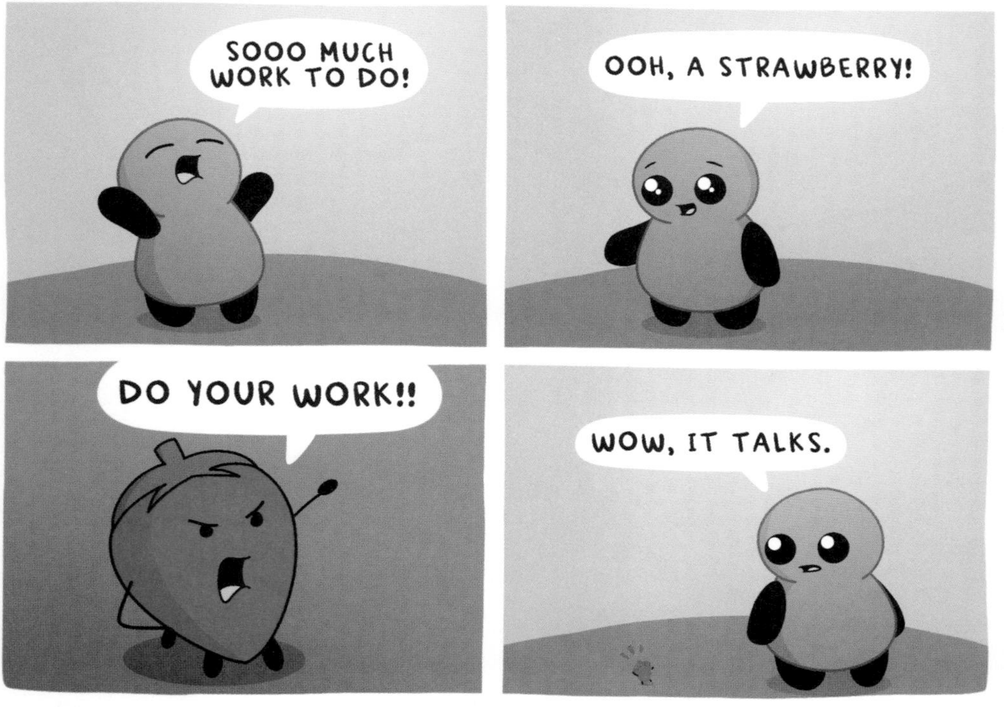
SOOO MUCH WORK TO DO!
OOH, A STRAWBERRY!
DO YOUR WORK!!
WOW, IT TALKS.

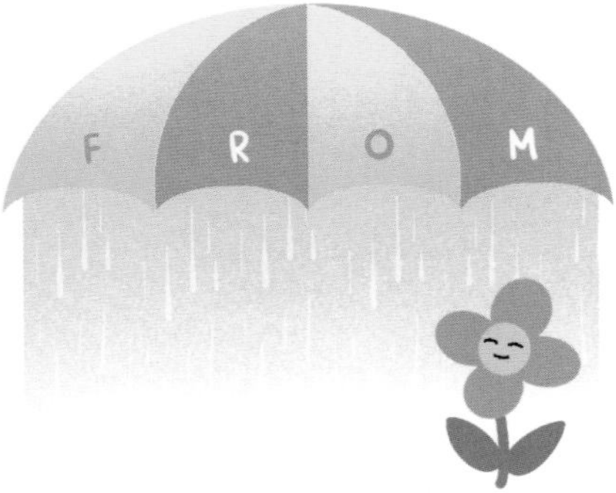
F R O M

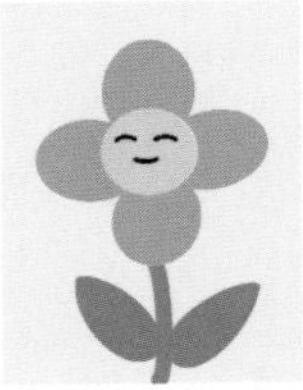

TO

FROM

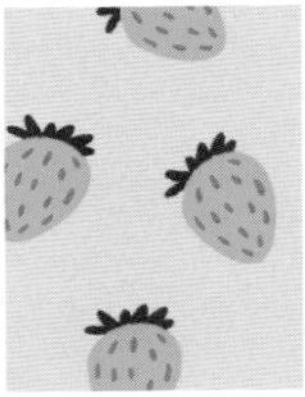

HAVE A BERRY
GOOD DAY!

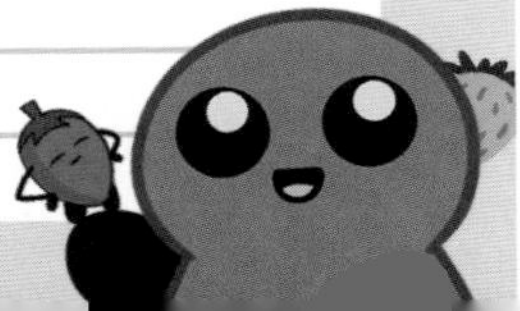

TO

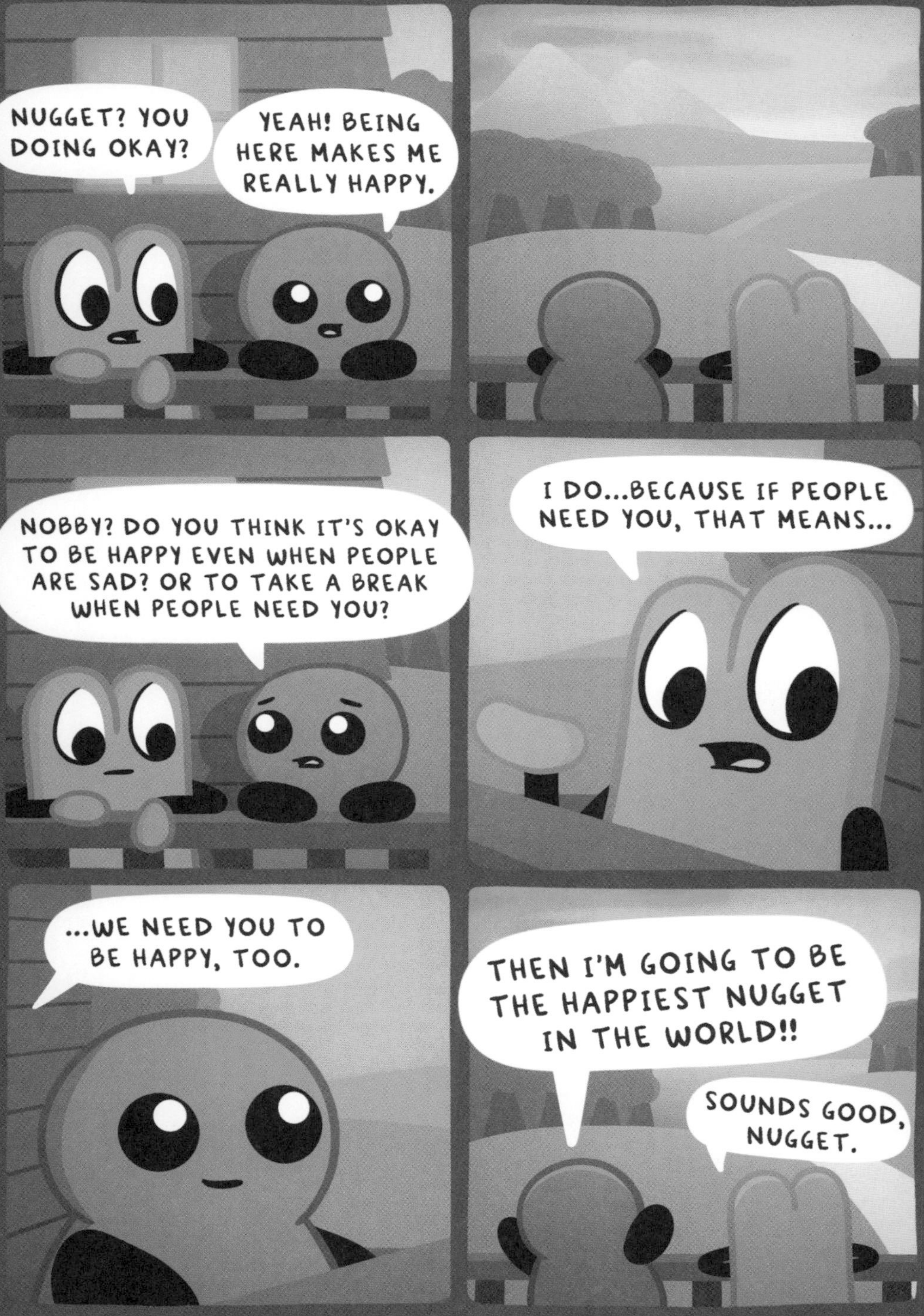
NUGGET? YOU DOING OKAY?
YEAH! BEING HERE MAKES ME REALLY HAPPY.
NOBBY? DO YOU THINK IT'S OKAY TO BE HAPPY EVEN WHEN PEOPLE ARE SAD? OR TO TAKE A BREAK WHEN PEOPLE NEED YOU?
I DO...BECAUSE IF PEOPLE NEED YOU, THAT MEANS...
...WE NEED YOU TO BE HAPPY, TOO.
THEN I'M GOING TO BE THE HAPPIEST NUGGET IN THE WORLD!!
SOUNDS GOOD, NUGGET.

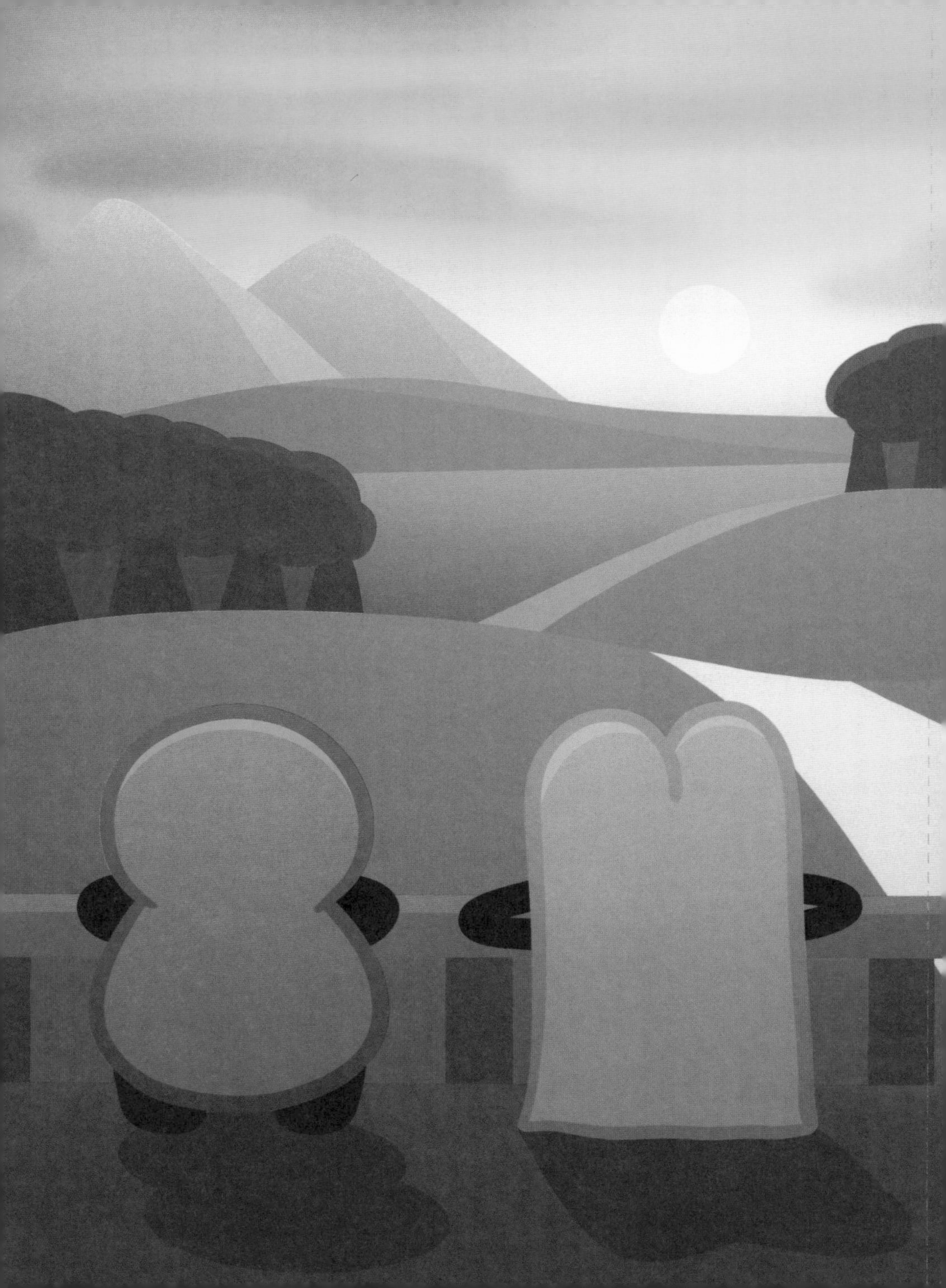

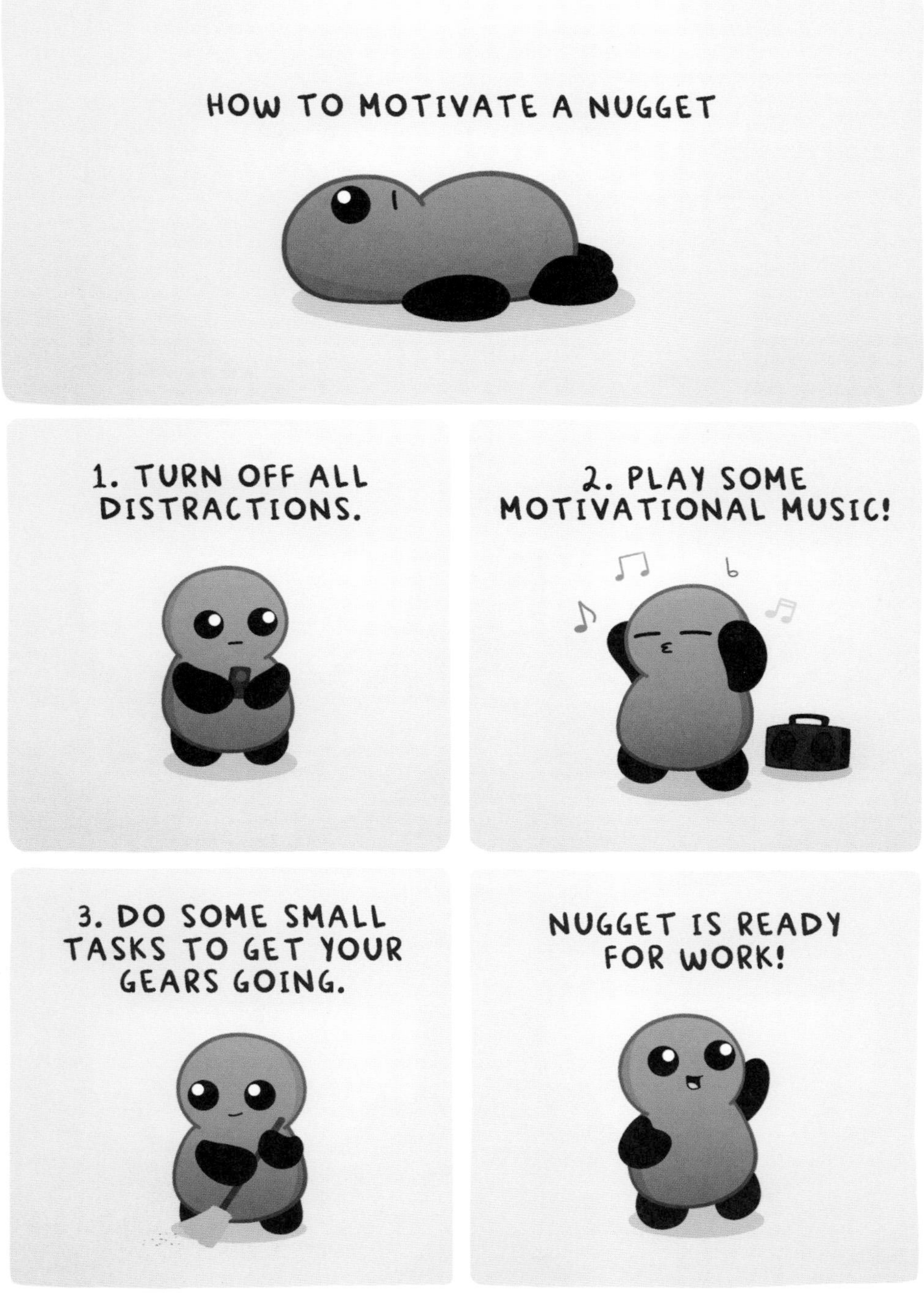
HOW TO MOTIVATE A NUGGET
1. TURN OFF ALL DISTRACTIONS.
2. PLAY SOME MOTIVATIONAL MUSIC!
3. DO SOME SMALL TASKS TO GET YOUR GEARS GOING.
NUGGET IS READY FOR WORK!

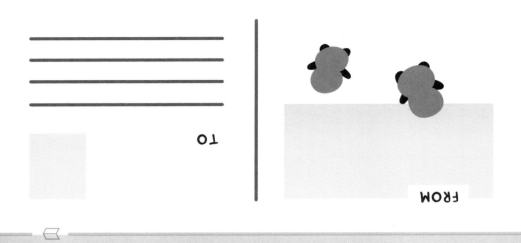

TO

FROM

SHHH...I'M GETTING MOTIVATED.

JUST CHECKING IN ON YOU!

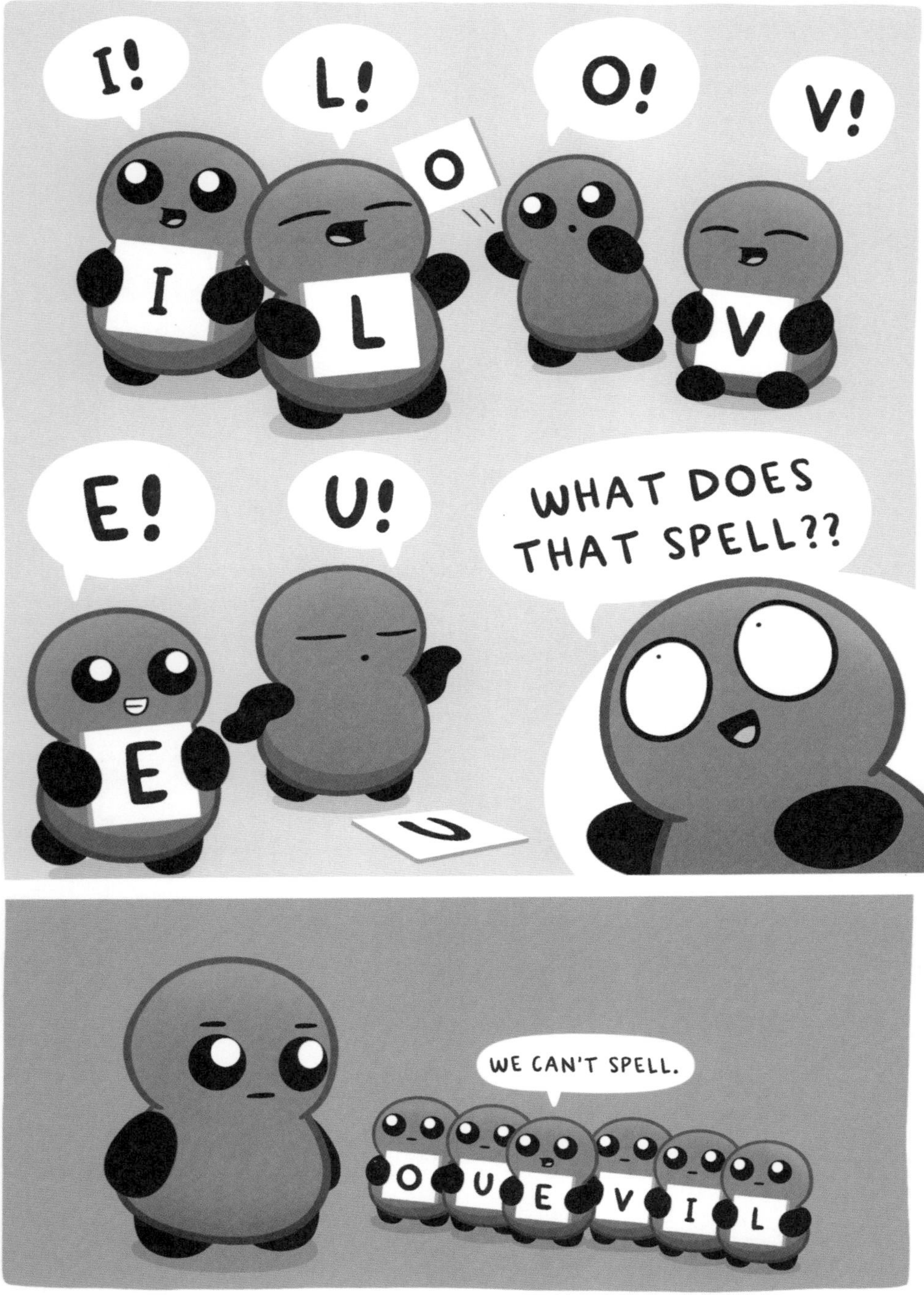

I!
L!
O!
V!
E!
U!
WHAT DOES THAT SPELL??
WE CAN'T SPELL.

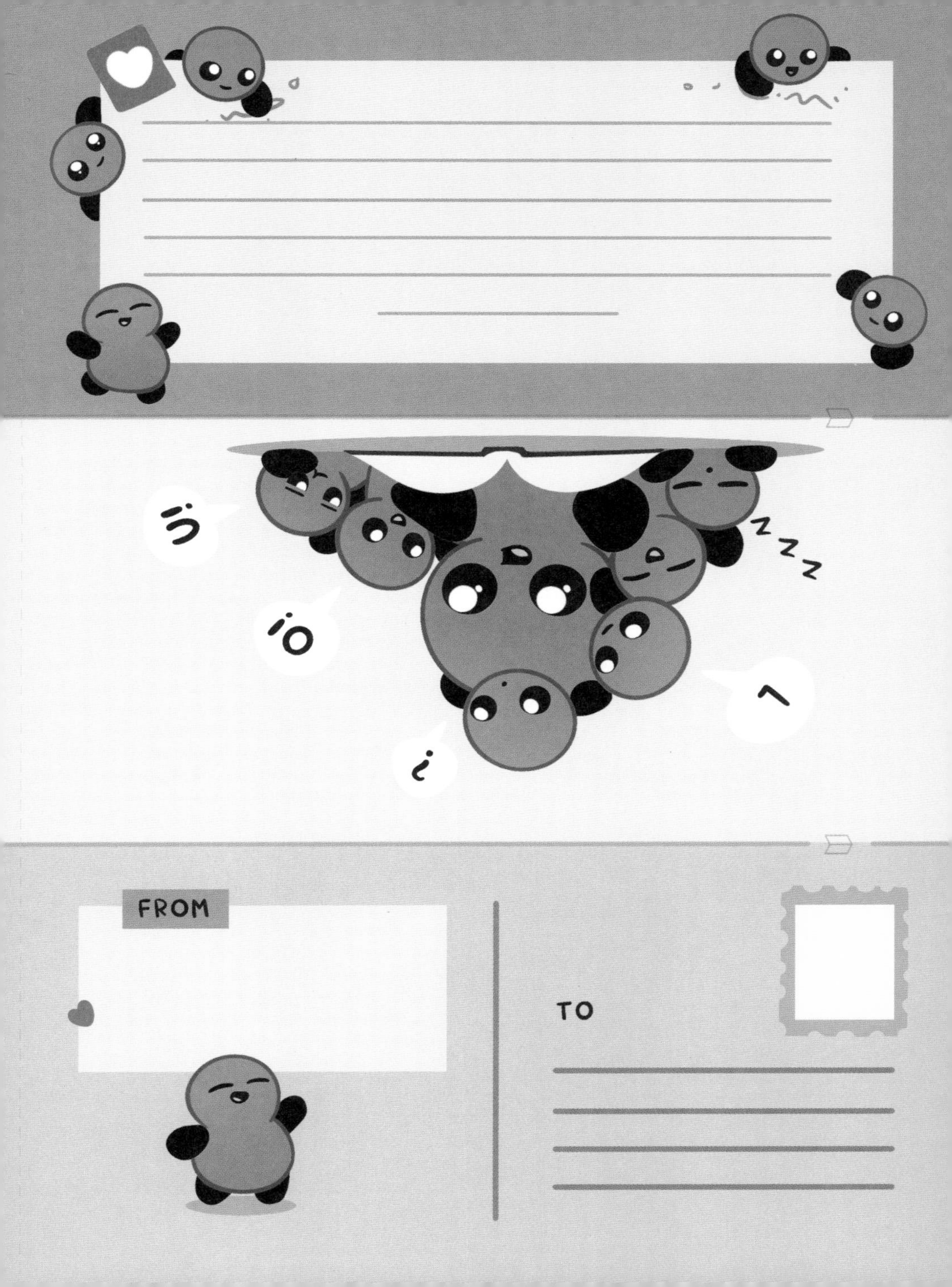
FROM
TO

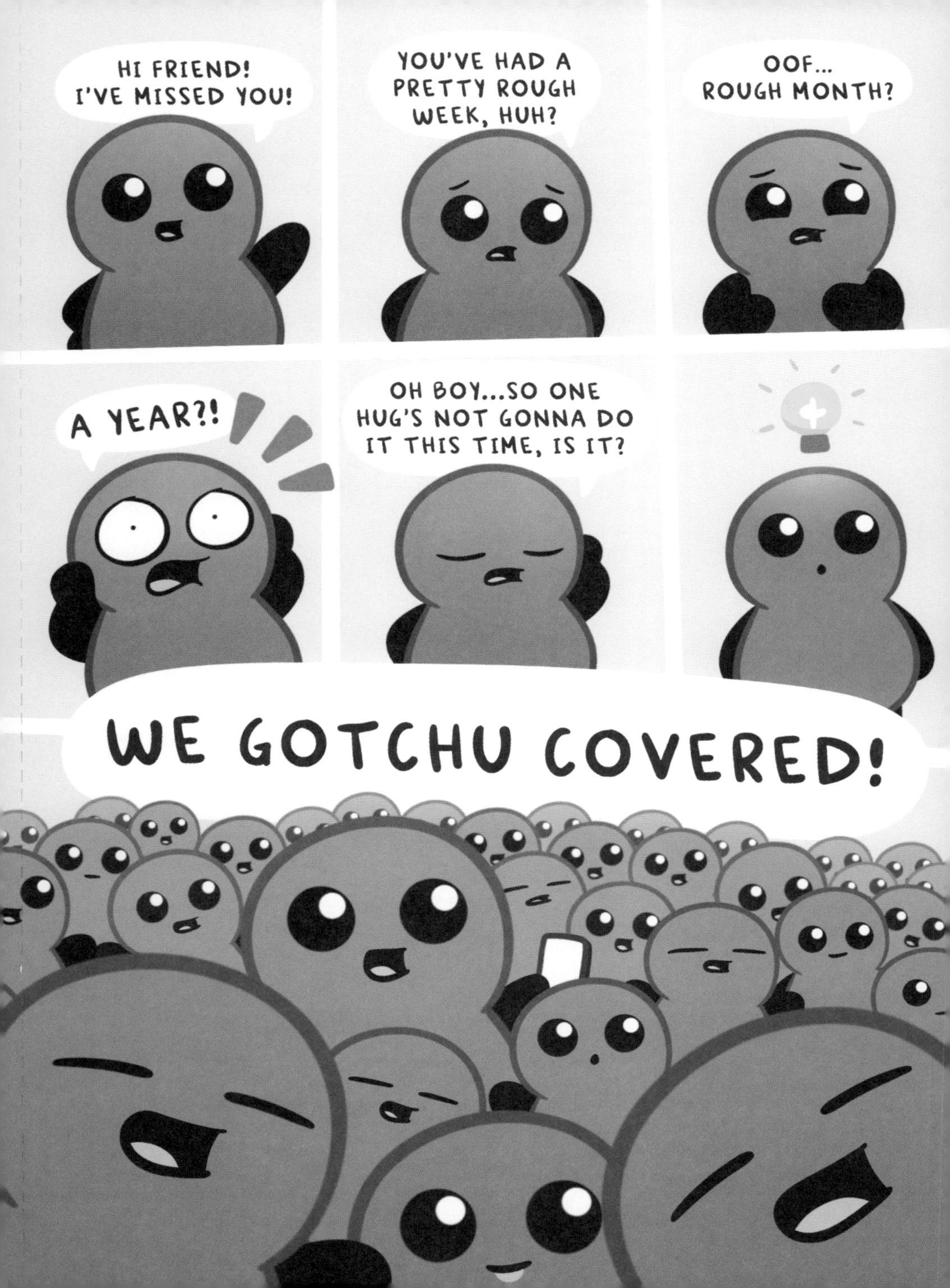
HI FRIEND! I'VE MISSED YOU!
YOU'VE HAD A PRETTY ROUGH WEEK, HUH?
OOF... ROUGH MONTH?
A YEAR?!
OH BOY...SO ONE HUG'S NOT GONNA DO IT THIS TIME, IS IT?
WE GOTCHU COVERED!

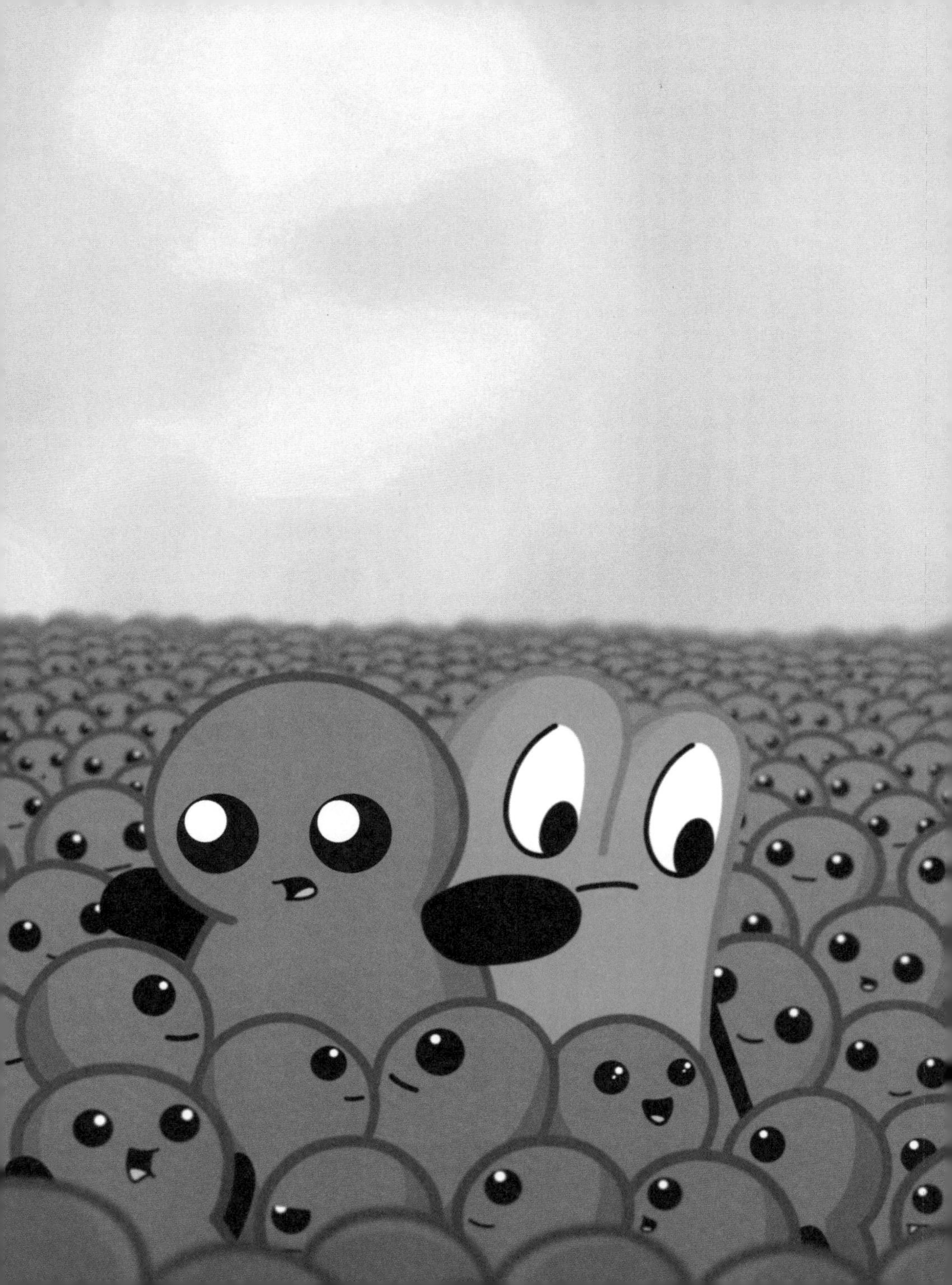

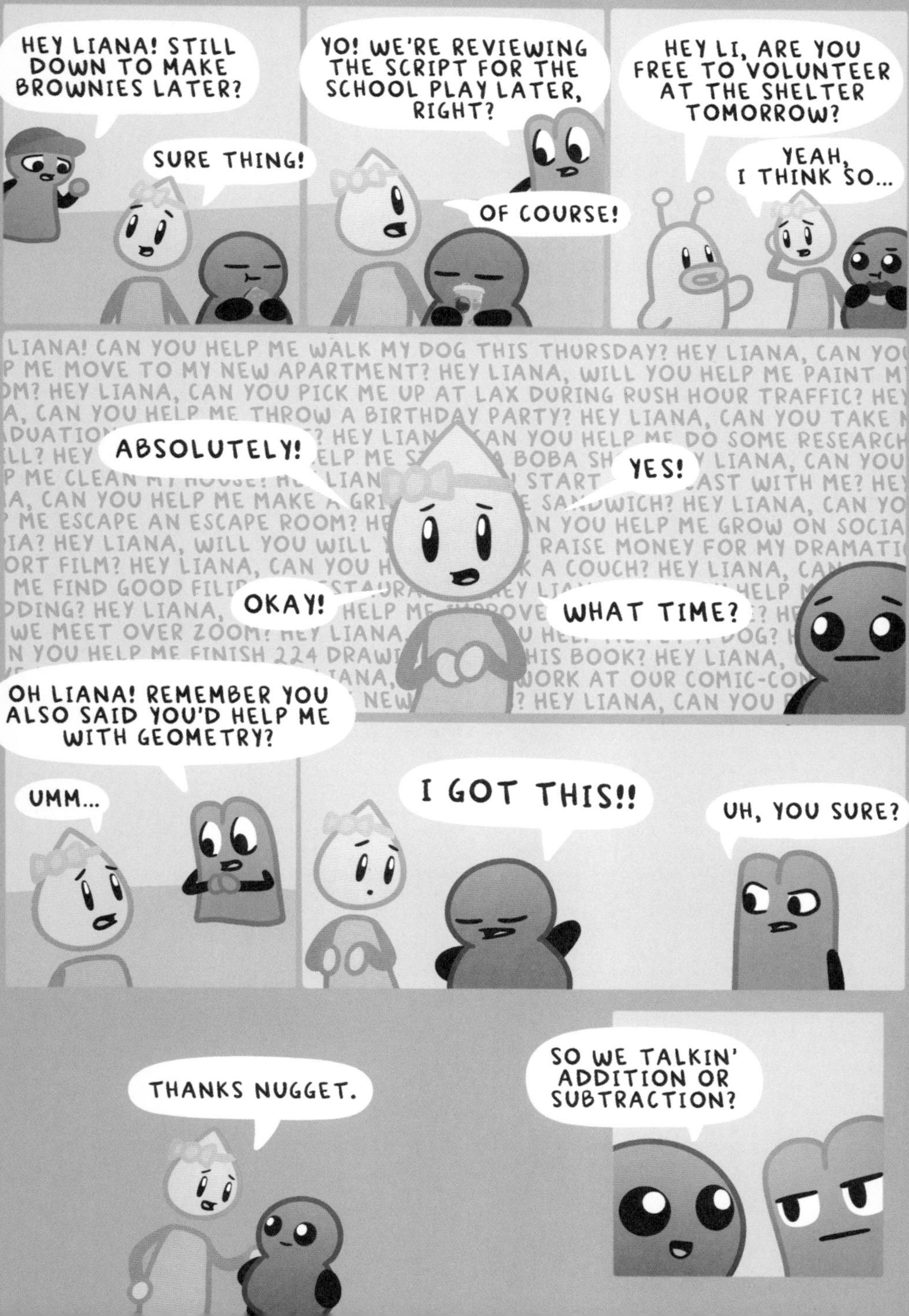
HEY LIANA! STILL DOWN TO MAKE BROWNIES LATER?
SURE THING!
YO! WE'RE REVIEWING THE SCRIPT FOR THE SCHOOL PLAY LATER, RIGHT?
OF COURSE!
HEY LI, ARE YOU FREE TO VOLUNTEER AT THE SHELTER TOMORROW?
YEAH, I THINK SO...
LIANA! CAN YOU HELP ME WALK MY DOG THIS THURSDAY? HEY LIANA, CAN YOU
ME MOVE TO MY NEW APARTMENT? HEY LIANA, WILL YOU HELP ME PAINT MY
HEY LIANA, CAN YOU PICK ME UP AT LAX DURING RUSH HOUR TRAFFIC?
CAN YOU HELP ME THROW A BIRTHDAY PARTY? HEY LIANA, CAN YOU TAKE
ABSOLUTELY!
YES!
OKAY!
WHAT TIME?
OH LIANA! REMEMBER YOU ALSO SAID YOU'D HELP ME WITH GEOMETRY?
UMM...
I GOT THIS!!
UH, YOU SURE?
THANKS NUGGET.
SO WE TALKIN' ADDITION OR SUBTRACTION?

TO

FROM

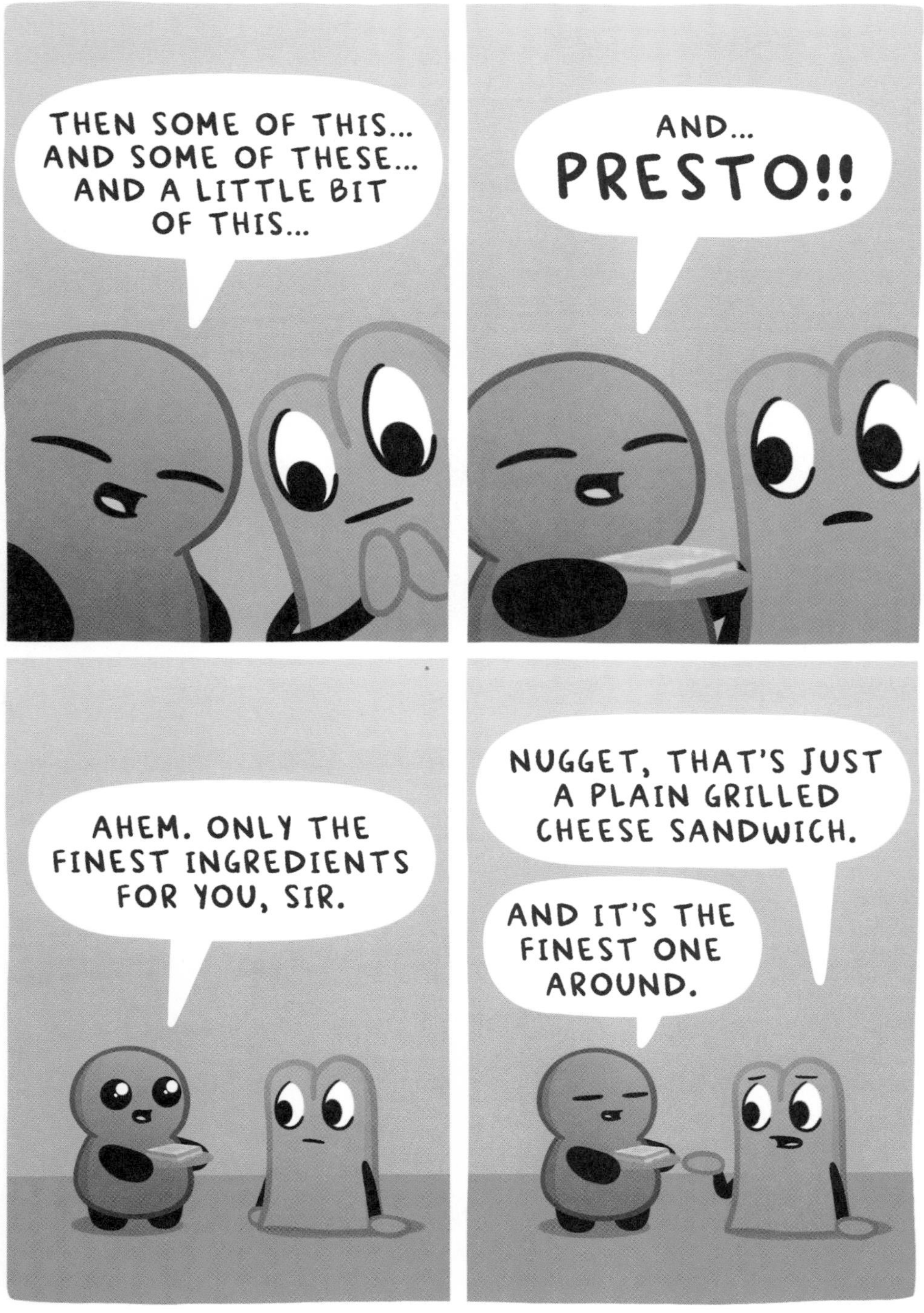
THEN SOME OF THIS... AND SOME OF THESE... AND A LITTLE BIT OF THIS...
AND... PRESTO!!
AHEM. ONLY THE FINEST INGREDIENTS FOR YOU, SIR.
NUGGET, THAT'S JUST A PLAIN GRILLED CHEESE SANDWICH.
AND IT'S THE FINEST ONE AROUND.

TUBBY'S FANCY GRILLED CHEESE RECIPE!

IT'S HARD TO GO WRONG WITH A YUMMY GRILLED CHEESE SANDWICH — SO HERE'S A RECIPE FOR AN EXTRA YUMMY ONE YOU MIGHT WANNA MAKE FOR SOMEONE SPECIAL! (LIKE YOU!)

INGREDIENTS:

2 SLICES OF YOUR FAVORITE FANCY BREAD
(LIKE FRENCH BAGUETTE, SOURDOUGH, OR BRIOCHE)

GHEE, BROWN BUTTER,
OR YOUR BUTTER OF CHOICE

KEWPIE MAYO, OR YOUR MAYO OF CHOICE

2 SLICES EACH OF CHEDDAR, GOUDA, AND GRUYÈRE &
GRATED PARMESAN

DIRECTIONS:

1. COVER BOTH SIDES OF TWO SLICES OF BREAD WITH GHEE, BROWN BUTTER, OR YOUR BUTTER OF CHOICE! (MAKE SURE YOUR GHEE OR BUTTER IS ROOM TEMPERATURE BEFOREHAND — THIS WILL MAKE IT MUCH EASIER TO SPREAD!)

2. ON ONE SIDE OF EACH PIECE OF BREAD, SPREAD A GENEROUS AMOUNT OF KEWPIE MAYO, AND COVER WITH HALF OF YOUR CHEESE SLICES. (WE LIKE TO DO 1 SLICE OF BREAD WITH CHEDDAR & GOUDA, AND 1 SLICE OF BREAD WITH ALL GRUYÈRE CHEESE!) CLOSE YOUR SANDWICH.

3. NOW, MELT SOME OF YOUR GHEE OR BUTTER IN A PAN OVER MEDIUM HEAT, THEN PLACE YOUR SANDWICH RIGHT ON TOP. GIVE IT ABOUT 2 MINUTES BEFORE CHECKING TO SEE IF YOUR TOAST IS GOLDEN BROWN!

4. AND IF IT IS — IT'S TIME TO FLIP!

5. TOAST THE OTHER SIDE OF YOUR SANDWICH FOR ABOUT 2 MORE MINUTES, AND KEEP AN EYE ON YOUR TOAST SO IT DOESN'T BURN! A GOOD WAY TO TELL THAT YOUR CHEESE IS PERFECTLY MELTED IS TO SLIGHTLY PULL UP ON ONE SIDE OF THE BREAD TO SEE IF IT STICKS TO THE CHEESE.

AND WHEN YOUR TOAST IS AS PERFECTLY GOLDEN BROWN AS YOU LIKE IT...

6. TAKE IT OUT OF THE PAN! NOW, SPRINKLE SOME DELICIOUS, FRESHLY GRATED PARMESAN ON TOP OF YOUR SANDWICH, AND SERVE.

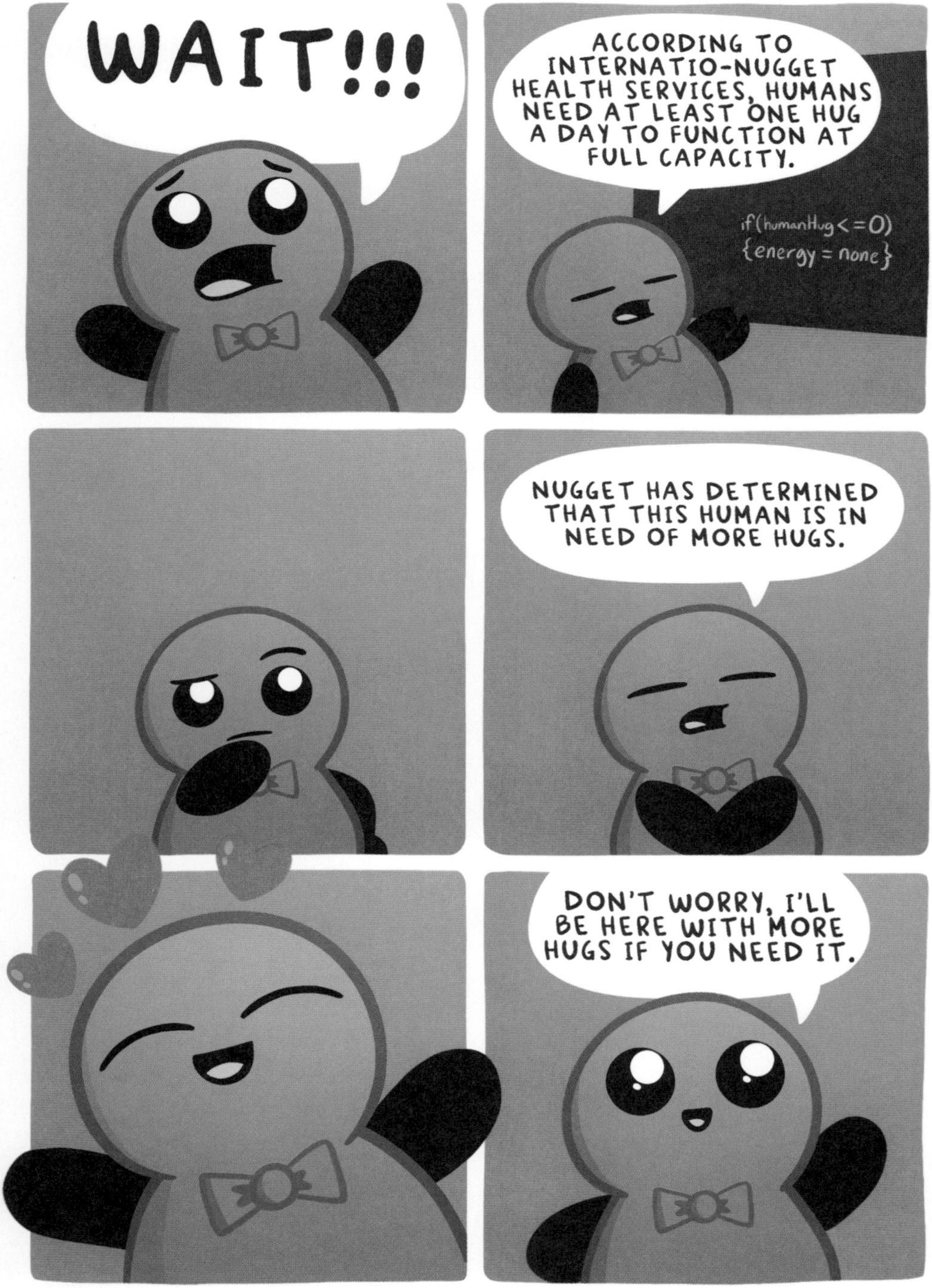
WAIT!!!
ACCORDING TO INTERNATIO-NUGGET HEALTH SERVICES, HUMANS NEED AT LEAST ONE HUG A DAY TO FUNCTION AT FULL CAPACITY.
if(humanHug<=0)
{energy = none}
NUGGET HAS DETERMINED THAT THIS HUMAN IS IN NEED OF MORE HUGS.
DON'T WORRY, I'LL BE HERE WITH MORE HUGS IF YOU NEED IT.

FROM

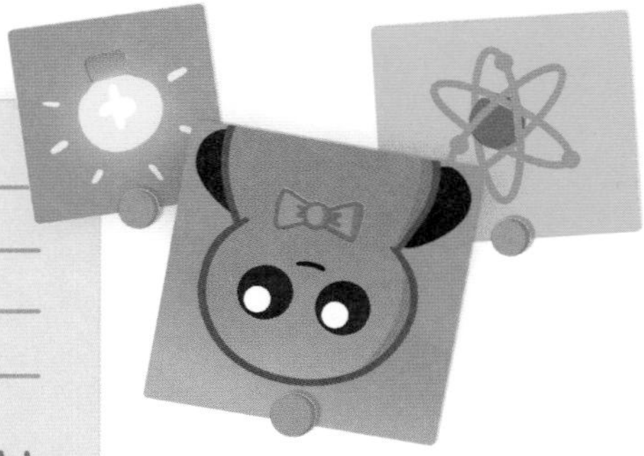

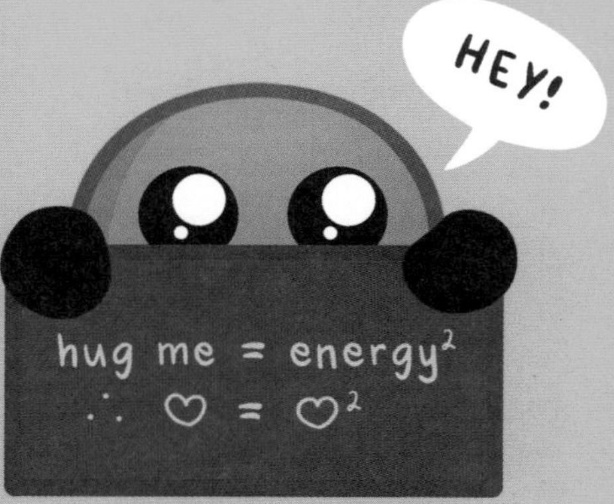
HEY!
hug me = energy²
∴ ♡ = ♡²

TO

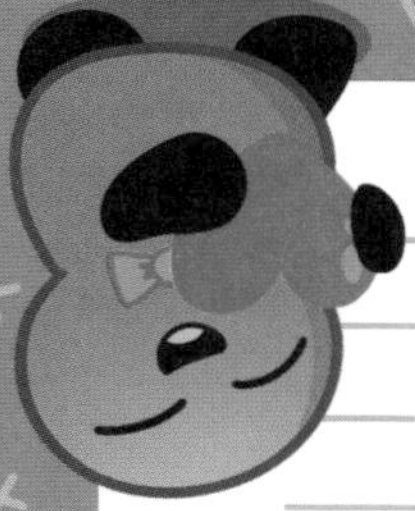

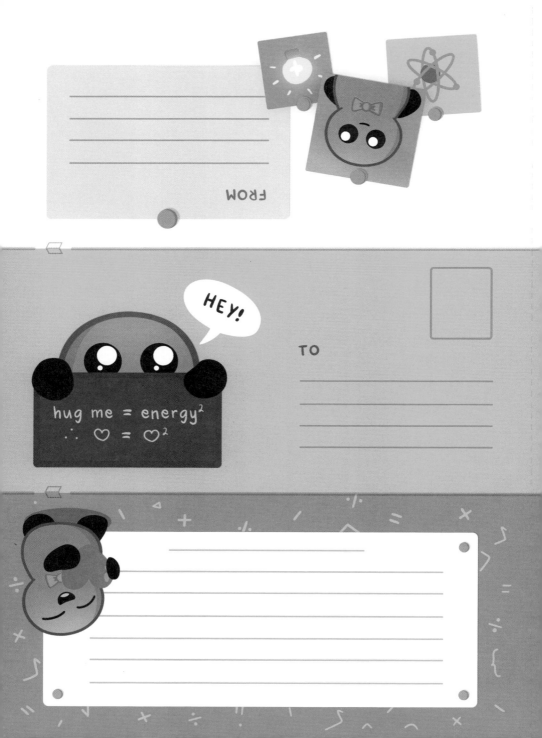

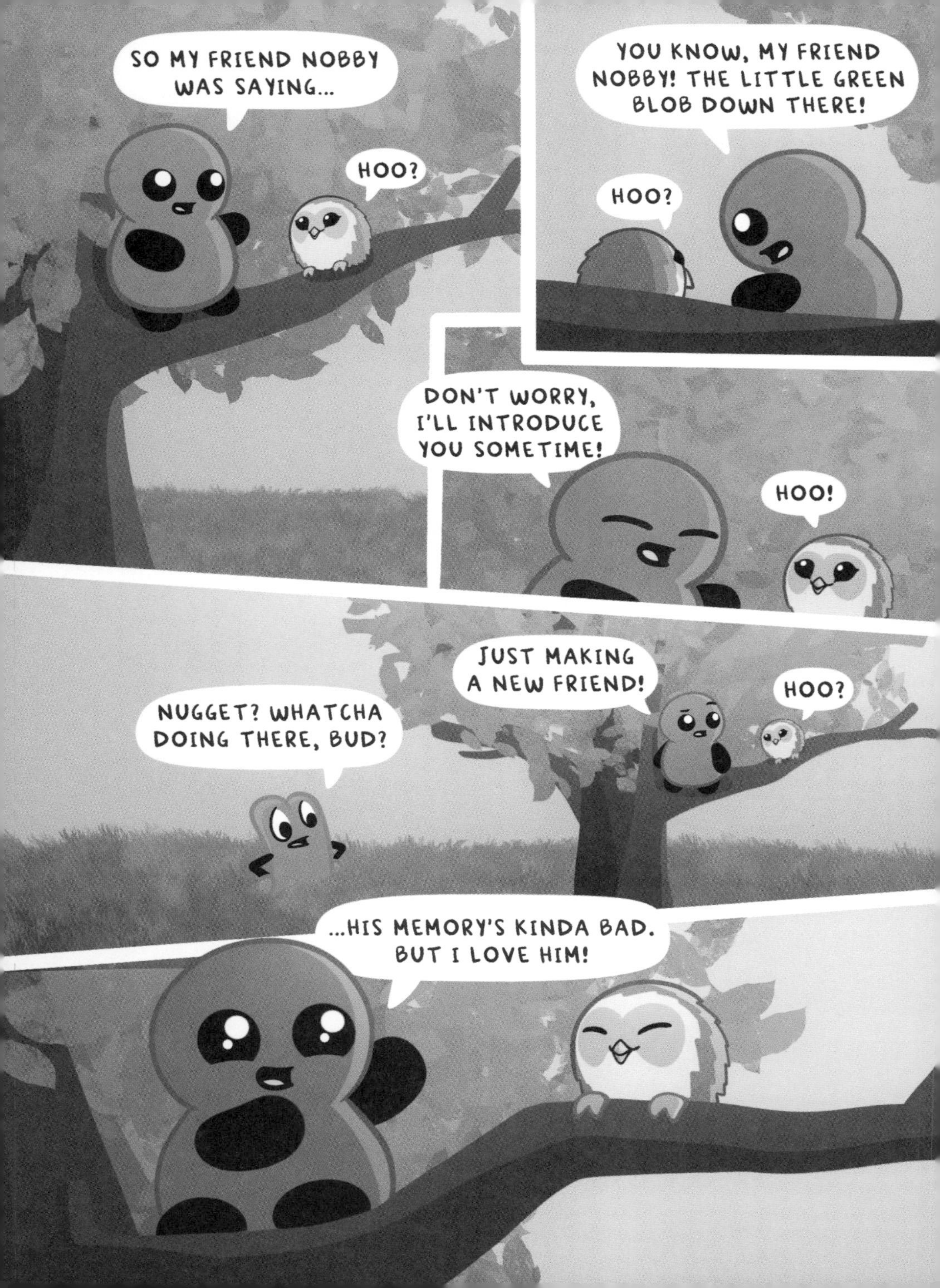
SO MY FRIEND NOBBY WAS SAYING...
HOO?
YOU KNOW, MY FRIEND NOBBY! THE LITTLE GREEN BLOB DOWN THERE!
HOO?
DON'T WORRY, I'LL INTRODUCE YOU SOMETIME!
HOO!
NUGGET? WHATCHA DOING THERE, BUD?
JUST MAKING A NEW FRIEND!
HOO?
...HIS MEMORY'S KINDA BAD. BUT I LOVE HIM!

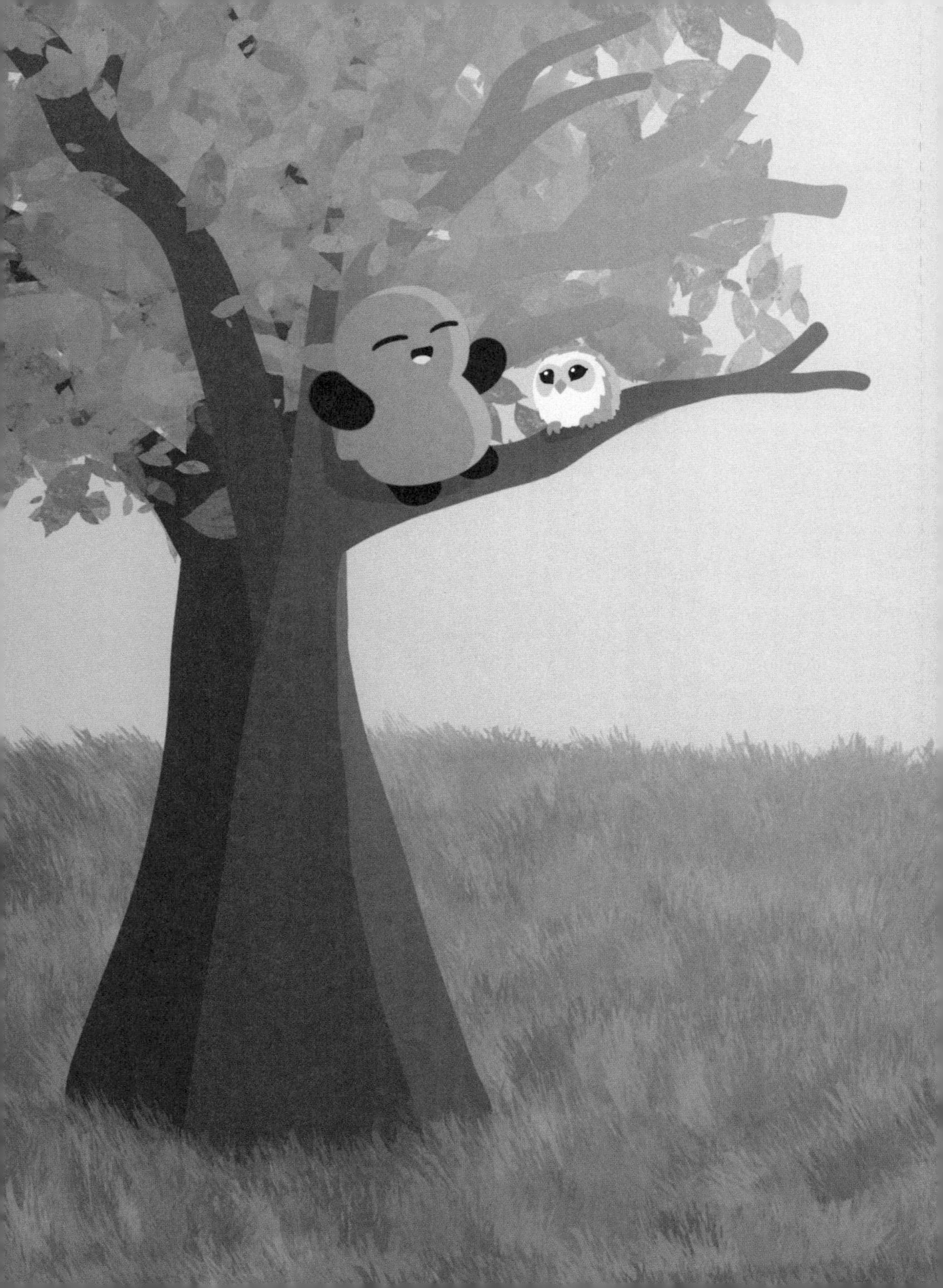

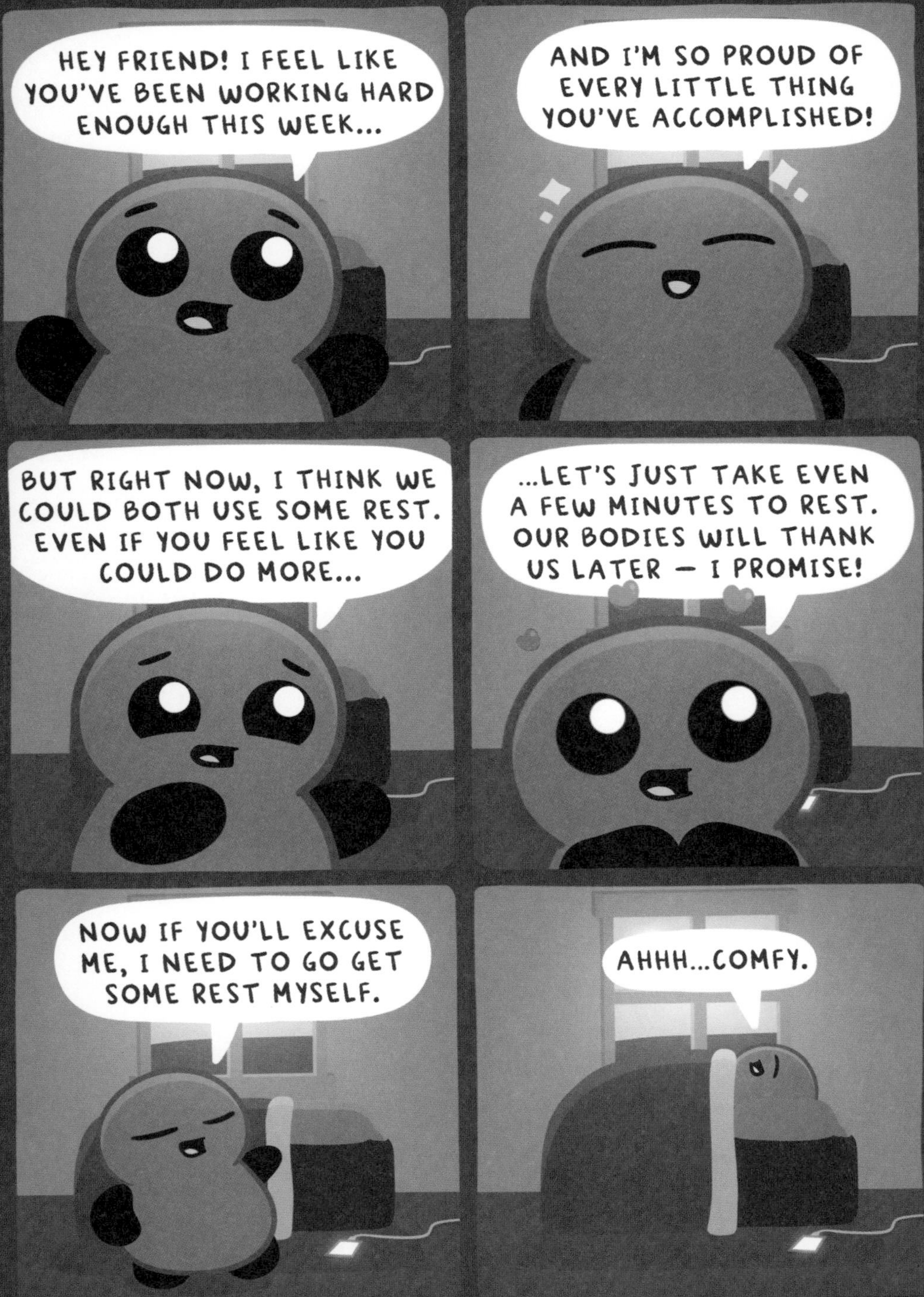
HEY FRIEND! I FEEL LIKE YOU'VE BEEN WORKING HARD ENOUGH THIS WEEK...
AND I'M SO PROUD OF EVERY LITTLE THING YOU'VE ACCOMPLISHED!
BUT RIGHT NOW, I THINK WE COULD BOTH USE SOME REST. EVEN IF YOU FEEL LIKE YOU COULD DO MORE...
...LET'S JUST TAKE EVEN A FEW MINUTES TO REST. OUR BODIES WILL THANK US LATER — I PROMISE!
NOW IF YOU'LL EXCUSE ME, I NEED TO GO GET SOME REST MYSELF.
AHHH...COMFY.

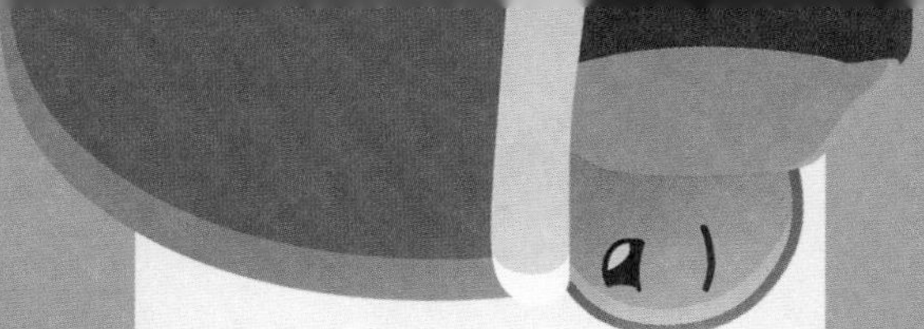

TO

FROM

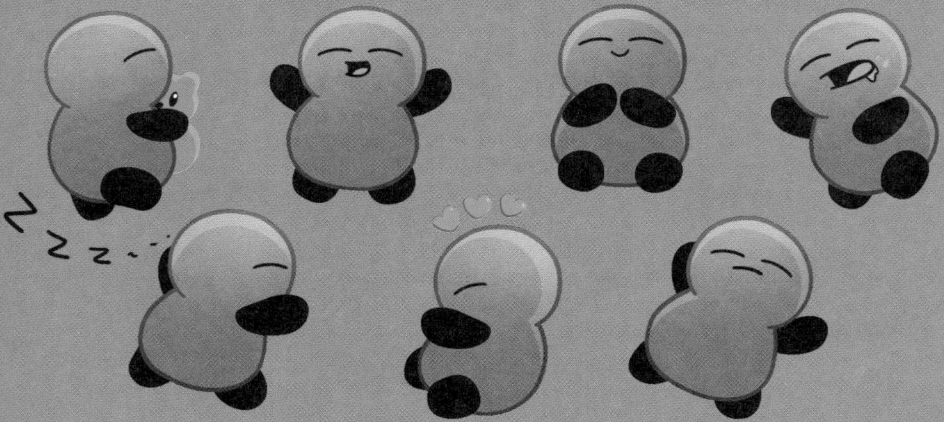

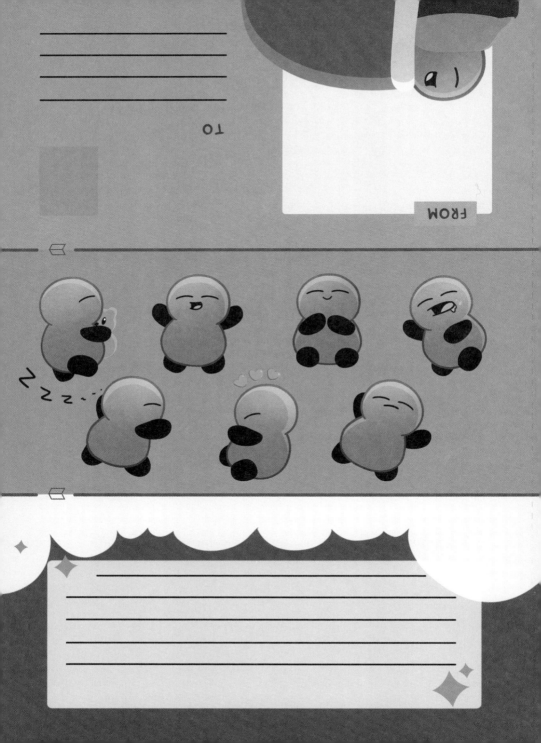

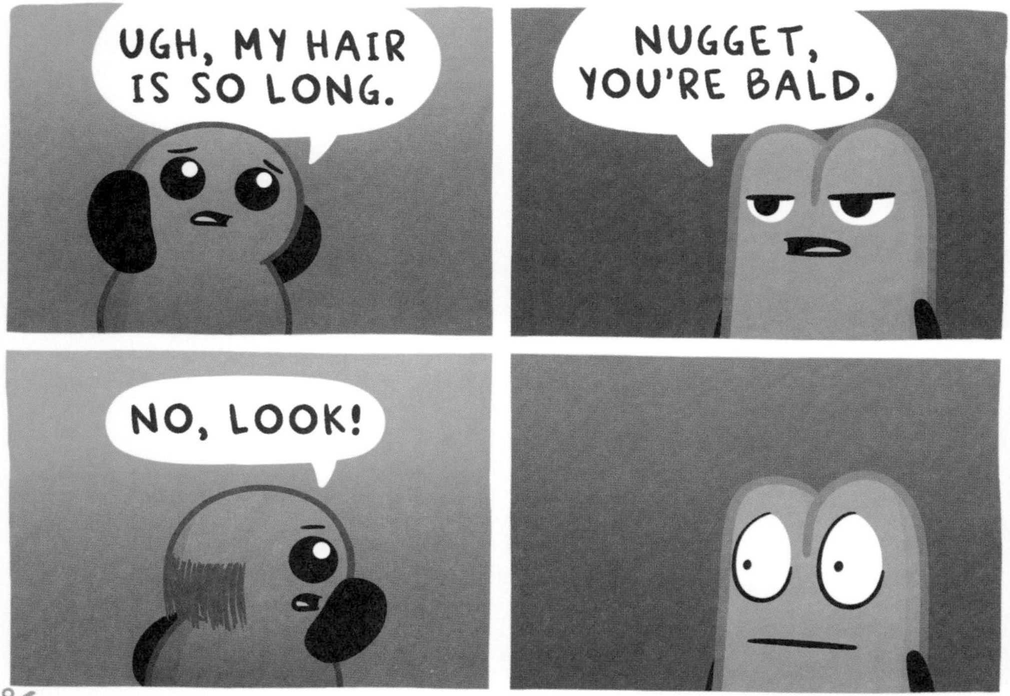
UGH, MY HAIR IS SO LONG.
NUGGET, YOU'RE BALD.
NO, LOOK!

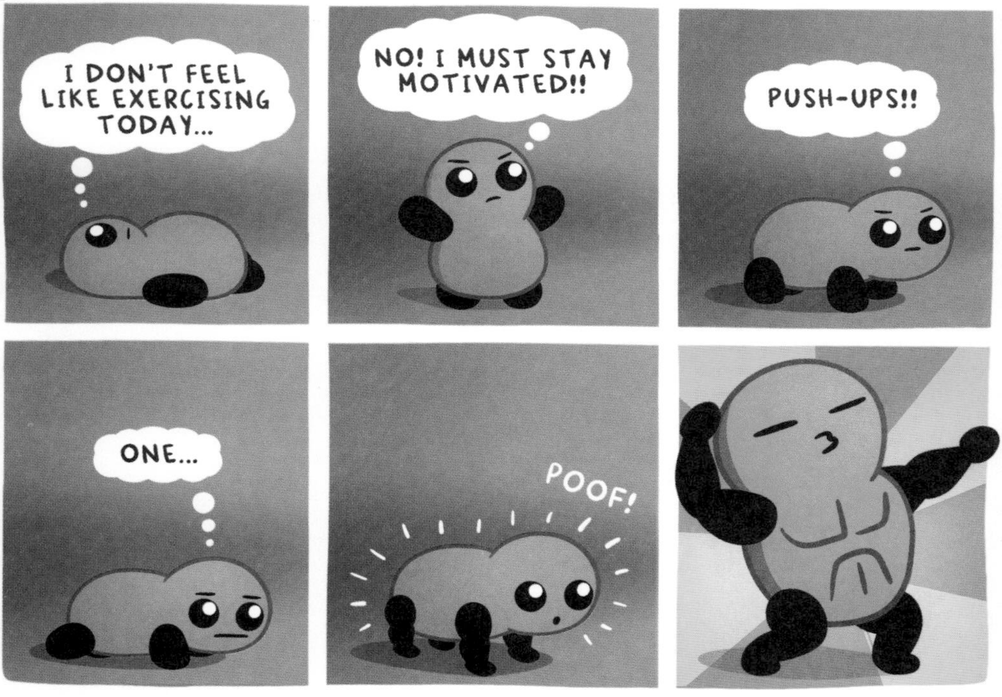
I DON'T FEEL LIKE EXERCISING TODAY...
NO! I MUST STAY MOTIVATED!!
PUSH-UPS!!
ONE...
POOF!

FROM

TO

_____

_____
_____
_____
_____
_____
_____
_____

- - - - - - - - ✂ -

FROM

WELL THAT WAS EASY.

TO

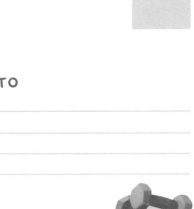

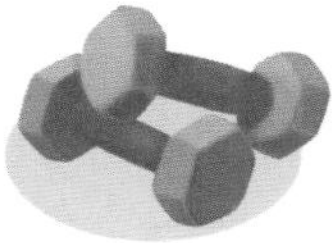

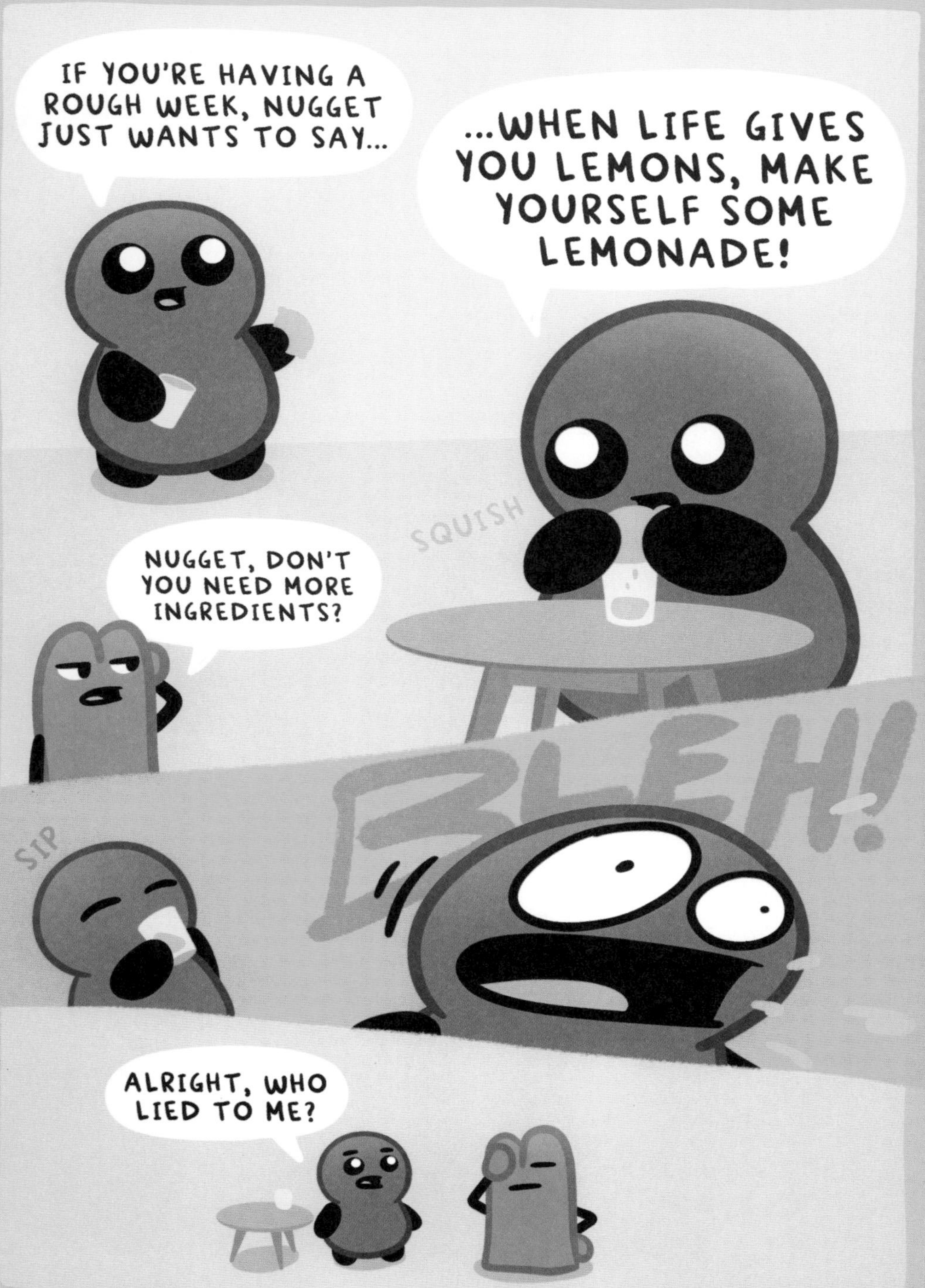
IF YOU'RE HAVING A ROUGH WEEK, NUGGET JUST WANTS TO SAY...
...WHEN LIFE GIVES YOU LEMONS, MAKE YOURSELF SOME LEMONADE!
SQUISH
NUGGET, DON'T YOU NEED MORE INGREDIENTS?
SIP
BLEH!
ALRIGHT, WHO LIED TO ME?

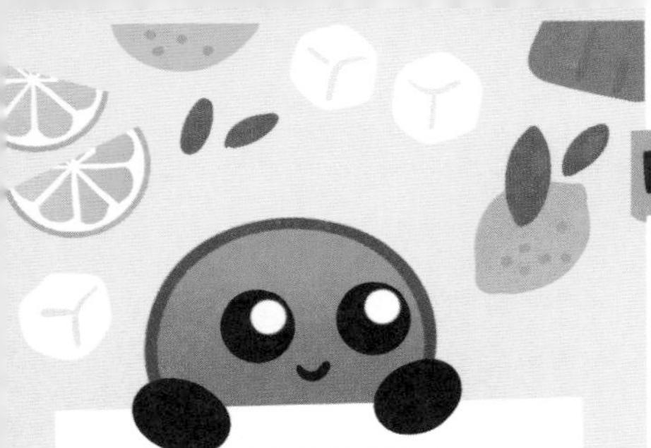

TUBBY'S HONEY CITRUS LEMONADE!

This yummy drink is bright, sweet, and special — just like you! And it yields one full pitcher (or about 1/2 gallon's worth) of lemonade!

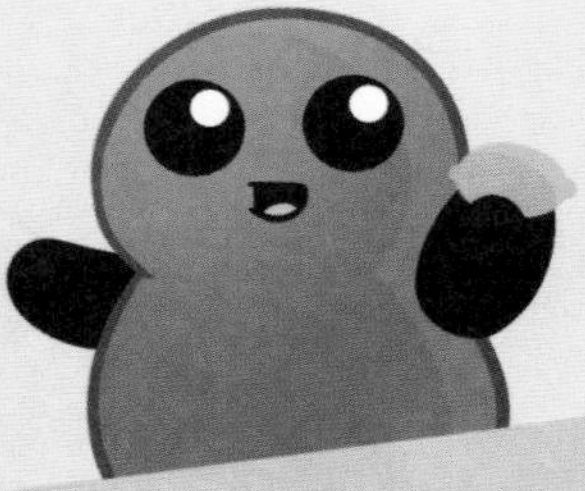

INGREDIENTS:

4-6 lemons

3-5 ripe oranges

1/2 cup of your favorite honey

4 cups of ice cold water

Ice cubes

DIRECTIONS:

1. Juice your lemons along with 3-4 of your ripe oranges. Use a strainer to help remove all the pulp and seeds.

2. In a pitcher, combine your fruit juices with your honey, and stir until the honey is completely dissolved.

3. Add in 4 cups of ice cold water, then stir thoroughly once again.

4. Taste test your mix, and adjust the sweetness to your liking!

5. For added flavor (and a pretty pitcher), peel and take apart your last orange, then place the segments inside the pitcher. (Make sure to thoroughly remove the peel and pith to help avoid any bitterness!)

6. Add some ice cubes and stir thoroughly once more to chill the mix.

7. And — you're finished! :) Serve your yummy drink over ice with a lemon or orange wedge for a delicious garnish.

AND ENJOY!

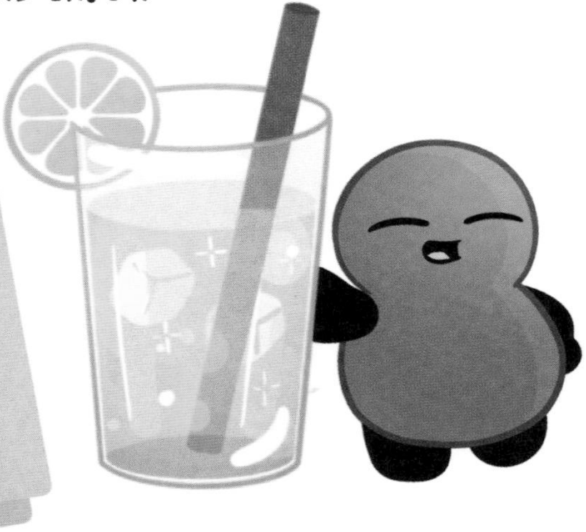

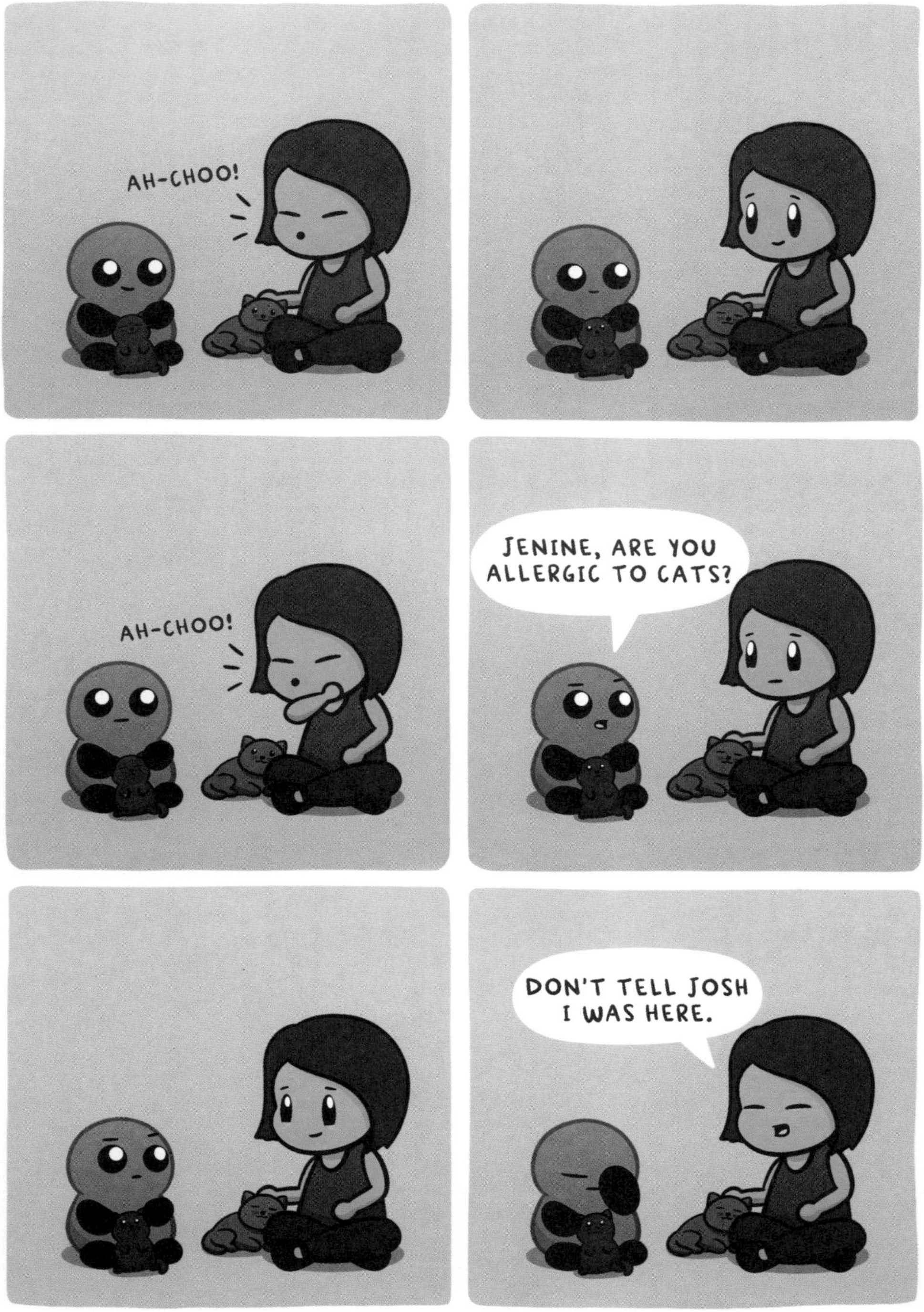
AH-CHOO!
AH-CHOO!
JENINE, ARE YOU ALLERGIC TO CATS?
DON'T TELL JOSH I WAS HERE.

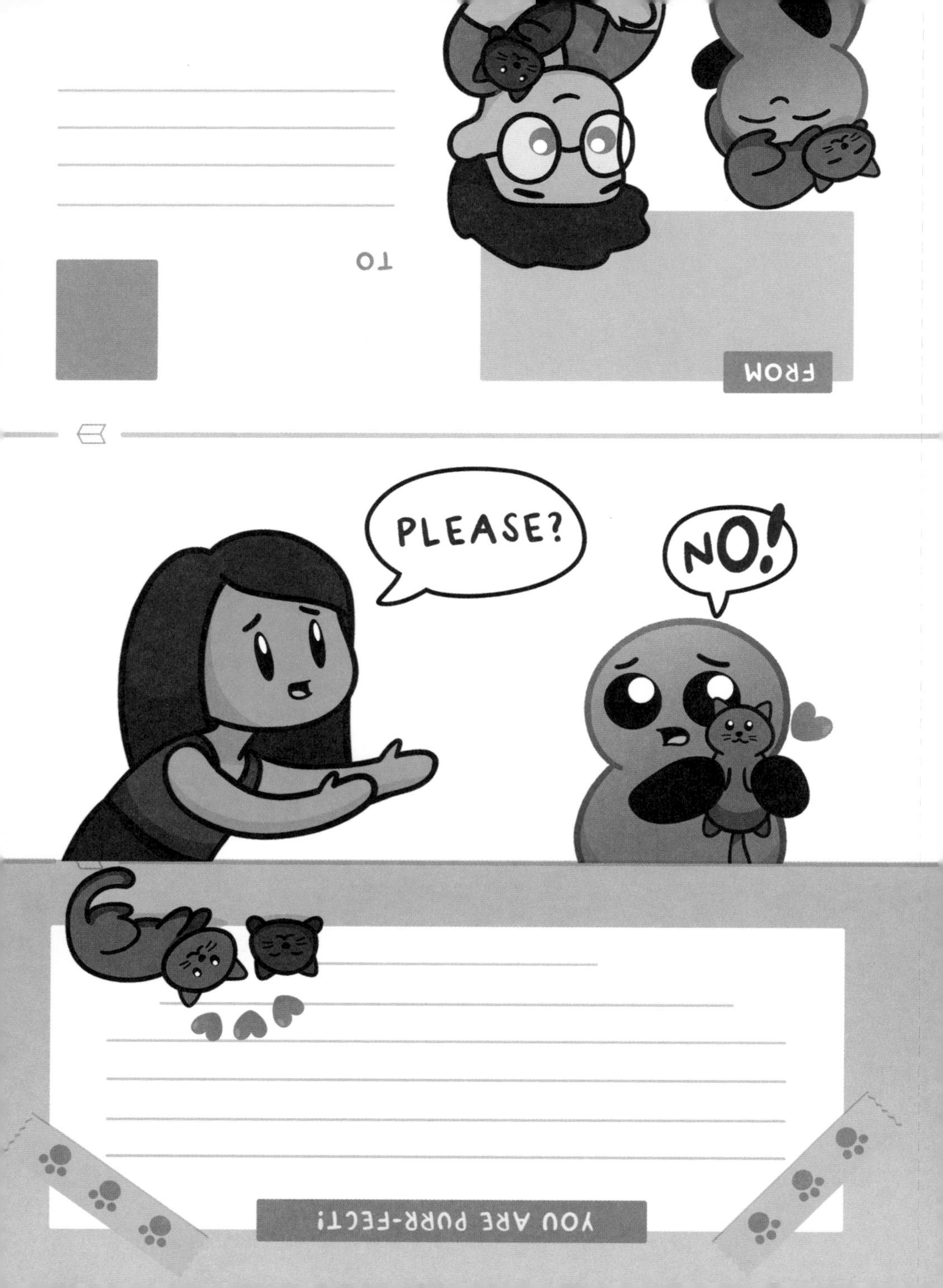
TO
FROM
PLEASE?
NO!
YOU ARE PURR-FECT!

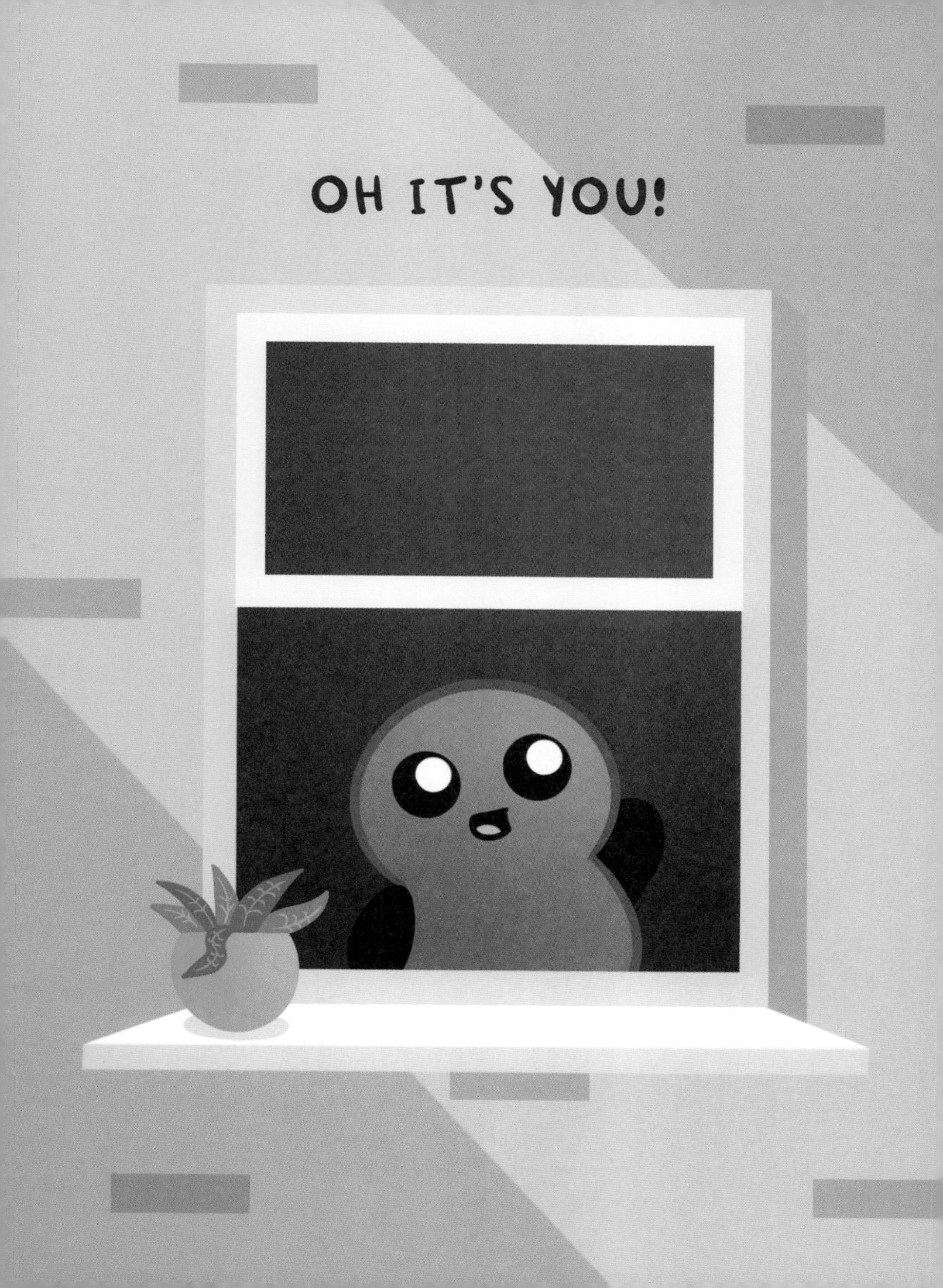
OH IT'S YOU!

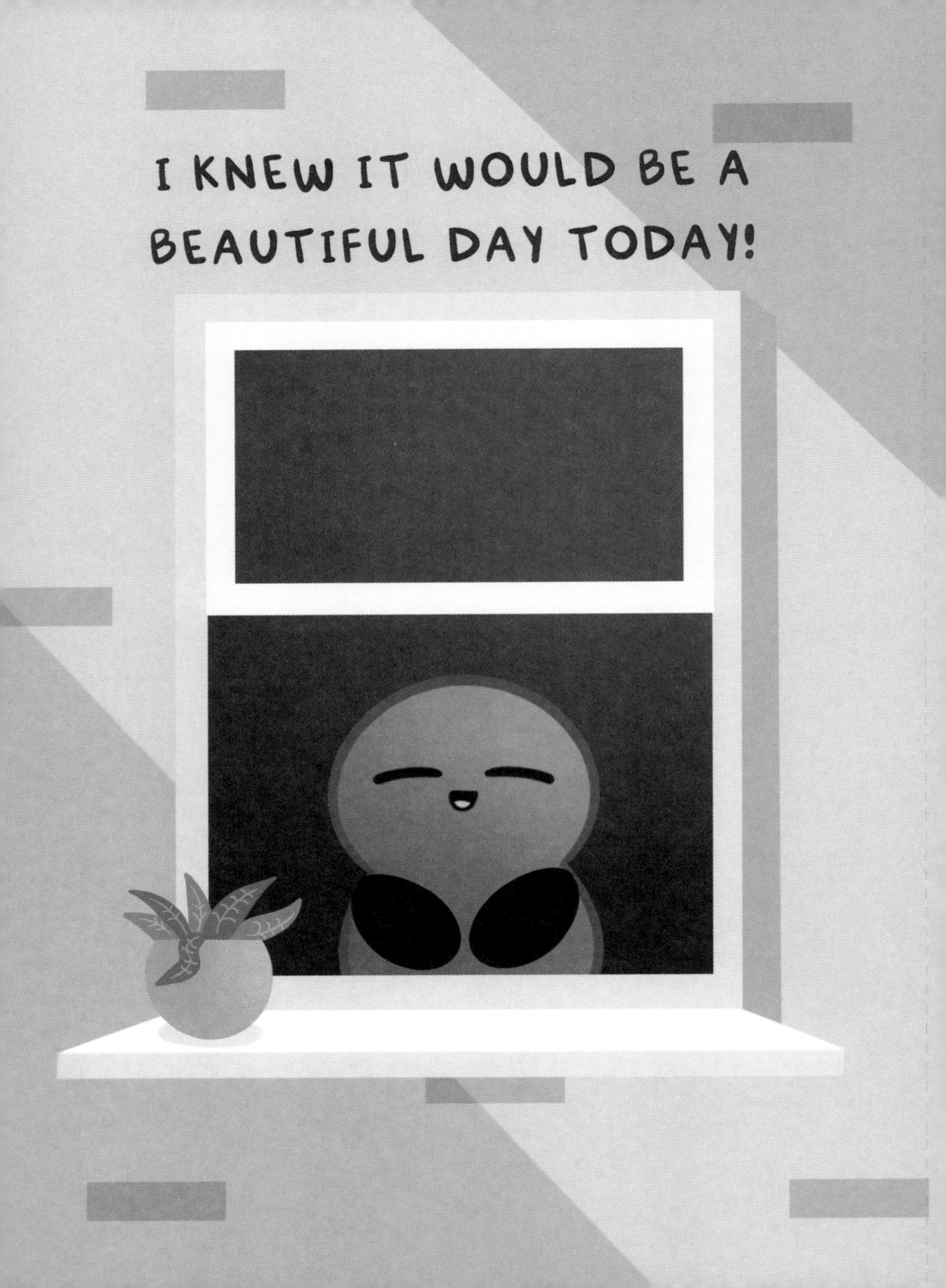
I KNEW IT WOULD BE A BEAUTIFUL DAY TODAY!

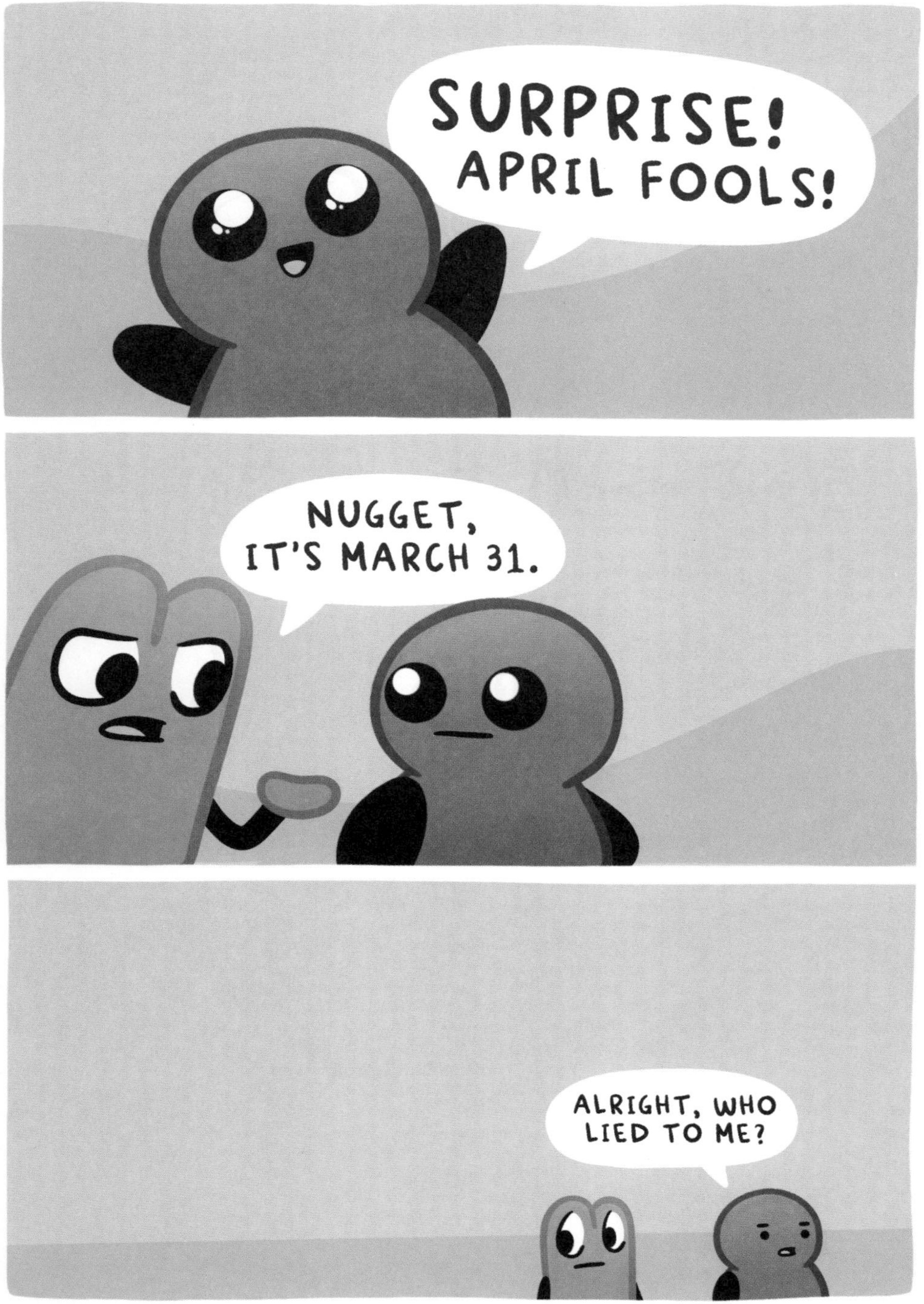
SURPRISE! APRIL FOOLS!
NUGGET, IT'S MARCH 31.
ALRIGHT, WHO LIED TO ME?

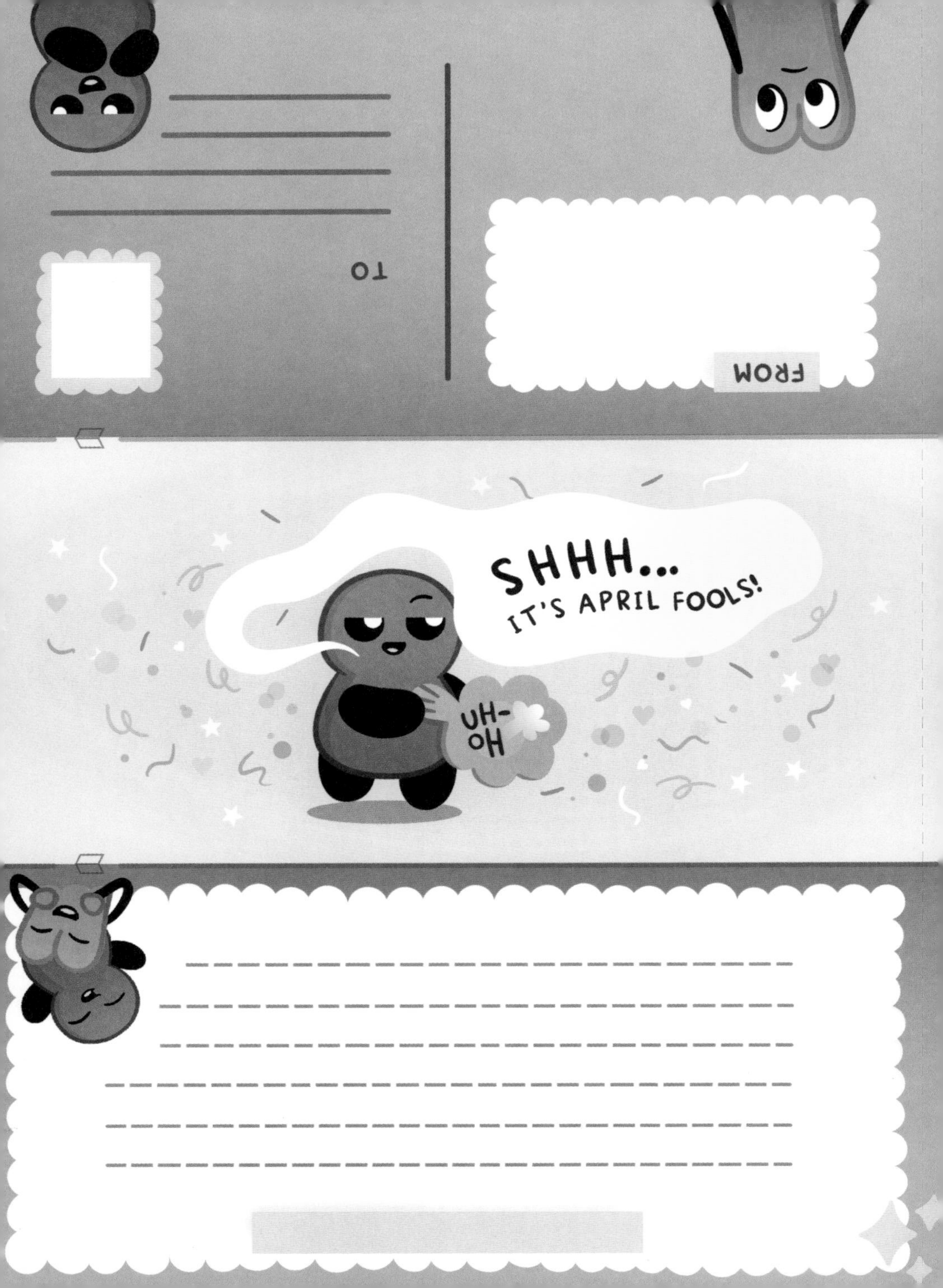
TO
FROM
SHHH...
IT'S APRIL FOOLS!
UH-OH

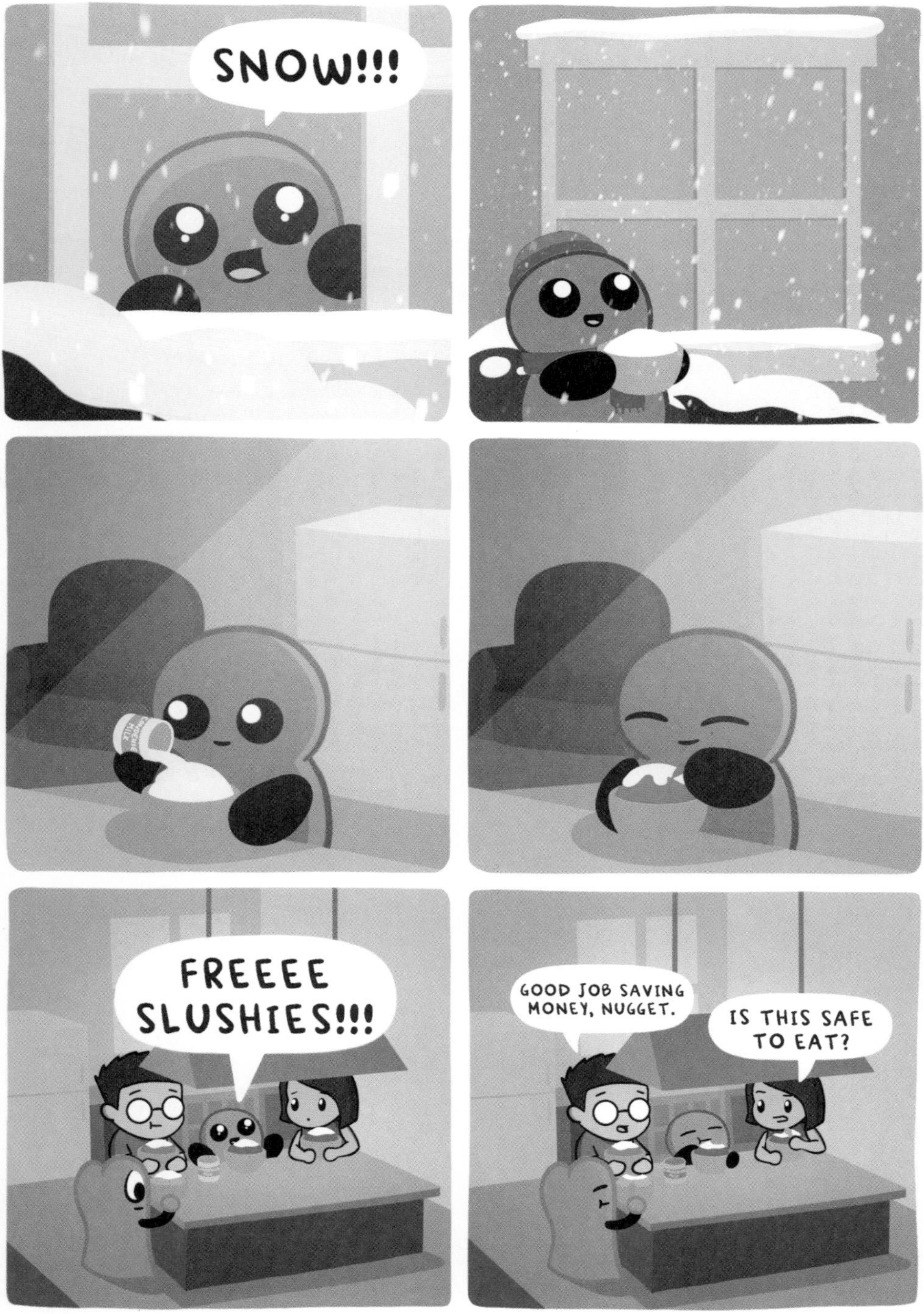
SNOW!!!
FREEEE SLUSHIES!!!
GOOD JOB SAVING MONEY, NUGGET.
IS THIS SAFE TO EAT?

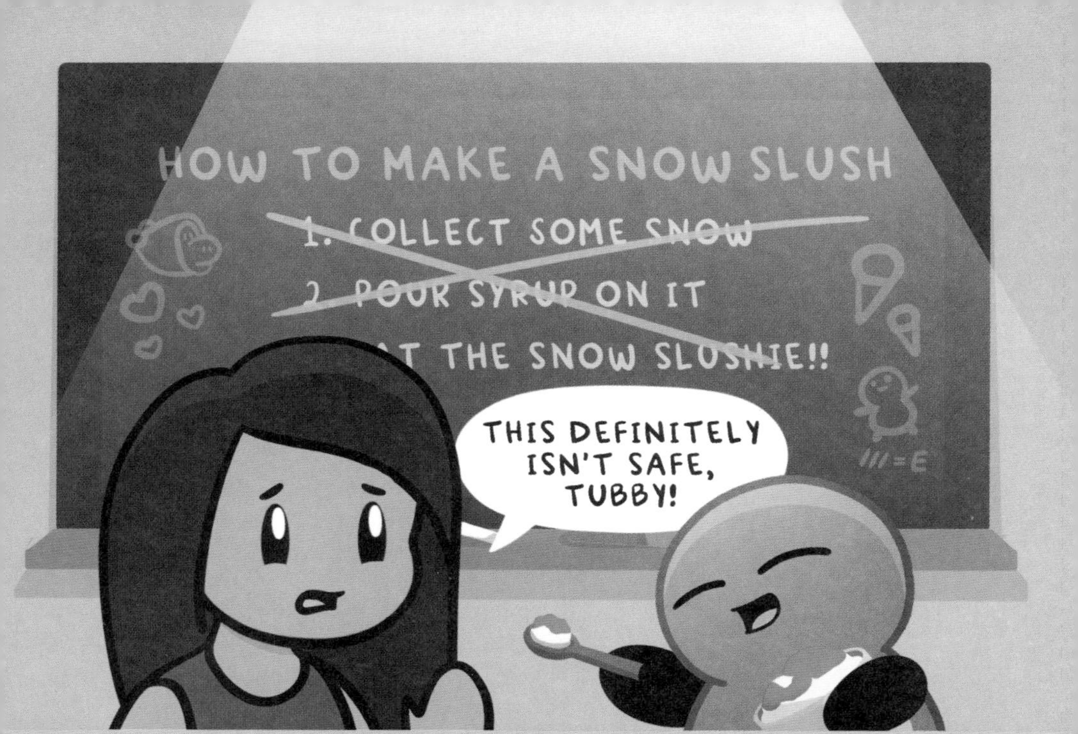
HOW TO MAKE A SNOW SLUSH
1. COLLECT SOME SNOW
2. POUR SYRUP ON IT
...AT THE SNOW SLOSHIE!!
THIS DEFINITELY ISN'T SAFE, TUBBY!

JENINE-APPROVED DELICIOUS "SWEET SNOW"

We all love a good slushie! Here's a list of fun toppings we can get to upgrade ours together!

(But...let's maybe not get our snow from outdoors.)

FRUITY TOPPINGS

- Strawberries
- Mangoes
- Bananas
- Melons
- Kiwi

SWEET TOPPINGS

- Mini mochi
- Chia seeds
- Granola or cereal
- Graham cracker crumbs
- Yogurt
- Chocolate chips

DRIZZLES

- Condensed milk
- Honey or agave
- Chocolate sauce
- Matcha syrup
- Caramel syrup

Circle the ones you like best!

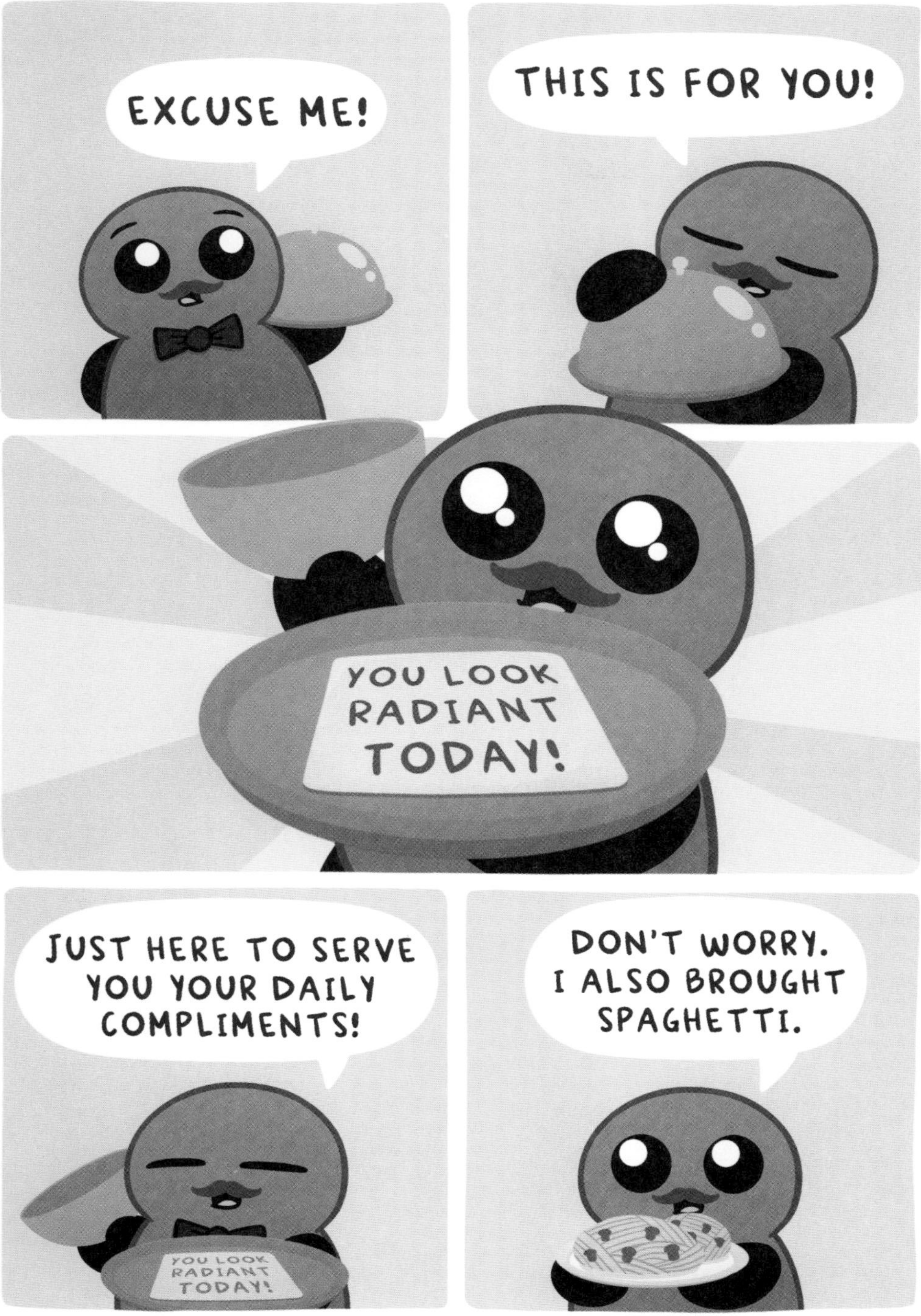
EXCUSE ME!
THIS IS FOR YOU!
YOU LOOK RADIANT TODAY!
JUST HERE TO SERVE YOU YOUR DAILY COMPLIMENTS!
YOU LOOK RADIANT TODAY!
DON'T WORRY. I ALSO BROUGHT SPAGHETTI.

TO

FROM

ESPECIALLY FOR YOU

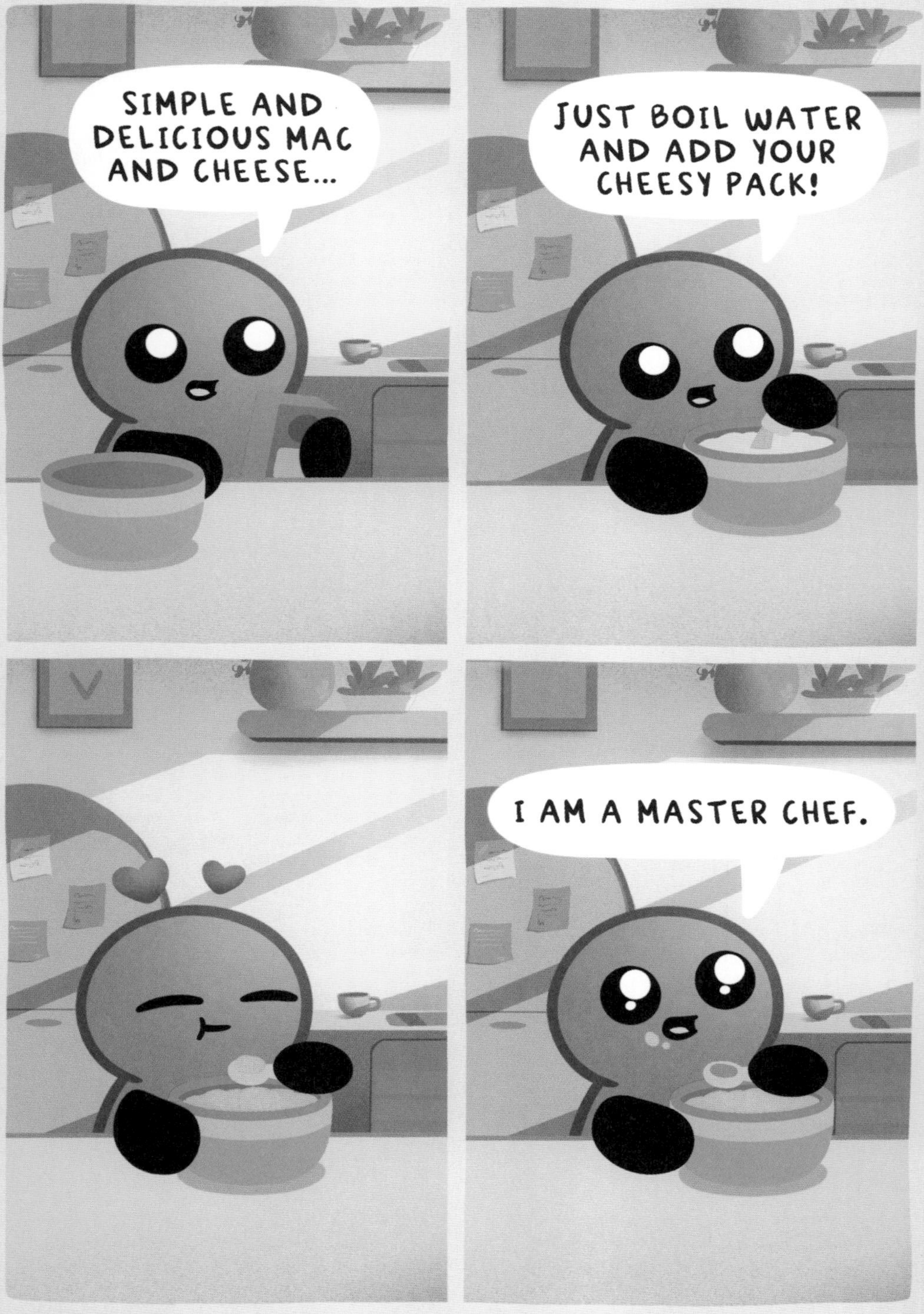
SIMPLE AND DELICIOUS MAC AND CHEESE...
JUST BOIL WATER AND ADD YOUR CHEESY PACK!
I AM A MASTER CHEF.

MEEPLE'S JALAPEÑO MAC AND CHEESE RECIPE

INGREDIENTS:

1 BOX OF ELBOW MACARONI (OR YOUR FAVORITE PASTA SHELLS)
4–5 JALAPEÑOS
1 TOMATO
1/4 CUP OF UNSALTED BUTTER
1/4 CUP OF ALL-PURPOSE FLOUR
1 CUP OF MILK OR HALF-AND-HALF
2 CUPS OF SHREDDED SHARP CHEDDAR CHEESE

1 CUP OF SHREDDED MONTEREY JACK CHEESE
1/2 CUP OF CREAM CHEESE
SALT AND BLACK PEPPER
1/4 CUP OF YOUR FAVORITE SALSA
1/4 CUP OF CRUSHED TORTILLA CHIPS
1/4 CUP OF CRUMBLED COTIJA CHEESE OR GRATED PARMESAN CHEESE
CHOPPED FRESH CILANTRO FOR GARNISHING!

DIRECTIONS:

1. IN A LARGE POT, COOK THE ELBOW MACARONI IN BOILING WATER ACCORDING TO THE PACKAGE DIRECTIONS. DRAIN, TRANSFER TO A LARGE BAKING DISH, AND SET ASIDE.

2. MEANWHILE, PREP YOUR VEGGIES. PEEL, DE-SEED (IF YOU LIKE), AND THINLY SLICE THE JALAPEÑOS. IN A SMALL COOKING PAN OVER HIGH HEAT, BLACKEN THE SLICES UNTIL THEY'RE NICE AND TOASTY, ABOUT 5 TO 10 MINUTES. REMOVE FROM THE HEAT AND SET ASIDE. DICE THE TOMATO.

3. PREHEAT THE OVEN TO 375 DEGREES FAHRENHEIT.

4. IN A SAUCEPAN OVER MEDIUM HEAT, MELT THE BUTTER. ADD THE FLOUR, AND WHISK FOR ABOUT 1–2 MINUTES.

5. WHEN THE MIXTURE IS GOLDEN, WHISK IN THE MILK UNTIL EVERYTHING IS INCORPORATED. KEEP WHISKING UNTIL THE SAUCE BECOMES THICKENED.

6. STIR IN THE CHEDDAR, MONTEREY JACK, AND CREAM CHEESE. CONTINUE STIRRING UNTIL THE CHEESES ARE FULLY MELTED, AND SEASON WITH SALT AND PEPPER.

7. POUR THE CHEESE SAUCE OVER THE PASTA IN THE BAKING DISH. ADD THE JALAPEÑOS, TOMATO, AND SALSA, AND MIX WELL.

8. IN A SMALL BOWL, COMBINE THE CRUSHED TORTILLA CHIPS WITH THE COTIJA CHEESE. GENEROUSLY SPRINKLE THE CRUMB MIXTURE OVER THE TOP OF THE MAC AND CHEESE.

9. BAKE FOR 30–40 MINUTES OR UNTIL THE TOP CRUST IS GOLDEN AND CRISPY.

10. GARNISH WITH CILANTRO, AND SERVE!

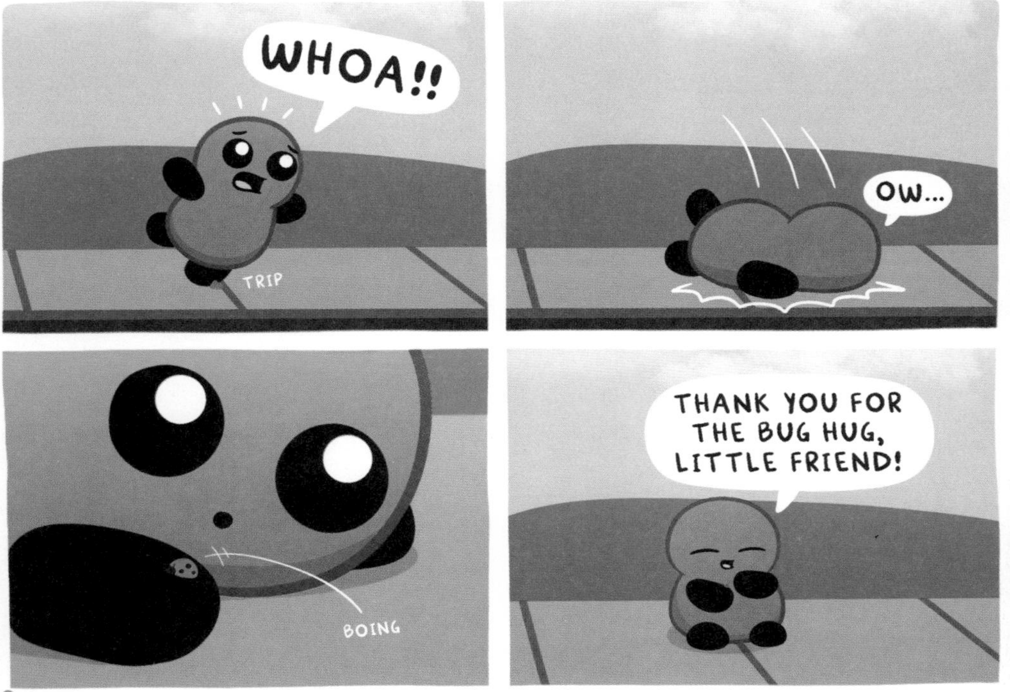
WHOA!!
TRIP
OW...
BOING
THANK YOU FOR THE BUG HUG, LITTLE FRIEND!

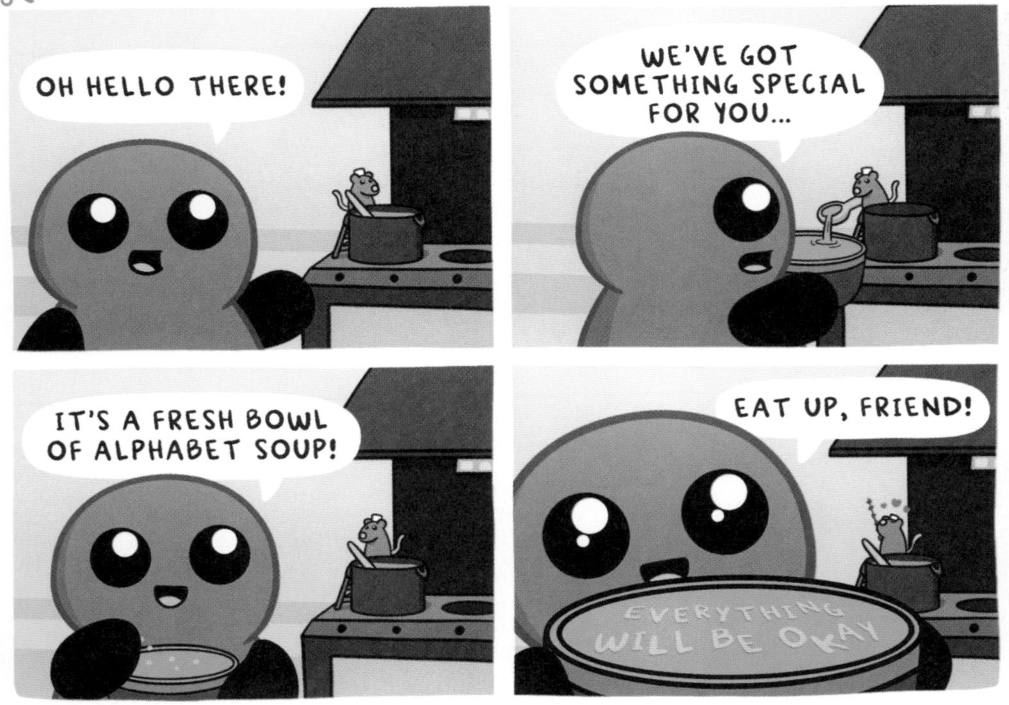
OH HELLO THERE!
WE'VE GOT SOMETHING SPECIAL FOR YOU...
IT'S A FRESH BOWL OF ALPHABET SOUP!
EAT UP, FRIEND!
EVERYTHING WILL BE OKAY

BUG HUG FROM

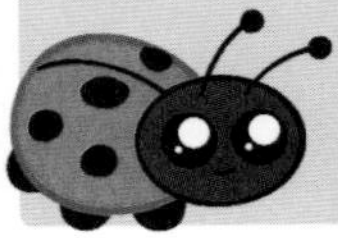

TO

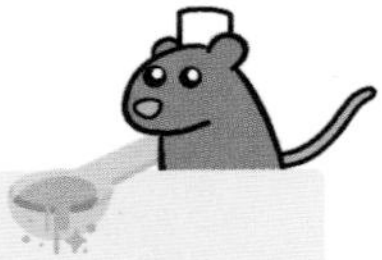

SPICE OF LIFE
COURTESY OF

TO

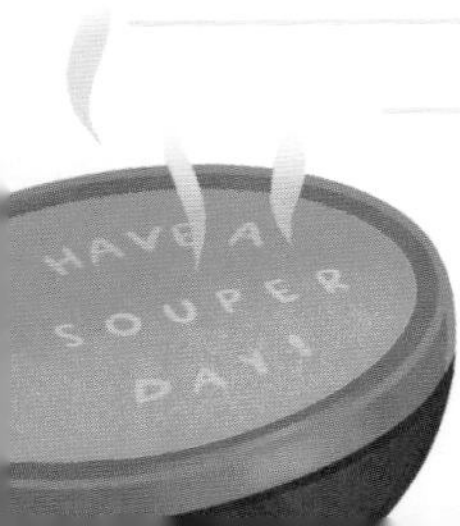
HAVE A
SOUPER
DAY!

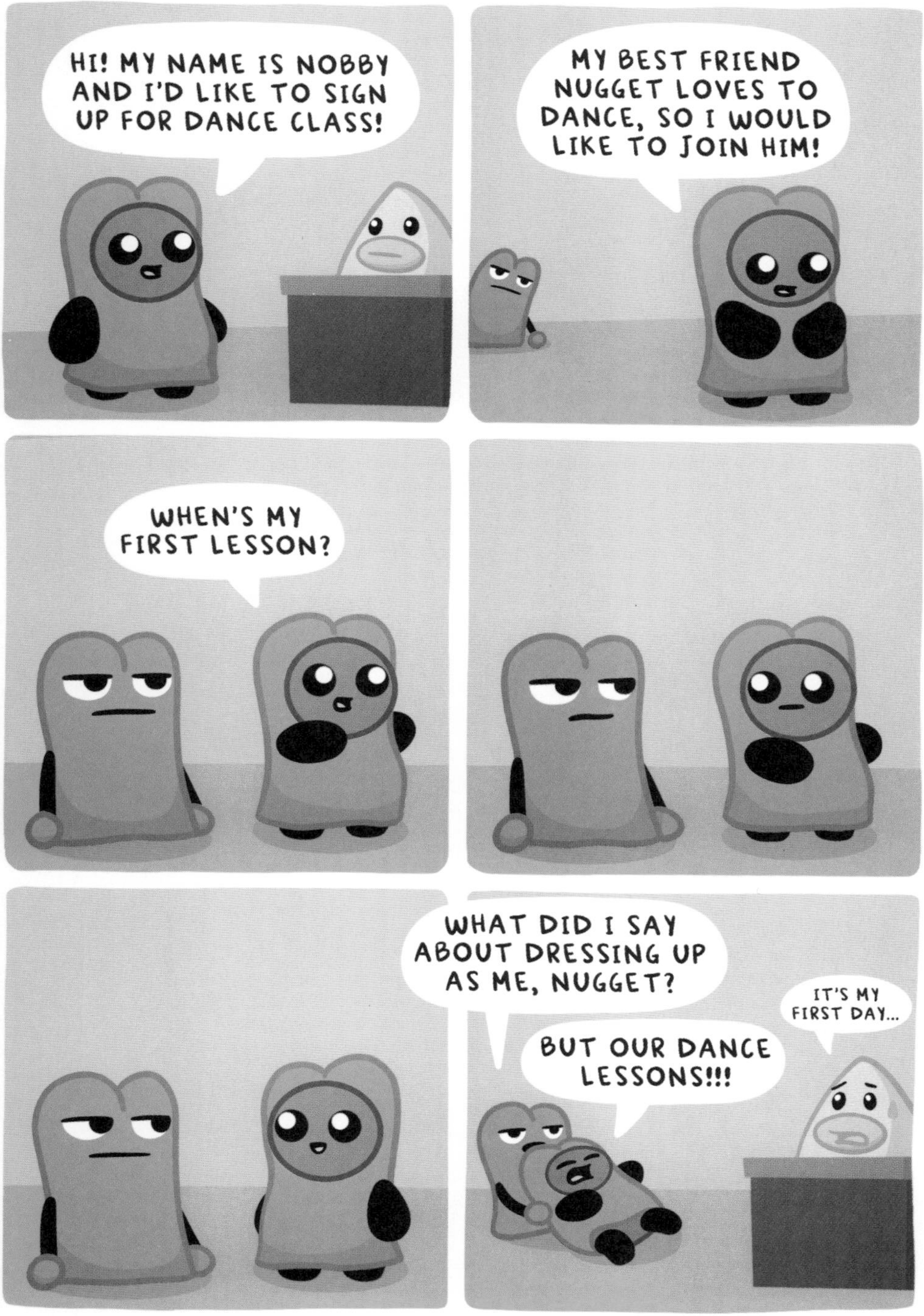
HI! MY NAME IS NOBBY AND I'D LIKE TO SIGN UP FOR DANCE CLASS!
MY BEST FRIEND NUGGET LOVES TO DANCE, SO I WOULD LIKE TO JOIN HIM!
WHEN'S MY FIRST LESSON?
WHAT DID I SAY ABOUT DRESSING UP AS ME, NUGGET?
BUT OUR DANCE LESSONS!!!
IT'S MY FIRST DAY...

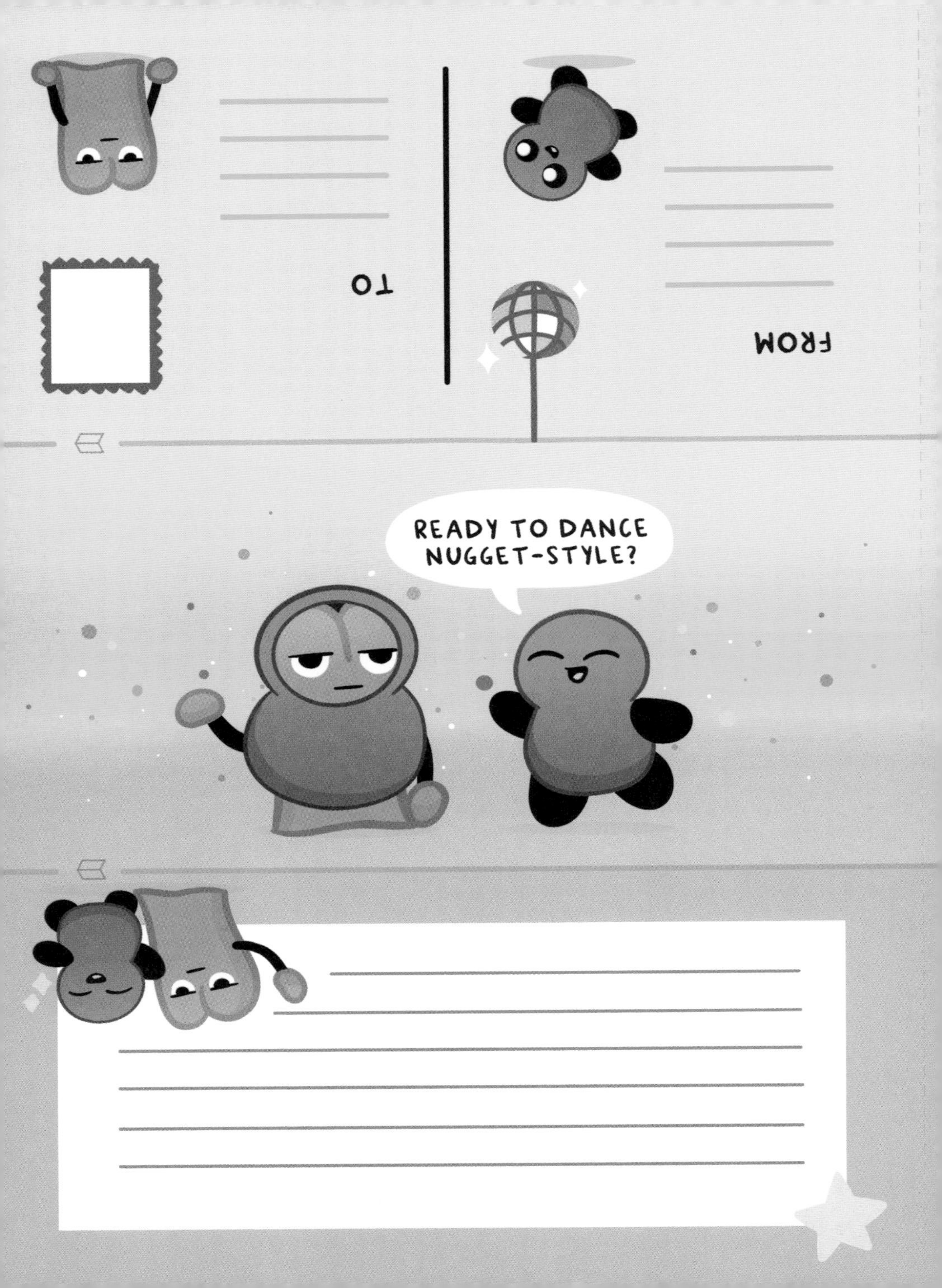
TO
FROM
READY TO DANCE NUGGET-STYLE?

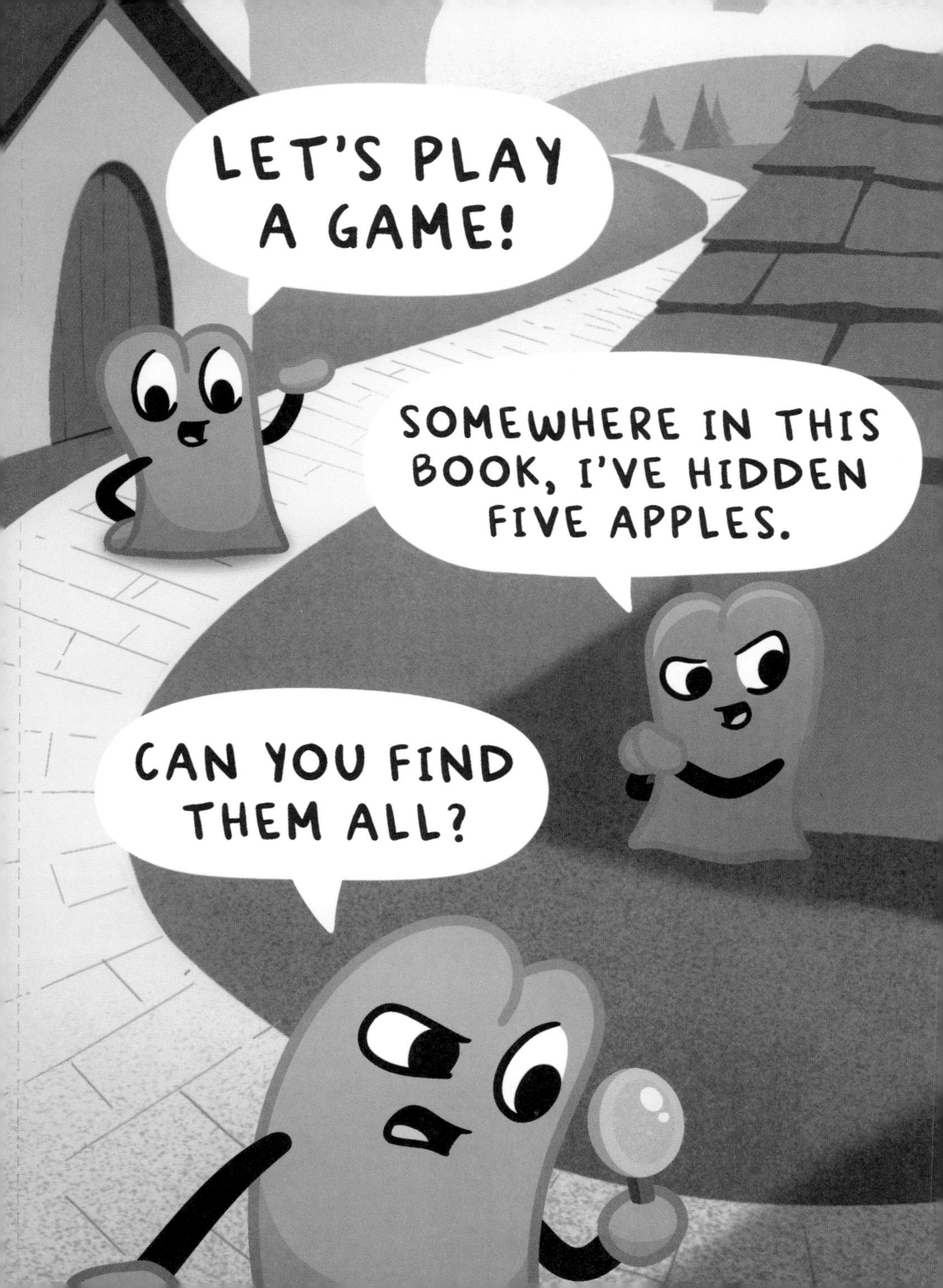
LET'S PLAY A GAME!
SOMEWHERE IN THIS BOOK, I'VE HIDDEN FIVE APPLES.
CAN YOU FIND THEM ALL?

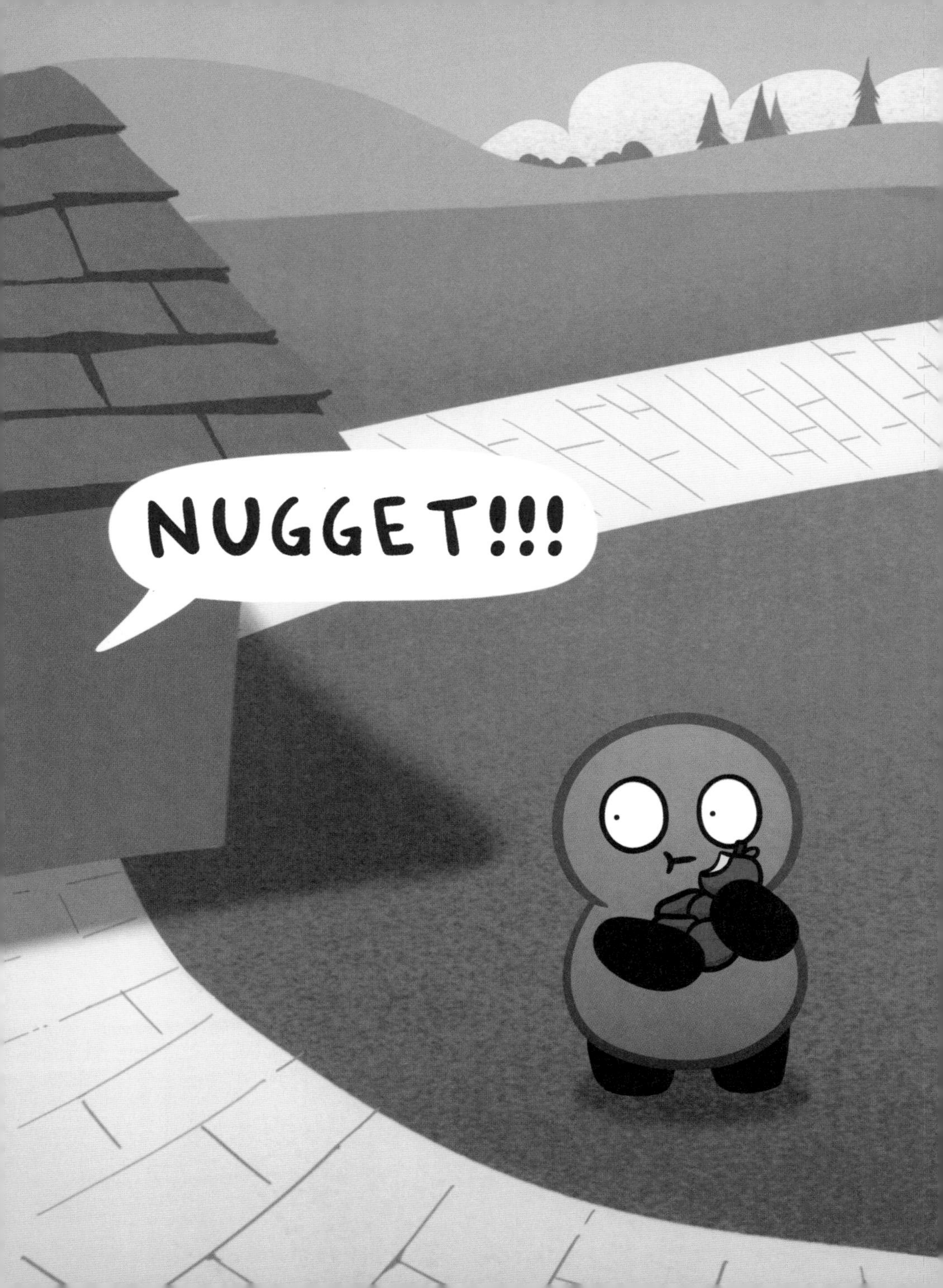
NUGGET!!!

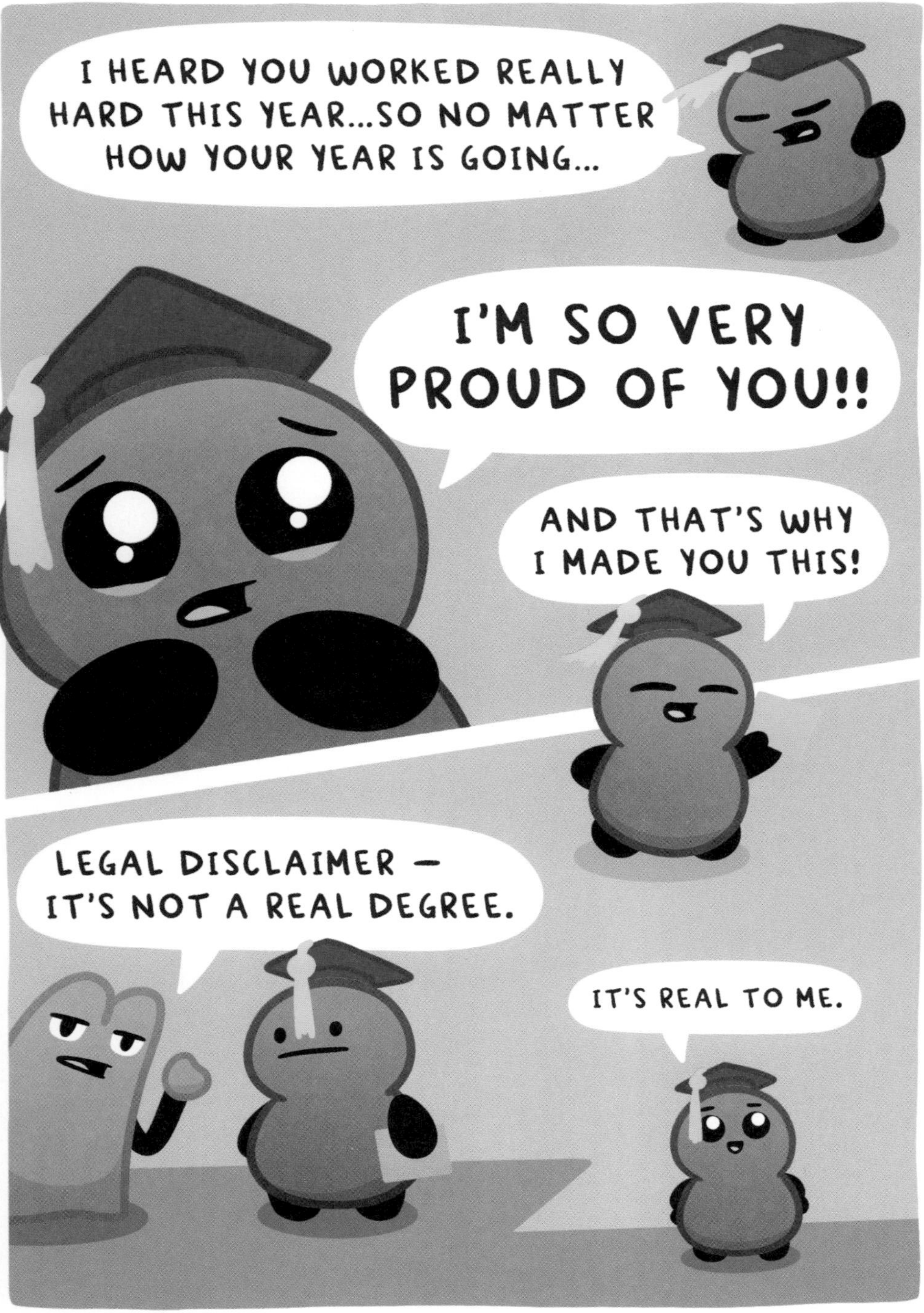
I HEARD YOU WORKED REALLY HARD THIS YEAR...SO NO MATTER HOW YOUR YEAR IS GOING...
I'M SO VERY PROUD OF YOU!!
AND THAT'S WHY I MADE YOU THIS!
LEGAL DISCLAIMER — IT'S NOT A REAL DEGREE.
IT'S REAL TO ME.

NUGGET'S DEGREE OF WONDERFULNESS

On nomination of the faculty of

Nuggeton "Not-A-Real" College

We have conferred upon you,

the degree of Bachelor of Wonderfulness!

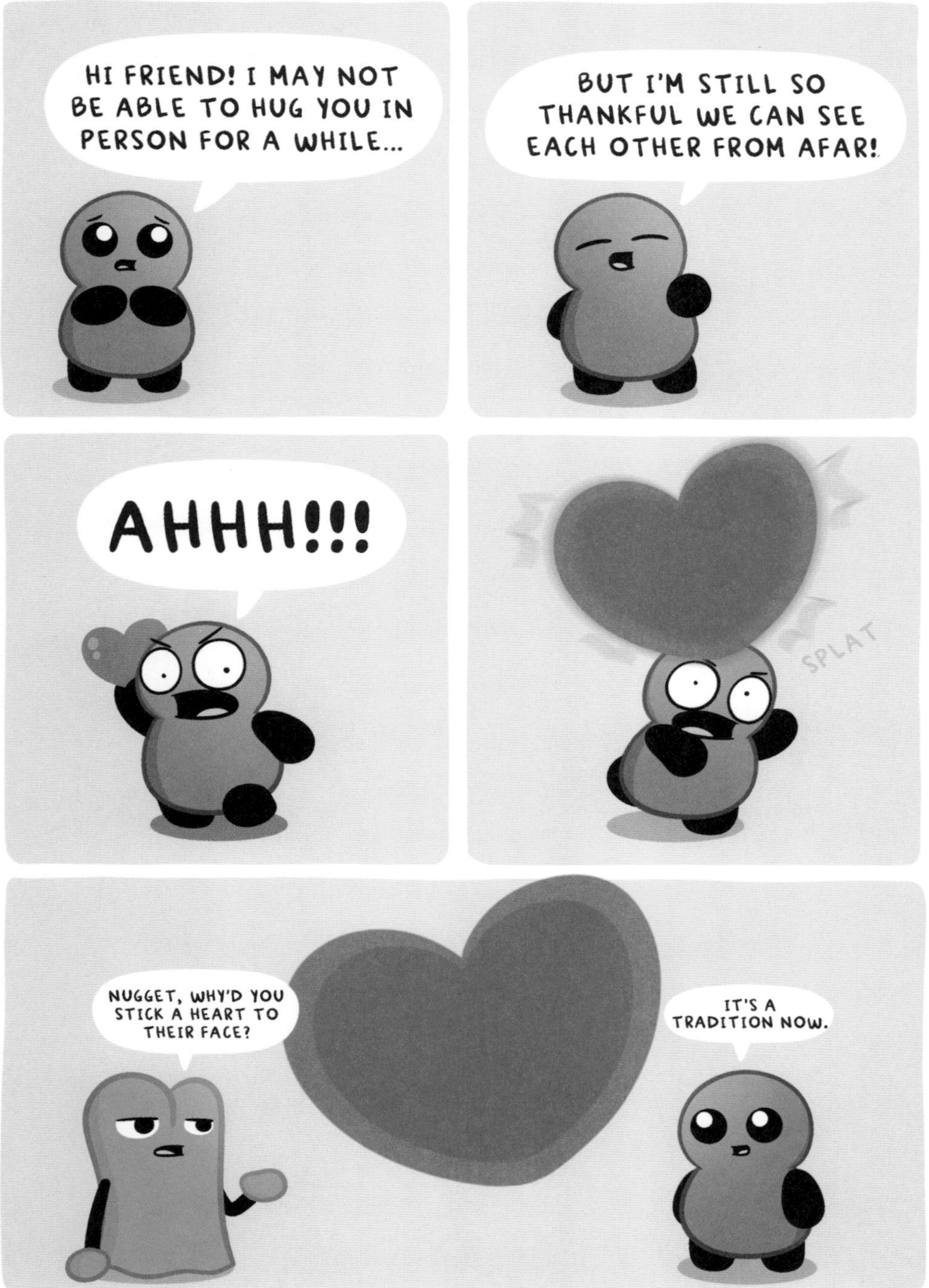
HI FRIEND! I MAY NOT BE ABLE TO HUG YOU IN PERSON FOR A WHILE...
BUT I'M STILL SO THANKFUL WE CAN SEE EACH OTHER FROM AFAR!
AHHH!!!
SPLAT
NUGGET, WHY'D YOU STICK A HEART TO THEIR FACE?
IT'S A TRADITION NOW.

FROM

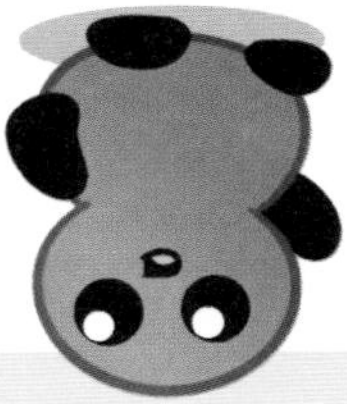

TO

INCOMING: LONG-DISTANCE HUG

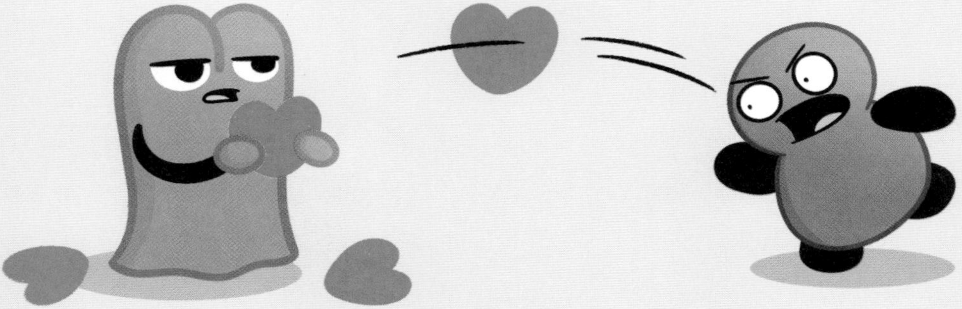

SENDING HUGS & LOVE

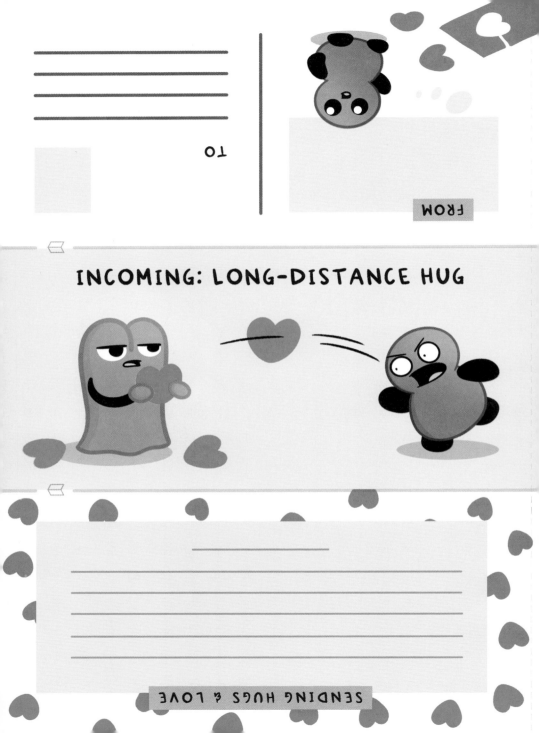

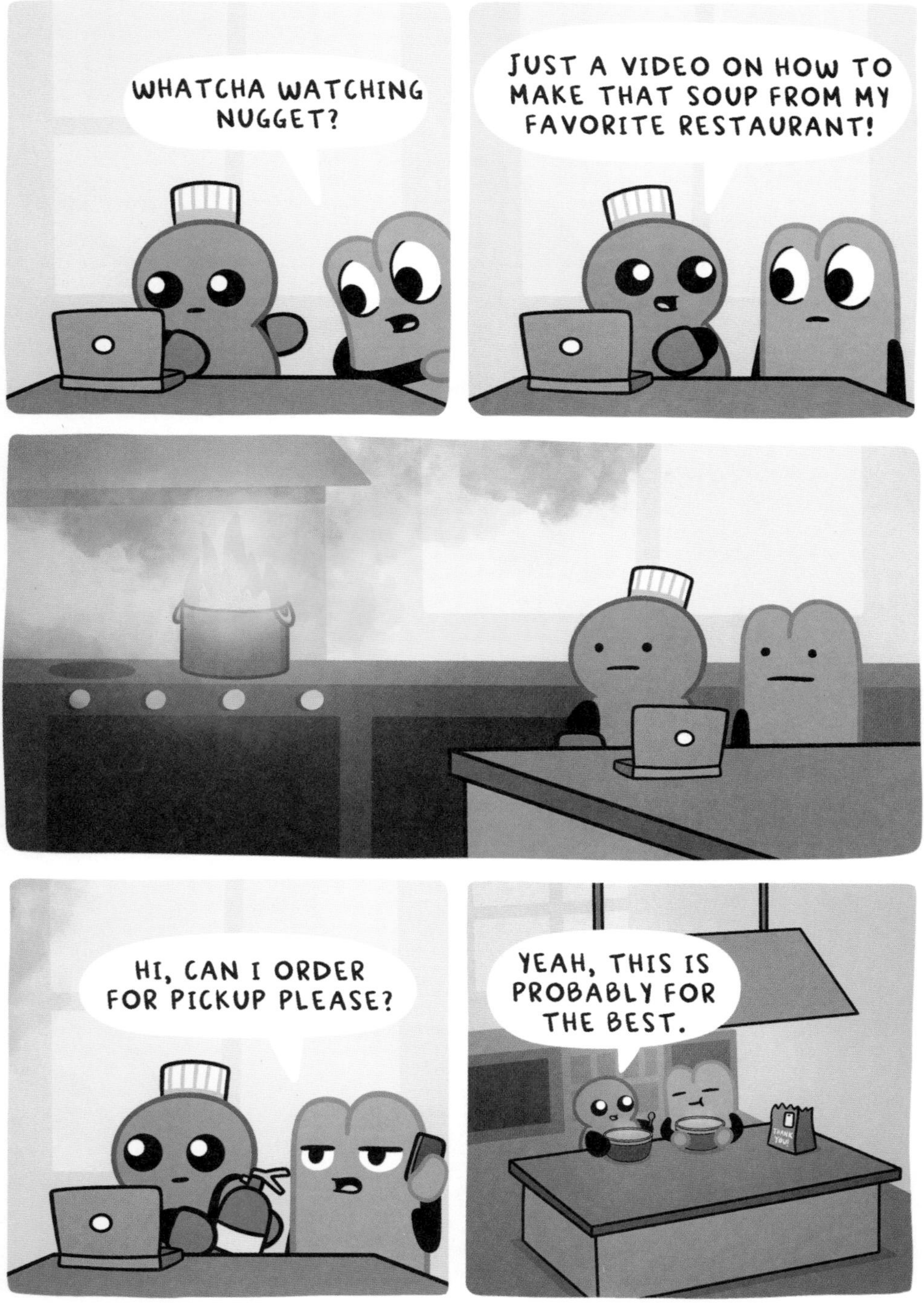
WHATCHA WATCHING NUGGET?
JUST A VIDEO ON HOW TO MAKE THAT SOUP FROM MY FAVORITE RESTAURANT!
HI, CAN I ORDER FOR PICKUP PLEASE?
YEAH, THIS IS PROBABLY FOR THE BEST.

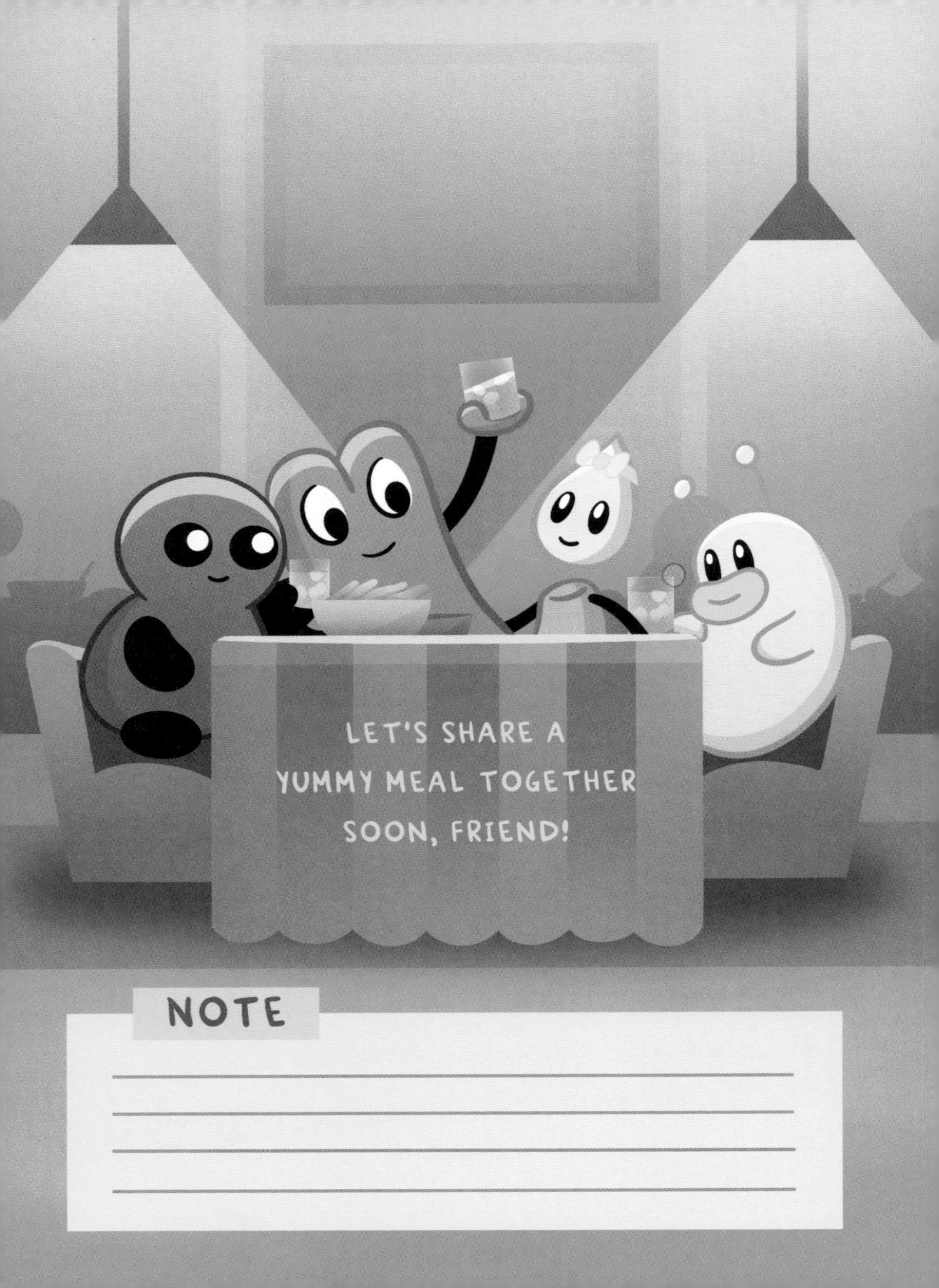
LET'S SHARE A
YUMMY MEAL TOGETHER
SOON, FRIEND!

NOTE

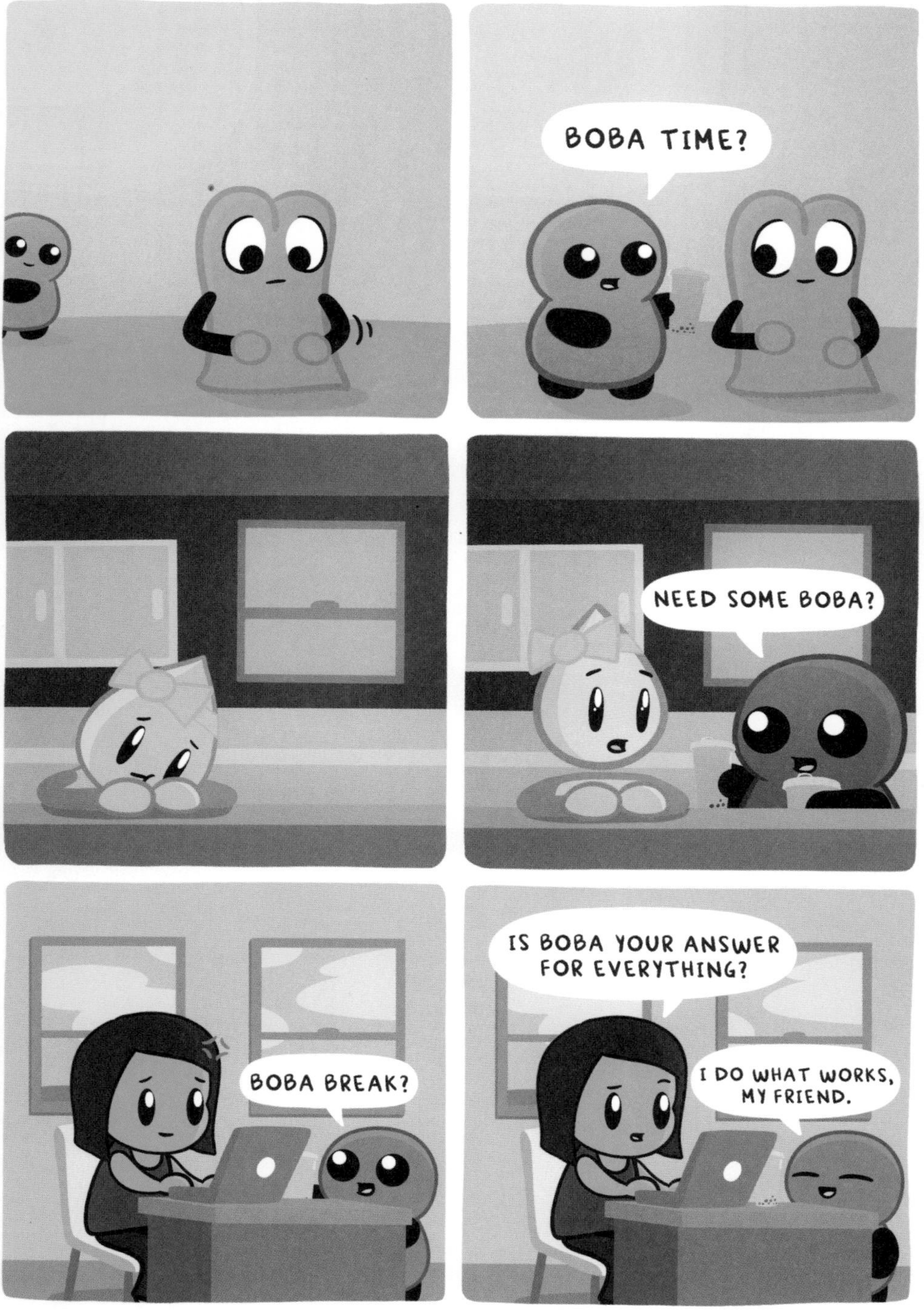
BOBA TIME?
NEED SOME BOBA?
BOBA BREAK?
IS BOBA YOUR ANSWER FOR EVERYTHING?
I DO WHAT WORKS, MY FRIEND.

WILL YOU JOIN ME FOR BOBA?

DATE: ____________________

TIME: ____________________

LOCATION: ________________

____________________ TO

HI BEST-TEA!

FROM

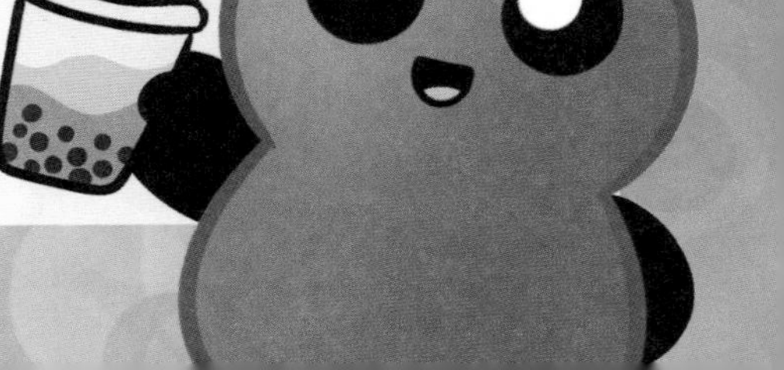

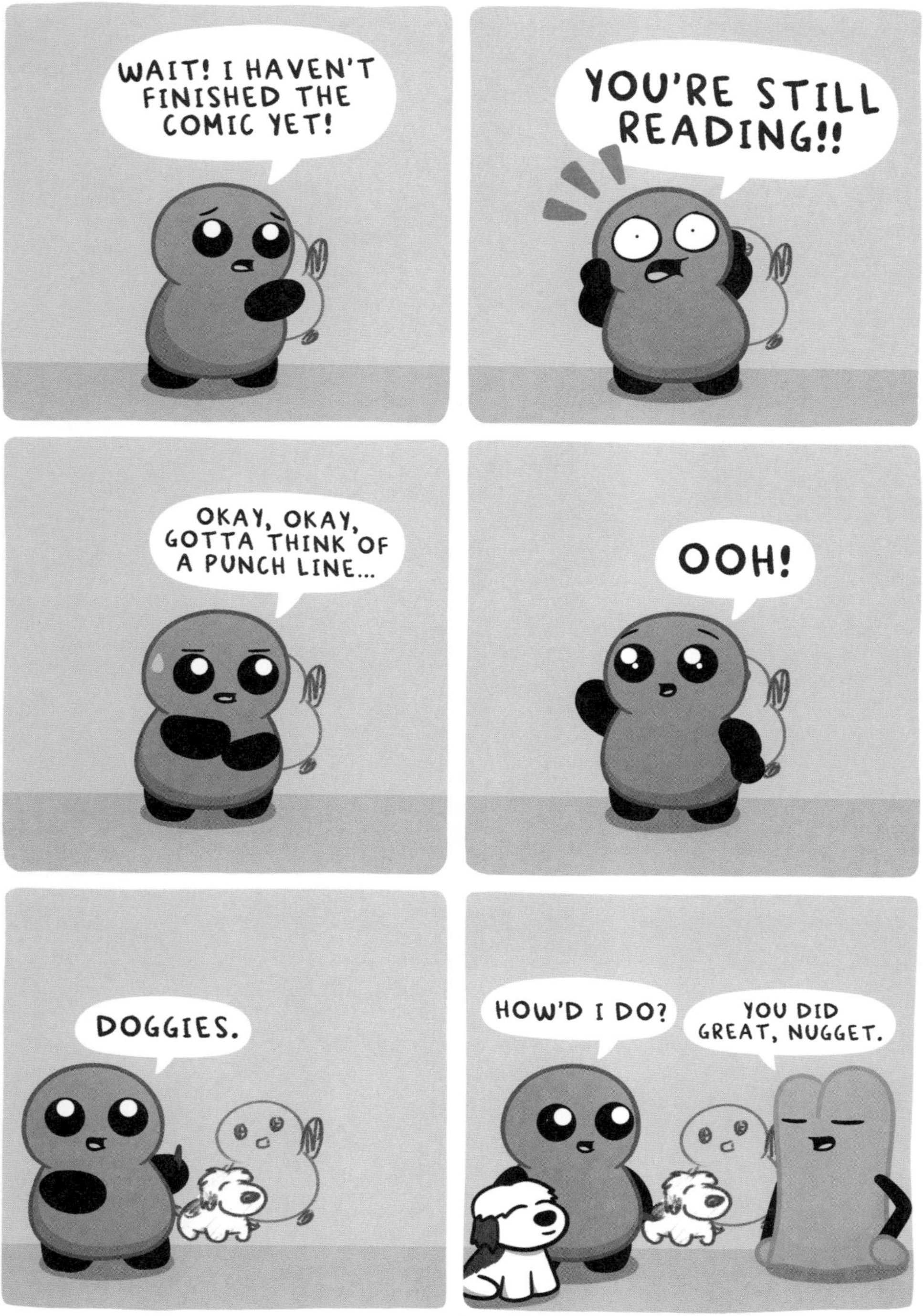
WAIT! I HAVEN'T FINISHED THE COMIC YET!
YOU'RE STILL READING!!
OKAY, OKAY, GOTTA THINK OF A PUNCH LINE...
OOH!
DOGGIES.
HOW'D I DO?
YOU DID GREAT, NUGGET.

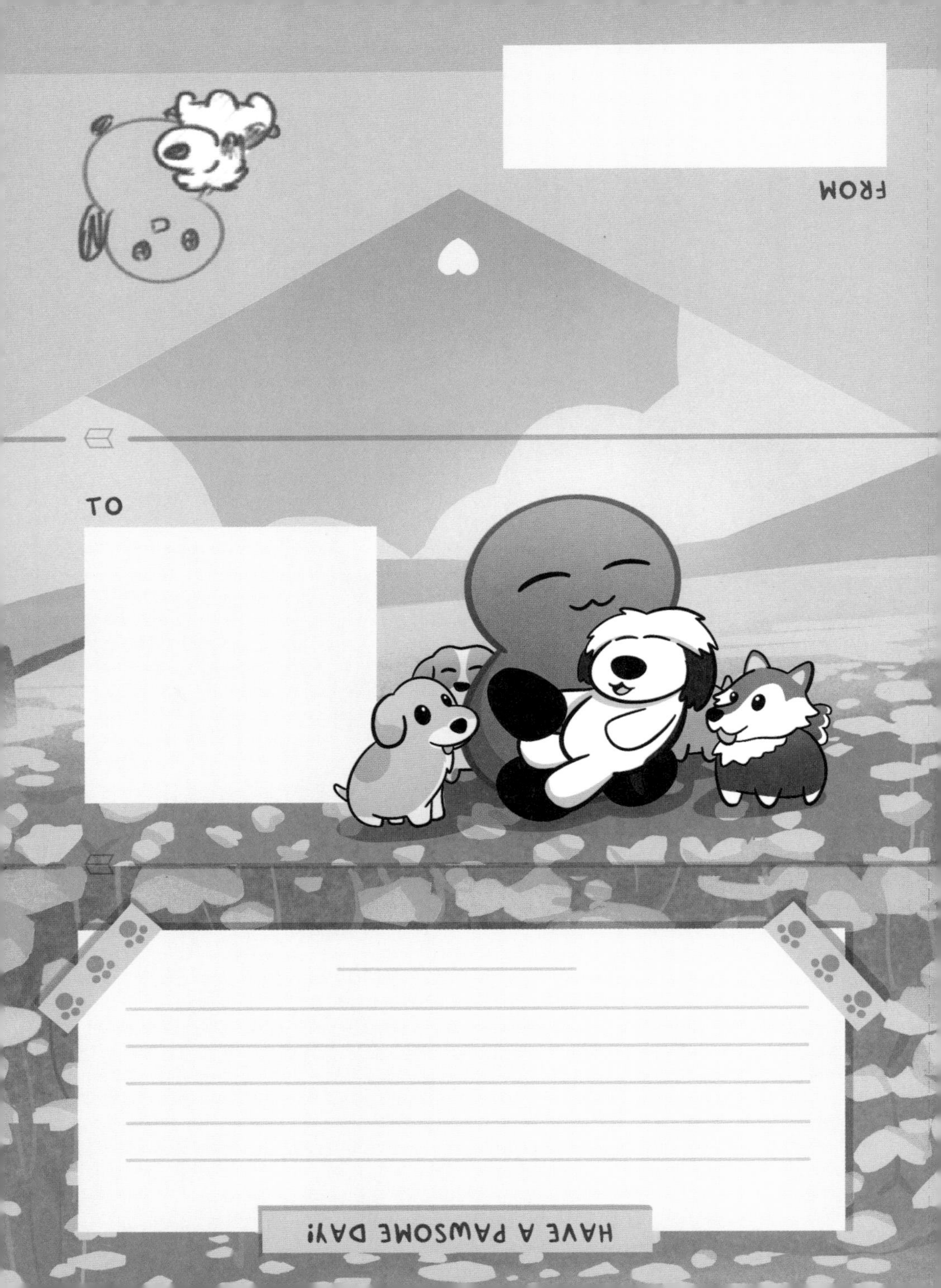
FROM
TO
HAVE A PAWSOME DAY!

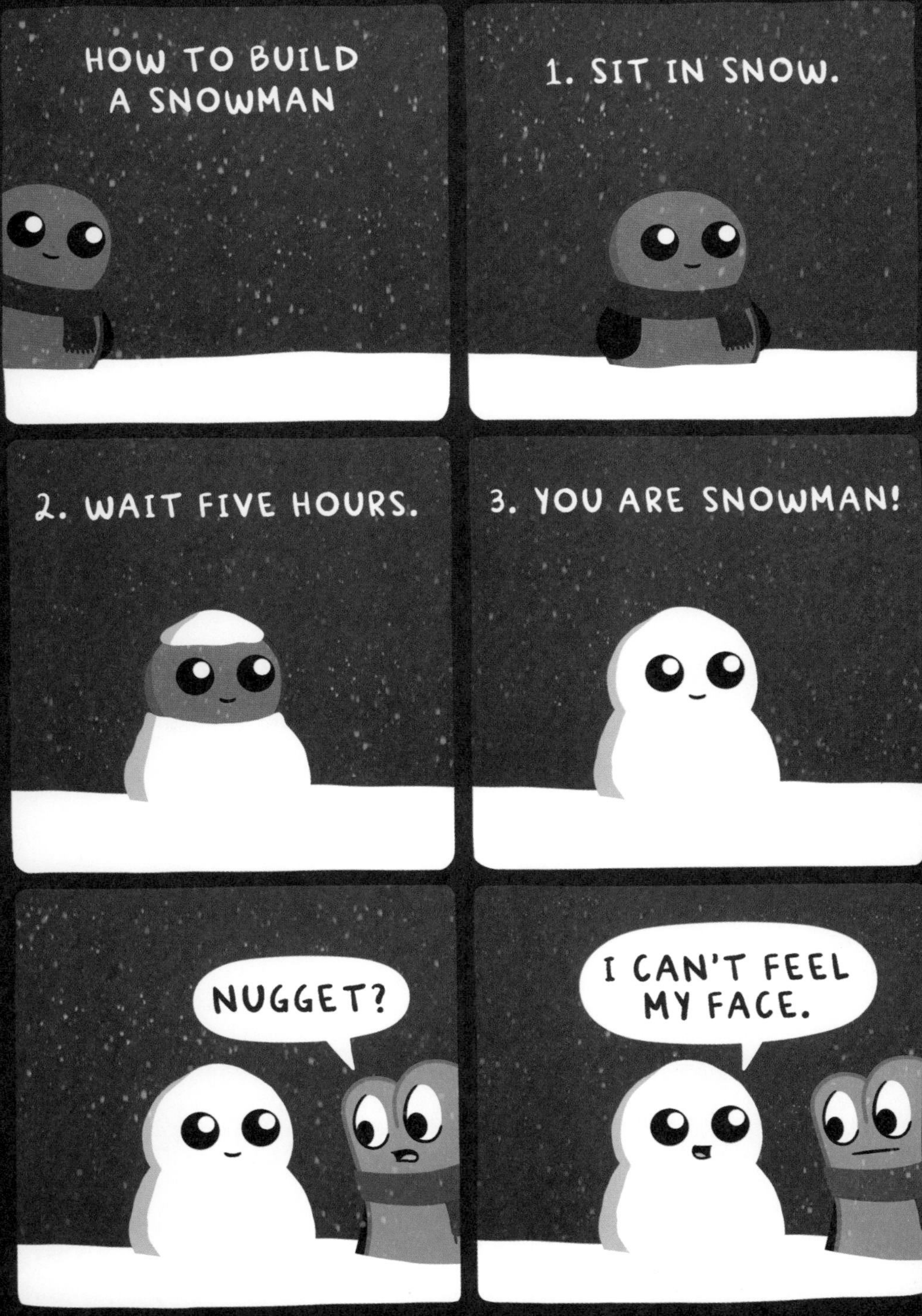
HOW TO BUILD A SNOWMAN
1. SIT IN SNOW.
2. WAIT FIVE HOURS.
3. YOU ARE SNOWMAN!
NUGGET?
I CAN'T FEEL MY FACE.

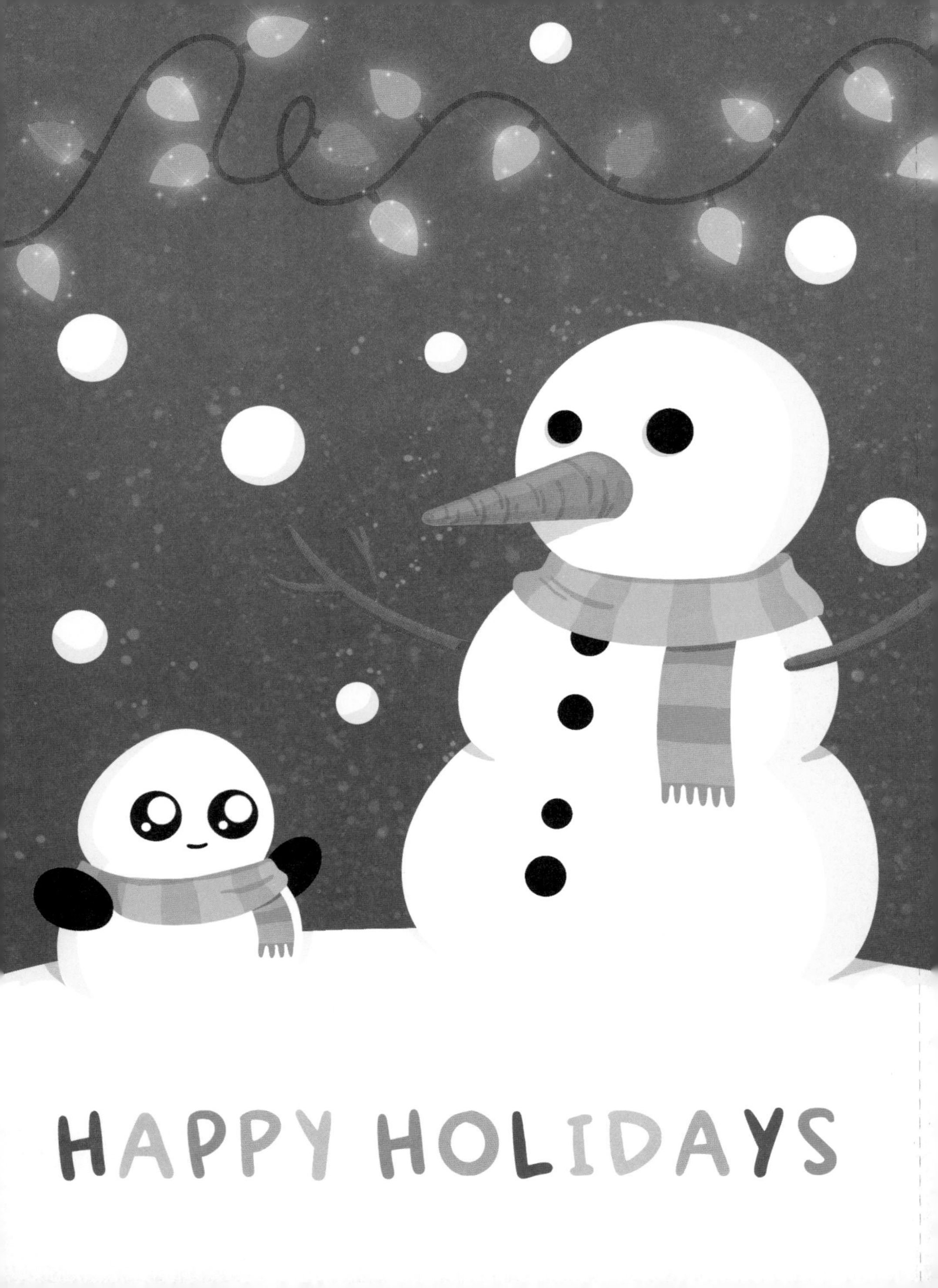
HAPPY HOLIDAYS

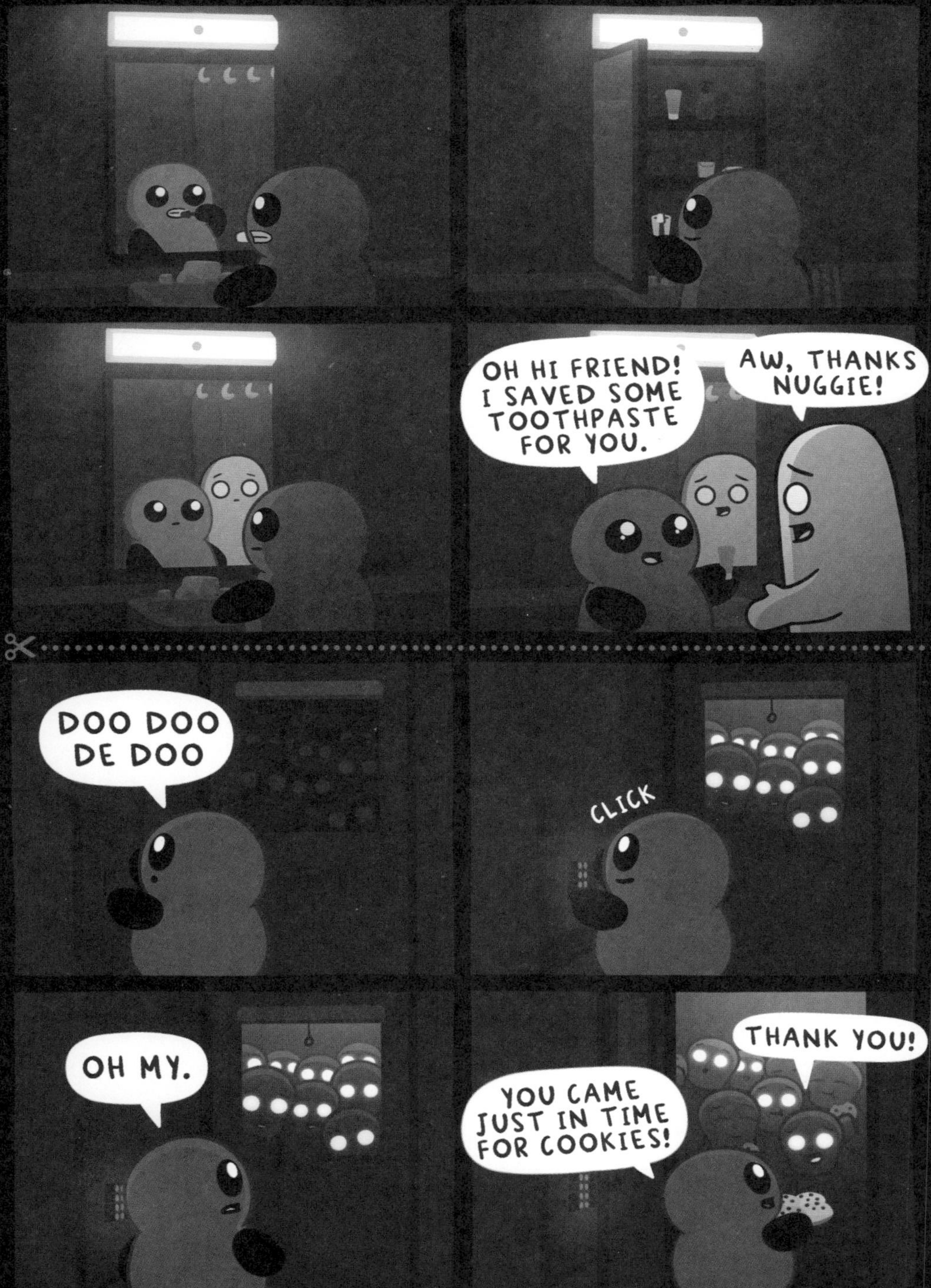
OH HI FRIEND! I SAVED SOME TOOTHPASTE FOR YOU.
AW, THANKS NUGGIE!
DOO DOO DE DOO
CLICK
OH MY.
THANK YOU!
YOU CAME JUST IN TIME FOR COOKIES!

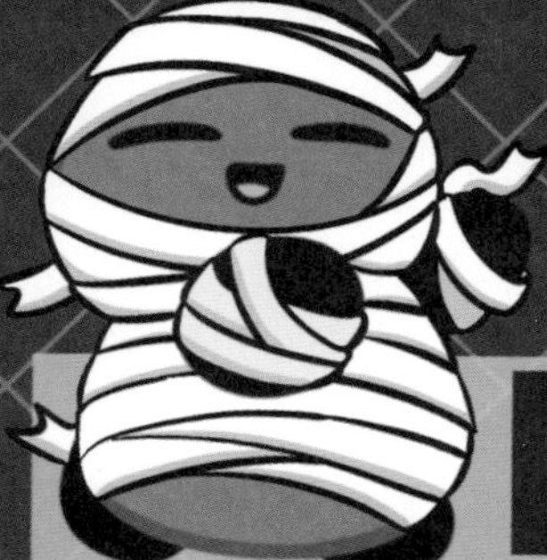

YOU'RE INVITED!

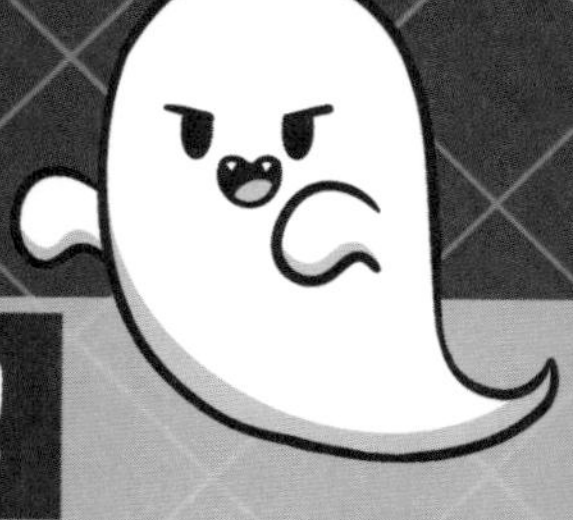

FROM

TO

FROM

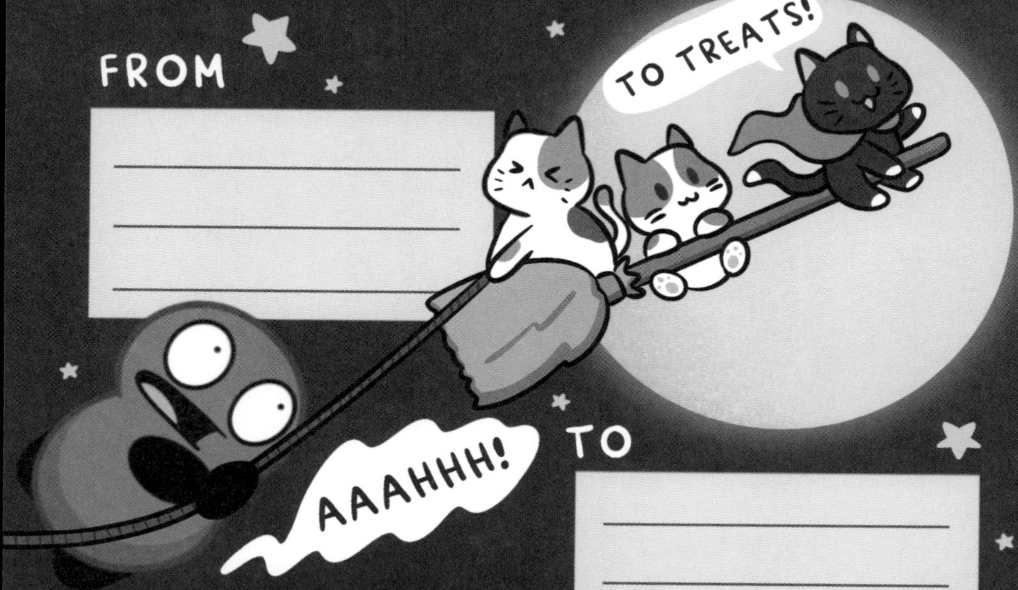
TO TREATS!
AAAHHH!

TO

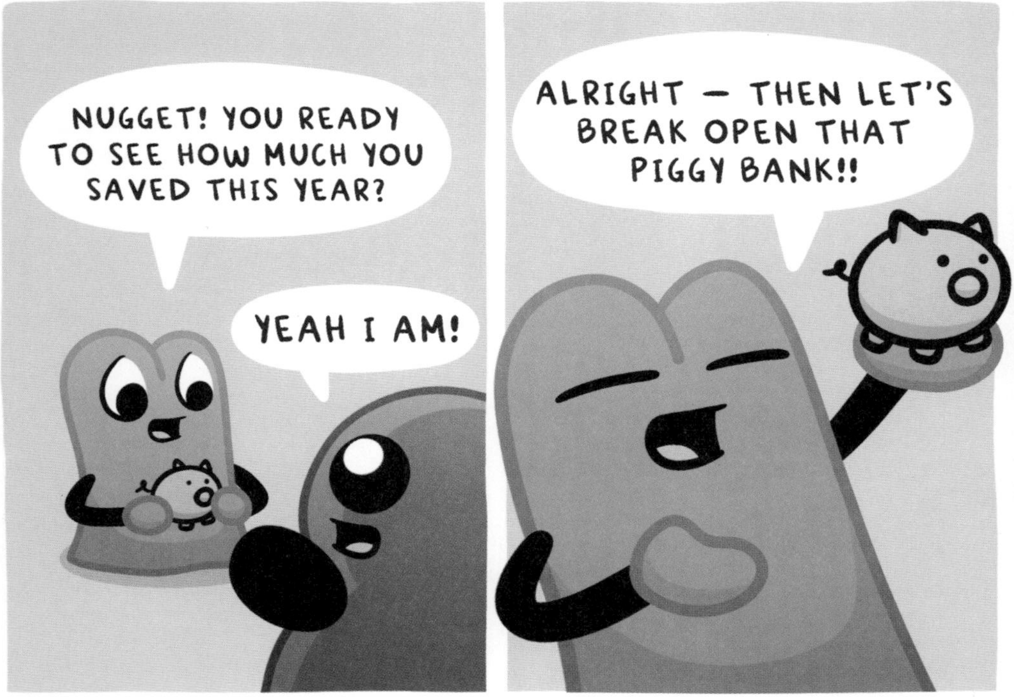
NUGGET! YOU READY TO SEE HOW MUCH YOU SAVED THIS YEAR?
YEAH I AM!
ALRIGHT — THEN LET'S BREAK OPEN THAT PIGGY BANK!!

HERE'S SOME NUGGET-APPROVED CURRENCY TO USE!! (VALID ONLY IN EXCHANGE FOR FRIENDSHIP, AND COOL NUGGETY VIBES)

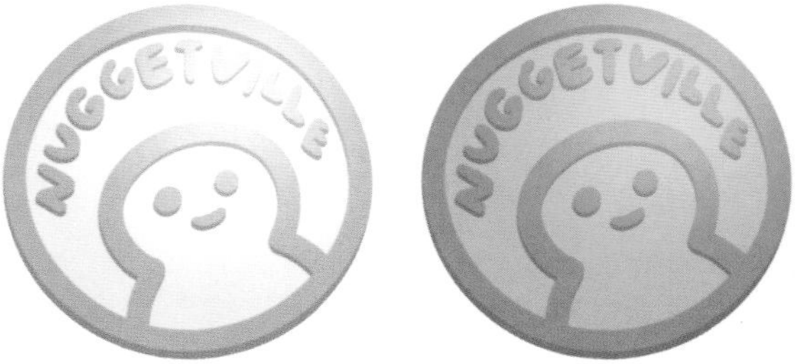
NUGGETVILLE
NUGGETVILLE

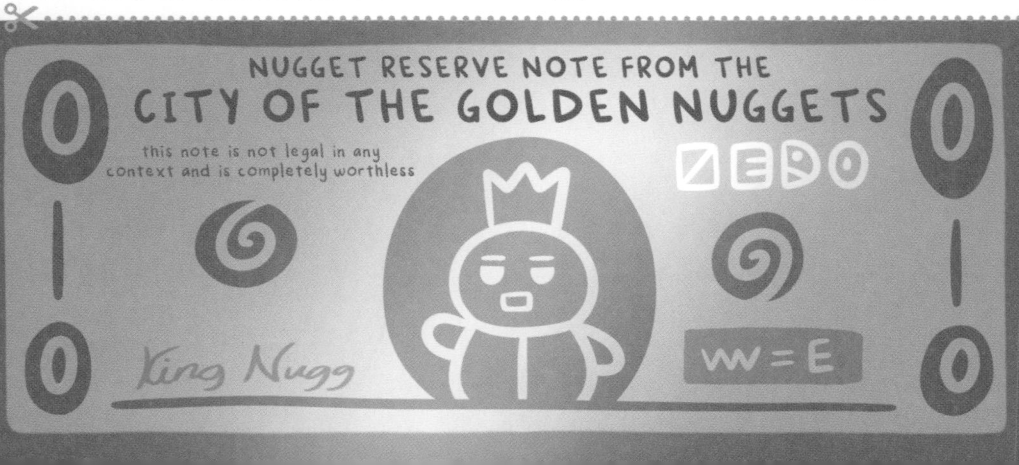
NUGGET RESERVE NOTE FROM THE
CITY OF THE GOLDEN NUGGETS
this note is not legal in any context and is completely worthless
ZERO
0
0
0
0
King Nugg

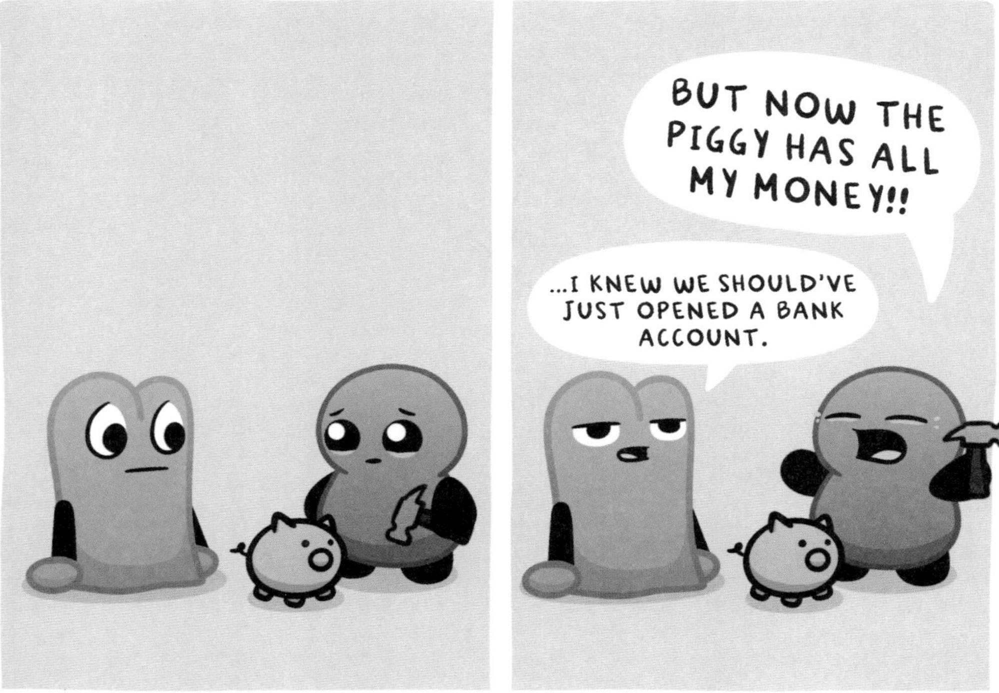
BUT NOW THE PIGGY HAS ALL MY MONEY!!
...I KNEW WE SHOULD'VE JUST OPENED A BANK ACCOUNT.

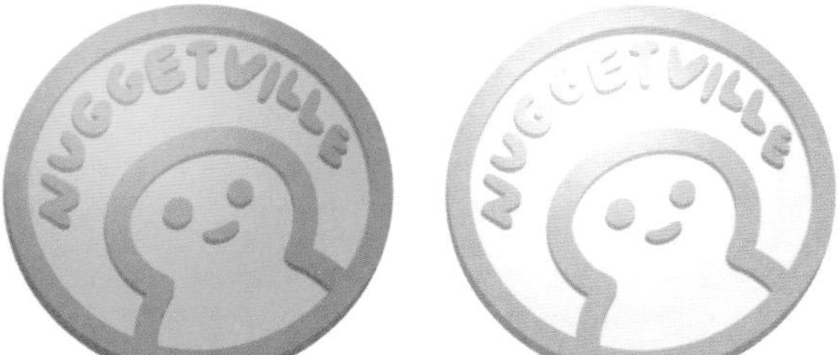
NUGGETVILLE
NUGGETVILLE

NUGGETVILLE CURRENCY:

PELL = DOLLAR
PEBBLE = COIN

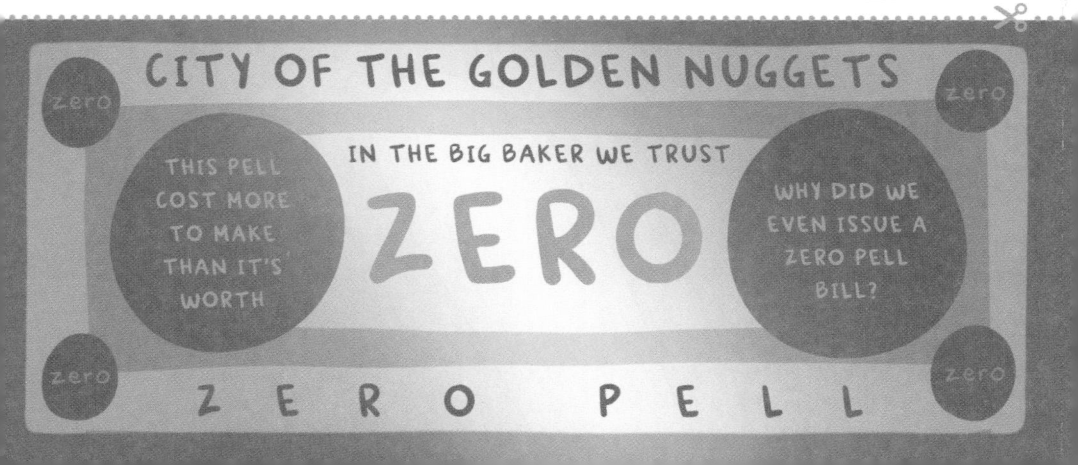
CITY OF THE GOLDEN NUGGETS
zero
zero
IN THE BIG BAKER WE TRUST
THIS PELL COST MORE TO MAKE THAN IT'S WORTH
ZERO
WHY DID WE EVEN ISSUE A ZERO PELL BILL?
zero
zero
ZERO PELL

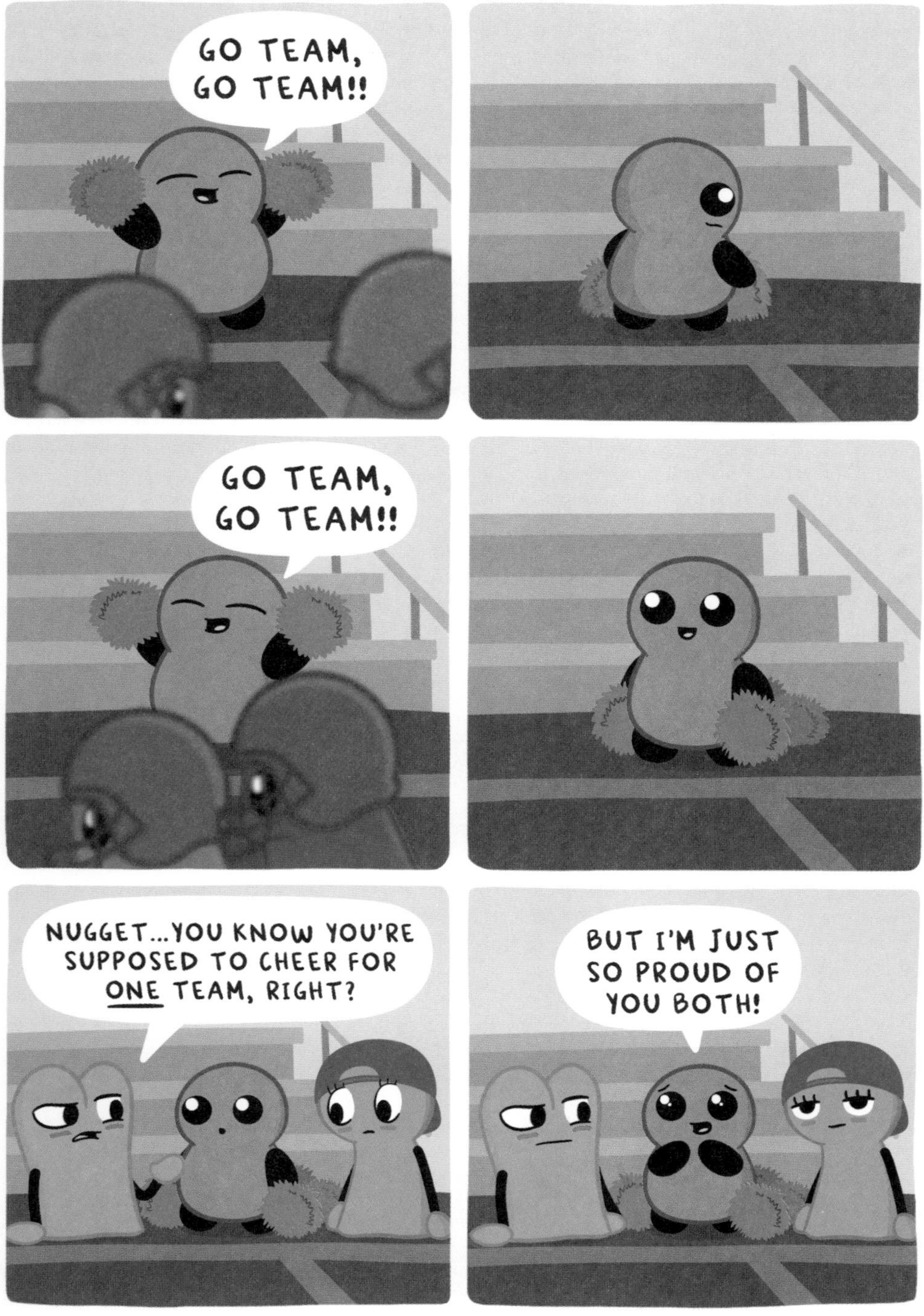
GO TEAM, GO TEAM!!
GO TEAM, GO TEAM!!
NUGGET...YOU KNOW YOU'RE SUPPOSED TO CHEER FOR ONE TEAM, RIGHT?
BUT I'M JUST SO PROUD OF YOU BOTH!

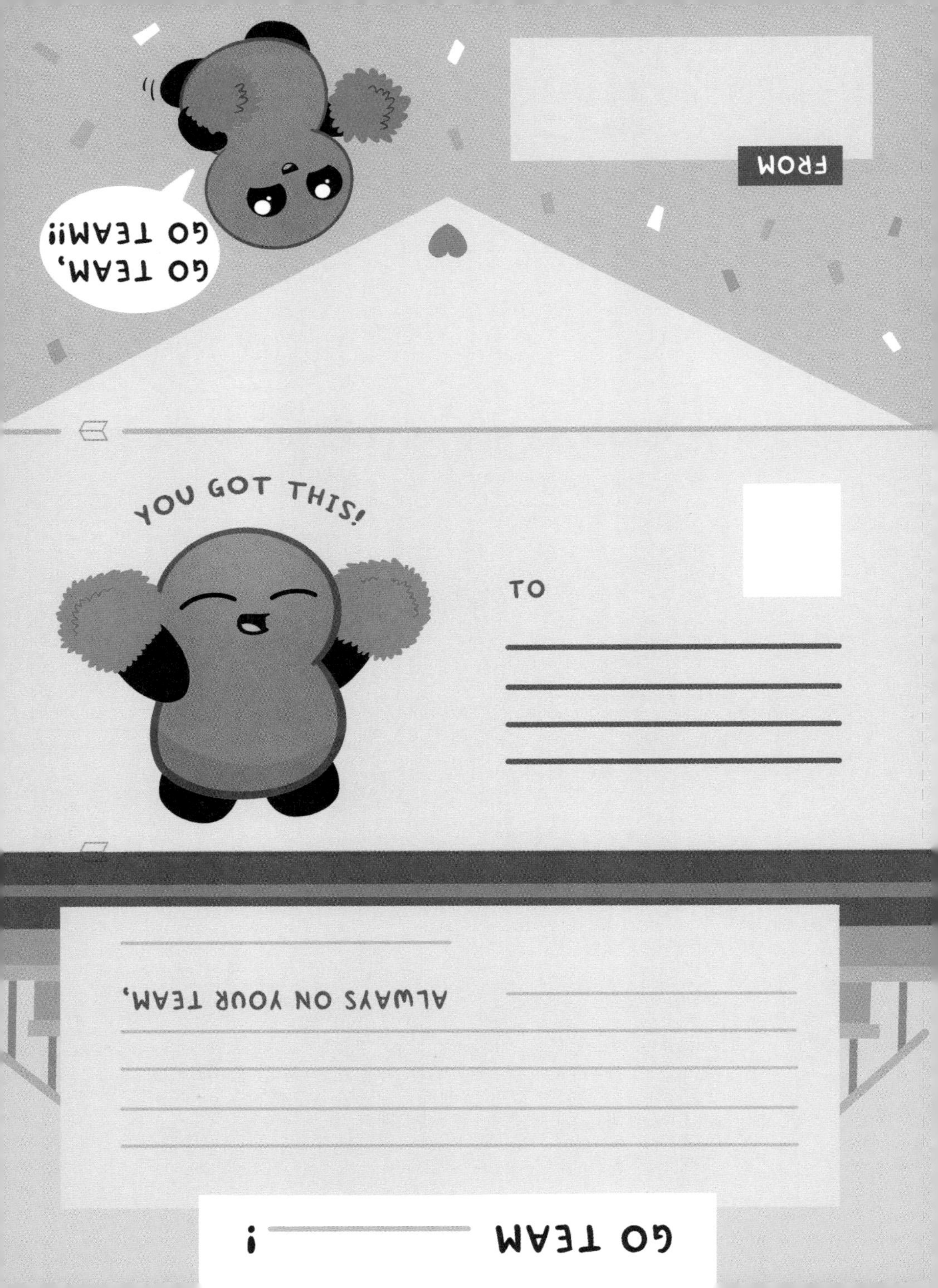
GO TEAM,
GO TEAM!!
FROM
YOU GOT THIS!
TO
ALWAYS ON YOUR TEAM,
GO TEAM ______!

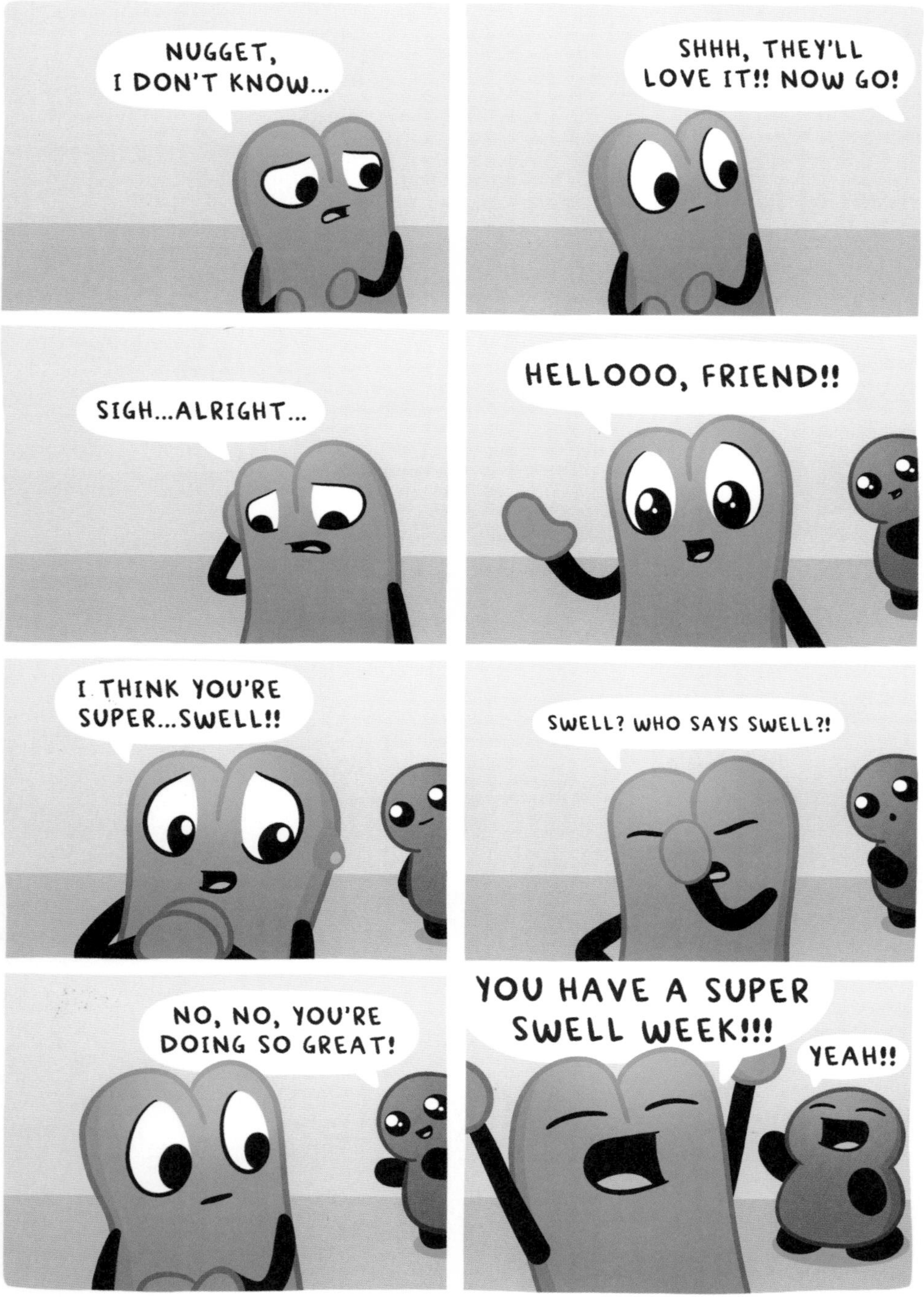
NUGGET, I DON'T KNOW...
SHHH, THEY'LL LOVE IT!! NOW GO!
SIGH...ALRIGHT...
HELLOOO, FRIEND!!
I THINK YOU'RE SUPER...SWELL!!
SWELL? WHO SAYS SWELL?!
NO, NO, YOU'RE DOING SO GREAT!
YOU HAVE A SUPER SWELL WEEK!!!
YEAH!!

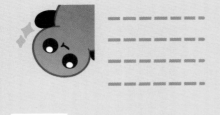

TO

FROM

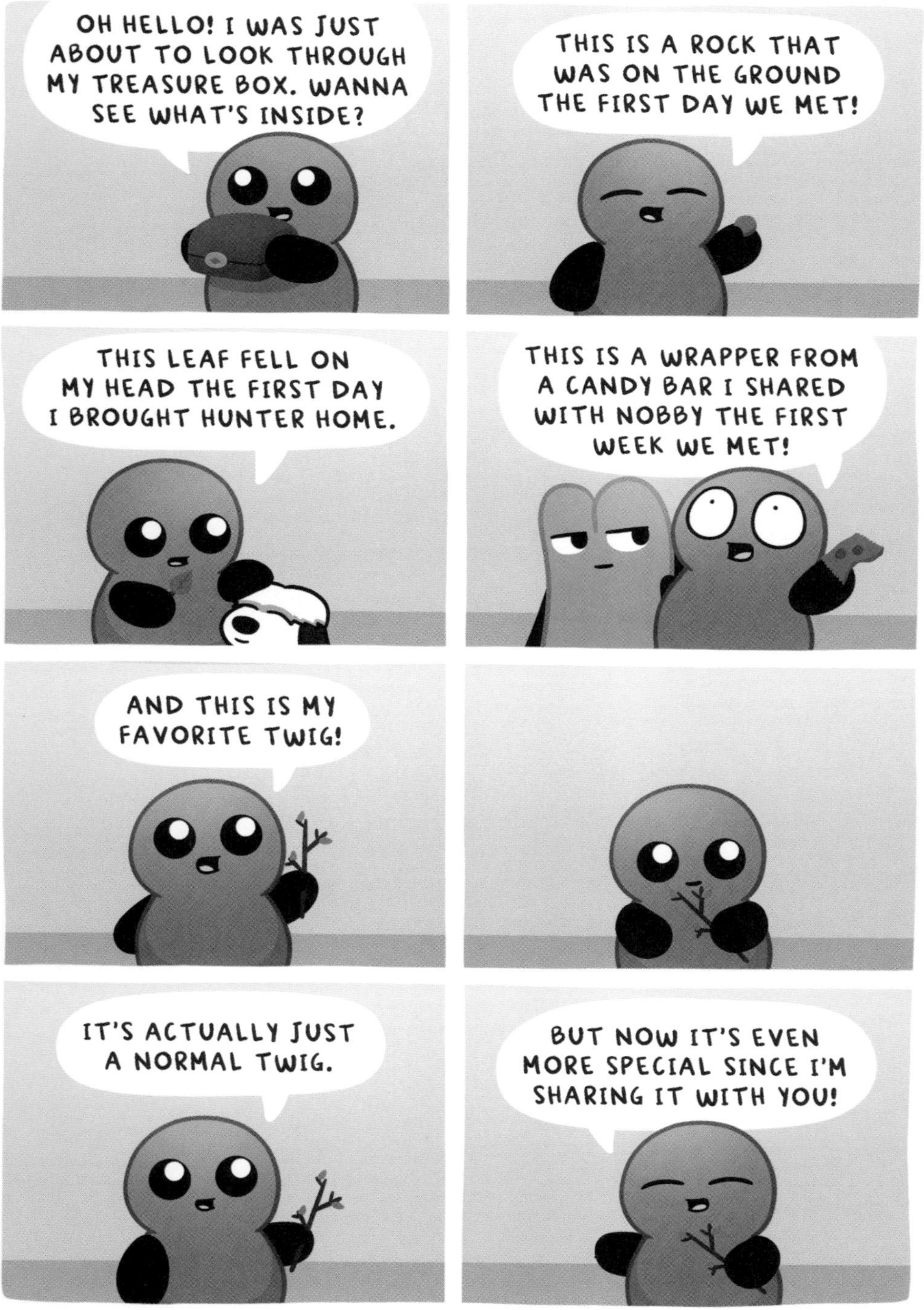
OH HELLO! I WAS JUST ABOUT TO LOOK THROUGH MY TREASURE BOX. WANNA SEE WHAT'S INSIDE?
THIS IS A ROCK THAT WAS ON THE GROUND THE FIRST DAY WE MET!
THIS LEAF FELL ON MY HEAD THE FIRST DAY I BROUGHT HUNTER HOME.
THIS IS A WRAPPER FROM A CANDY BAR I SHARED WITH NOBBY THE FIRST WEEK WE MET!
AND THIS IS MY FAVORITE TWIG!
IT'S ACTUALLY JUST A NORMAL TWIG.
BUT NOW IT'S EVEN MORE SPECIAL SINCE I'M SHARING IT WITH YOU!

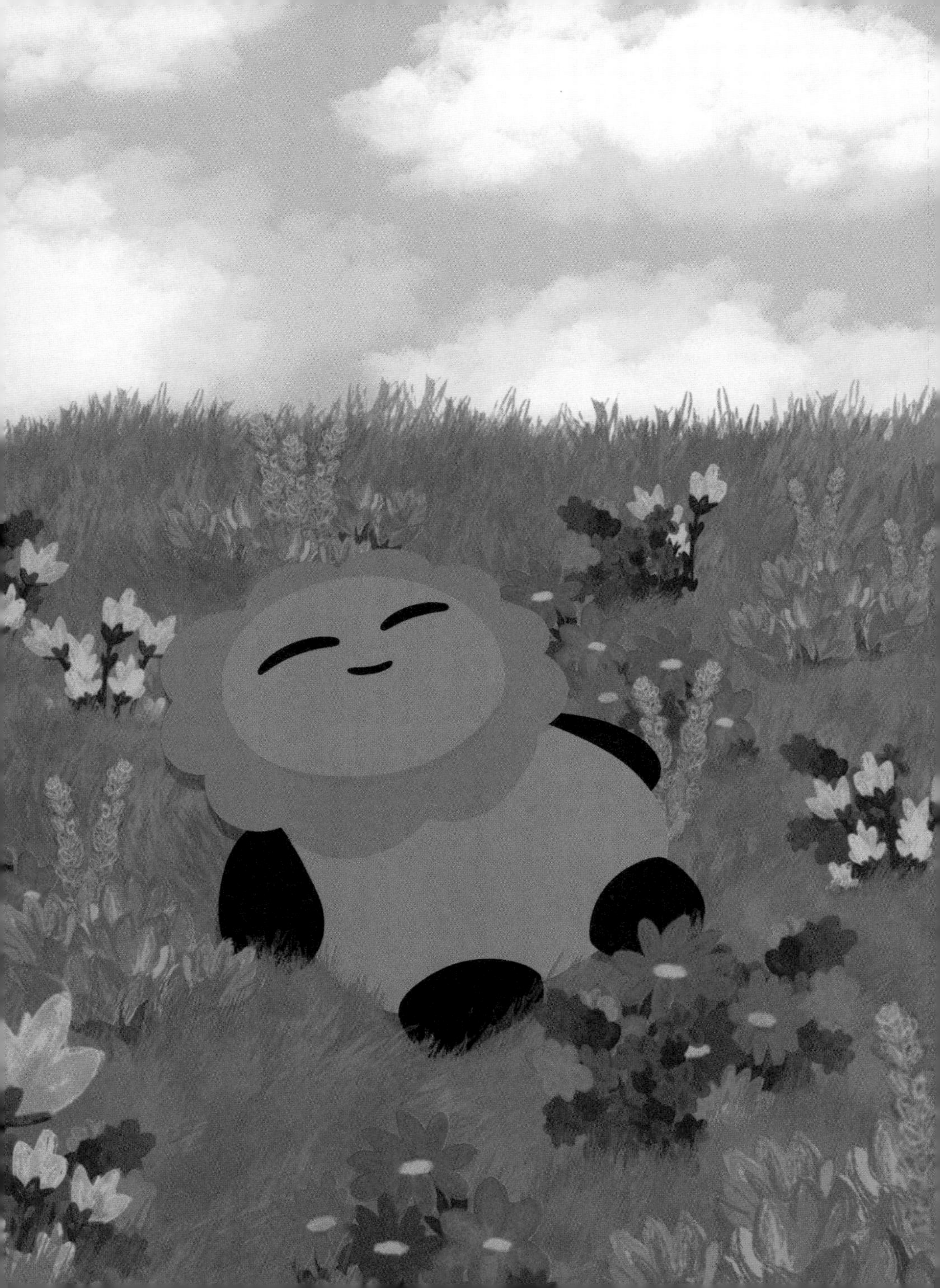

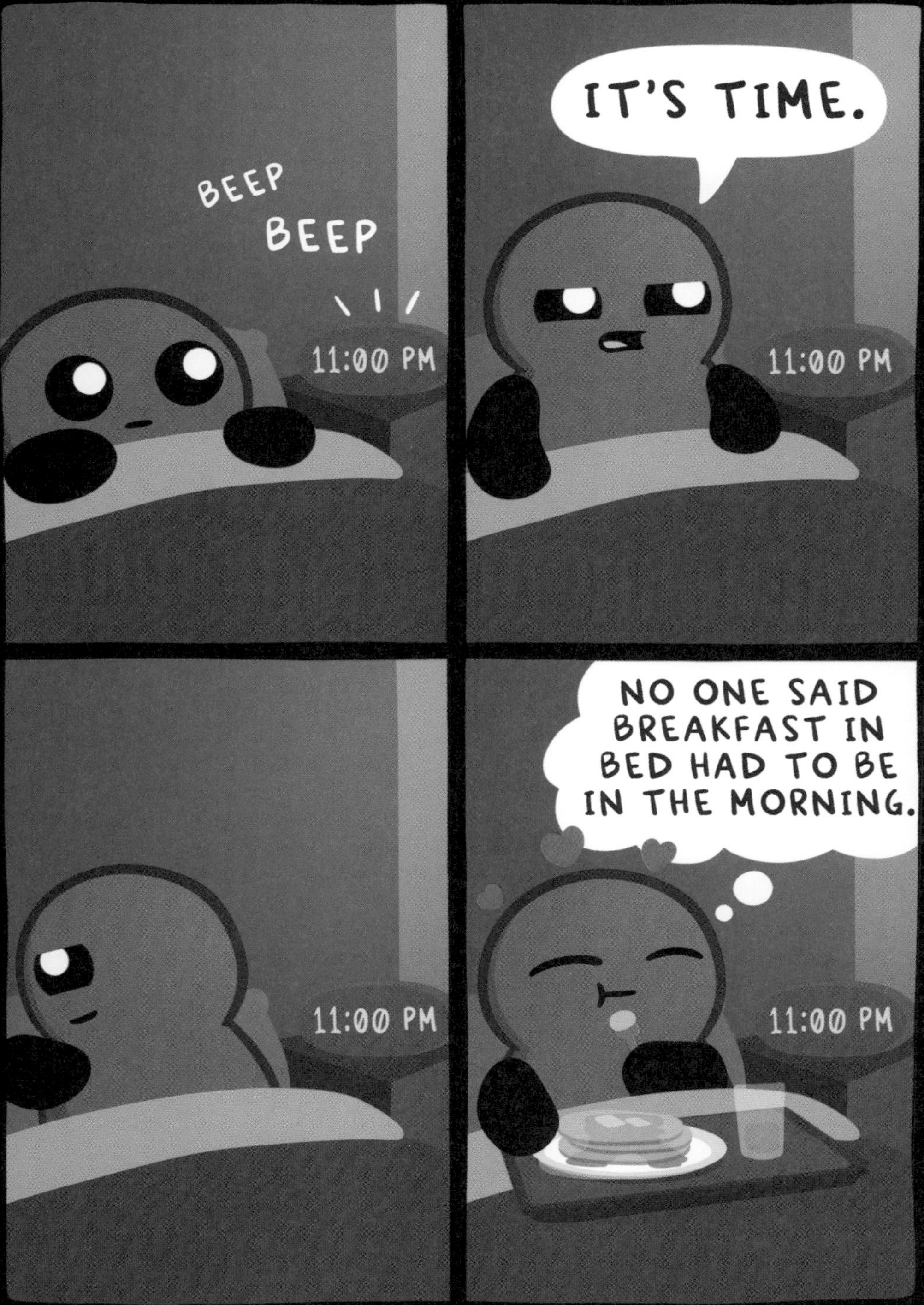
BEEP
BEEP
11:00 PM
IT'S TIME.
11:00 PM
11:00 PM
NO ONE SAID BREAKFAST IN BED HAD TO BE IN THE MORNING.
11:00 PM

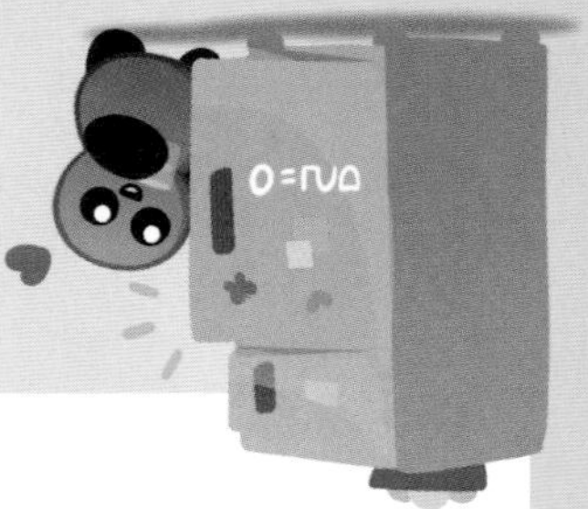

TO

FROM

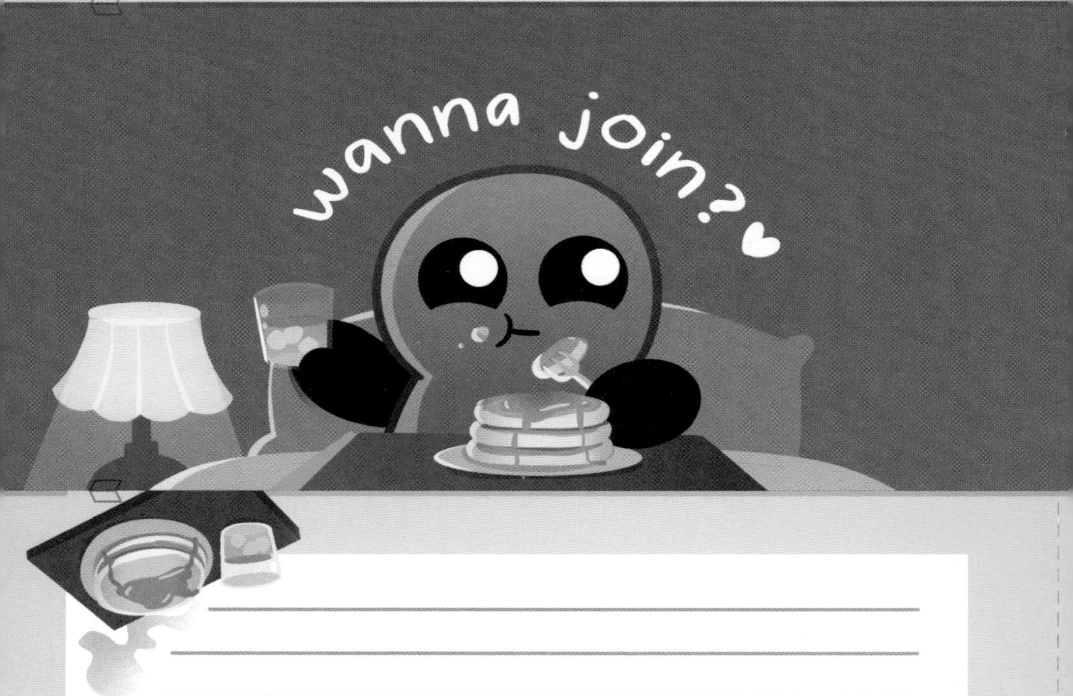
wanna join?

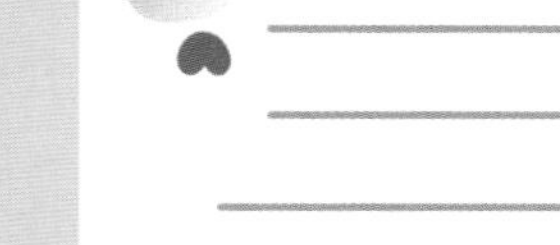

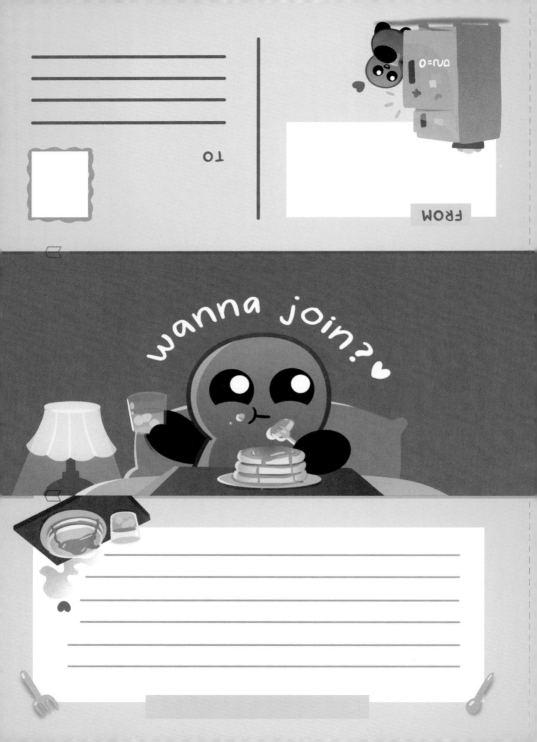

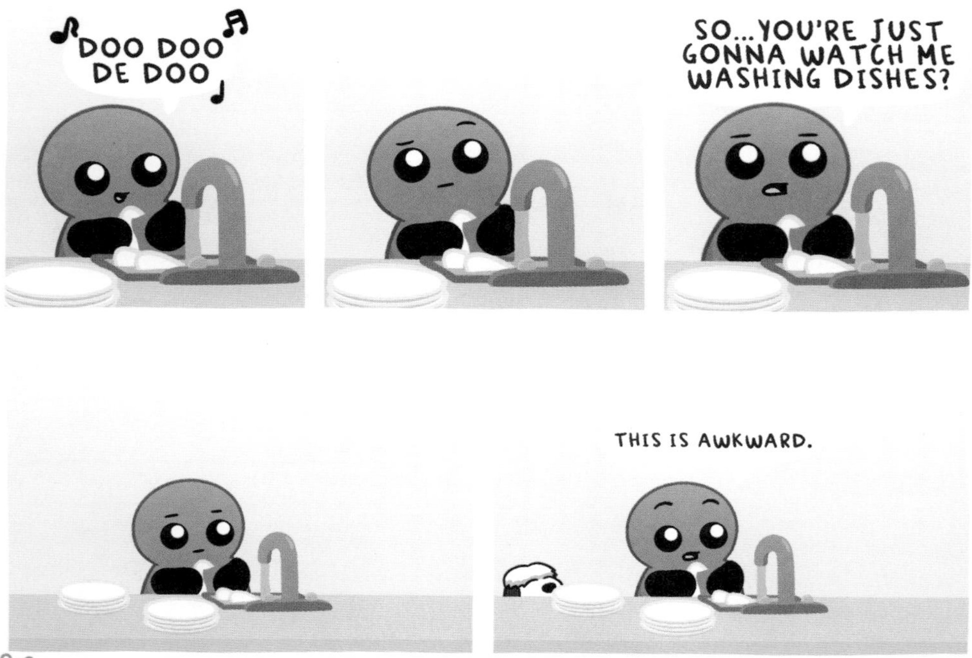
DOO DOO DE DOO
SO...YOU'RE JUST GONNA WATCH ME WASHING DISHES?
THIS IS AWKWARD.

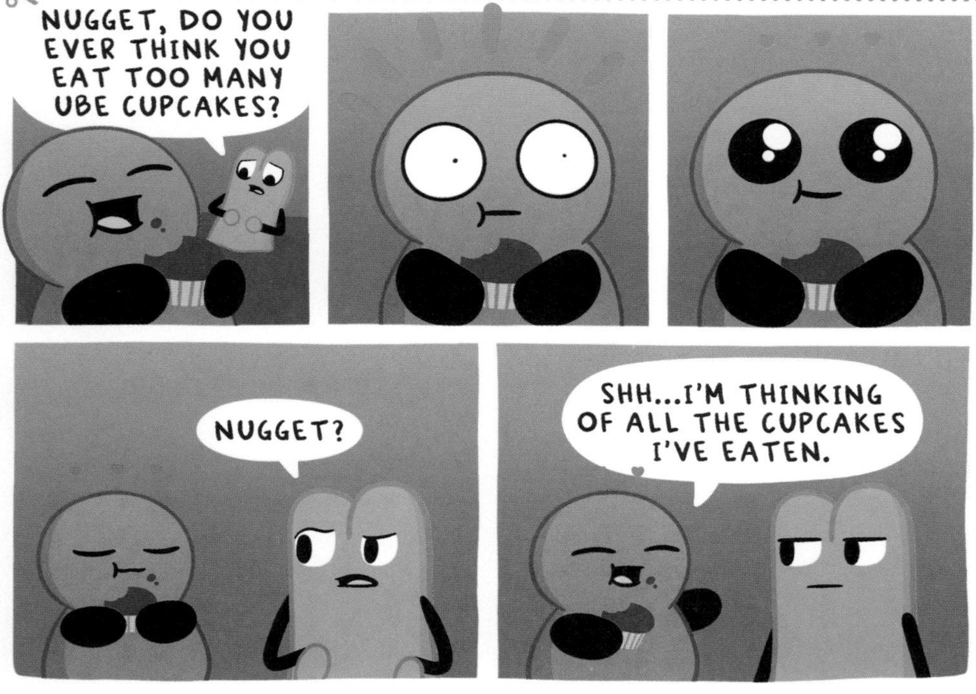
NUGGET, DO YOU EVER THINK YOU EAT TOO MANY UBE CUPCAKES?
NUGGET?
SHH...I'M THINKING OF ALL THE CUPCAKES I'VE EATEN.

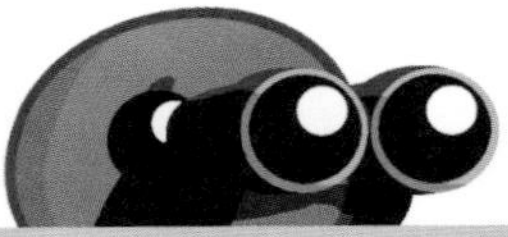

FROM

TO

FROM

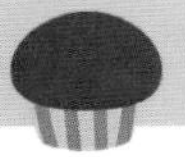

TO

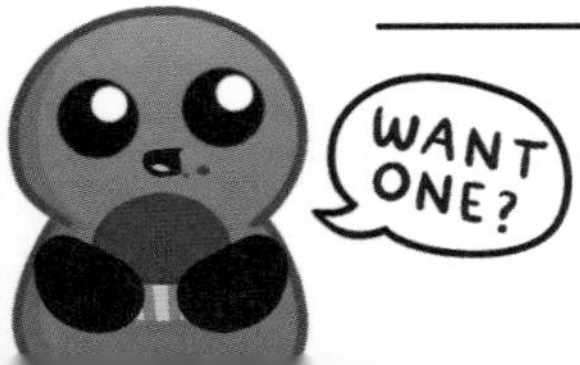
WANT ONE?

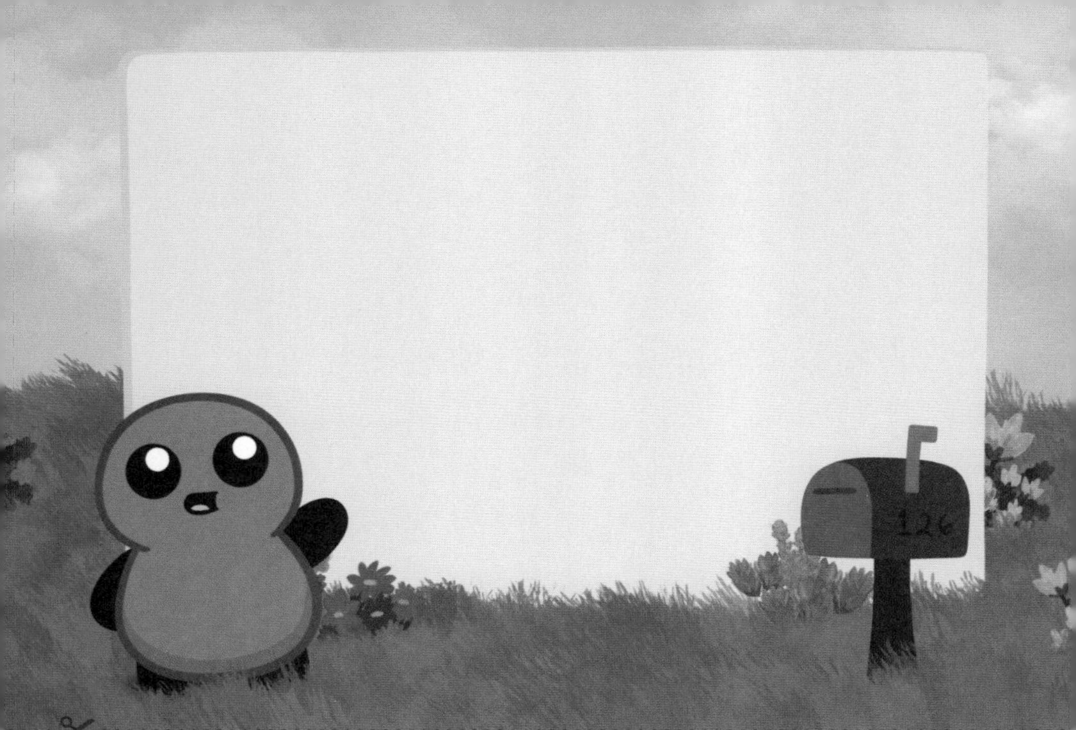
126

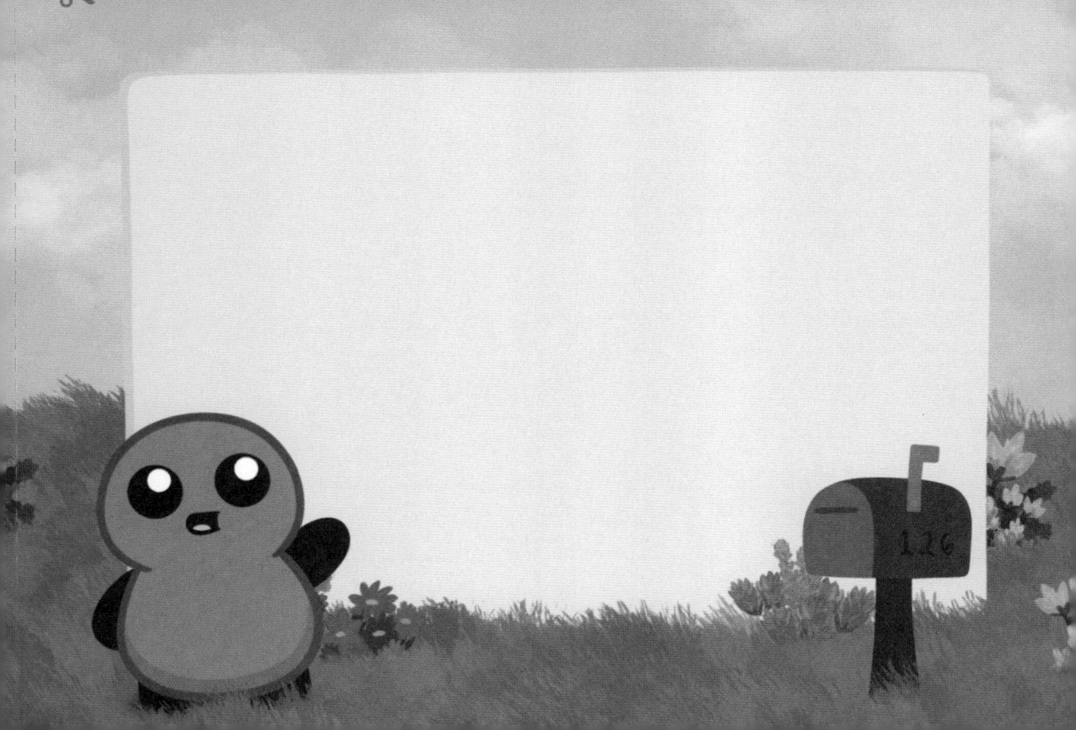
126

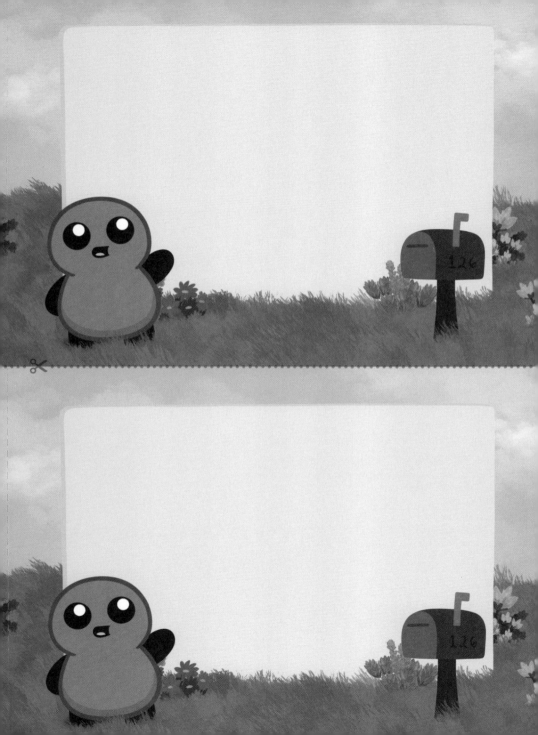

TO

_____

_____

_____

TO

_____

_____

_____

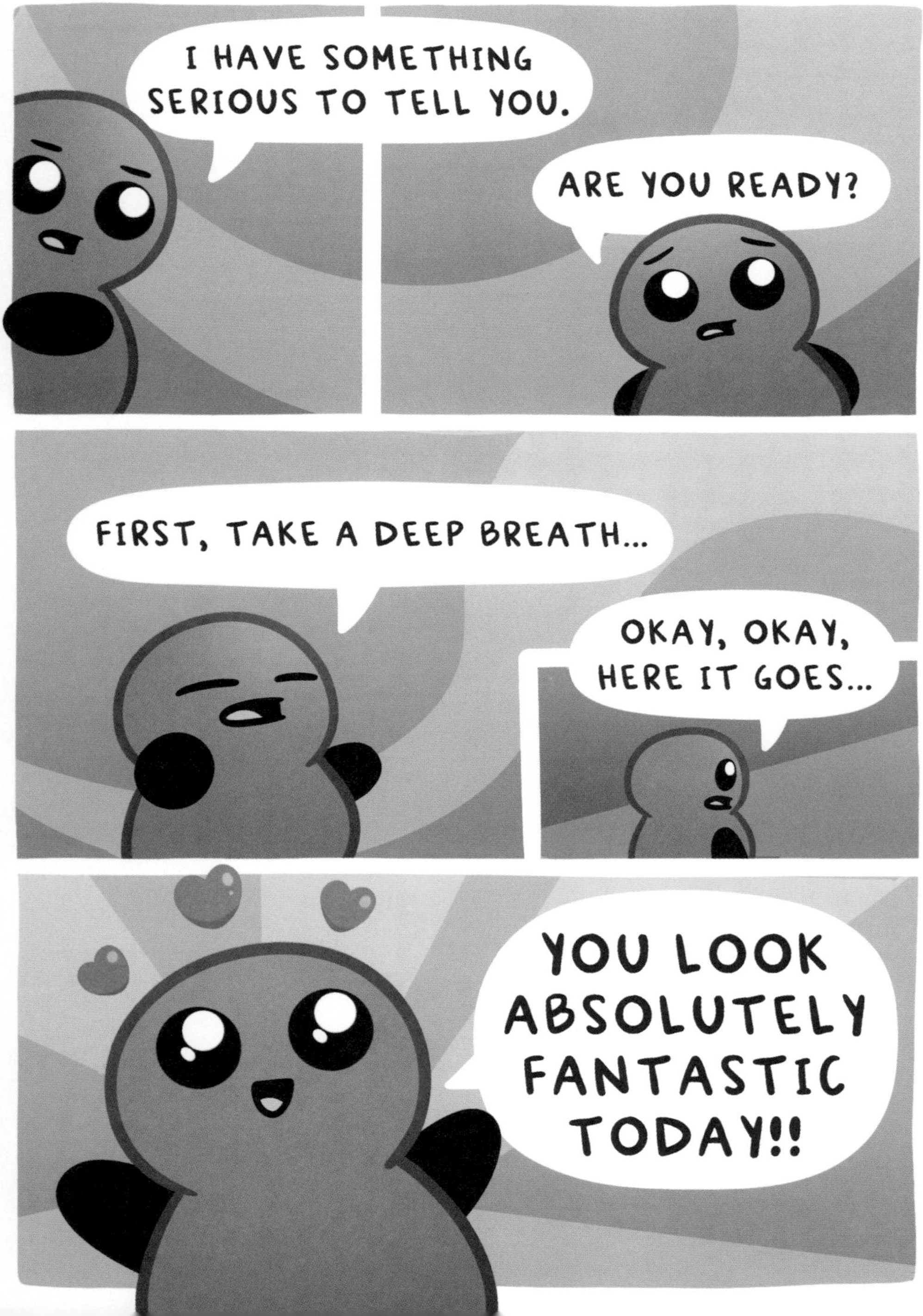
I HAVE SOMETHING SERIOUS TO TELL YOU.
ARE YOU READY?
FIRST, TAKE A DEEP BREATH...
OKAY, OKAY, HERE IT GOES...
YOU LOOK ABSOLUTELY FANTASTIC TODAY!!

YOU LOOK
SOOOOOOO...
BEAUTIFUL!

FROM

TO

HEY!
HEY!
HEY!!

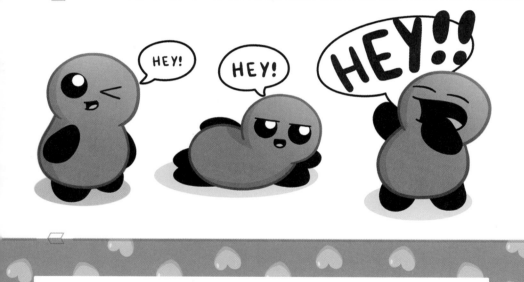

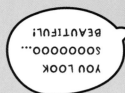

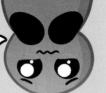

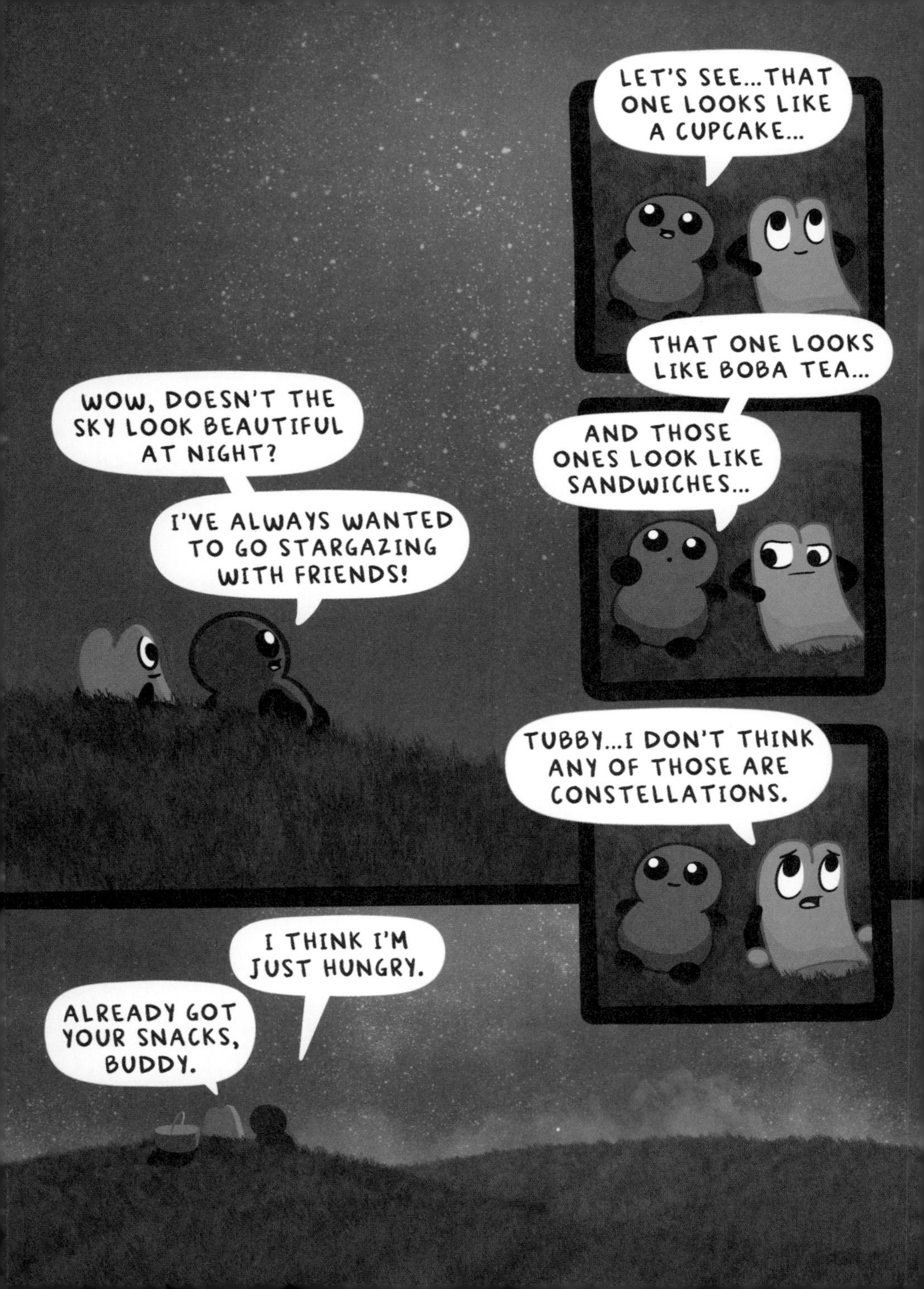
WOW, DOESN'T THE SKY LOOK BEAUTIFUL AT NIGHT?
I'VE ALWAYS WANTED TO GO STARGAZING WITH FRIENDS!
LET'S SEE...THAT ONE LOOKS LIKE A CUPCAKE...
THAT ONE LOOKS LIKE BOBA TEA...
AND THOSE ONES LOOK LIKE SANDWICHES...
TUBBY...I DON'T THINK ANY OF THOSE ARE CONSTELLATIONS.
I THINK I'M JUST HUNGRY.
ALREADY GOT YOUR SNACKS, BUDDY.

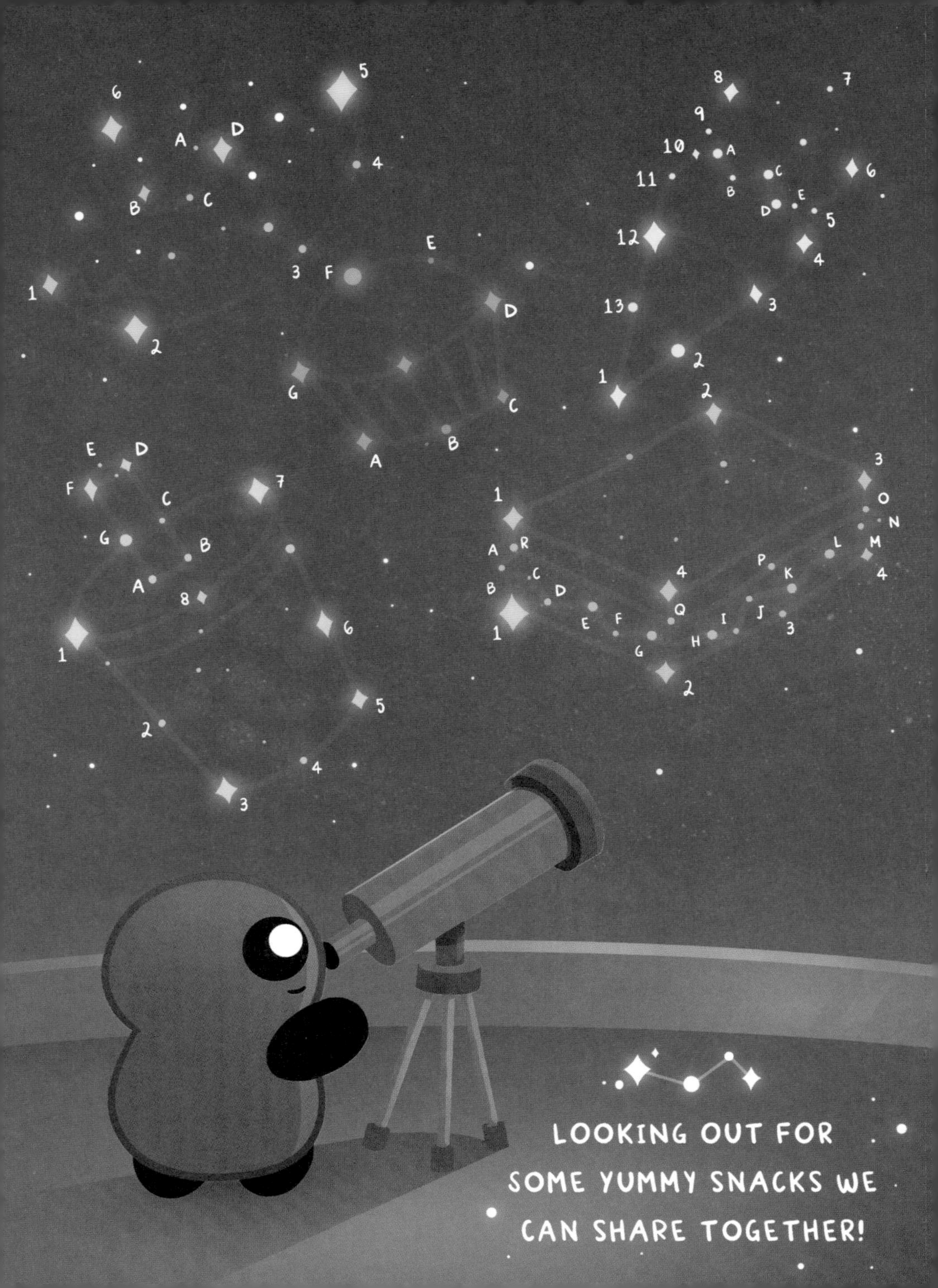
LOOKING OUT FOR
SOME YUMMY SNACKS WE
CAN SHARE TOGETHER!

INTERACTIVE PAGES

Do you have lots of ideas that you can't wait to put on paper? Then the second half of this book is PERFECT for you!

Tubby will guide you along the way with fun little prompts to help you get creative with your special letters.

Personalize these pages with inside jokes, notes, and affirmations for your favorite people!

🤍 🤍 🤍

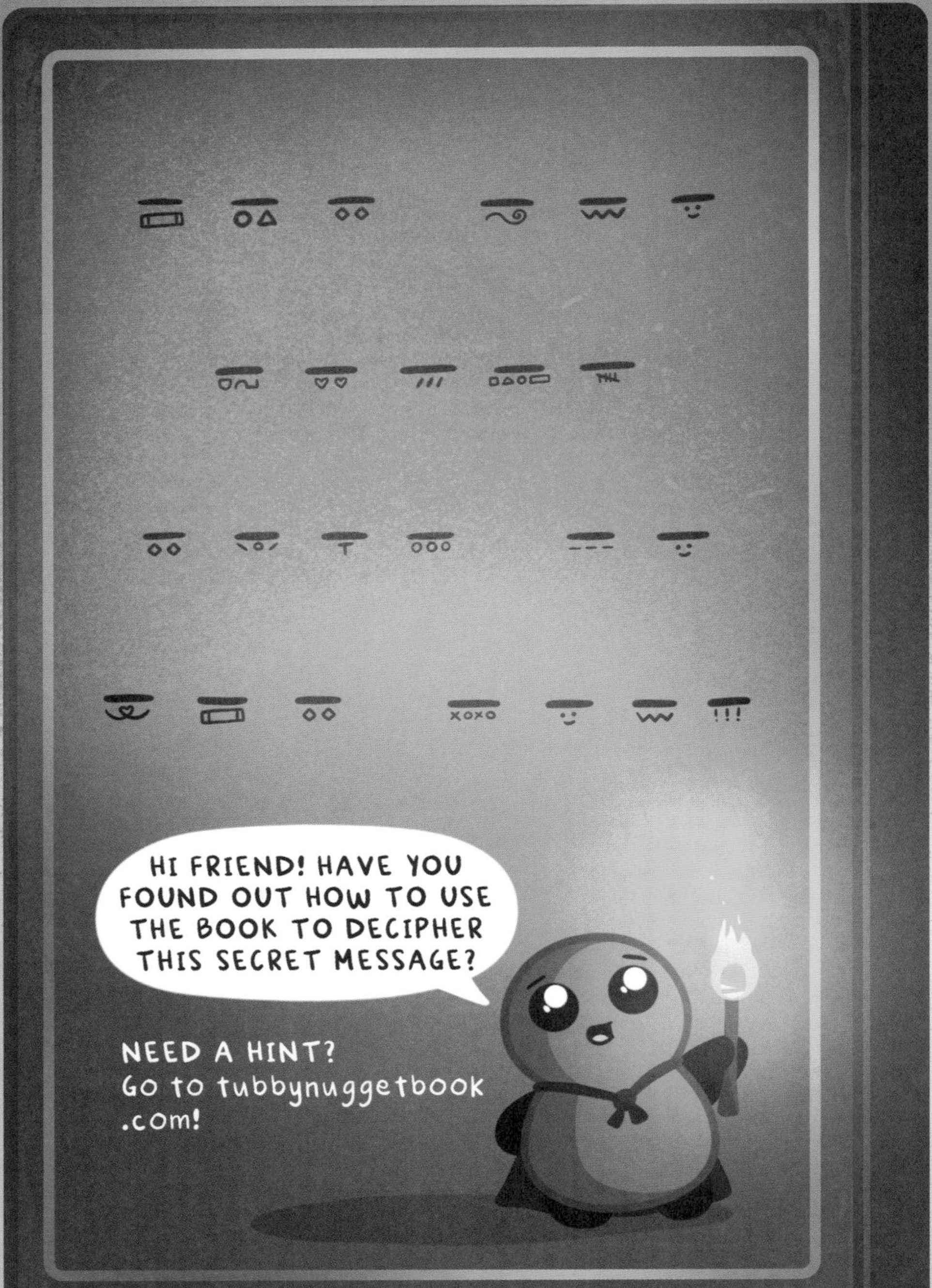
HI FRIEND! HAVE YOU FOUND OUT HOW TO USE THE BOOK TO DECIPHER THIS SECRET MESSAGE?
NEED A HINT?
Go to tubbynuggetbook.com!

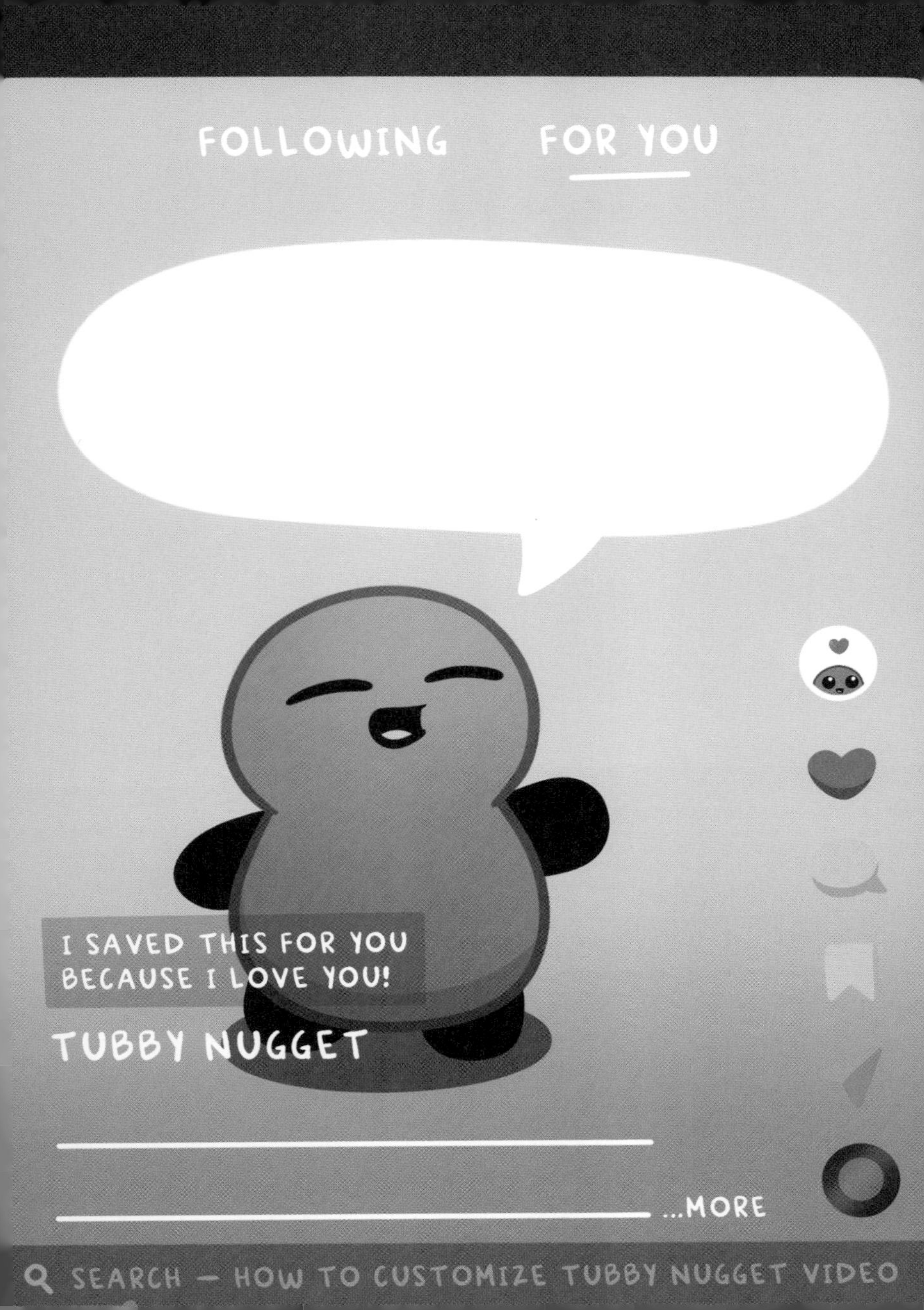
FOLLOWING
FOR YOU
I SAVED THIS FOR YOU
BECAUSE I LOVE YOU!
TUBBY NUGGET
...MORE
SEARCH — HOW TO CUSTOMIZE TUBBY NUGGET VIDEO

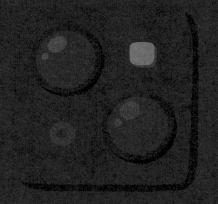

nugPhone

it's a phone for nugs!
(also folds in half)

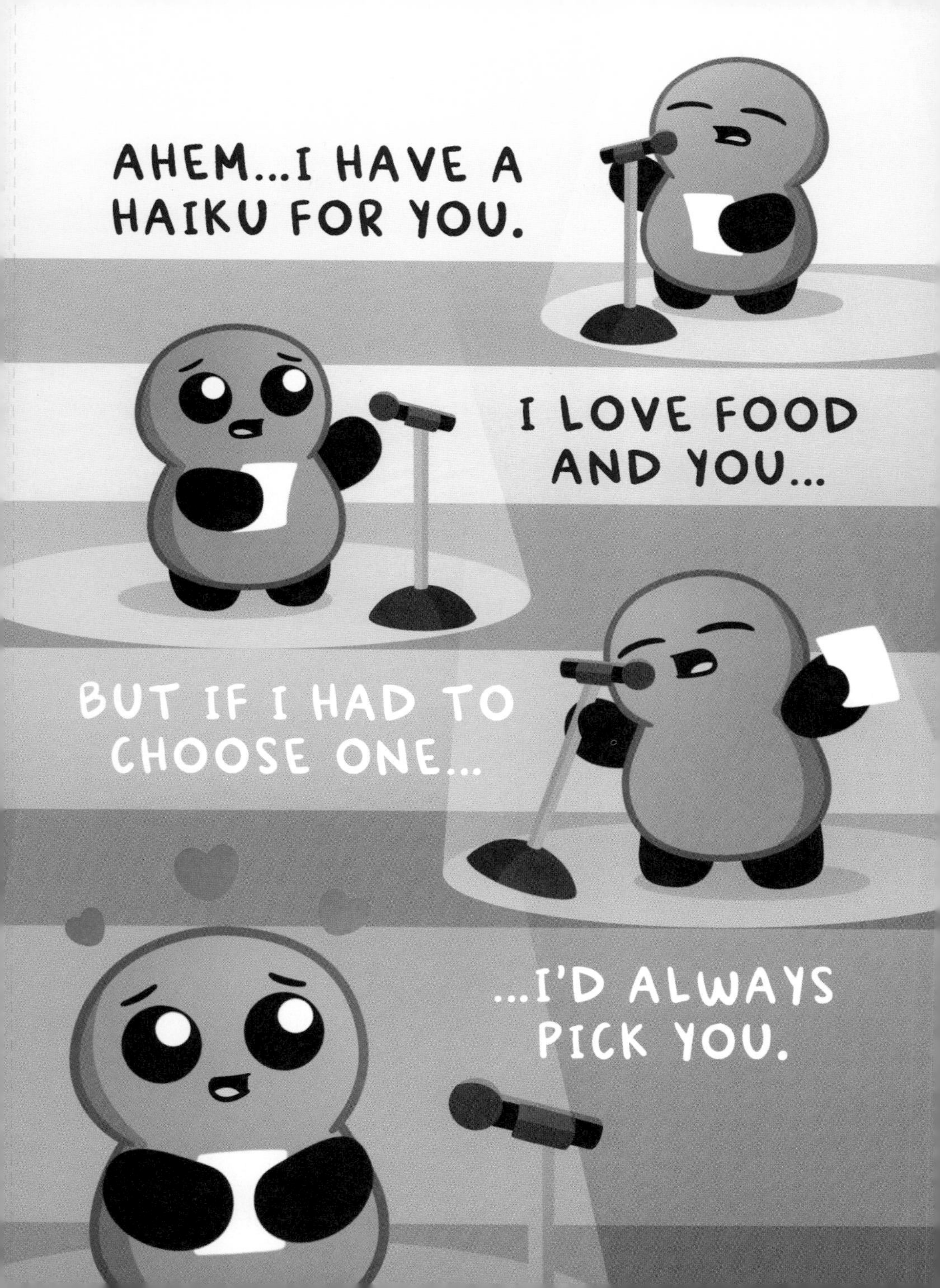
AHEM...I HAVE A HAIKU FOR YOU.
I LOVE FOOD AND YOU...
BUT IF I HAD TO CHOOSE ONE...
...I'D ALWAYS PICK YOU.

HERE'S HOW TO WRITE A SPECIAL HAIKU FOR YOUR FRIEND!

LINE 1: 5 SYLLABLES
LINE 2: 7 SYLLABLES
LINE 3: 5 SYLLABLES

I HAVE WRITTEN YOU
A HAIKU! *AHEM*

TO: ▭

FROM: ▭

_____

_____

_____

These songs made me think of you — I hope you like them!

"Playlist for you"

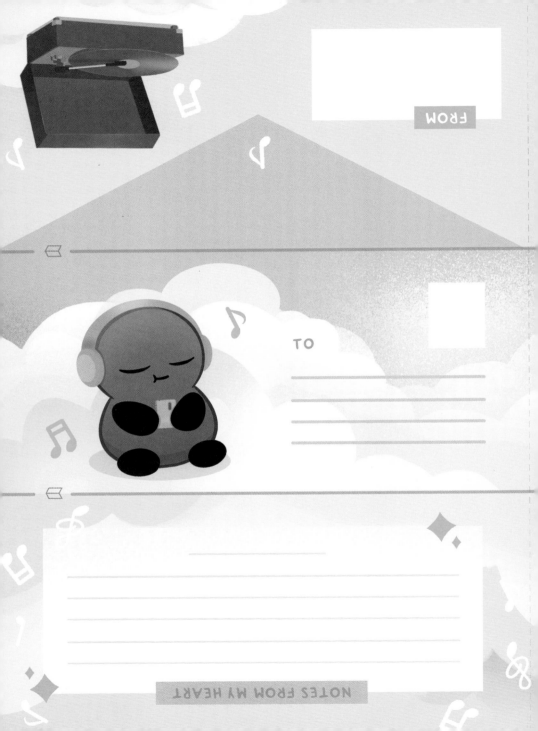

FROM

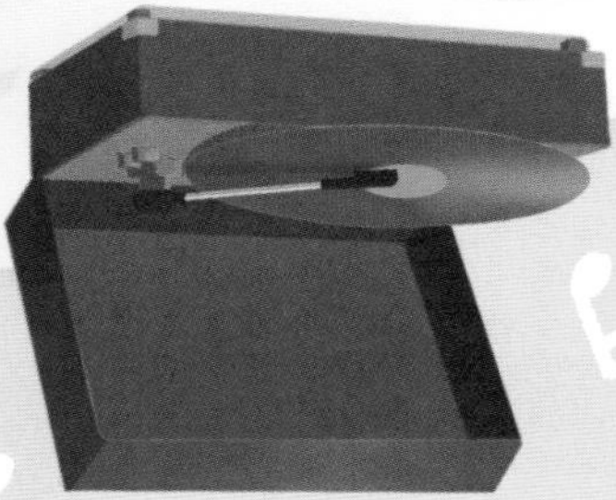

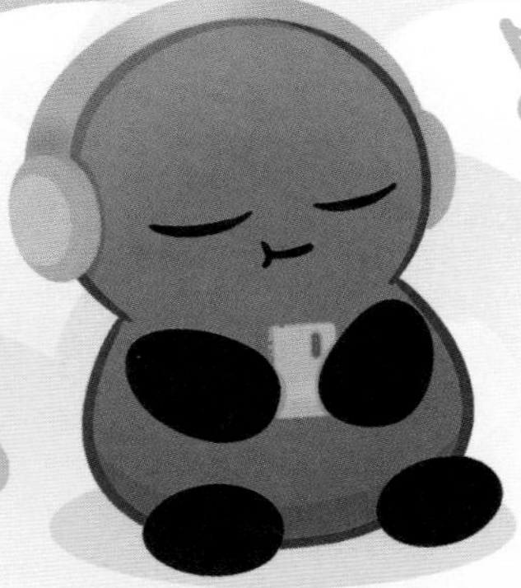

TO

NOTES FROM MY HEART

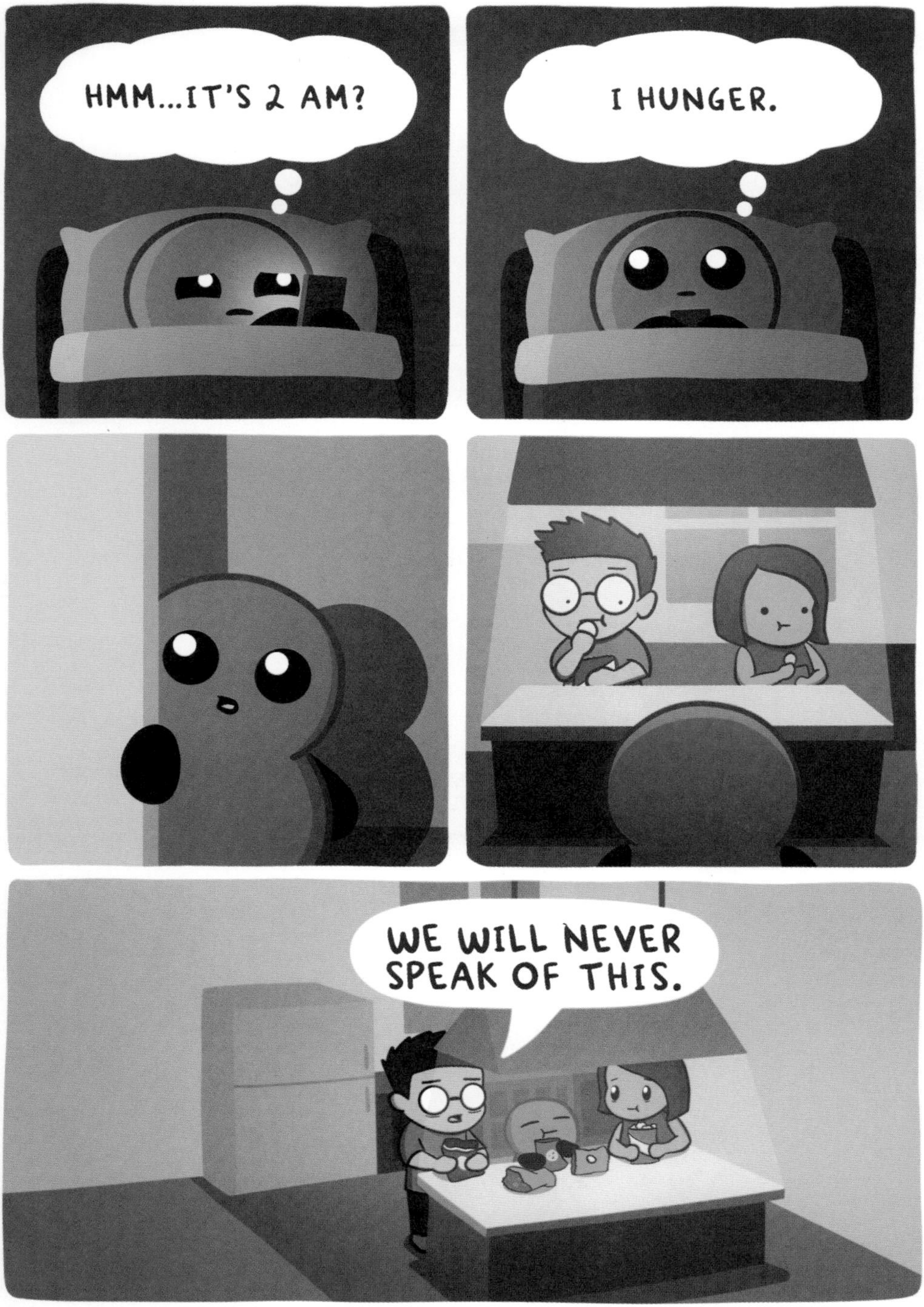
HMM...IT'S 2 AM?
I HUNGER.
WE WILL NEVER SPEAK OF THIS.

IT'S SNACK TIME!

Here's what we are stocking up on for our next midnight snackie mission

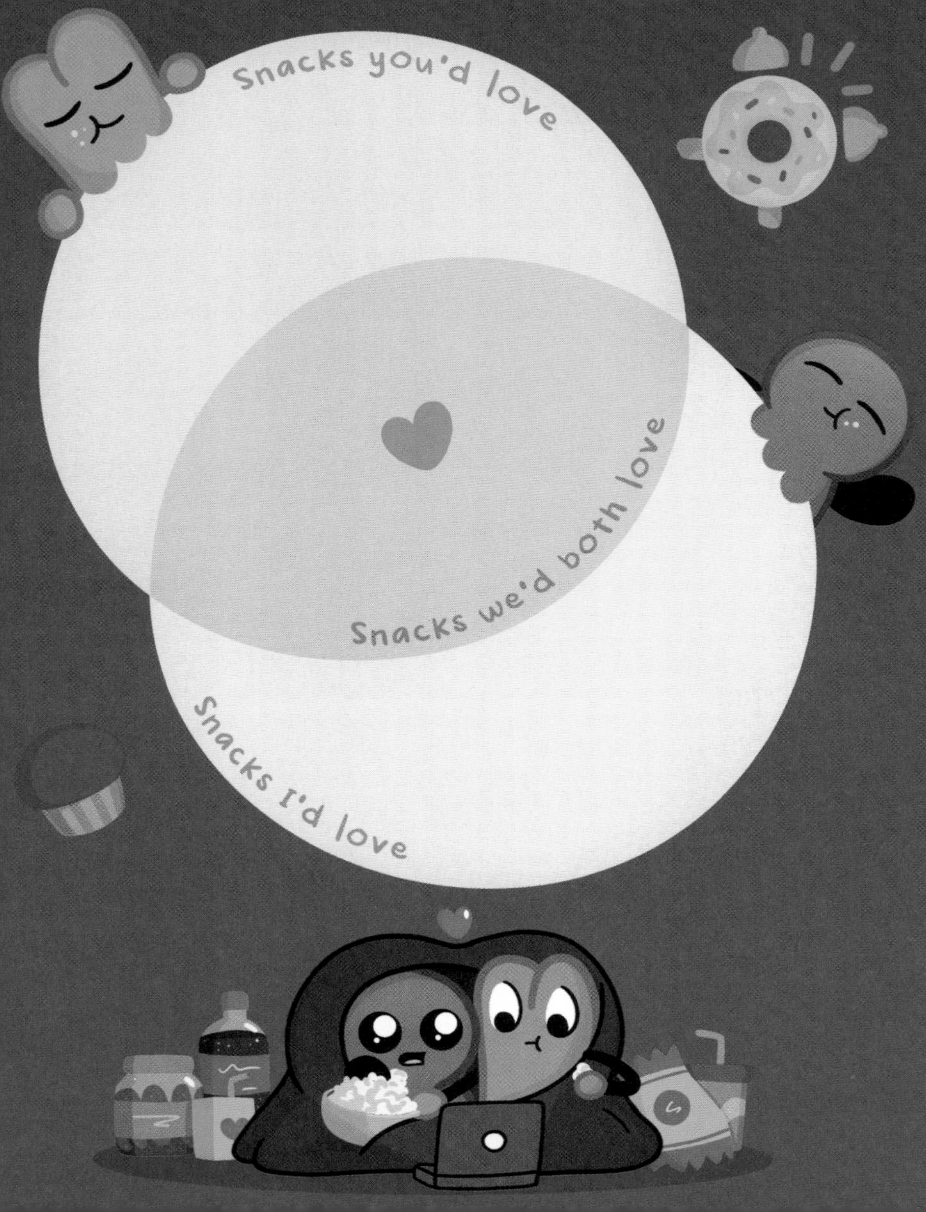
Snacks you'd love
Snacks we'd both love
Snacks I'd love

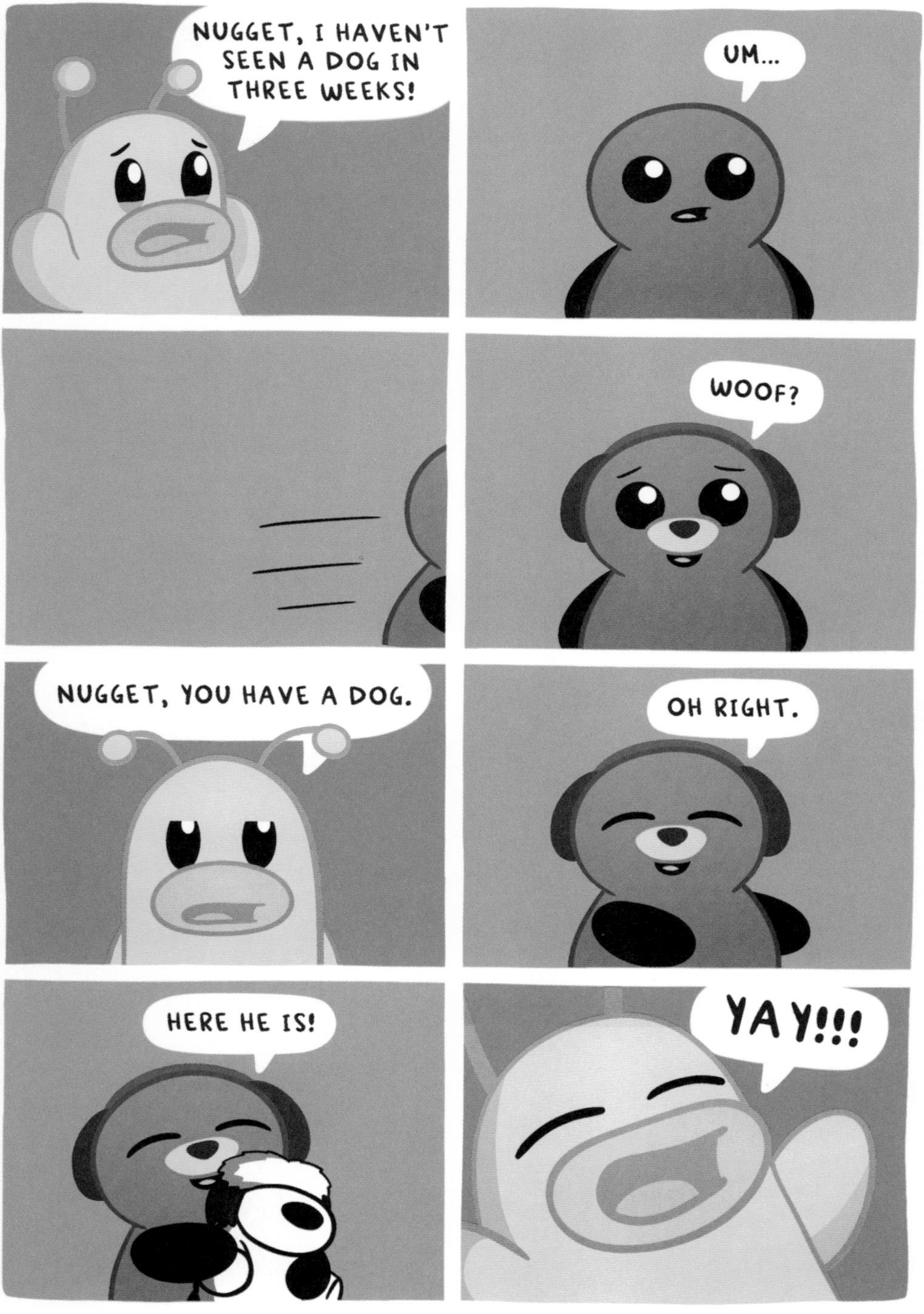
NUGGET, I HAVEN'T SEEN A DOG IN THREE WEEKS!
UM...
WOOF?
NUGGET, YOU HAVE A DOG.
OH RIGHT.
HERE HE IS!
YAY!!!

IF YOU WERE AN ANIMAL, YOU'D MAKE THE PERFECT...

____

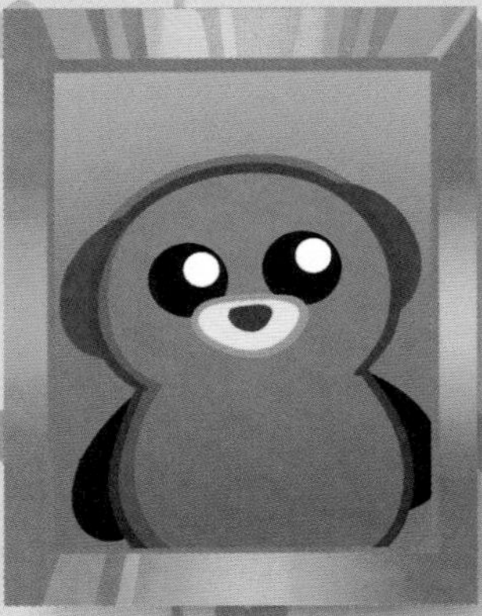

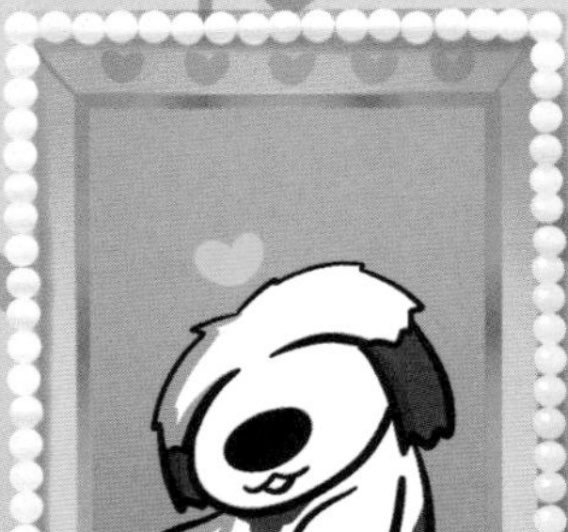

Draw animal here

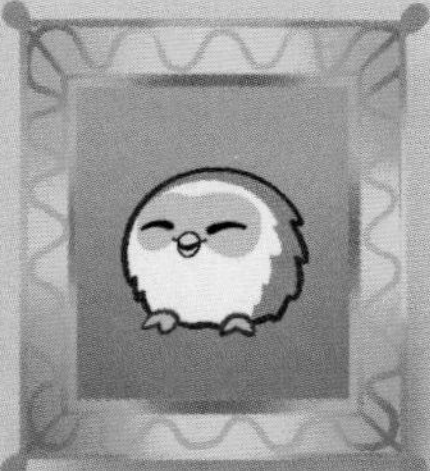

Why they match your energy:

____

____

____

PLACES I'VE BOOKMARKED FOR US

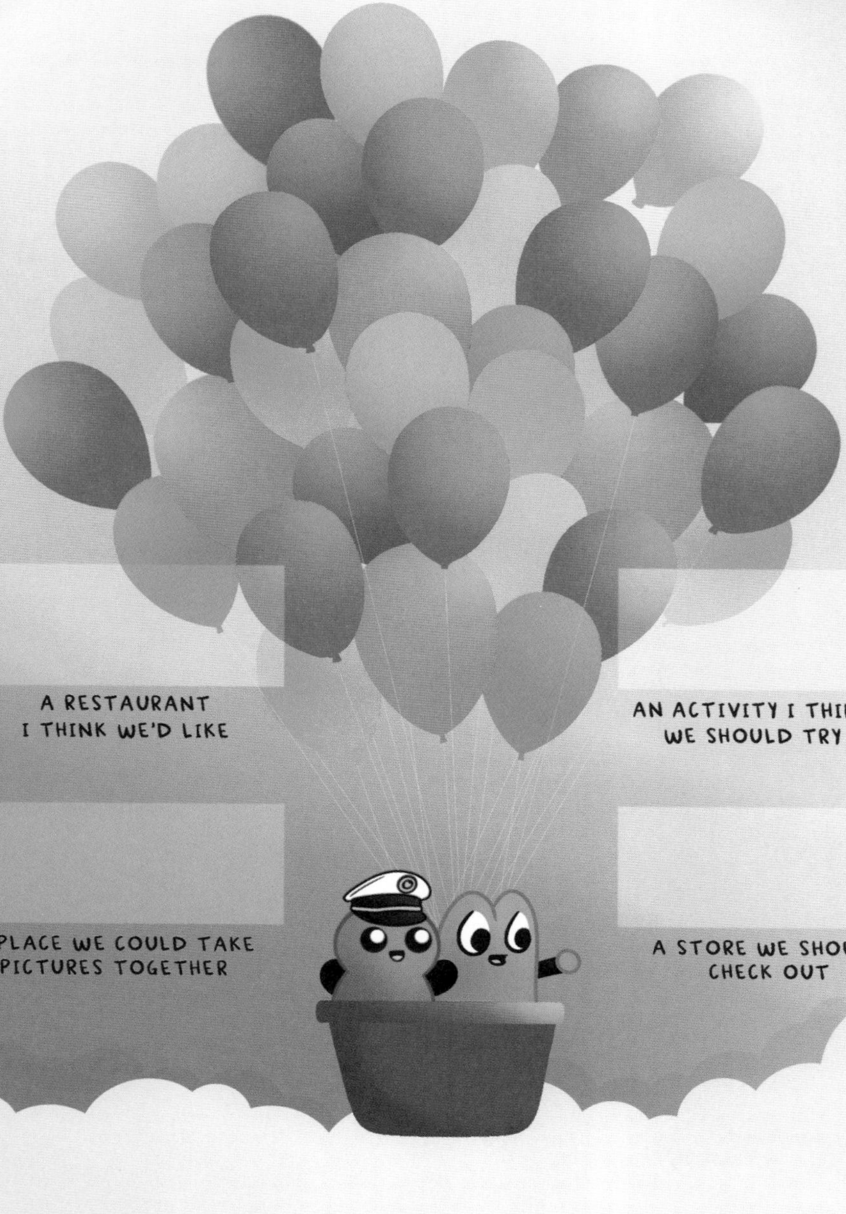

A RESTAURANT
I THINK WE'D LIKE

AN ACTIVITY I THINK
WE SHOULD TRY

A PLACE WE COULD TAKE
PICTURES TOGETHER

A STORE WE SHOULD
CHECK OUT

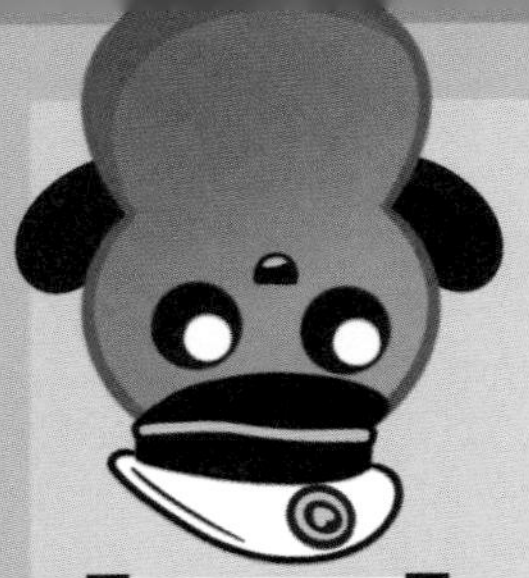

XOXO=R

NUGGET AIRLINES

BOARDING PASS

PASSENGER NAME:

FROM:

TO:

TIME:

SEAT:

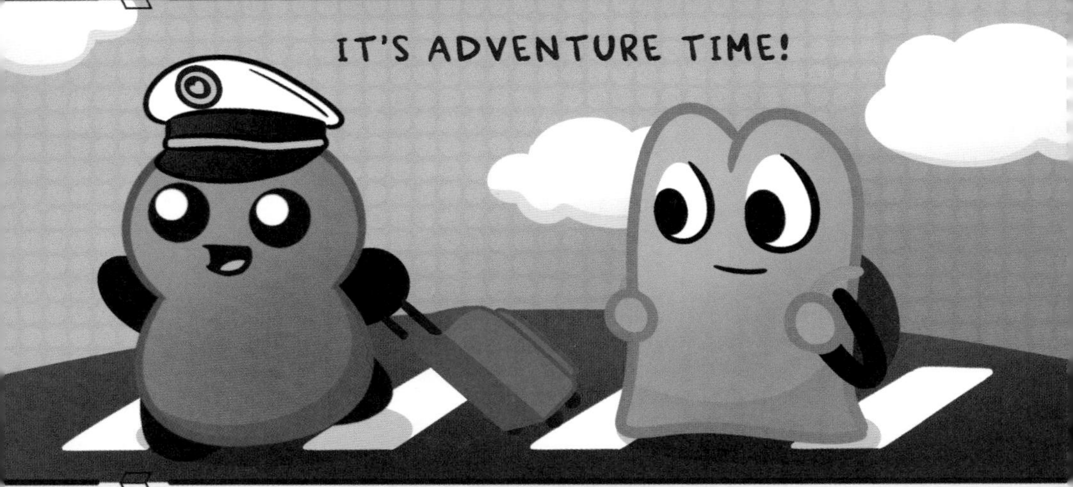
IT'S ADVENTURE TIME!

AN AFFIRMATION FOR EVERY DAY OF YOUR WEEK THIS WEEK!

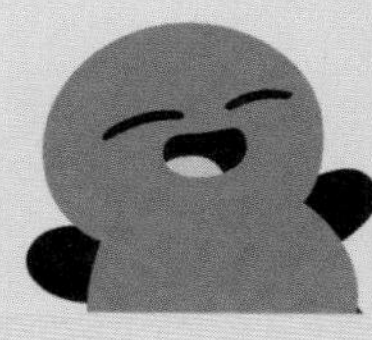

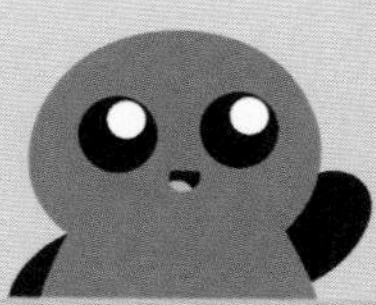

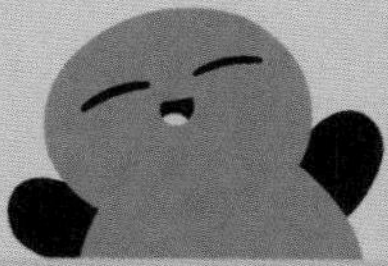

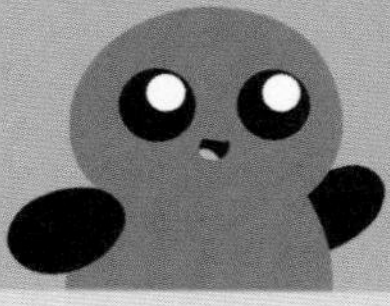

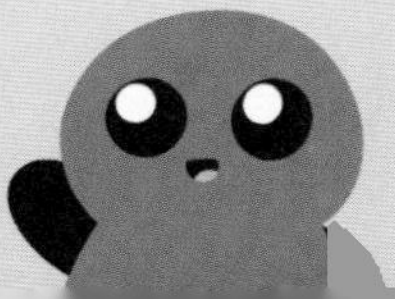

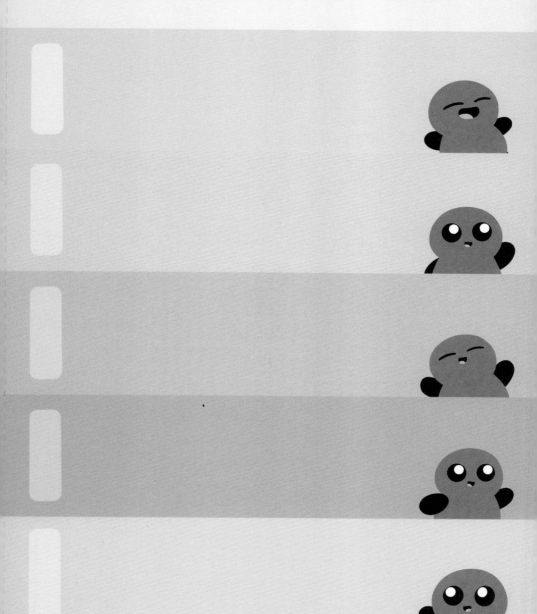

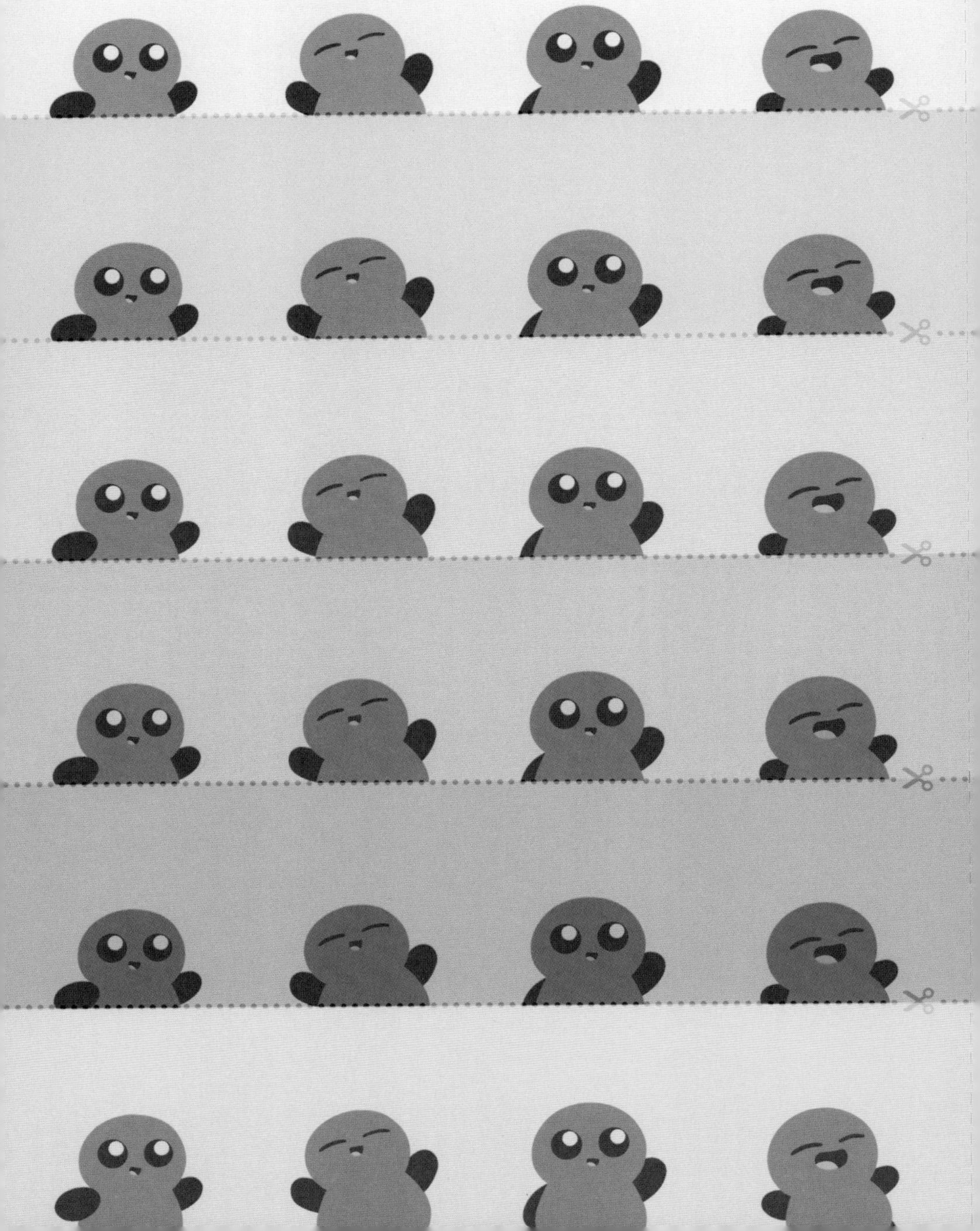

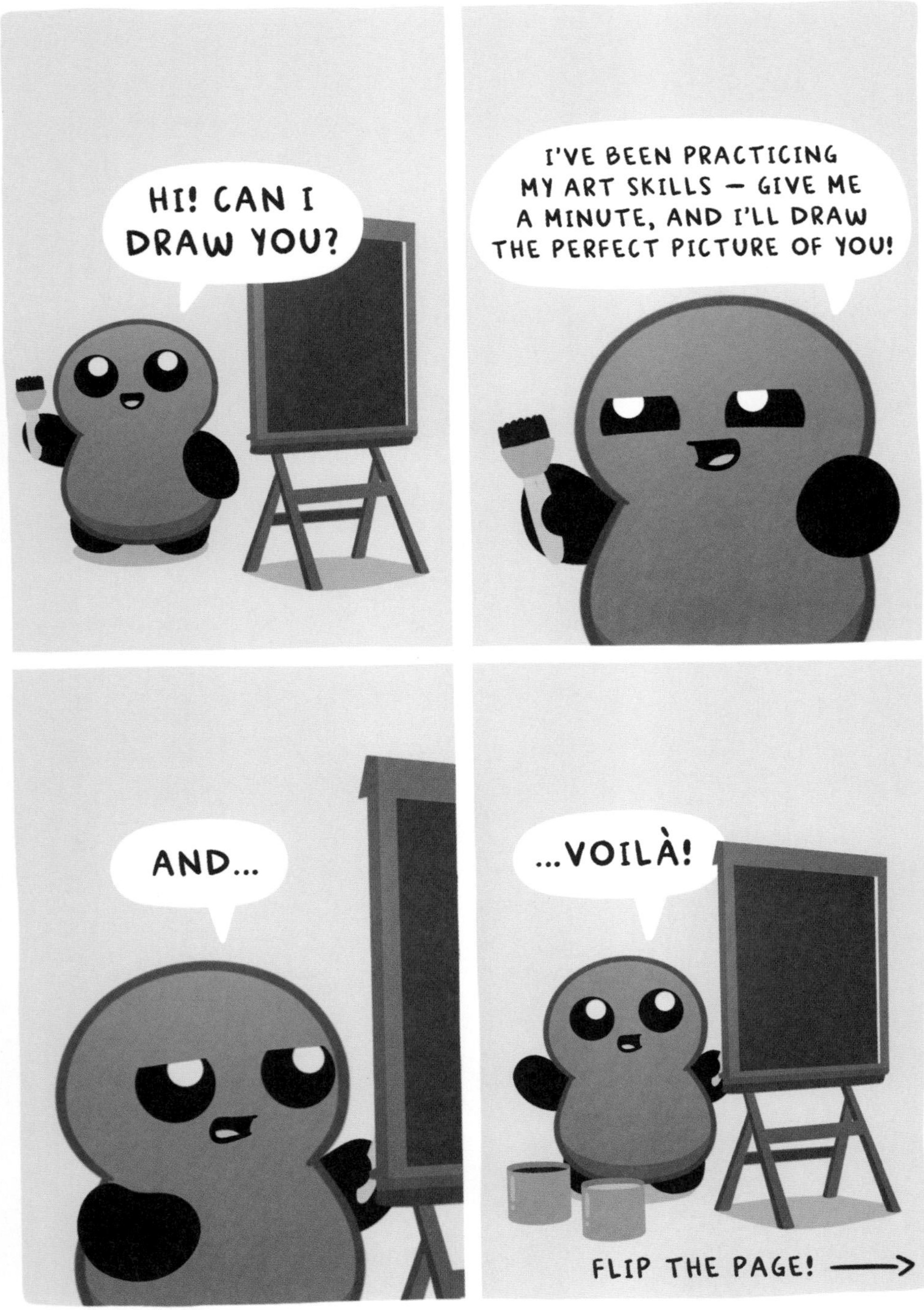
HI! CAN I DRAW YOU?
I'VE BEEN PRACTICING MY ART SKILLS — GIVE ME A MINUTE, AND I'LL DRAW THE PERFECT PICTURE OF YOU!
AND...
...VOILÀ!
FLIP THE PAGE!

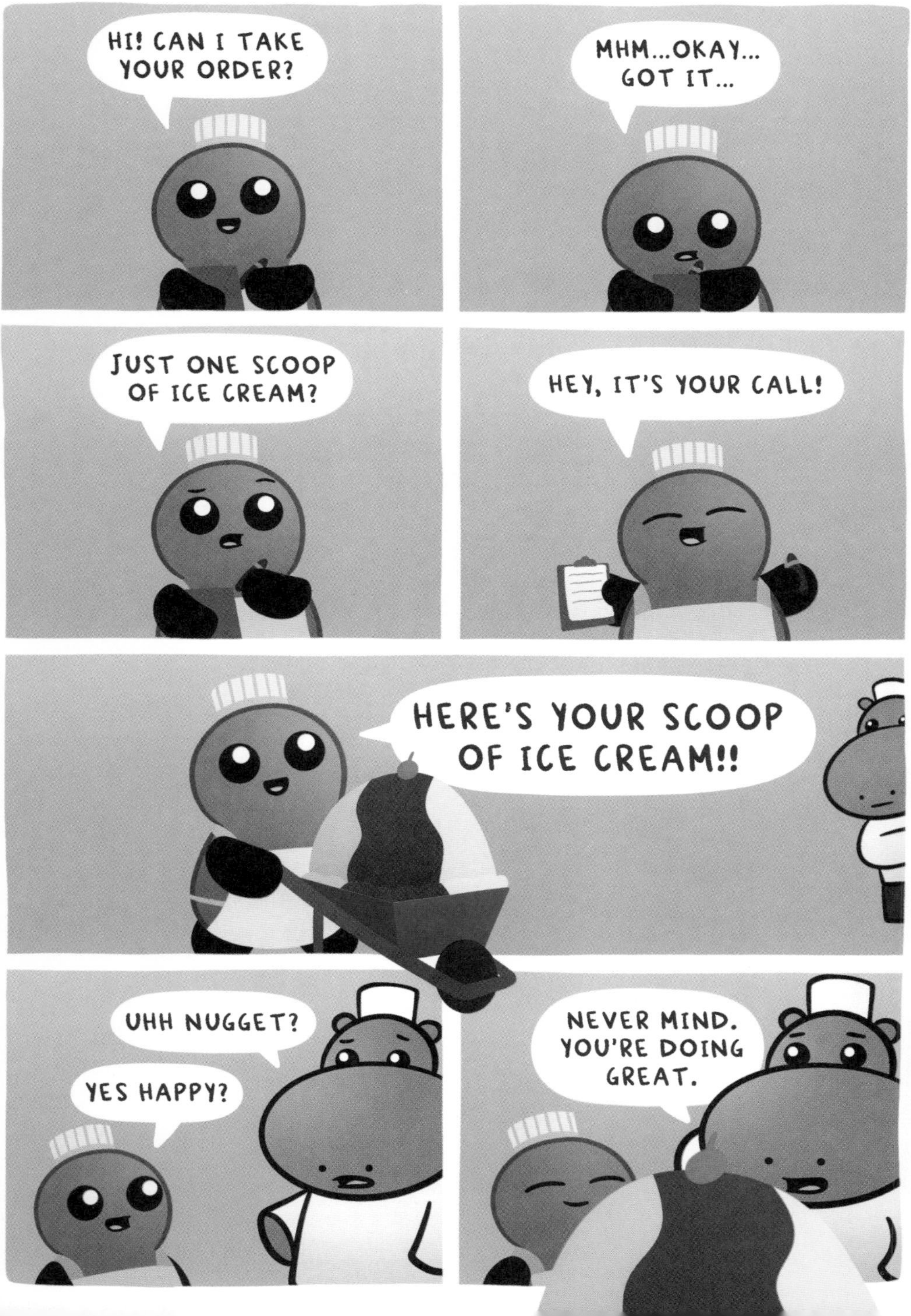
HI! CAN I TAKE YOUR ORDER?
MHM...OKAY... GOT IT...
JUST ONE SCOOP OF ICE CREAM?
HEY, IT'S YOUR CALL!
HERE'S YOUR SCOOP OF ICE CREAM!!
UHH NUGGET?
YES HAPPY?
NEVER MIND. YOU'RE DOING GREAT.

WRITE IN THE ICE CREAM SCOOPS

ICE CREAM TOPPED WITH SOME SWEET FACTS ABOUT YOU!

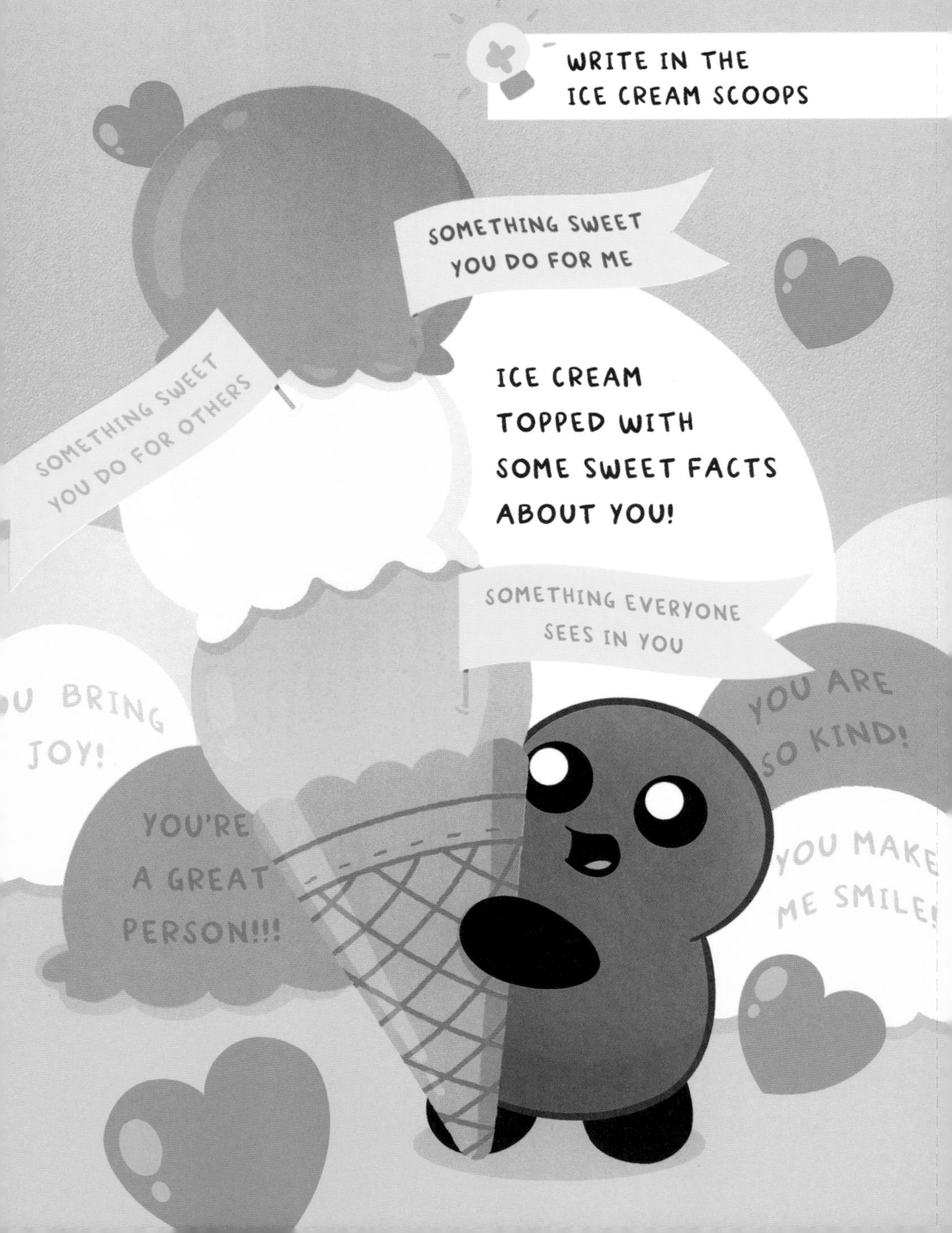

SOMETHING SWEET YOU DO FOR ME
SOMETHING SWEET YOU DO FOR OTHERS
SOMETHING EVERYONE SEES IN YOU
U BRING JOY!
YOU ARE SO KIND!
YOU'RE A GREAT PERSON!!!
YOU MAKE ME SMILE!

SAVE THE DATE!

IT'S TIME FOR OUR NEXT HANG!

I CAN'T WAIT TO SHARE ALL THE SNACKS WITH YOU!

WHEN:

WHERE:

TIME:

THEME:

SNACKS:

WHAT TO BRING:

YOU'RE CORDIALLY INVITED TO...

I WASN'T SURE WHAT TO BRING...SO I BROUGHT EVERYTHING!

A FUN-FILLED DAY FULL OF _____, _____, AND _____!

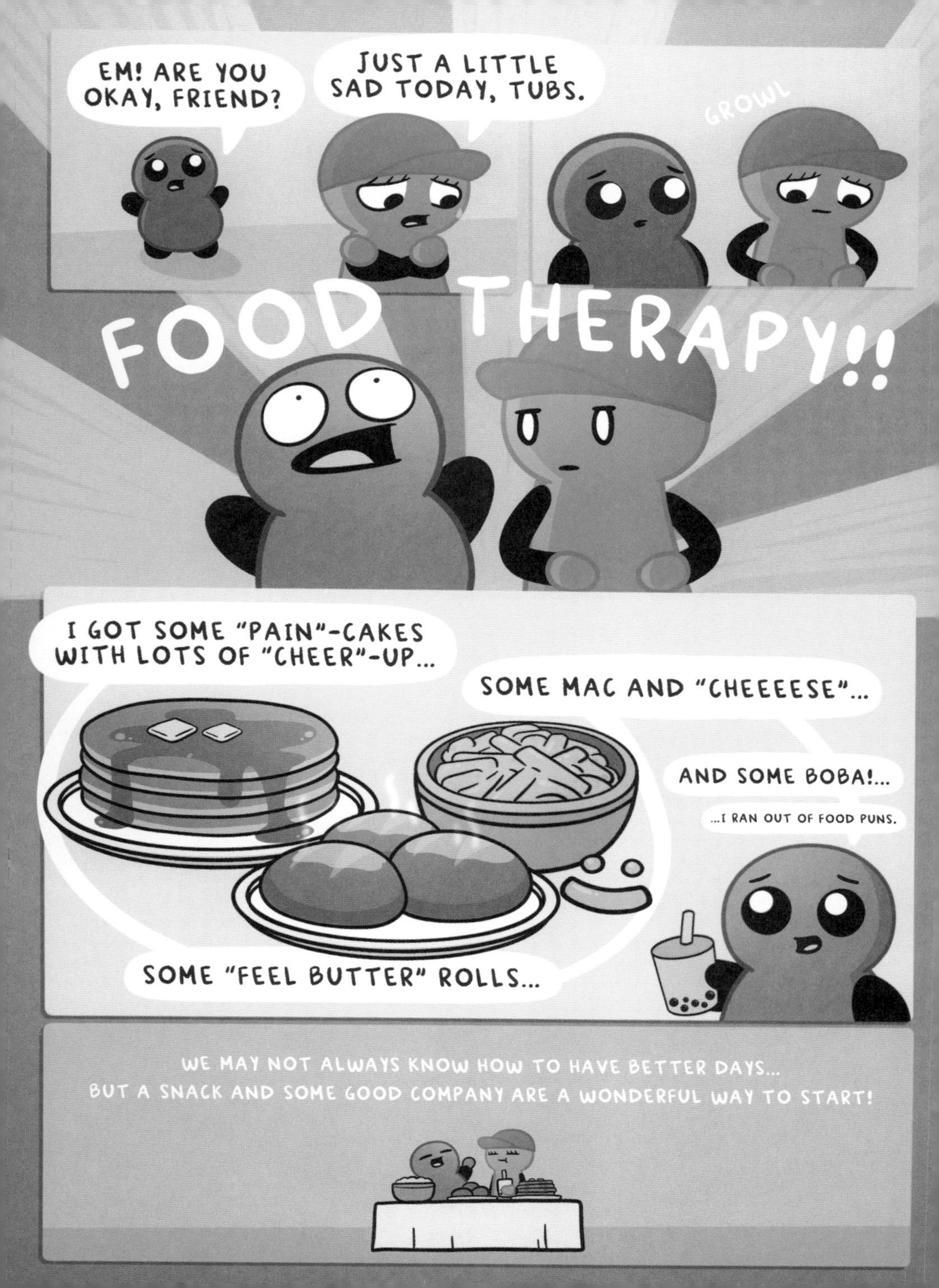
EM! ARE YOU OKAY, FRIEND?
JUST A LITTLE SAD TODAY, TUBS.
GROWL
FOOD THERAPY!!
I GOT SOME "PAIN"-CAKES WITH LOTS OF "CHEER"-UP...
SOME MAC AND "CHEEEESE"...
AND SOME BOBA!...
...I RAN OUT OF FOOD PUNS.
SOME "FEEL BUTTER" ROLLS...
WE MAY NOT ALWAYS KNOW HOW TO HAVE BETTER DAYS...
BUT A SNACK AND SOME GOOD COMPANY ARE A WONDERFUL WAY TO START!

PLANNING YOUR PERFECT COMFORT FEAST!

_____
the best drink

the best appetizer _____

_____
the best side dish

the best main course _____

_____
the best dessert

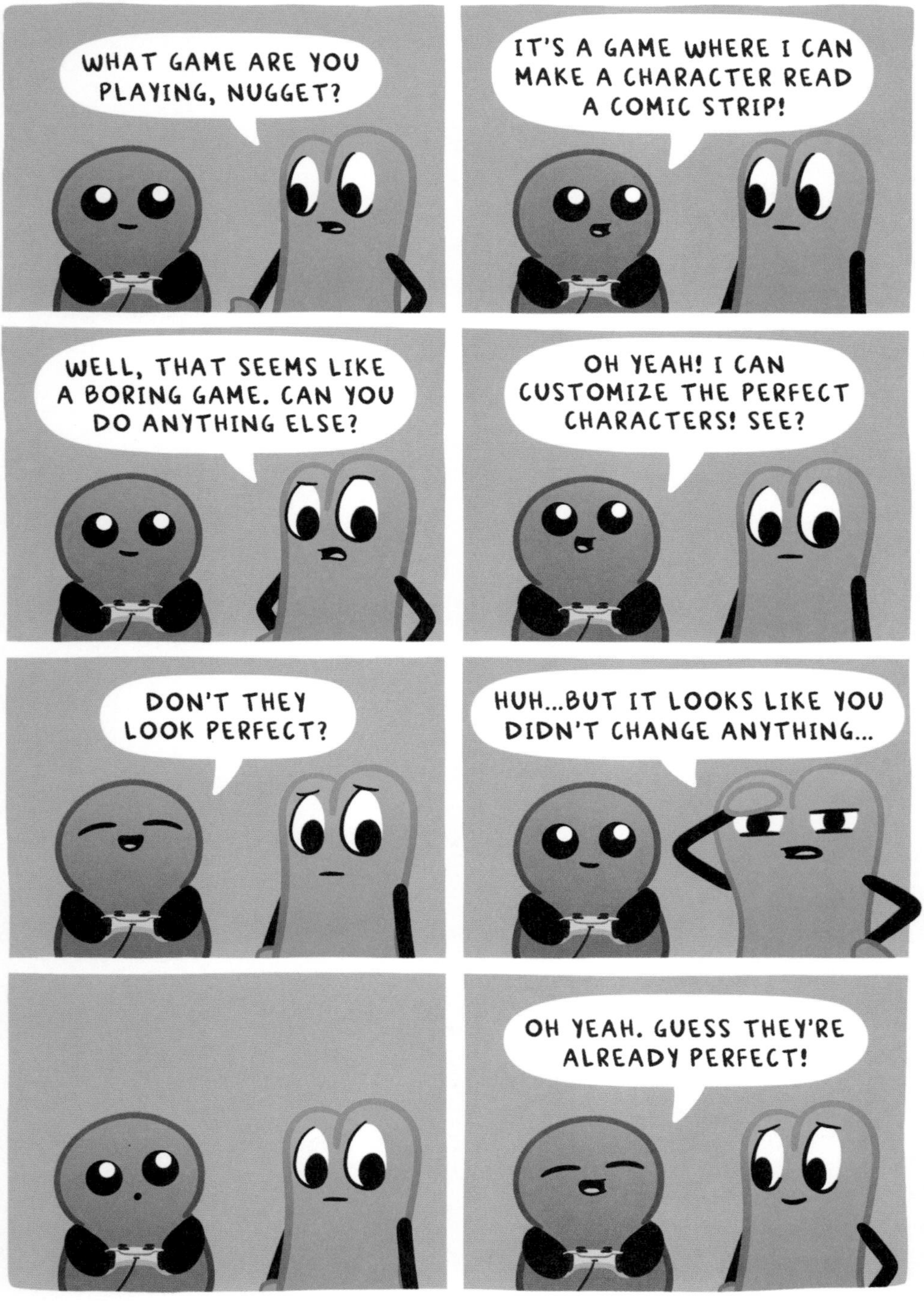
WHAT GAME ARE YOU PLAYING, NUGGET?
IT'S A GAME WHERE I CAN MAKE A CHARACTER READ A COMIC STRIP!
WELL, THAT SEEMS LIKE A BORING GAME. CAN YOU DO ANYTHING ELSE?
OH YEAH! I CAN CUSTOMIZE THE PERFECT CHARACTERS! SEE?
DON'T THEY LOOK PERFECT?
HUH...BUT IT LOOKS LIKE YOU DIDN'T CHANGE ANYTHING...
OH YEAH. GUESS THEY'RE ALREADY PERFECT!

HOW I'D DESIGN YOU AS A VIDEO GAME CHARACTER!

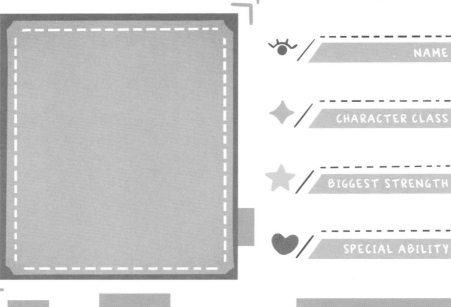

◡ / _____ NAME

◆ / _____ CHARACTER CLASS

★ / _____ BIGGEST STRENGTH

♥ / _____ SPECIAL ABILITY

BACKSTORY   000=S ☐

_____

_____

_____

_____

_____

_____

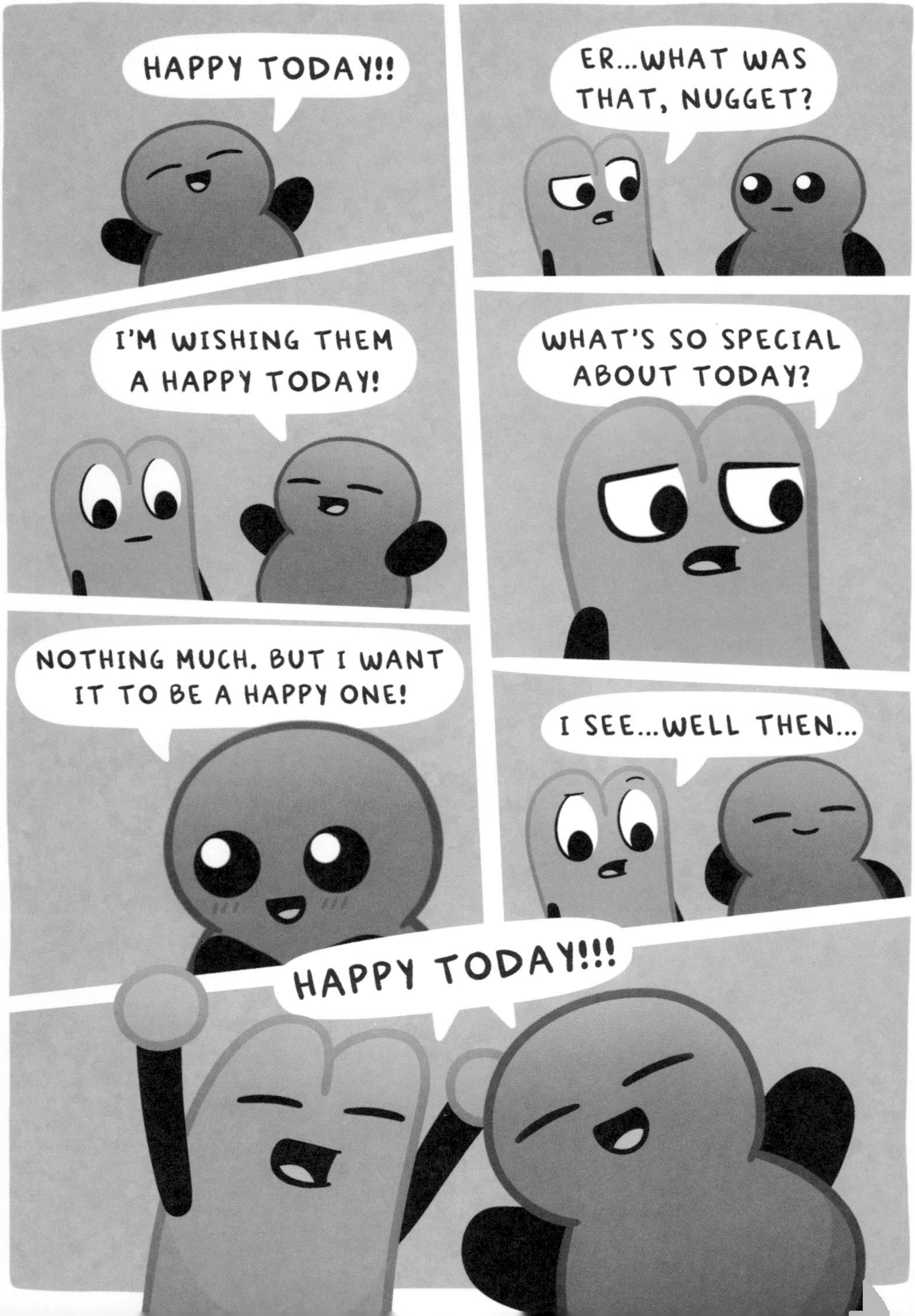
HAPPY TODAY!!
ER...WHAT WAS THAT, NUGGET?
I'M WISHING THEM A HAPPY TODAY!
WHAT'S SO SPECIAL ABOUT TODAY?
NOTHING MUCH. BUT I WANT IT TO BE A HAPPY ONE!
I SEE...WELL THEN...
HAPPY TODAY!!!

A SPECIAL DATE I LOVE CELEBRATING WITH YOU:

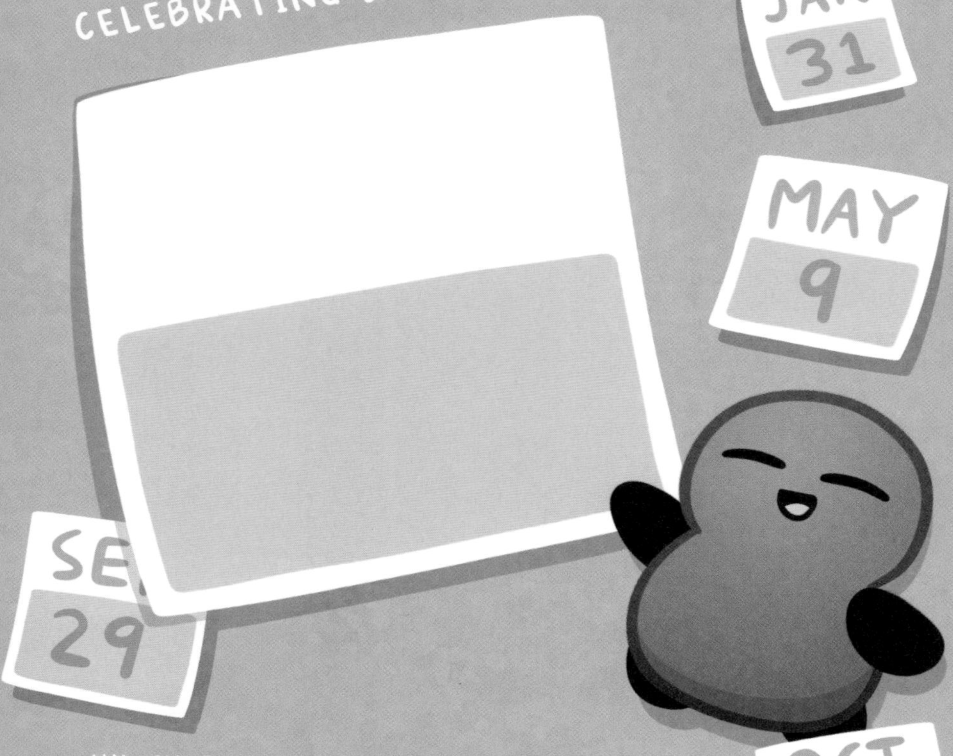
JAN
31
MAY
9
SE
29

WHY THIS DAY IS WORTH CELEBRATING:

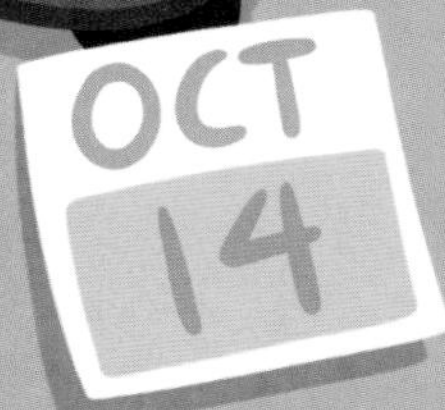
OCT
14

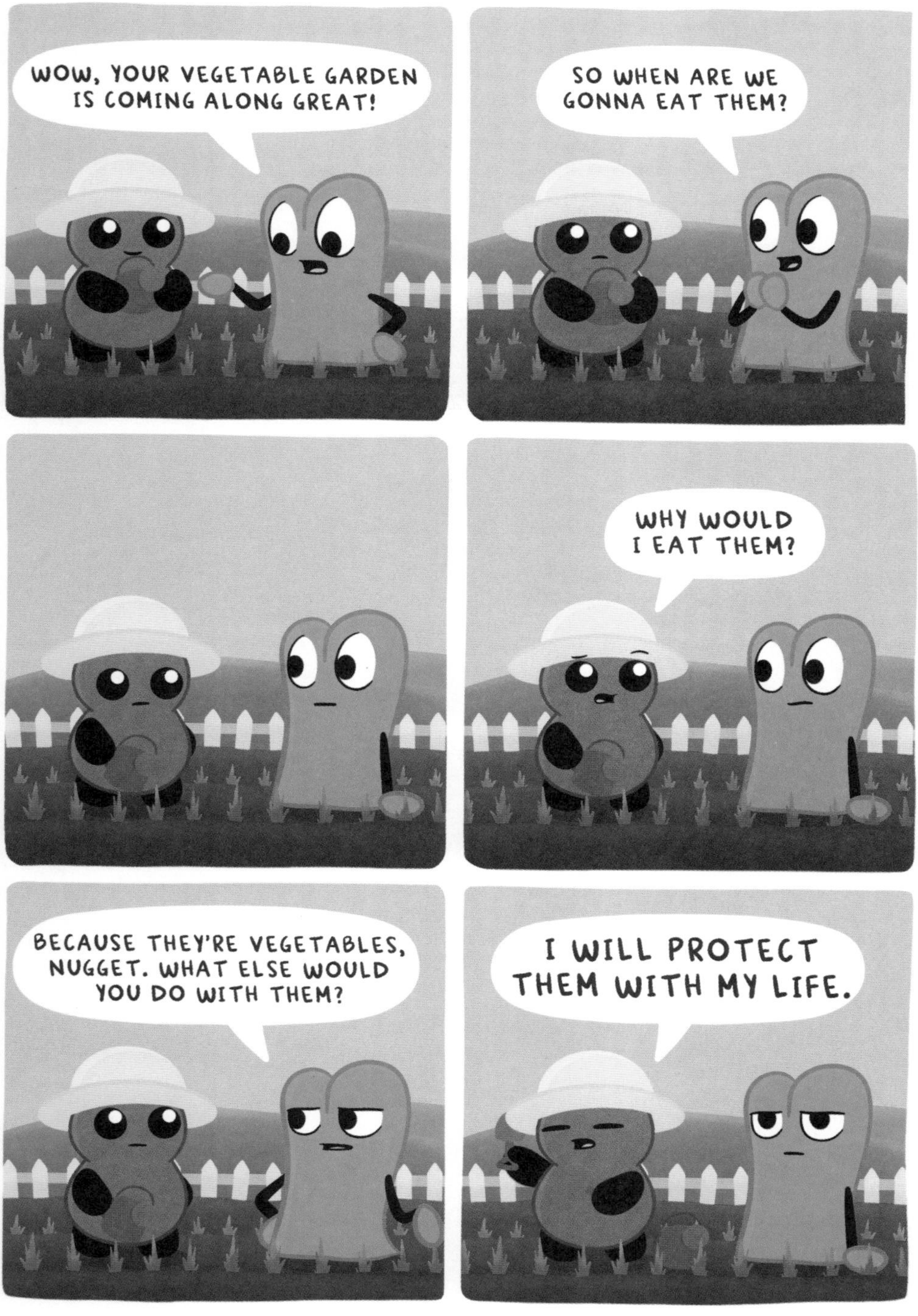
WOW, YOUR VEGETABLE GARDEN IS COMING ALONG GREAT!
SO WHEN ARE WE GONNA EAT THEM?
WHY WOULD I EAT THEM?
BECAUSE THEY'RE VEGETABLES, NUGGET. WHAT ELSE WOULD YOU DO WITH THEM?
I WILL PROTECT THEM WITH MY LIFE.

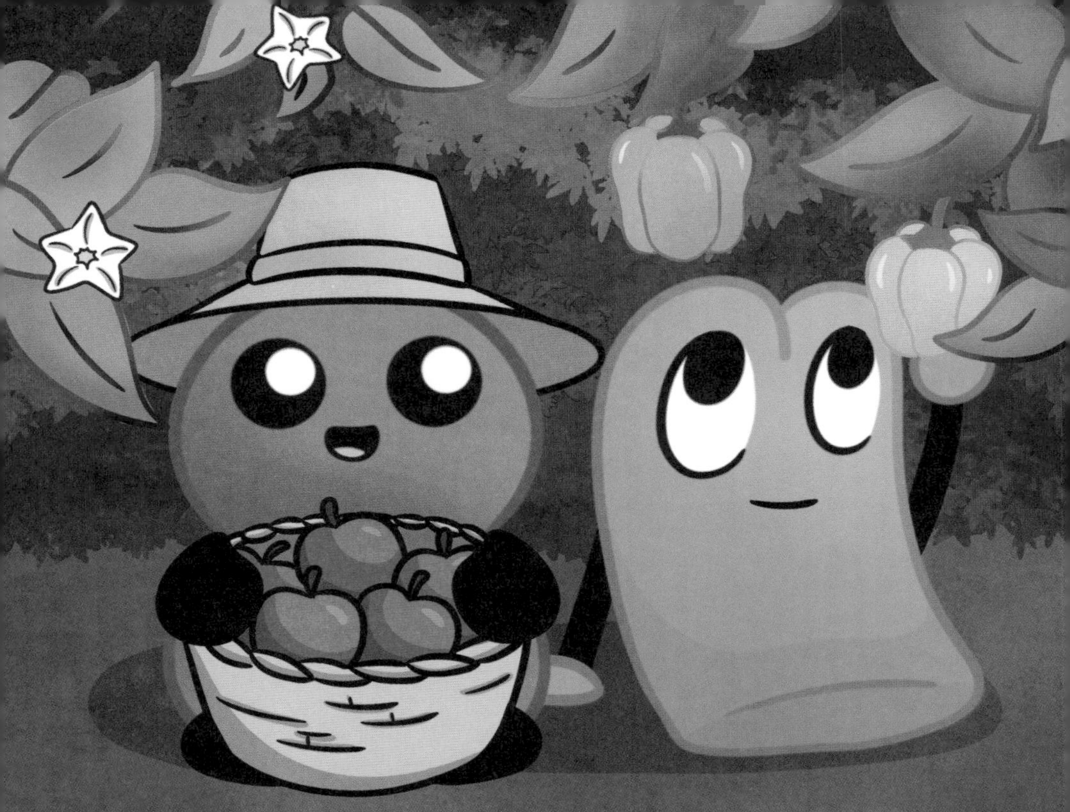

A FLOWER THAT
MATCHES YOUR VIBE

THE PERFECT SPICE TO
ADD TO YOUR LIFE

& THE PERFECT SIDE DISH
TO A MEAL WE CAN SHARE!

WANTED

(INSERT PHOTO HERE)

FOR THE CRIME OF BEING

THE BEST PERSON EVER!!!

1 BILLION NUG HUGS REWARD

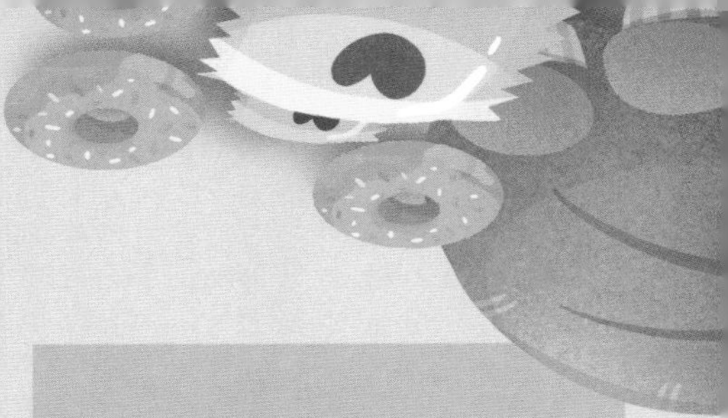

TO

FROM

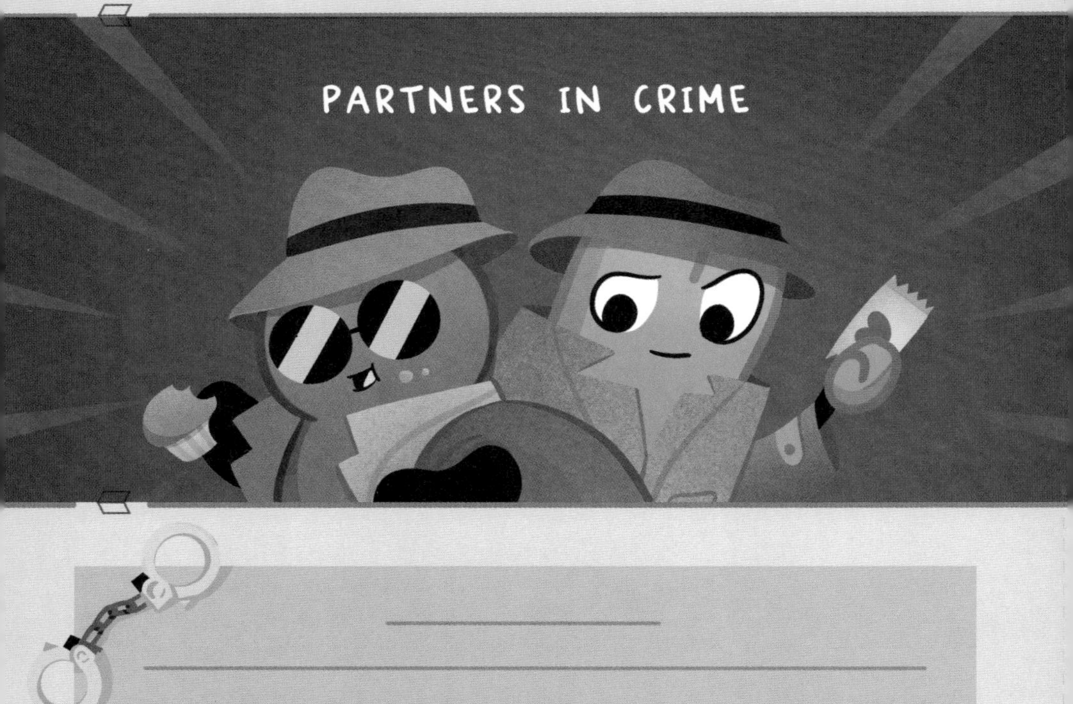
PARTNERS IN CRIME

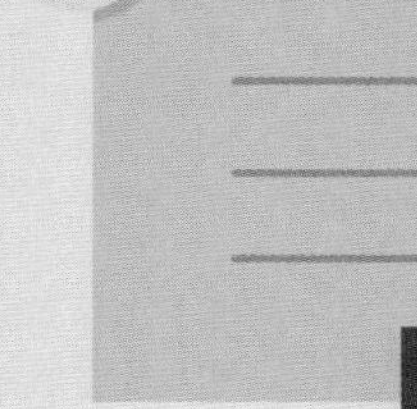

YOU ARE CRIMINALLY CUTE

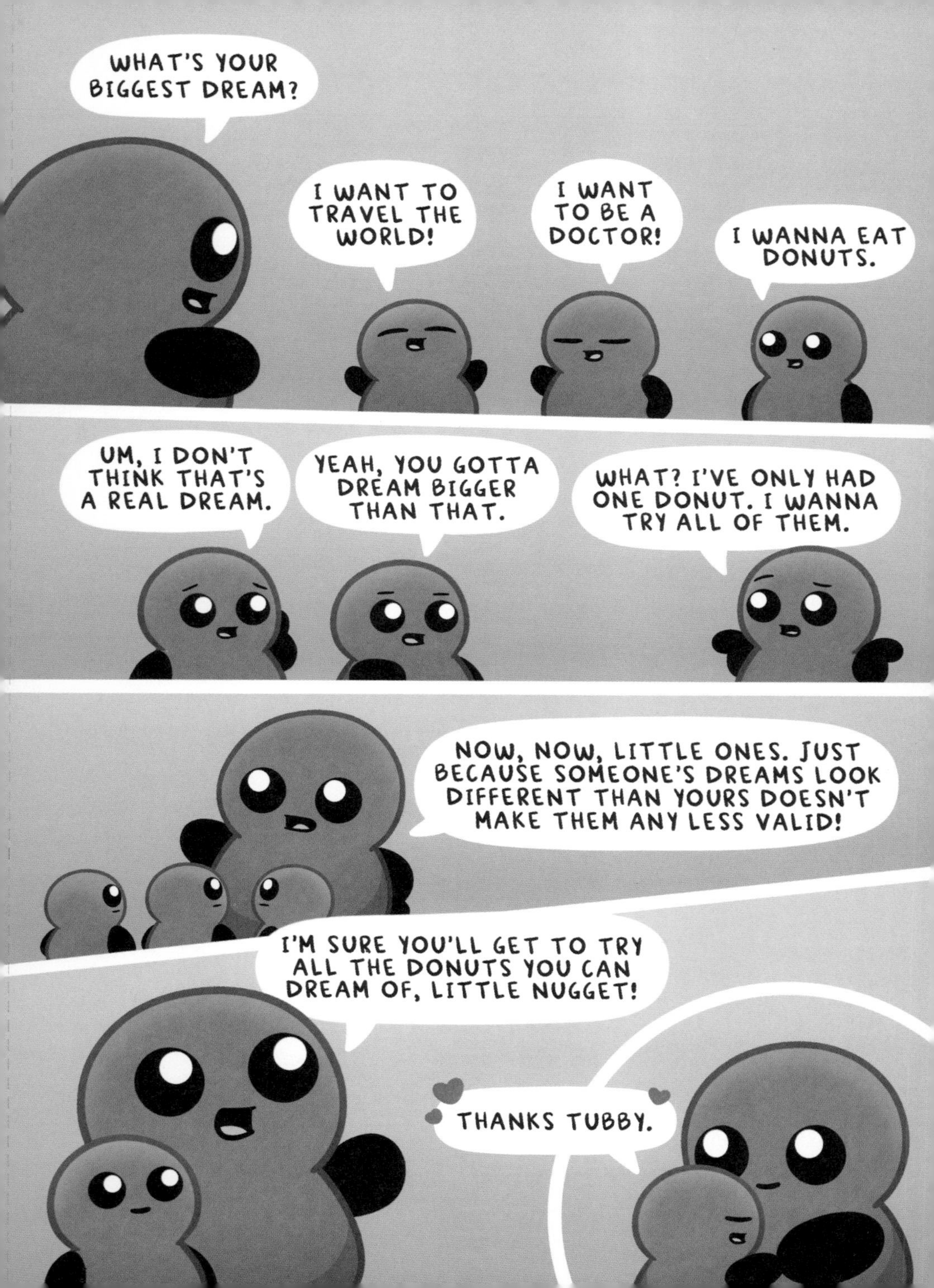
WHAT'S YOUR BIGGEST DREAM?
I WANT TO TRAVEL THE WORLD!
I WANT TO BE A DOCTOR!
I WANNA EAT DONUTS.
UM, I DON'T THINK THAT'S A REAL DREAM.
YEAH, YOU GOTTA DREAM BIGGER THAN THAT.
WHAT? I'VE ONLY HAD ONE DONUT. I WANNA TRY ALL OF THEM.
NOW, NOW, LITTLE ONES. JUST BECAUSE SOMEONE'S DREAMS LOOK DIFFERENT THAN YOURS DOESN'T MAKE THEM ANY LESS VALID!
I'M SURE YOU'LL GET TO TRY ALL THE DONUTS YOU CAN DREAM OF, LITTLE NUGGET!
THANKS TUBBY.

MY DREAM FOR OUR FUTURE

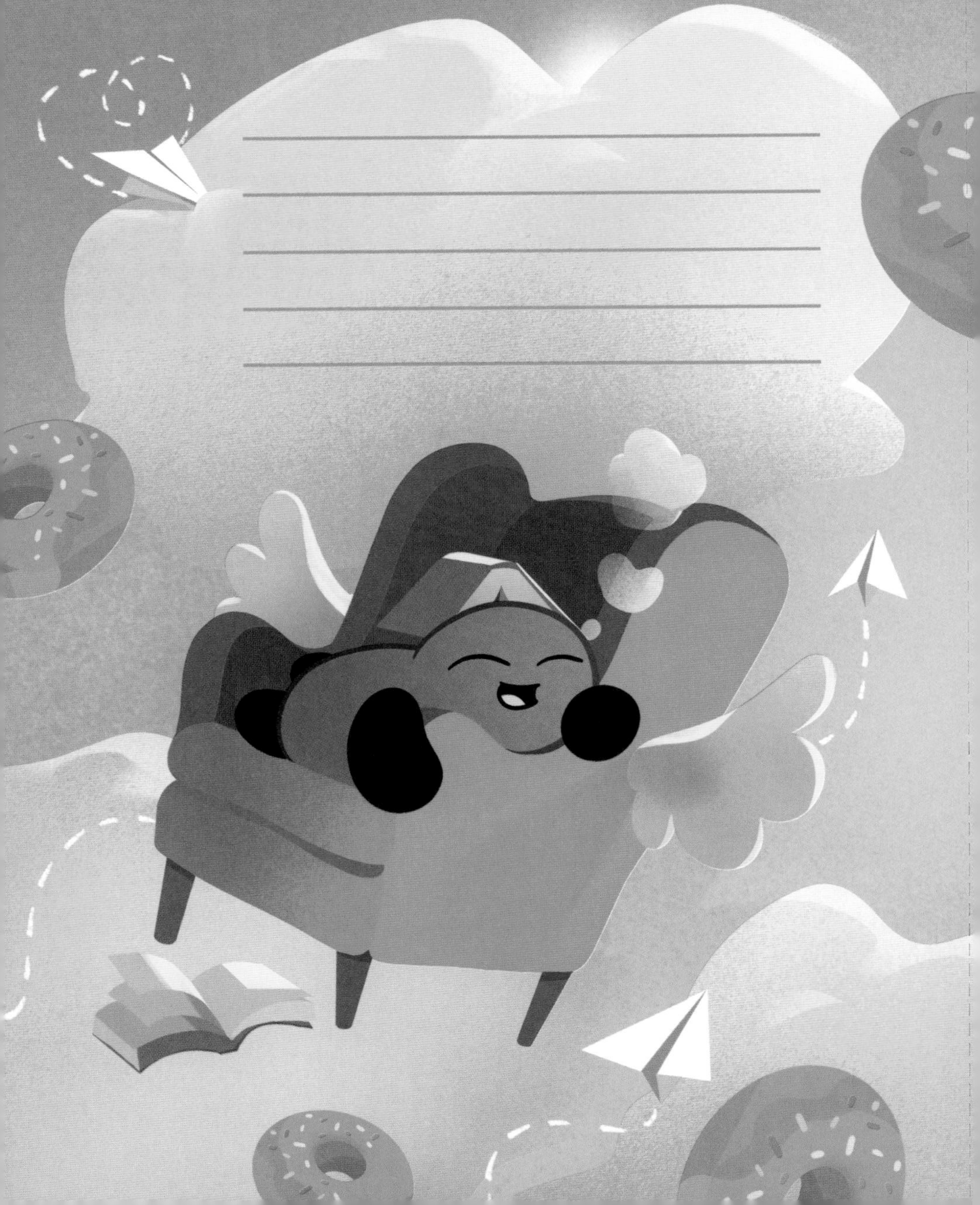

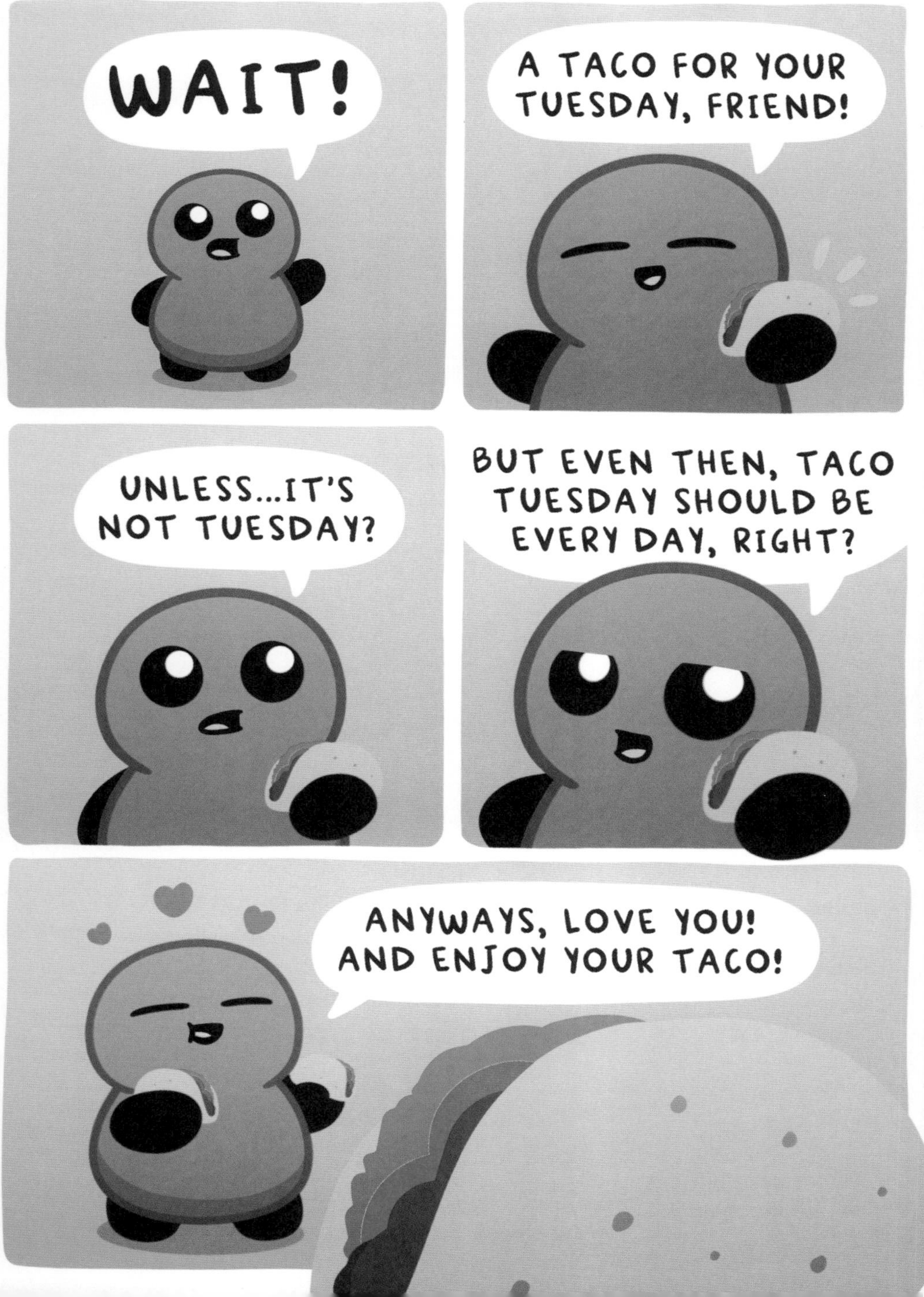
WAIT!
A TACO FOR YOUR TUESDAY, FRIEND!
UNLESS...IT'S NOT TUESDAY?
BUT EVEN THEN, TACO TUESDAY SHOULD BE EVERY DAY, RIGHT?
ANYWAYS, LOVE YOU! AND ENJOY YOUR TACO!

You're invited to:
TACO TUESDAY!!!

❤ where & when ❤

Place a check by all your favorite taco fillings so we can host the BEST taco night!

PROTEINS

MEAT-BASED
- [ ] Pollo Asado (Grilled Chicken)
- [ ] Carne Asada (Grilled Steak)
- [ ] Seasoned Ground Beef
- [ ] Lengua (Beef Tongue)
- [ ] Al Pastor (Marinated Pork)
- [ ] Carnitas (Slow-Cooked Pork)
- [ ] Chorizo (Spicy Sausage)
- [ ] Barbacoa or Birria (Slow-Cooked Meats)

TOPPINGS

VEGGIES
- [ ] White or Red Onions
- [ ] Diced Tomatoes
- [ ] Shredded Lettuce or Cabbage
- [ ] Sliced Avocado
- [ ] Grilled Bell Peppers
- [ ] Grilled Corn
- [ ] Sliced Radishes
- [ ] Jalapeños
- [ ] Pickled Veggies
- [ ] Fresh Cilantro
- [ ] Lime Wedges (for Squeezing)

SEAFOOD-BASED
- [ ] Whitefish (like Halibut, Tilapia, Mahi-Mahi)
- [ ] Shrimp
- [ ] Octopus
- [ ] Scallops

VEGETARIAN OR VEGAN FRIENDLY
- [ ] Mushrooms (Portobello, Shiitake, Chanterelle)
- [ ] Seitan (Made from Wheat Gluten)
- [ ] Tofu
- [ ] Beans

SAUCES AND CREAMS
- [ ] Salsa Roja (Red Salsa)
- [ ] Salsa Verde (Green Salsa)
- [ ] Crema Mexicana or Sour Cream
- [ ] Guacamole
- [ ] Hot Sauce of Choice

CHEESES
- [ ] Shredded Cheddar
- [ ] Queso Fresco or Cotija
- [ ] Queso (in Melted Dip Form)
- [ ] Vegan Cheese

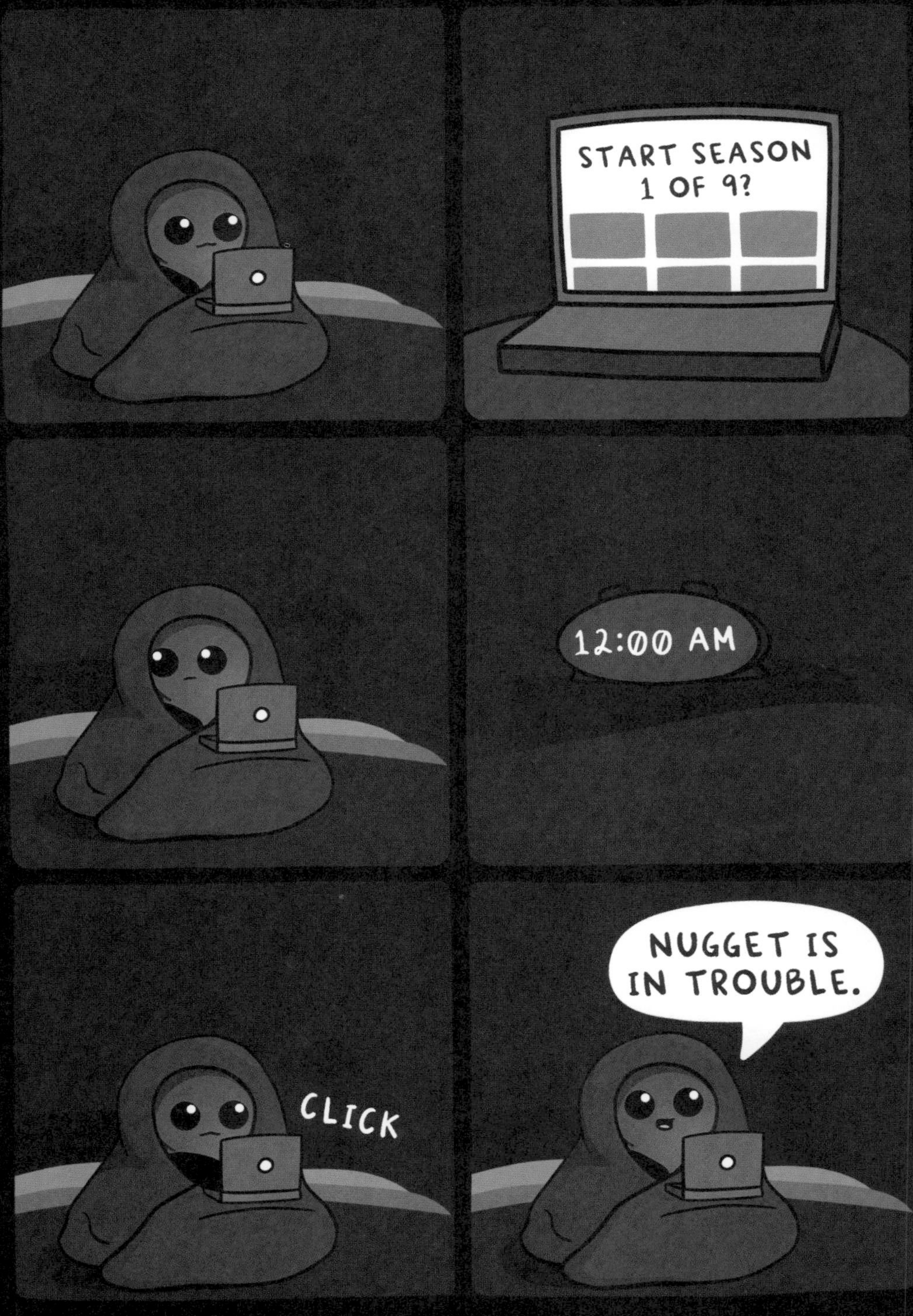
START SEASON 1 OF 9?
12:00 AM
CLICK
NUGGET IS IN TROUBLE.

SHOWS I THINK WE SHOULD START WATCHING TOGETHER

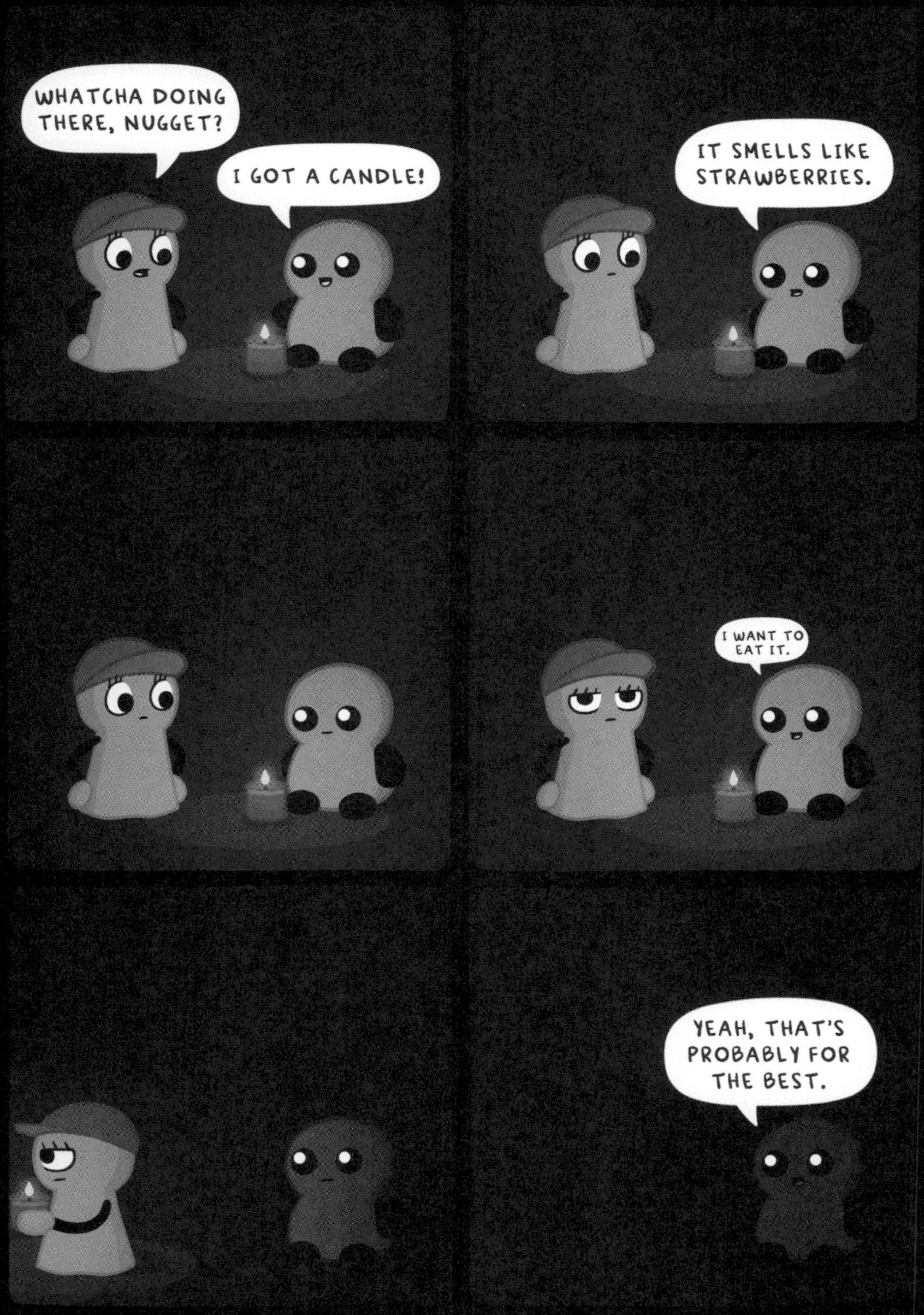
WHATCHA DOING THERE, NUGGET?
I GOT A CANDLE!
IT SMELLS LIKE STRAWBERRIES.
I WANT TO EAT IT.
YEAH, THAT'S PROBABLY FOR THE BEST.

WE MADE THE PERFECT SCENTED CANDLE FOR YOU!

TOP NOTE

MIDDLE NOTE

BASE NOTE

(CANDLE NAME)

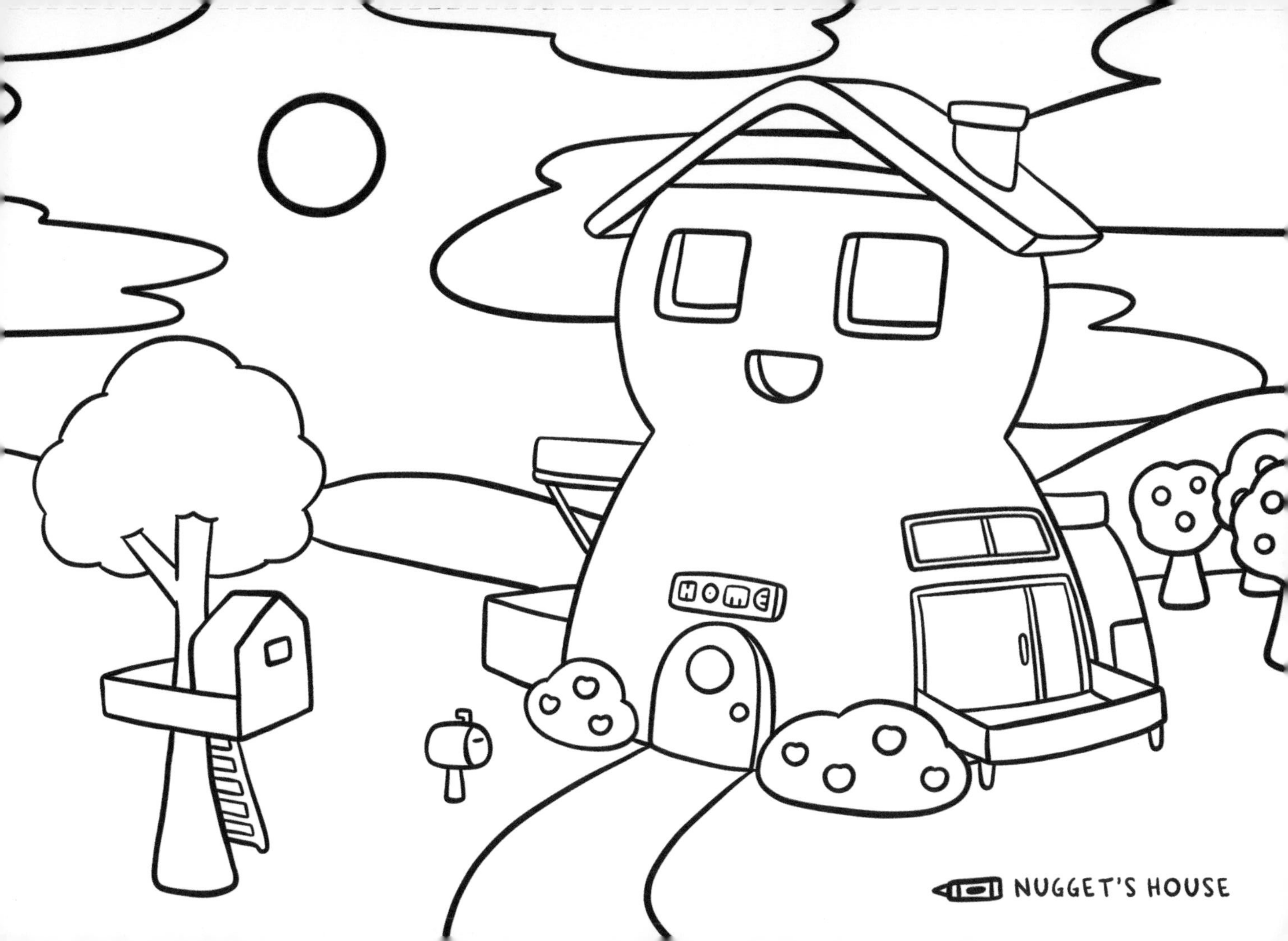
HOME

NUGGET'S HOUSE

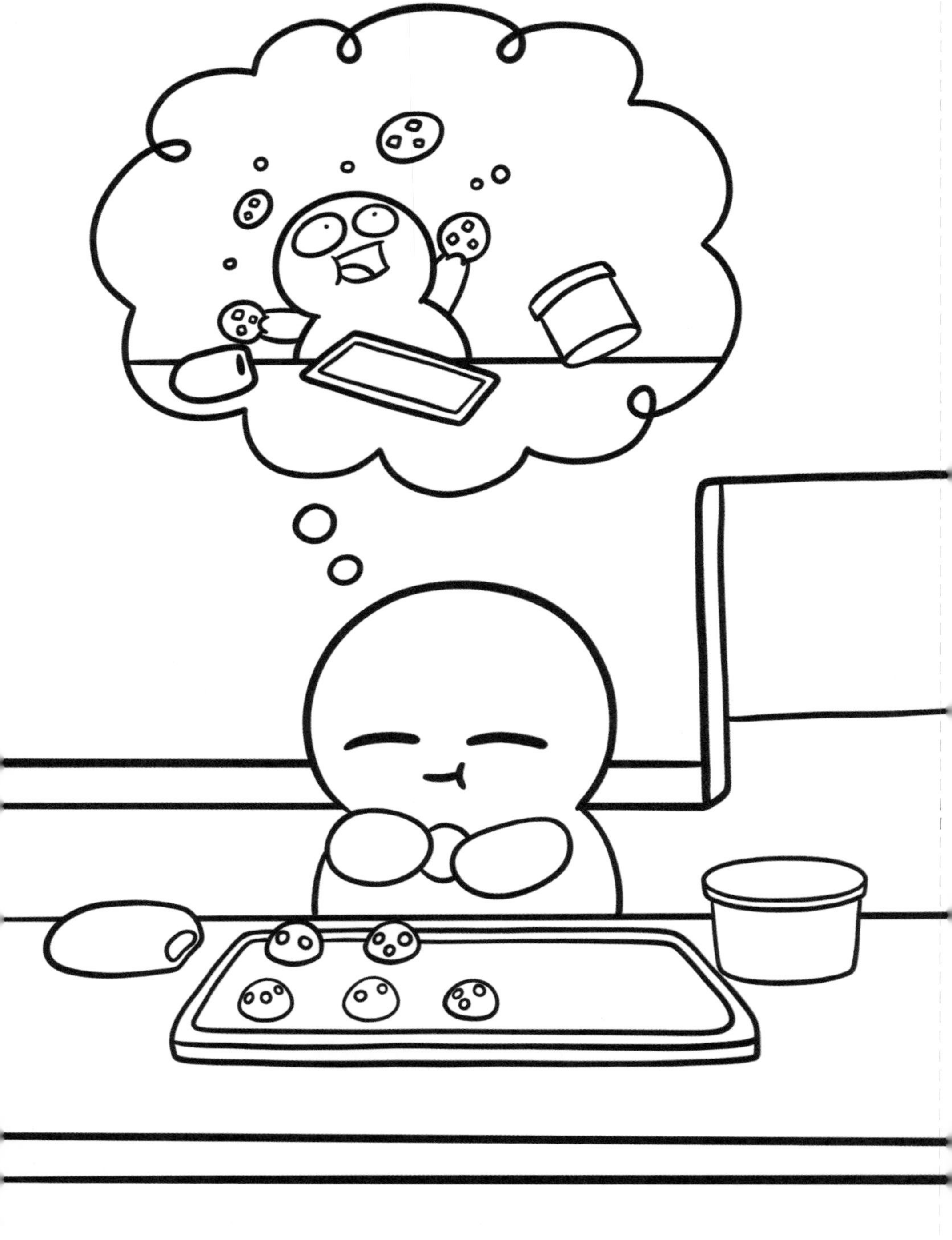

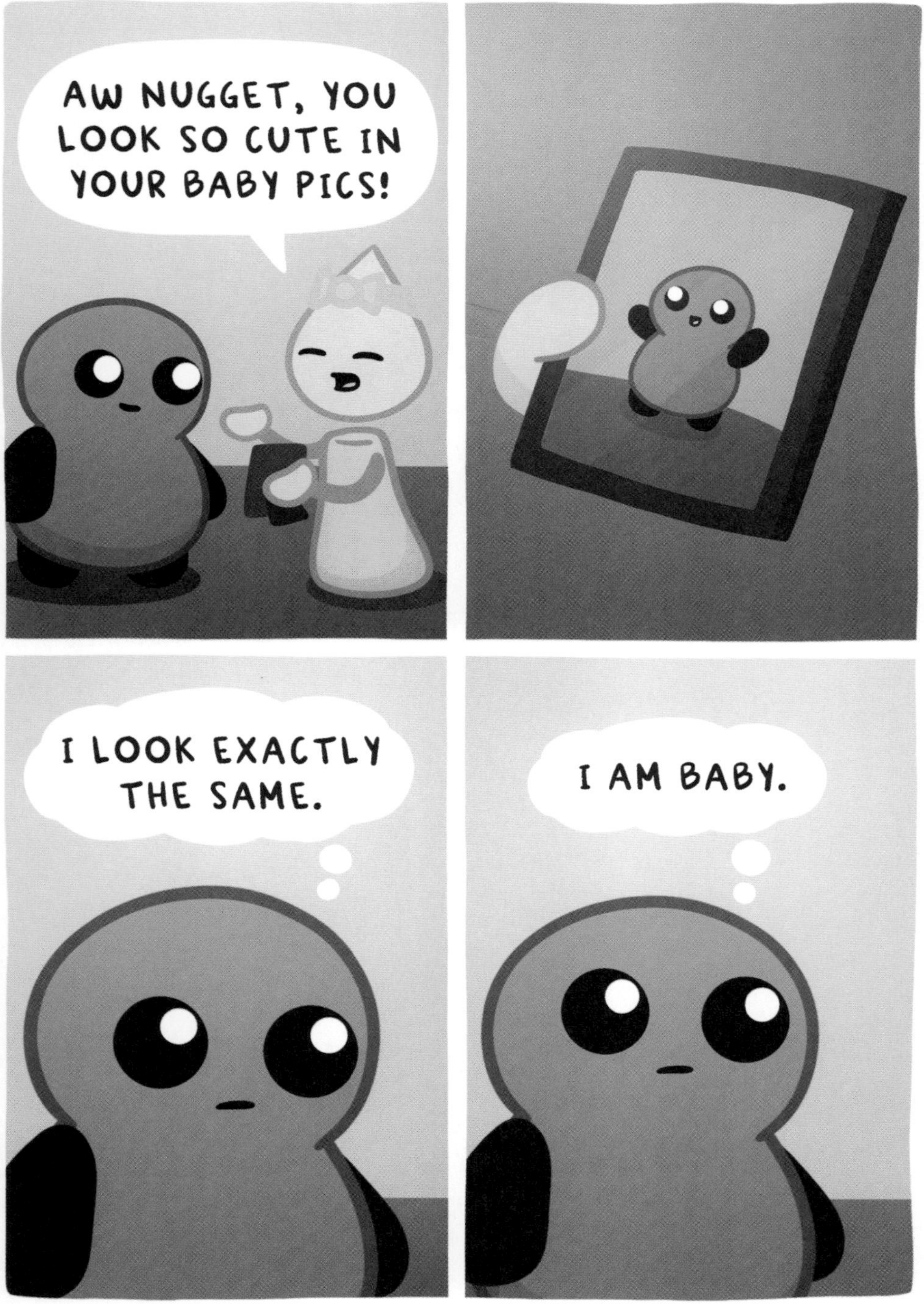
AW NUGGET, YOU LOOK SO CUTE IN YOUR BABY PICS!
I LOOK EXACTLY THE SAME.
I AM BABY.

Draw some of your favorite memories!

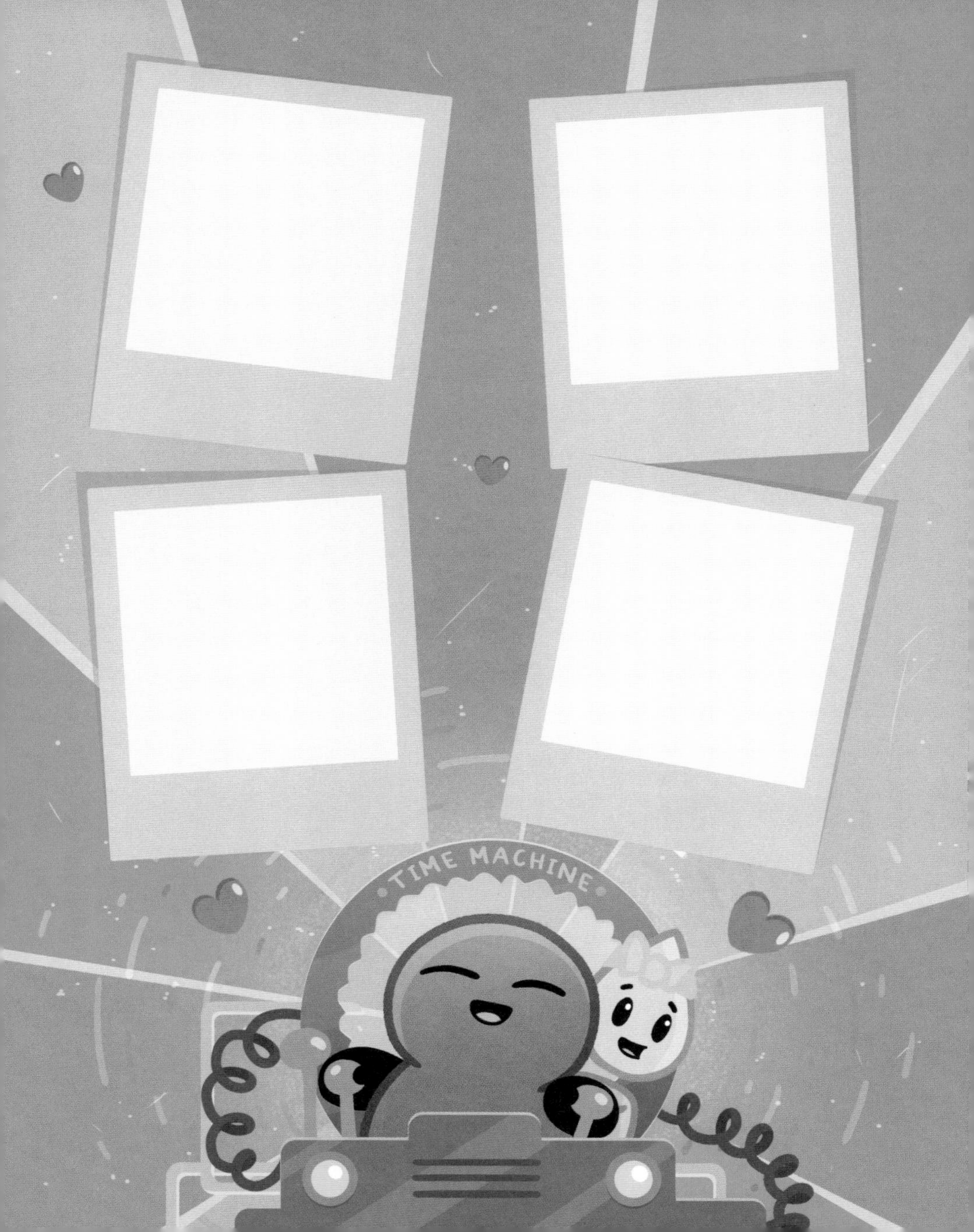
TIME MACHINE

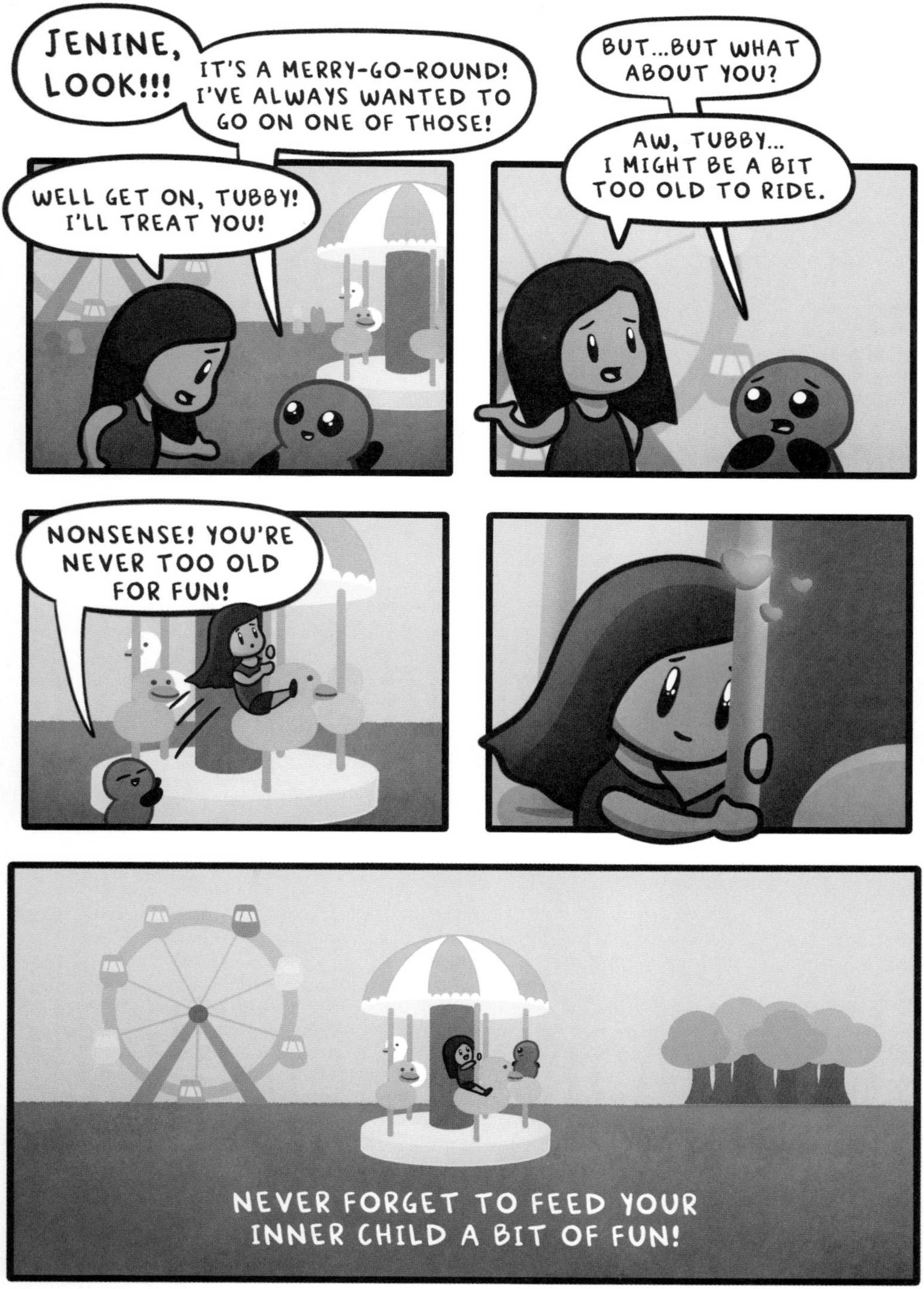
JENINE, LOOK!!!
IT'S A MERRY-GO-ROUND! I'VE ALWAYS WANTED TO GO ON ONE OF THOSE!
WELL GET ON, TUBBY! I'LL TREAT YOU!
BUT...BUT WHAT ABOUT YOU?
AW, TUBBY... I MIGHT BE A BIT TOO OLD TO RIDE.
NONSENSE! YOU'RE NEVER TOO OLD FOR FUN!
NEVER FORGET TO FEED YOUR INNER CHILD A BIT OF FUN!

MAKING PLANS FOR OUR INNER CHILD!

We'll never get too old to have fun together — so let's make plans our younger selves would've loved to do!

Some Examples

- Build a pillow fort
- Blow lots of bubbles
- Make friendship bracelets
- Have a coloring book date
- Create and fly paper airplanes

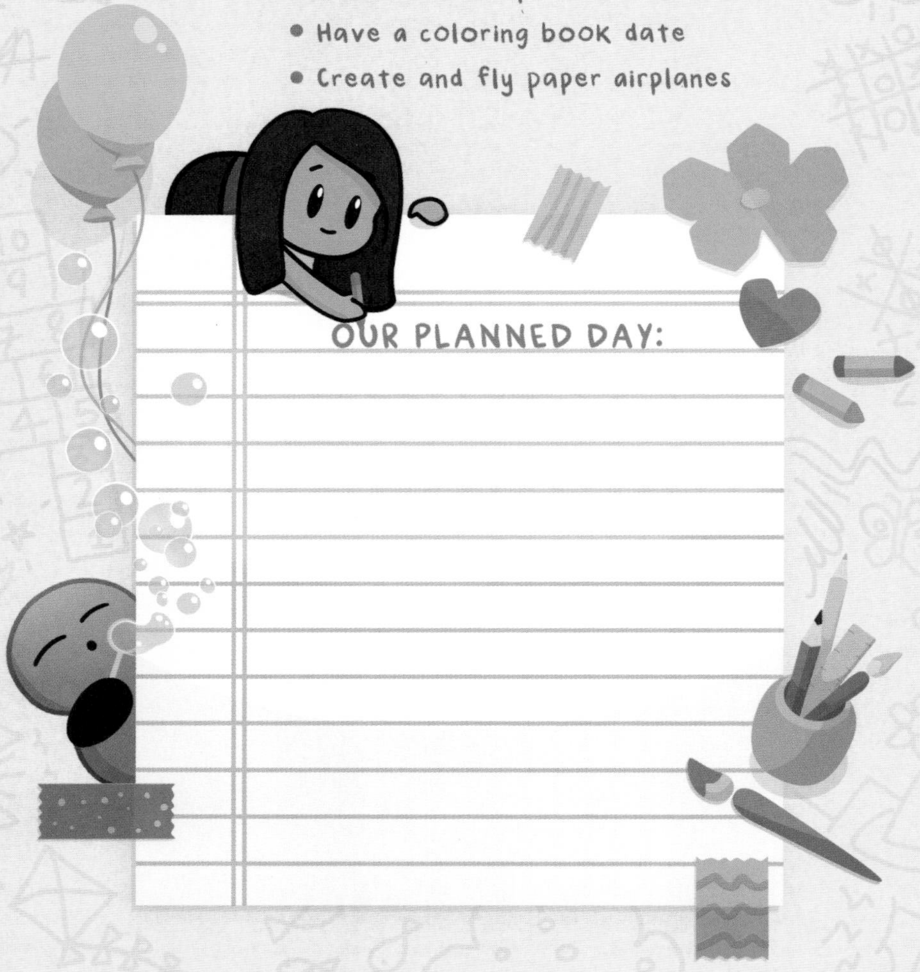
OUR PLANNED DAY:

GOING TO THE GROCERY

AND MAYBE I'LL GET A SNACK

GOTTA GET THE NECESSITIES

BUT MAYBE I'LL GET A SNACK

GOTTA GO GRAB SOME GOUDA CHEESE

OR MAYBE SOME PEPPER JACK

CAME BACK FROM THE GROCERY

AND ALL I GOT WERE SNACKS!

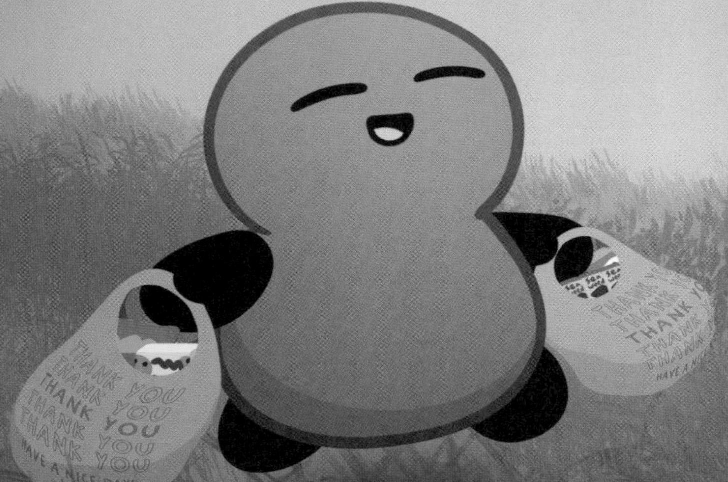
THANK YOU
THANK YOU
THANK YOU
THANK YOU
THANK YOU
HAVE A NICE DAY!

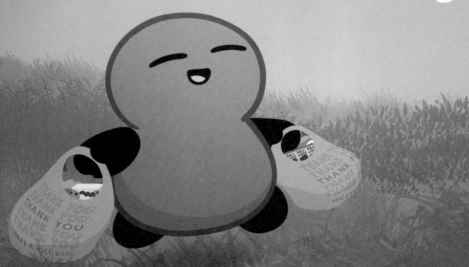

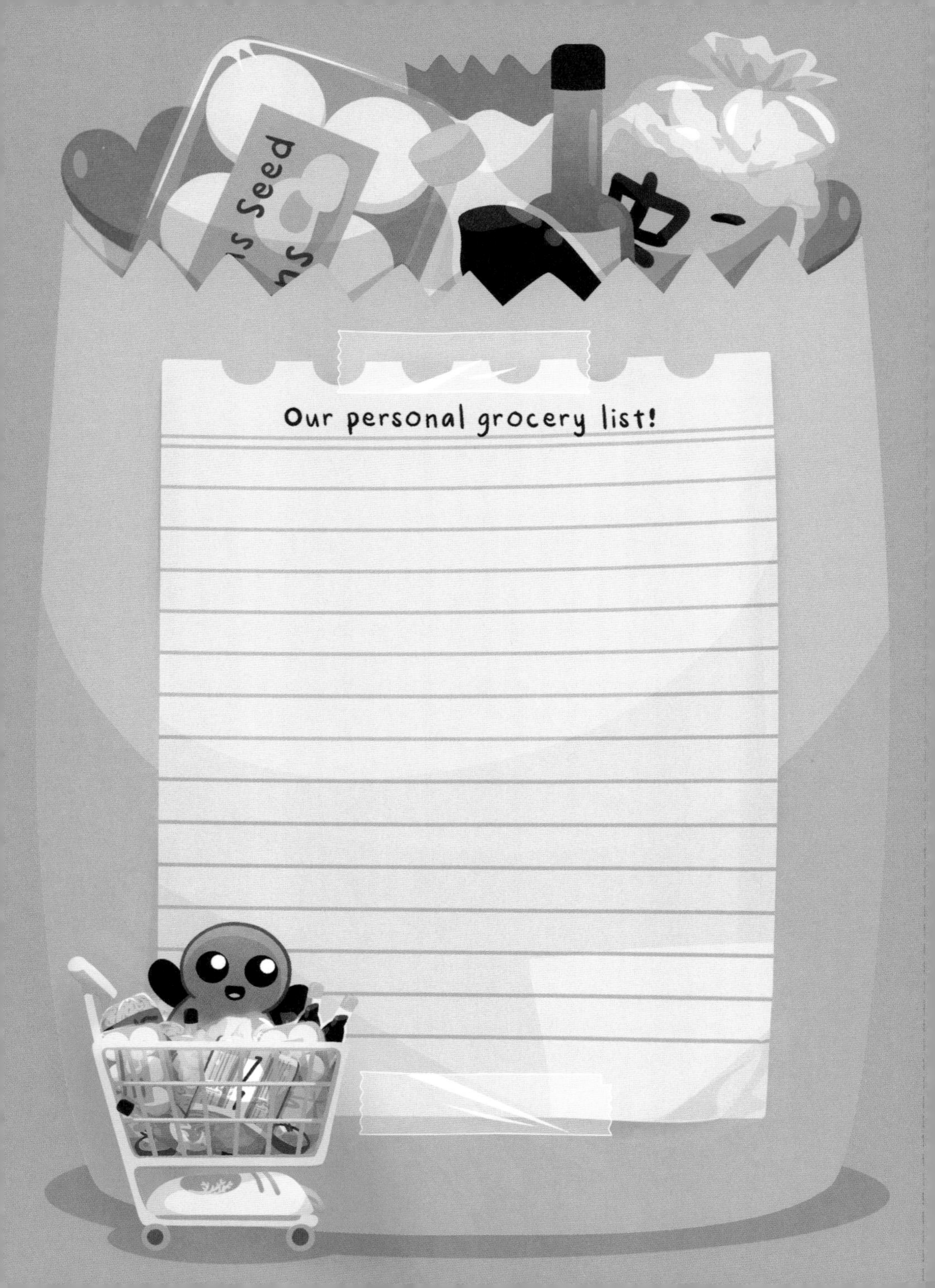
Seed
Our personal grocery list!

ALRIGHT FRIENDS, IF YOU SPOT SIGNS OF THE GHOST, MAKE SURE TO GRAB A PICTURE!

CLICK

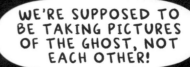
WE'RE SUPPOSED TO BE TAKING PICTURES OF THE GHOST, NOT EACH OTHER!

I JUST WANTED TO REMEMBER THIS MOMENT!

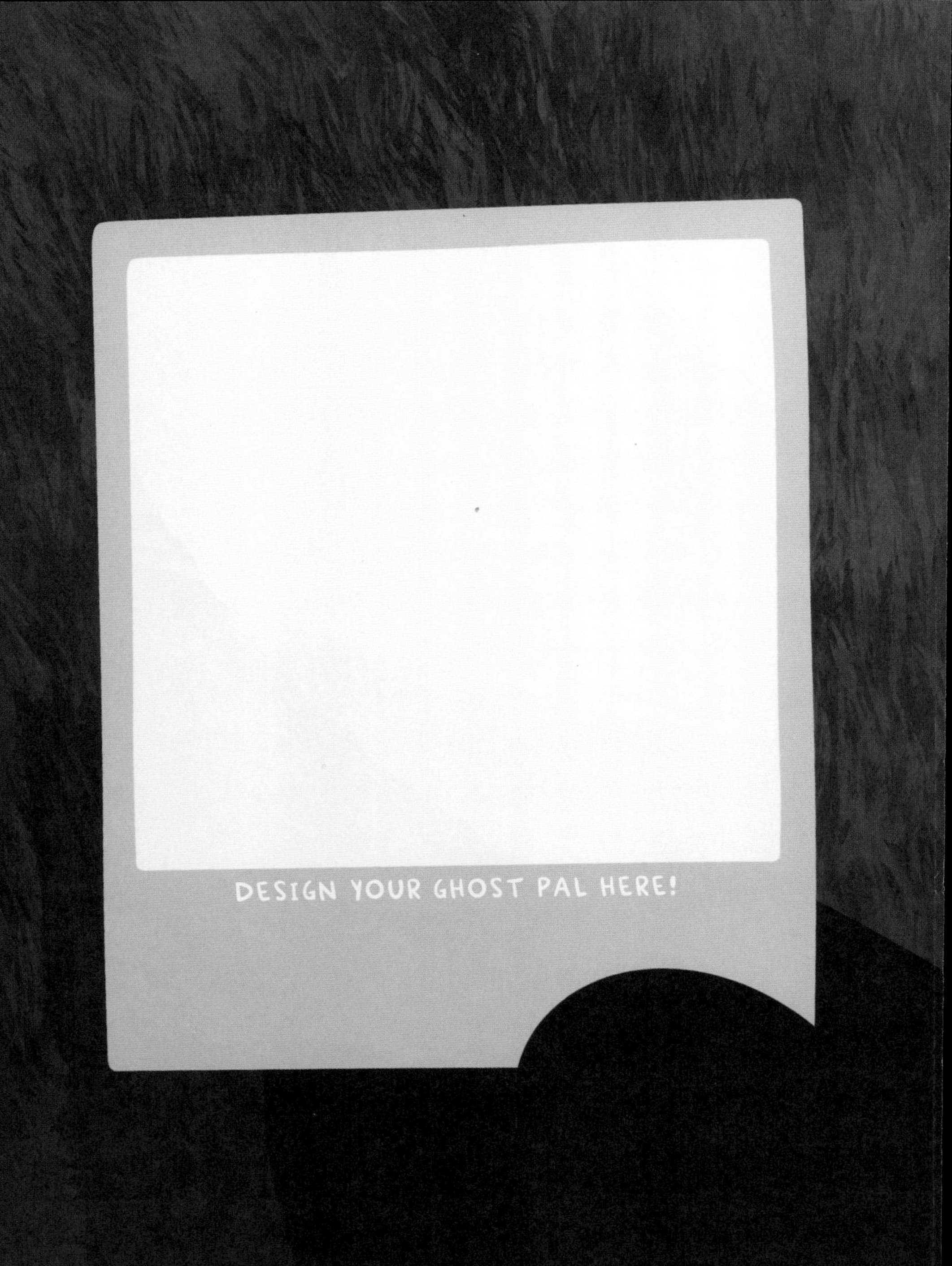
DESIGN YOUR GHOST PAL HERE!

HERE ARE SOME SILLY OR RANDOM FUN FACTS I JUST REALLY WANTED YOU TO KNOW!

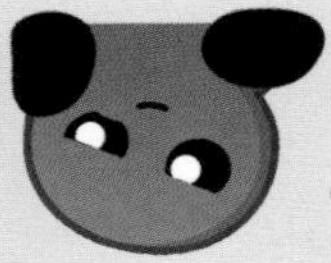

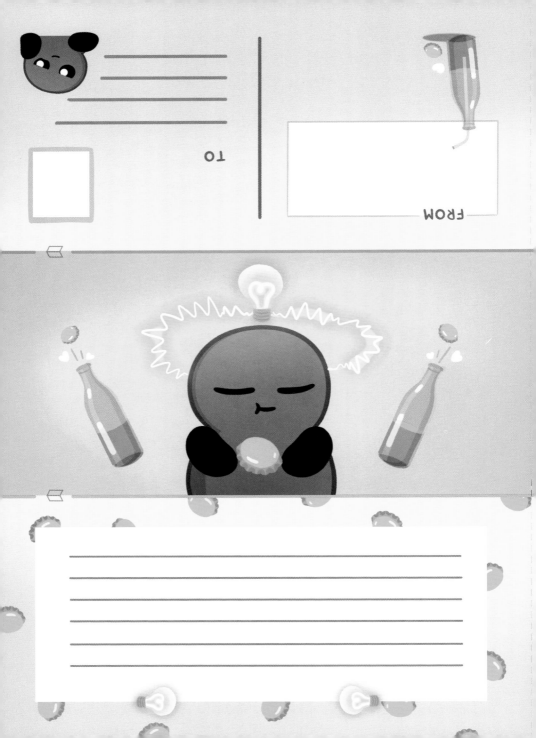

TO

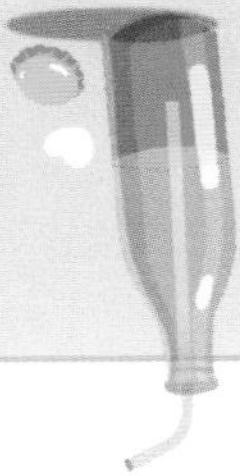

FROM

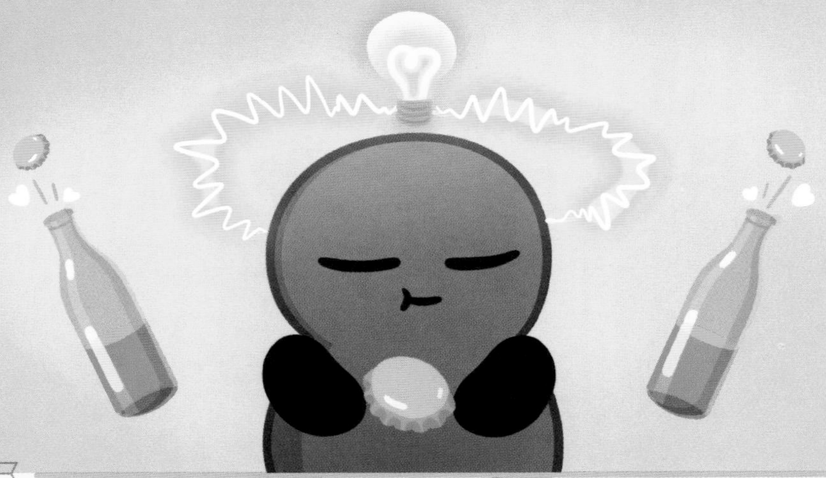

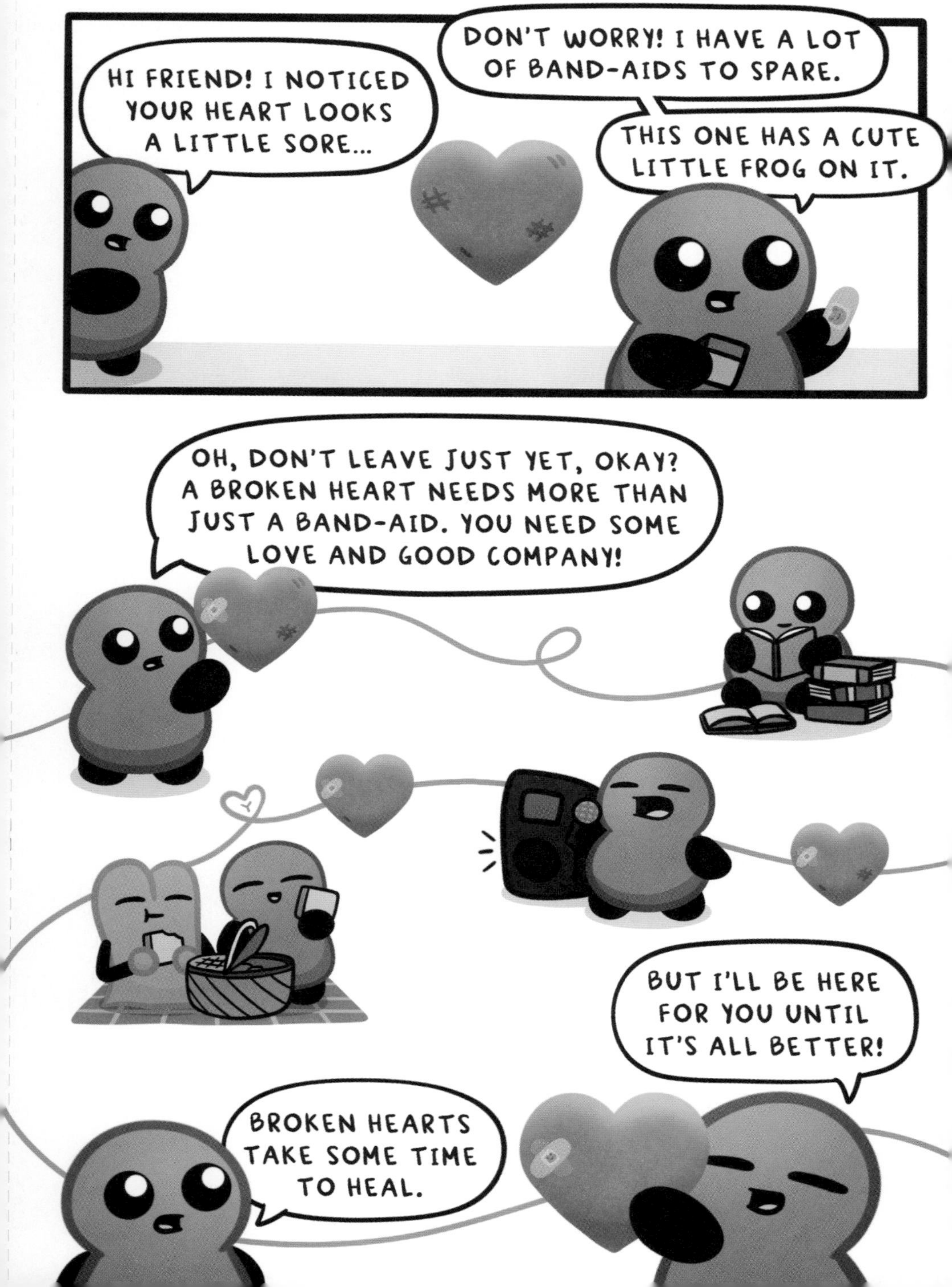
HI FRIEND! I NOTICED YOUR HEART LOOKS A LITTLE SORE...
DON'T WORRY! I HAVE A LOT OF BAND-AIDS TO SPARE.
THIS ONE HAS A CUTE LITTLE FROG ON IT.
OH, DON'T LEAVE JUST YET, OKAY? A BROKEN HEART NEEDS MORE THAN JUST A BAND-AID. YOU NEED SOME LOVE AND GOOD COMPANY!
BROKEN HEARTS TAKE SOME TIME TO HEAL.
BUT I'LL BE HERE FOR YOU UNTIL IT'S ALL BETTER!

a letter to heal your broken heart

FEATURING YOUR
LIFE MOVIE

Title: ＿ ＿ ＿ ＿ ＿ ＿ ＿ ＿

Genre: ＿ ＿ ＿ ＿ ＿ ＿ ＿ ＿

♥ STARRING ♥

PLOTLINE

＿ ＿ ＿ ＿ ＿ ＿ ＿ ＿ ＿ ＿ ＿ ＿

＿ ＿ ＿ ＿ ＿ ＿ ＿ ＿ ＿ ＿ ＿ ＿

＿ ＿ ＿ ＿ ＿ ＿ ＿ ＿ ＿ ＿ ＿ ＿

＿ ＿ ＿ ＿ ＿ ＿ ＿ ＿ ＿ ＿ ＿ ＿

＿ ＿ ＿ ＿ ＿ ＿ ＿ ＿ ＿ ＿ ＿ ＿

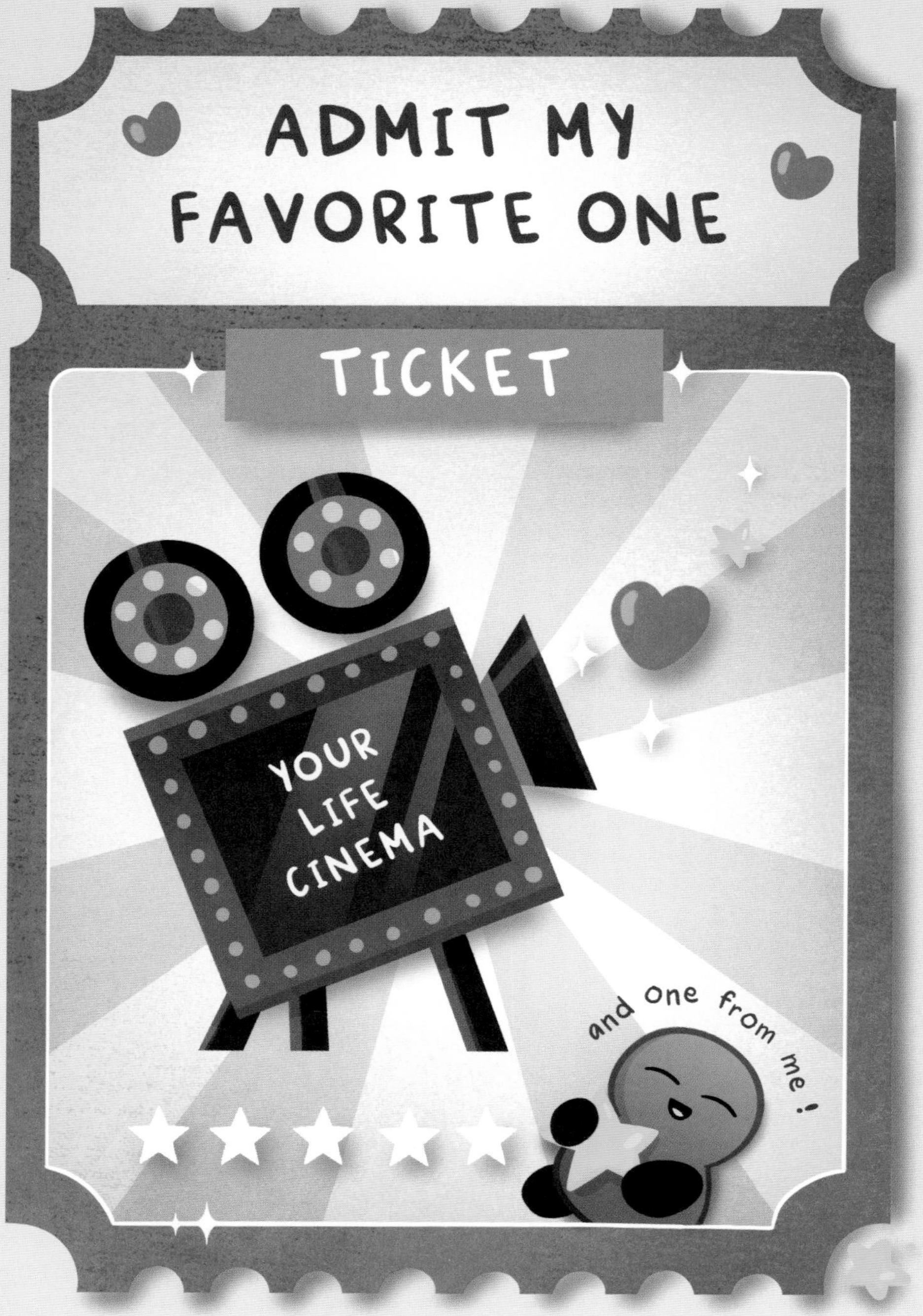
ADMIT MY
FAVORITE ONE
TICKET
YOUR
LIFE
CINEMA
and one from me!

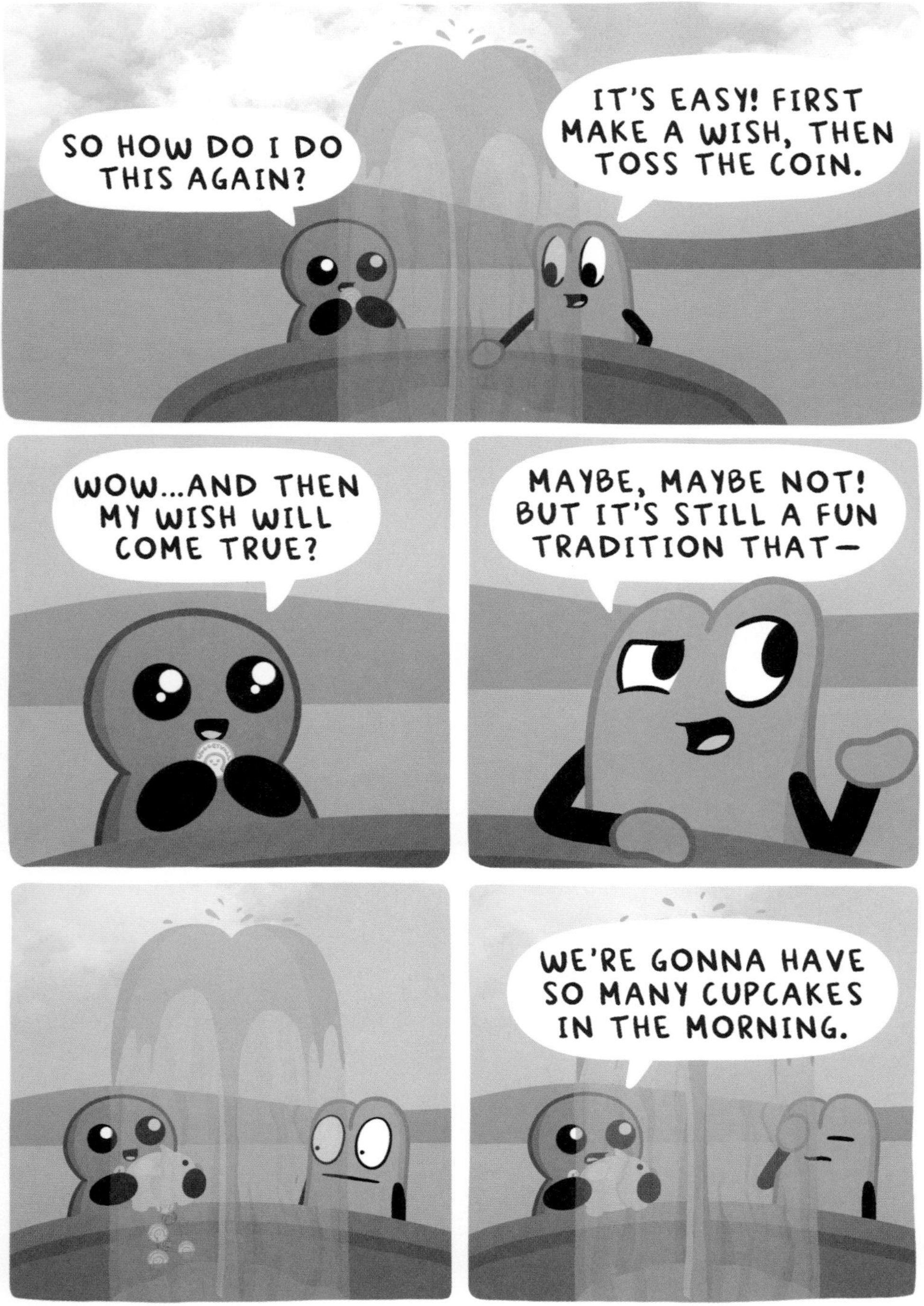

SO HOW DO I DO THIS AGAIN?
IT'S EASY! FIRST MAKE A WISH, THEN TOSS THE COIN.
WOW...AND THEN MY WISH WILL COME TRUE?
MAYBE, MAYBE NOT! BUT IT'S STILL A FUN TRADITION THAT—
WE'RE GONNA HAVE SO MANY CUPCAKES IN THE MORNING.

NUGGETVILLE

HERE'S A WISH I MADE FOR YOU:

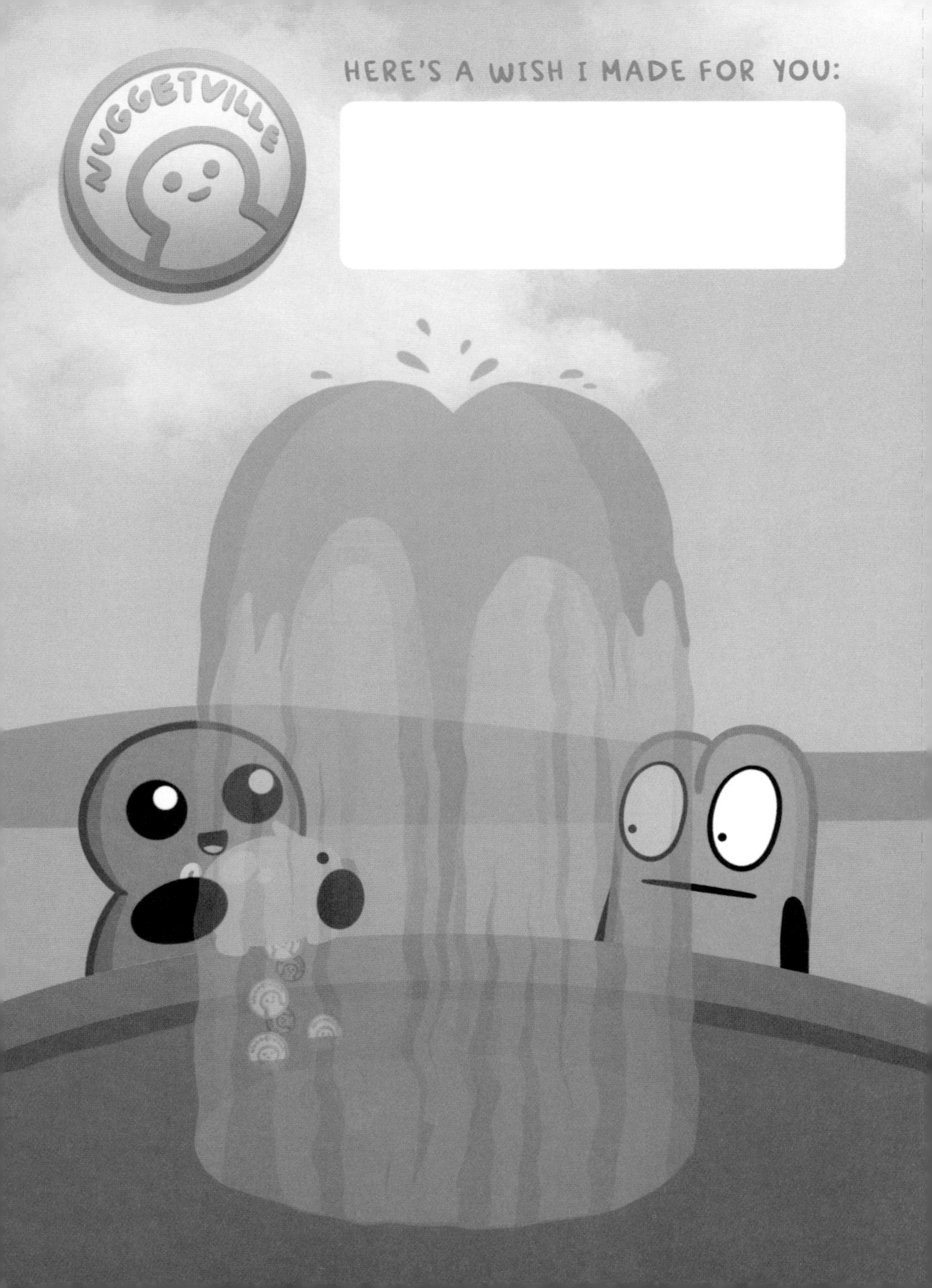

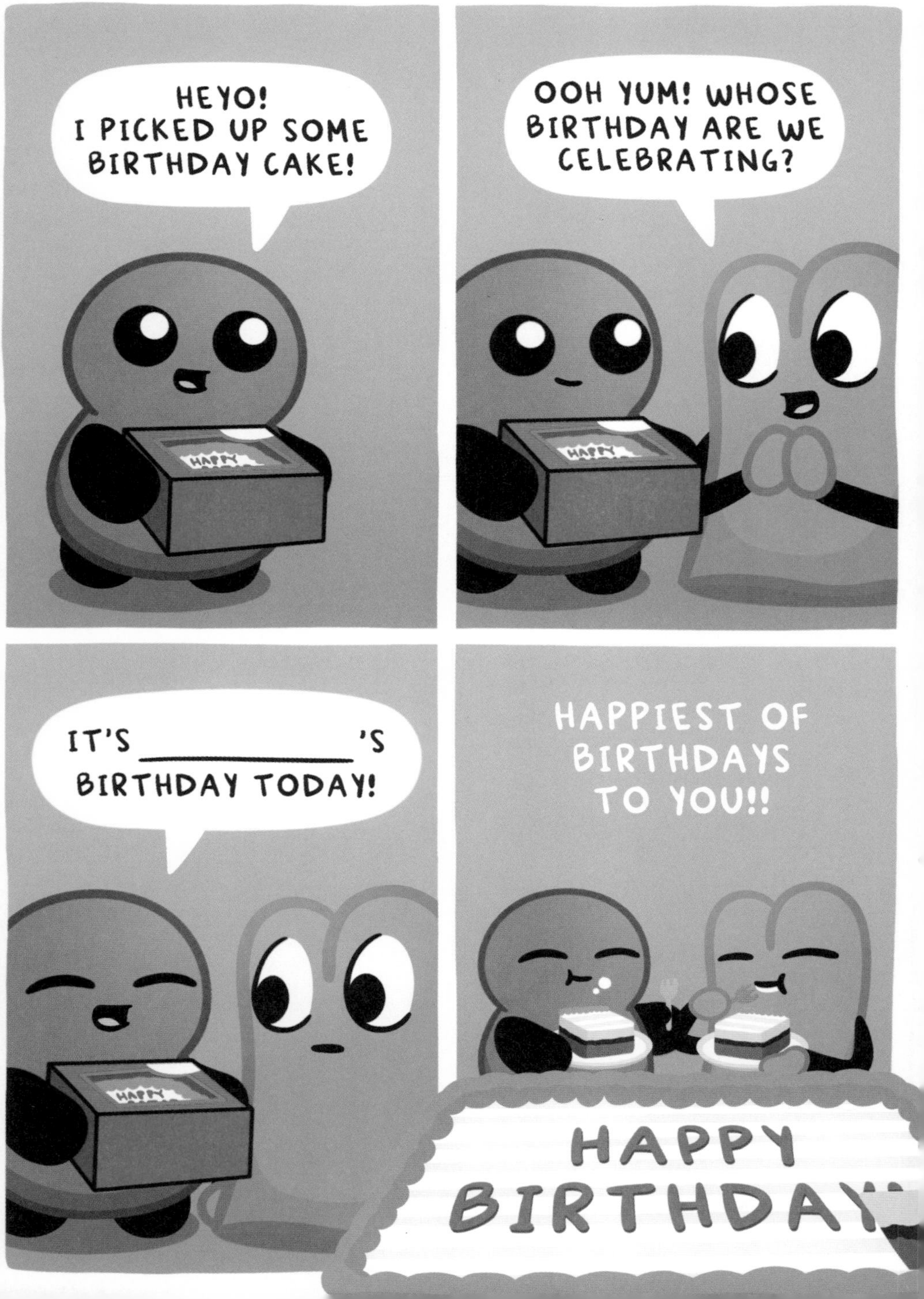
HEYO!
I PICKED UP SOME BIRTHDAY CAKE!
HAPPY
OOH YUM! WHOSE BIRTHDAY ARE WE CELEBRATING?
HAPPY
IT'S ____________'S BIRTHDAY TODAY!
HAPPY
HAPPIEST OF BIRTHDAYS TO YOU!!
HAPPY
BIRTHDA

YOUR "PERFECT PARTY" CHECKLIST!

EVERYONE HAS A DIFFERENT IDEA OF WHAT THE "PERFECT PARTY" LOOKS LIKE — AND I WANT TO KNOW HOW TO GET STARTED PLANNING YOURS! :)

WHERE?

- [ ] AT HOME
- [ ] LOCAL
- [ ] OUT OF TOWN

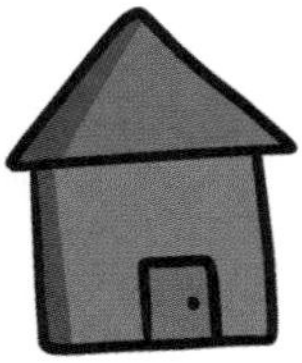

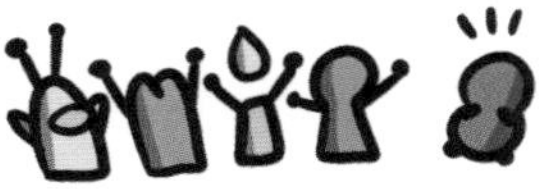

SURPRISE?

- [ ] YES — I WANT TO BE FULLY SURPRISED!
- [ ] NO — I WANT TO KNOW WHAT'S HAPPENING!

TIME OF DAY?

- [ ] MORNING
- [ ] AFTERNOON
- [ ] EVENING

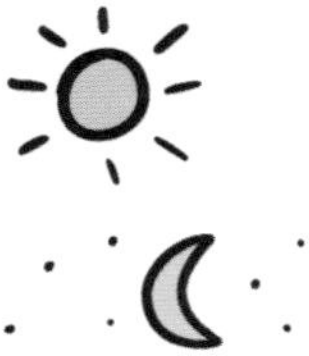

FOOD AND DRINKS?

- [ ] TAKEOUT
- [ ] POTLUCK
- [ ] HOME-COOKED

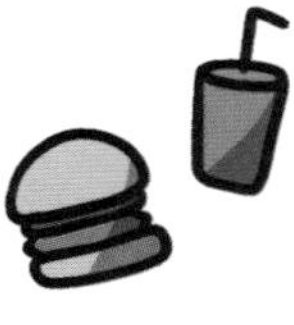

PARTY SIZE?

- [ ] LARGE
- [ ] MEDIUM
- [ ] SMALL

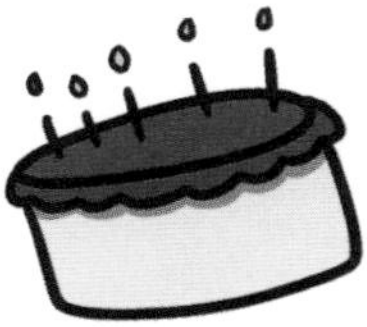

SPECIAL ACTIVITIES/GAMES?

- [ ] YES
- [ ] NO

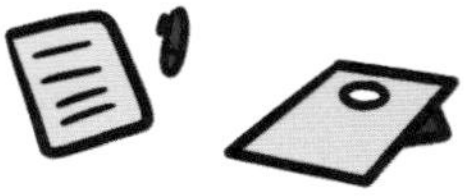

THEMED?

- [ ] YES (IF SO, WHAT THEME? ____________)
- [ ] NO

DECORATIONS

- [ ] YES — GO ALL OUT!
- [ ] YES — BUT PREFERABLY SOMETHING SIMPLE
- [ ] NO NEED :)

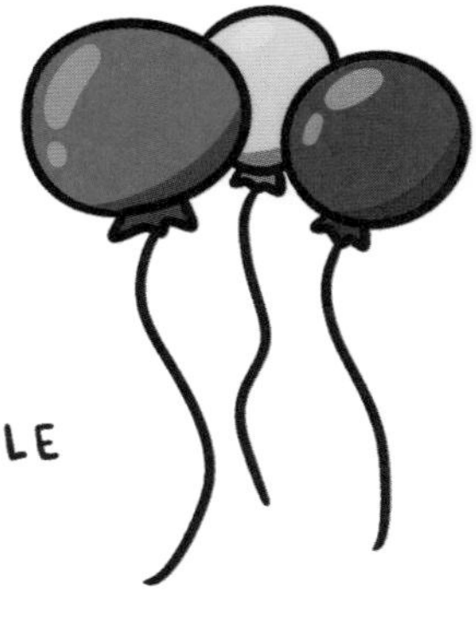

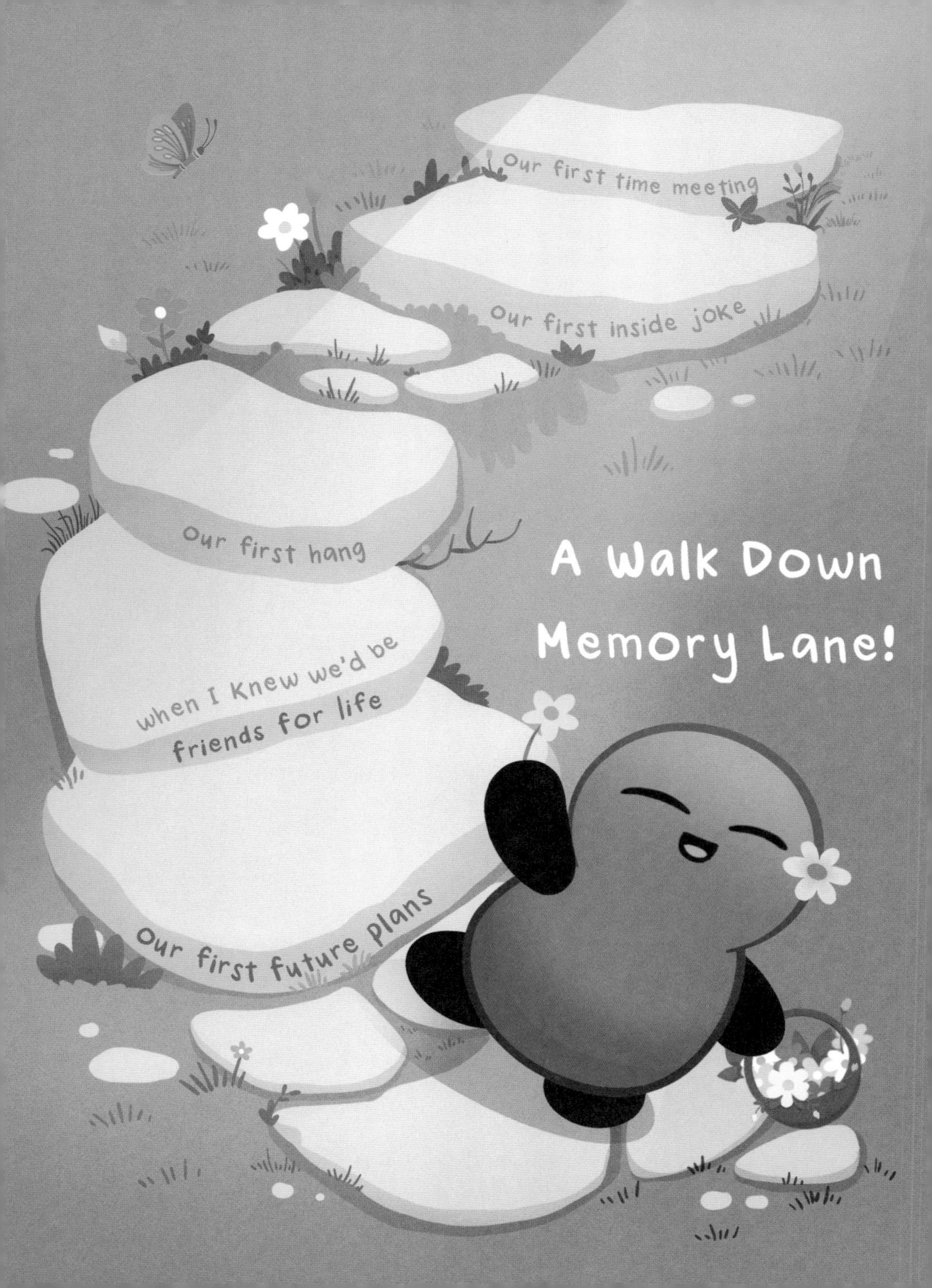
A Walk Down Memory Lane!
Our first time meeting
Our first inside joke
Our first hang
when I knew we'd be friends for life
Our first future plans

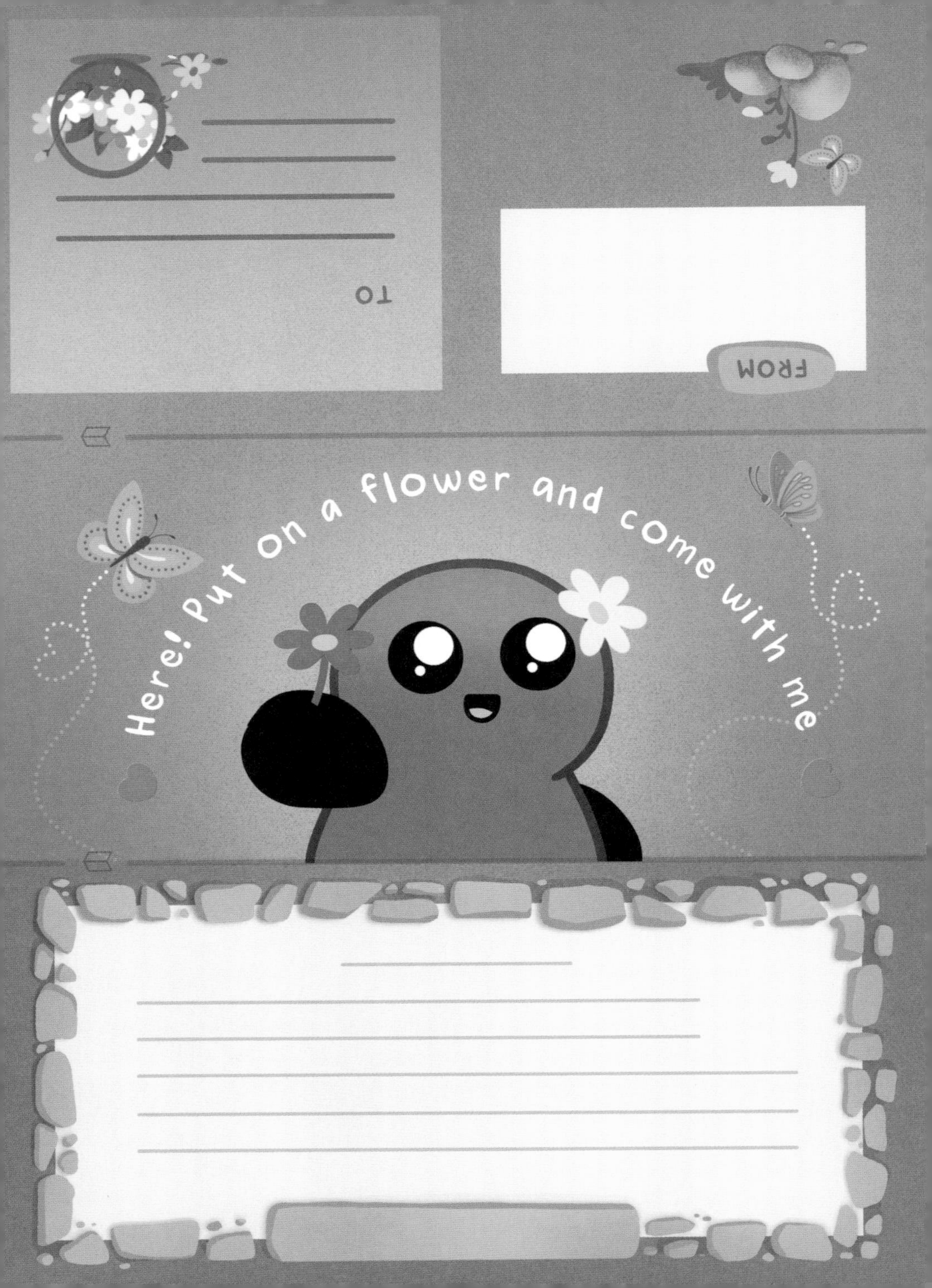
TO
FROM
Here! Put on a flower and come with me

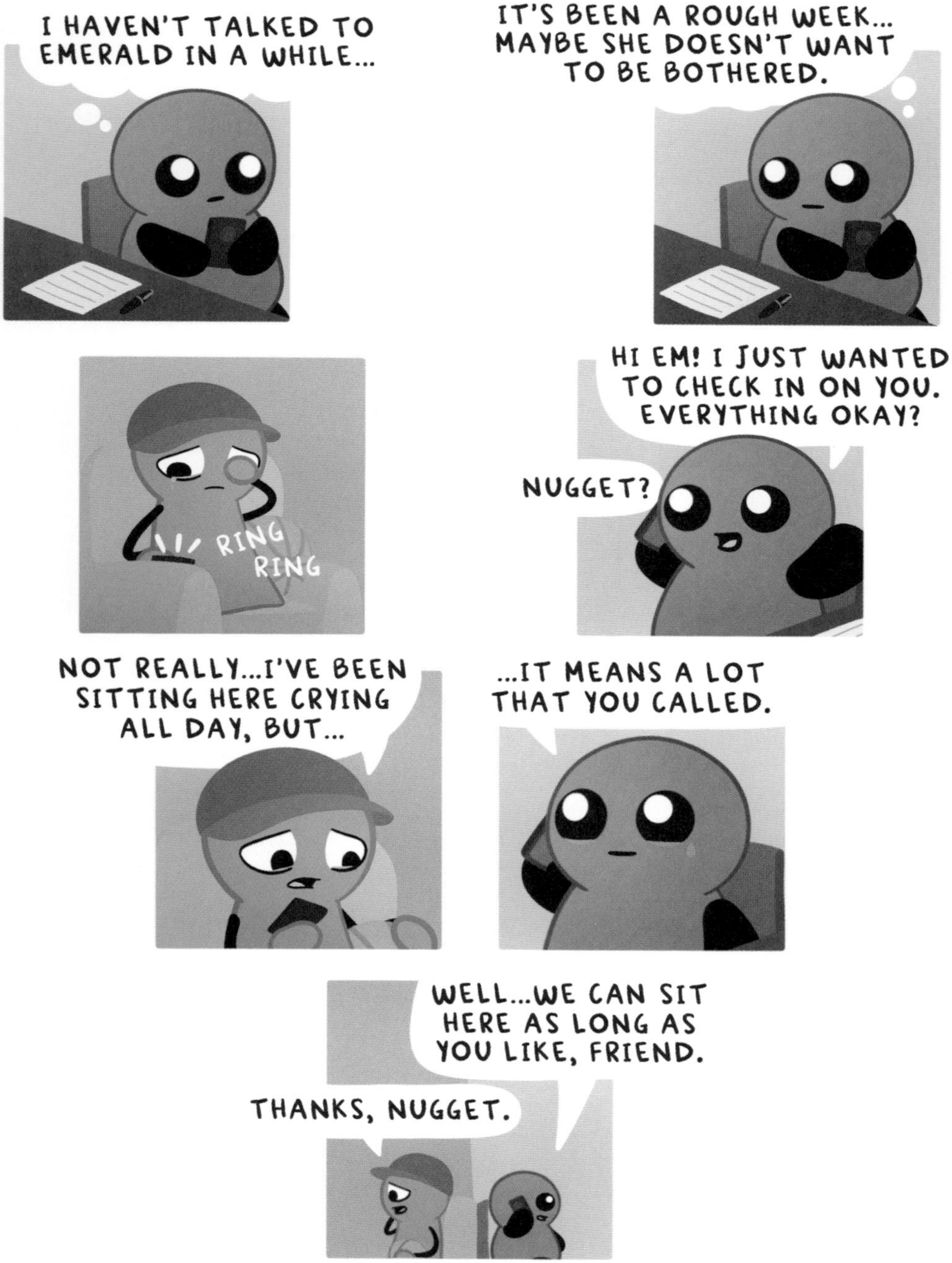
I HAVEN'T TALKED TO EMERALD IN A WHILE...
IT'S BEEN A ROUGH WEEK... MAYBE SHE DOESN'T WANT TO BE BOTHERED.
RING RING
HI EM! I JUST WANTED TO CHECK IN ON YOU. EVERYTHING OKAY?
NUGGET?
NOT REALLY...I'VE BEEN SITTING HERE CRYING ALL DAY, BUT...
...IT MEANS A LOT THAT YOU CALLED.
WELL...WE CAN SIT HERE AS LONG AS YOU LIKE, FRIEND.
THANKS, NUGGET.

A self-care checklist — made just for you!

Even though I can't always be there beside you,
I hope you remember to do all these things for
yourself today — because I love you!
And you deserve it! :)

- [ ] ______________________________
- [ ] ______________________________
- [ ] ______________________________
- [ ] ______________________________
- [ ] ______________________

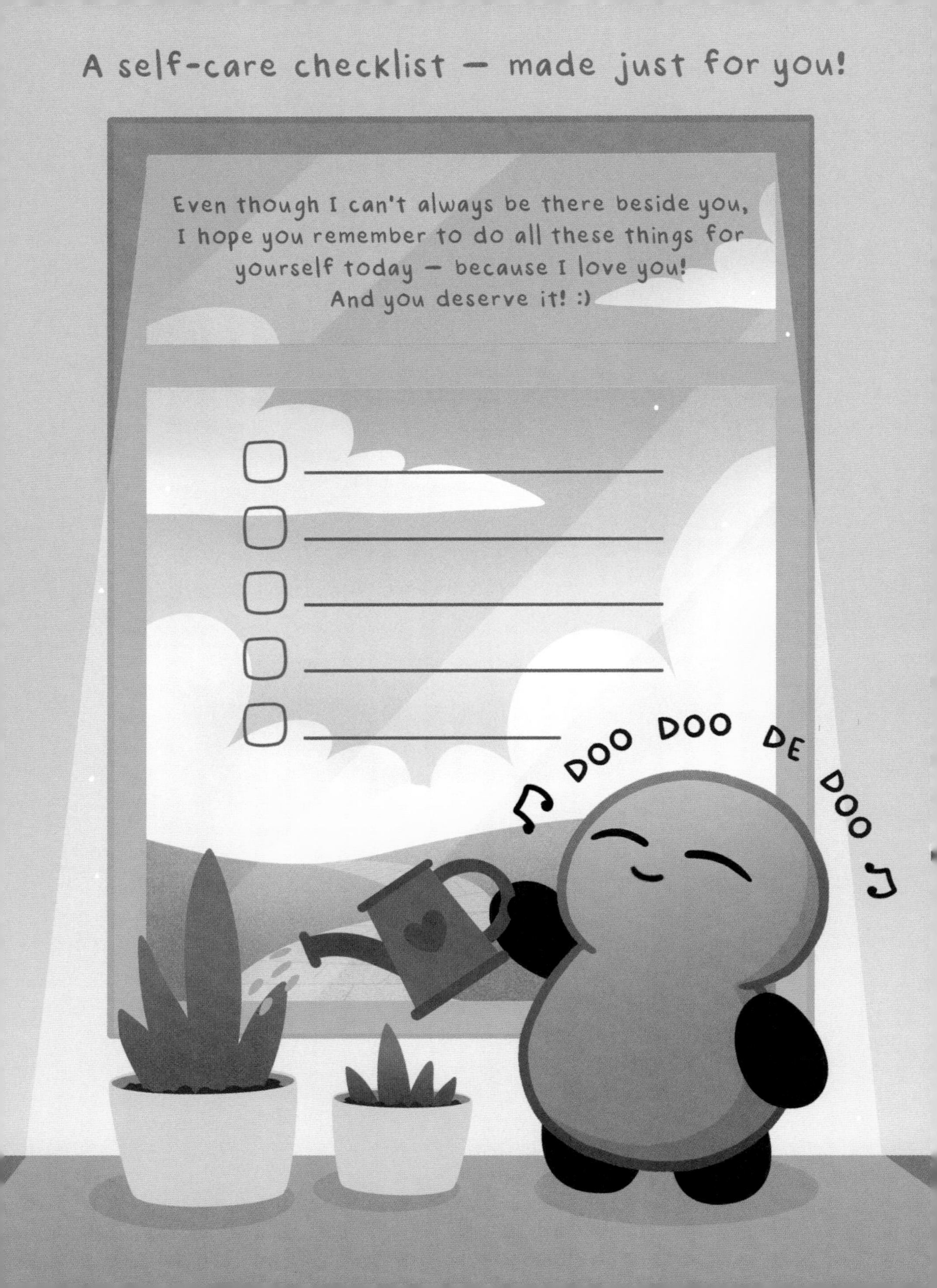
♪ DOO DOO DE DOO ♪

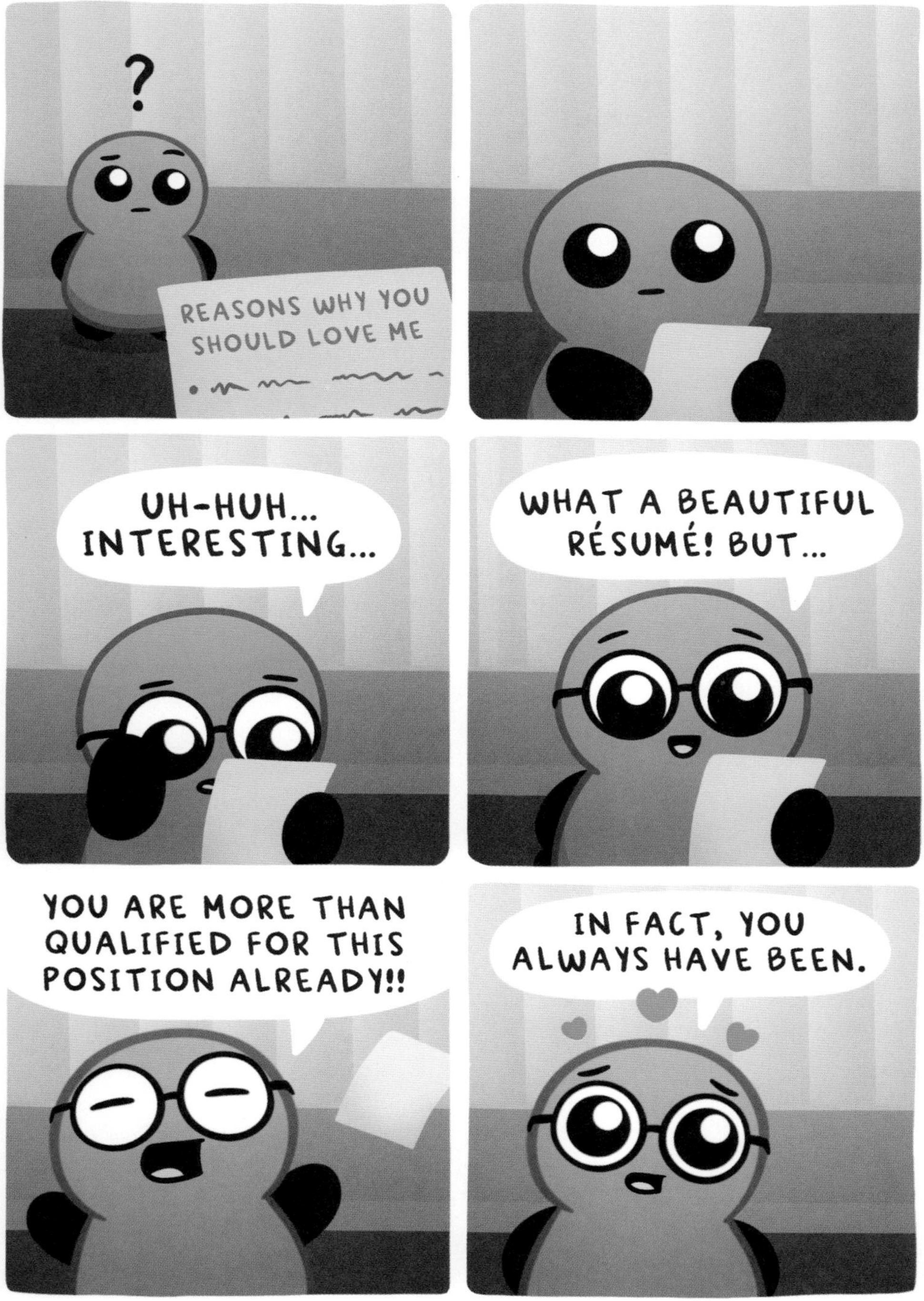
?
REASONS WHY YOU SHOULD LOVE ME
UH-HUH... INTERESTING...
WHAT A BEAUTIFUL RÉSUMÉ! BUT...
YOU ARE MORE THAN QUALIFIED FOR THIS POSITION ALREADY!!
IN FACT, YOU ALWAYS HAVE BEEN.

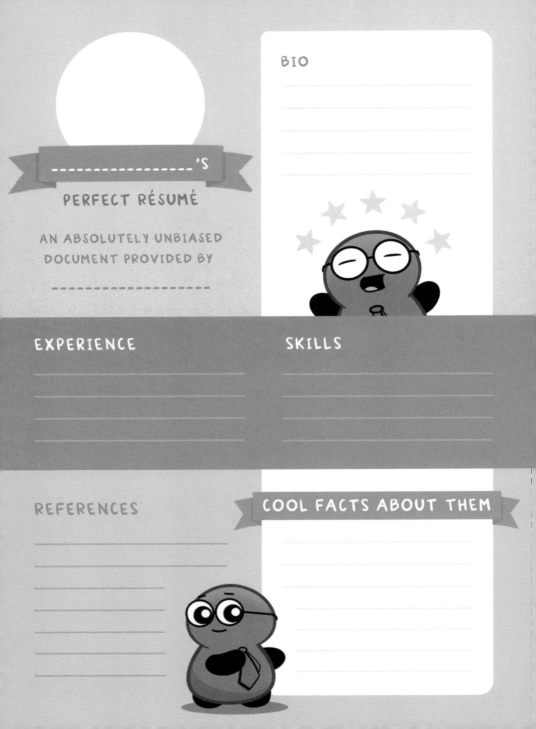

_____'S

PERFECT RÉSUMÉ

AN ABSOLUTELY UNBIASED
DOCUMENT PROVIDED BY

_____

BIO

EXPERIENCE

SKILLS

REFERENCES

COOL FACTS ABOUT THEM

PLACES I CAN'T WAIT TO TRAVEL WITH YOU

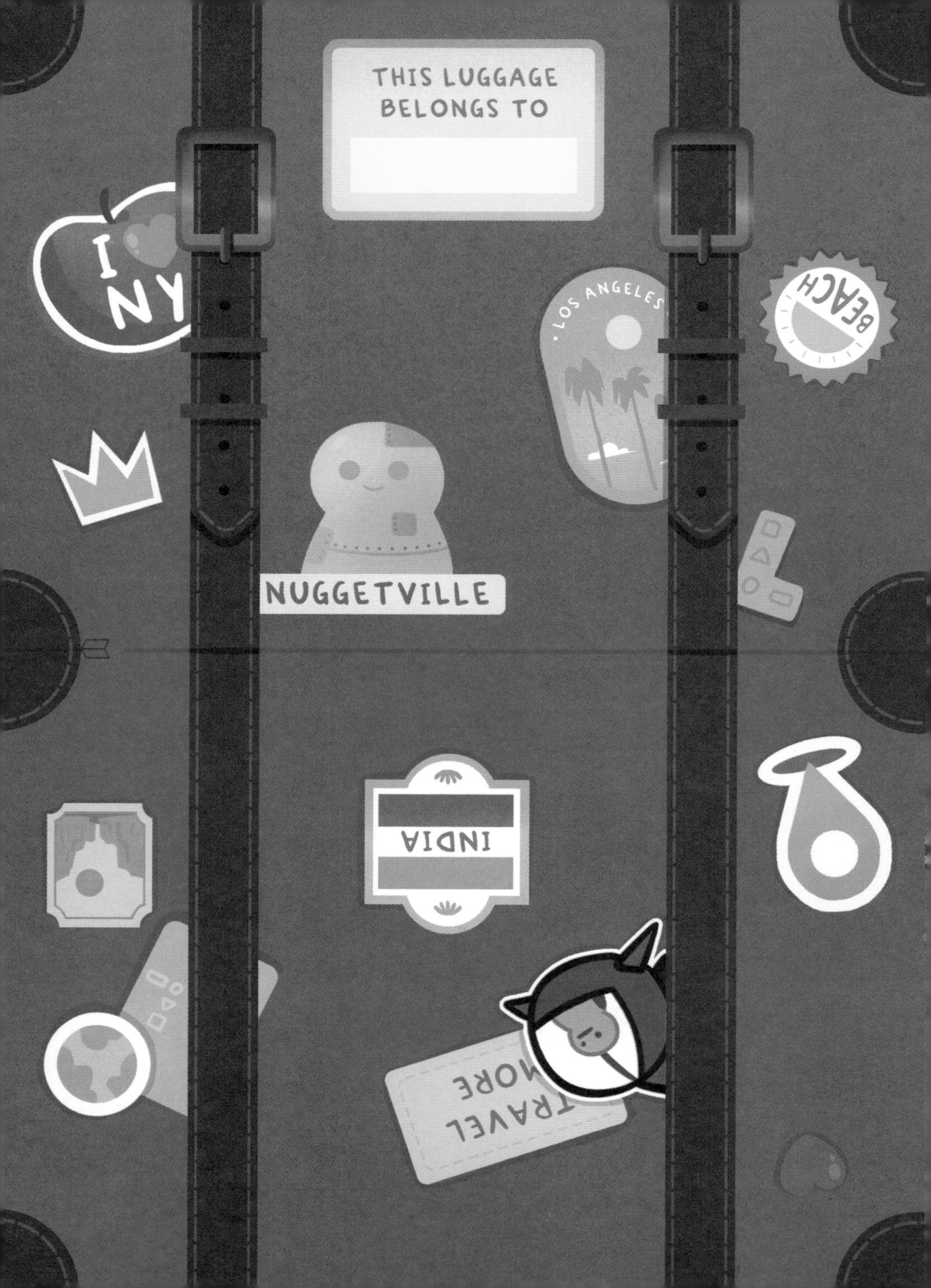
THIS LUGGAGE BELONGS TO
I NY
LOS ANGELES
BEACH
NUGGETVILLE
INDIA
TRAVEL MORE

AFTER ALL THIS TIME...
I'VE FINALLY COMPLETED MY PUZZLE!!

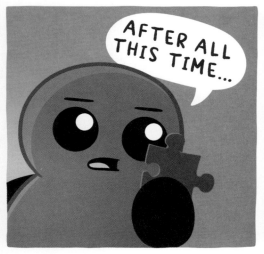

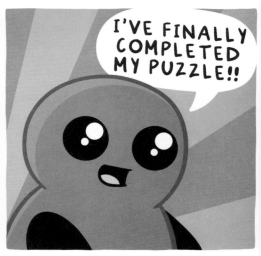

DRAW A PICTURE BELOW, THEN FOLLOW THE INSTRUCTIONS ON THE BACK OF THIS PAGE TO CREATE YOUR OWN PUZZLE!

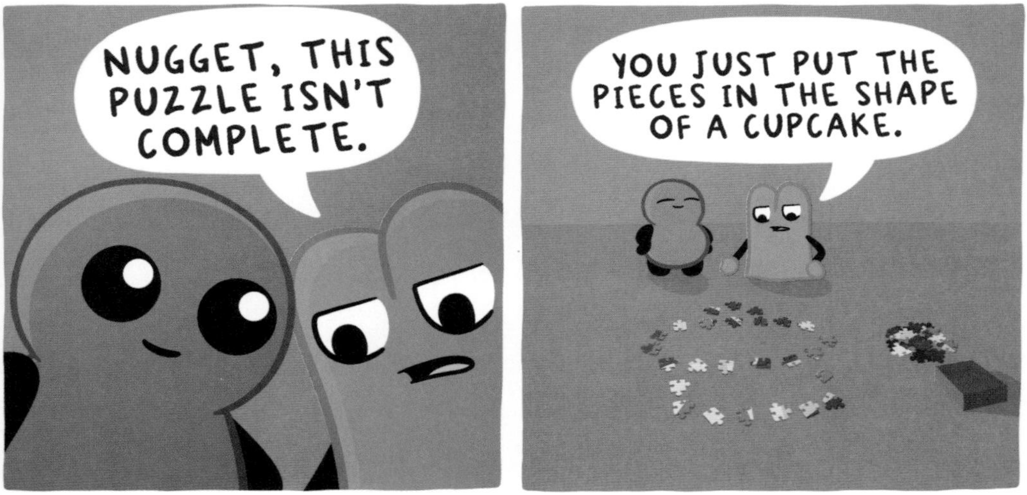
NUGGET, THIS PUZZLE ISN'T COMPLETE.
YOU JUST PUT THE PIECES IN THE SHAPE OF A CUPCAKE.

CUT ALONG THE DOTTED LINES TO CREATE YOUR OWN PUZZLE!

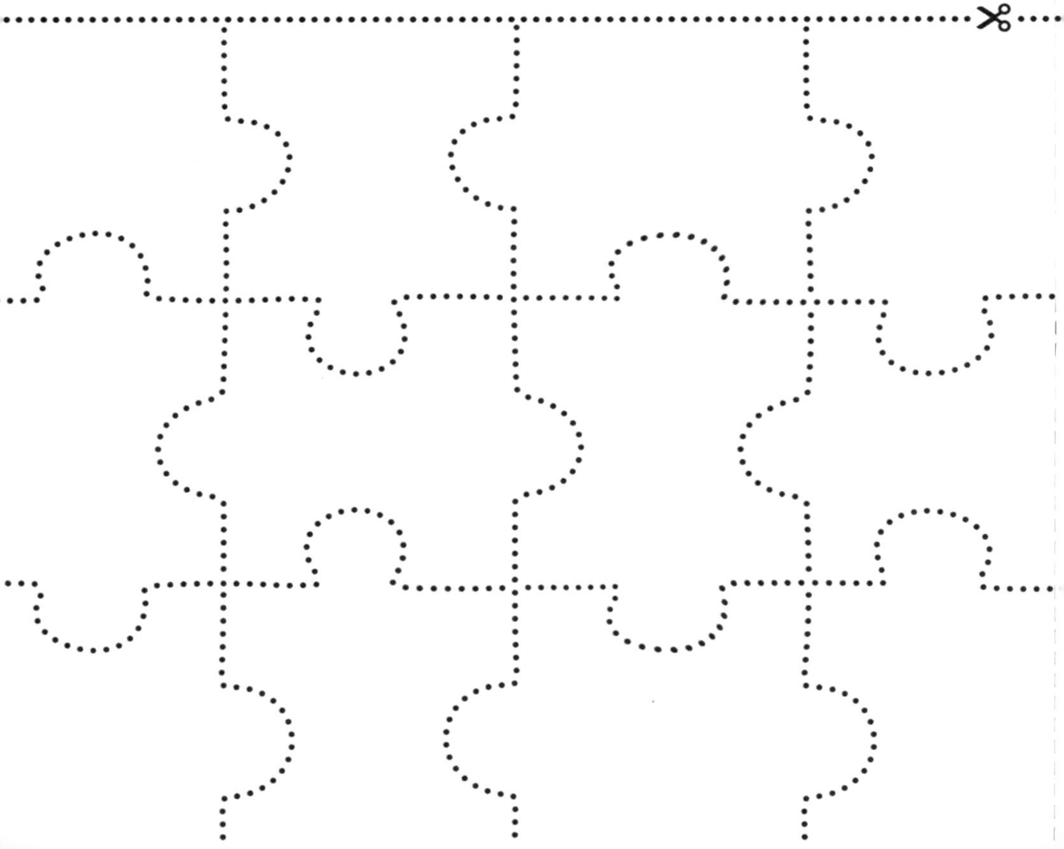

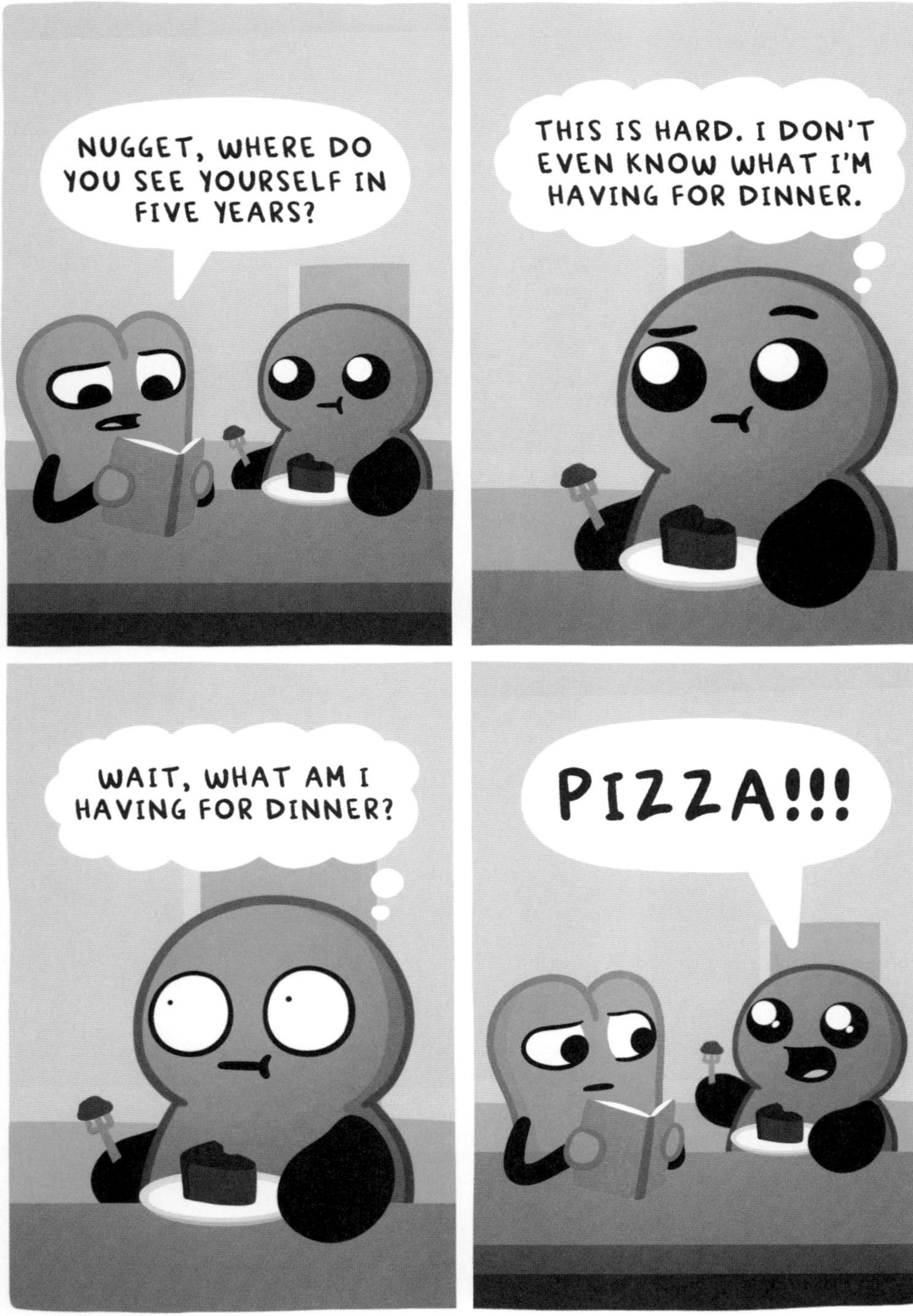
NUGGET, WHERE DO YOU SEE YOURSELF IN FIVE YEARS?
THIS IS HARD. I DON'T EVEN KNOW WHAT I'M HAVING FOR DINNER.
WAIT, WHAT AM I HAVING FOR DINNER?
PIZZA!!!

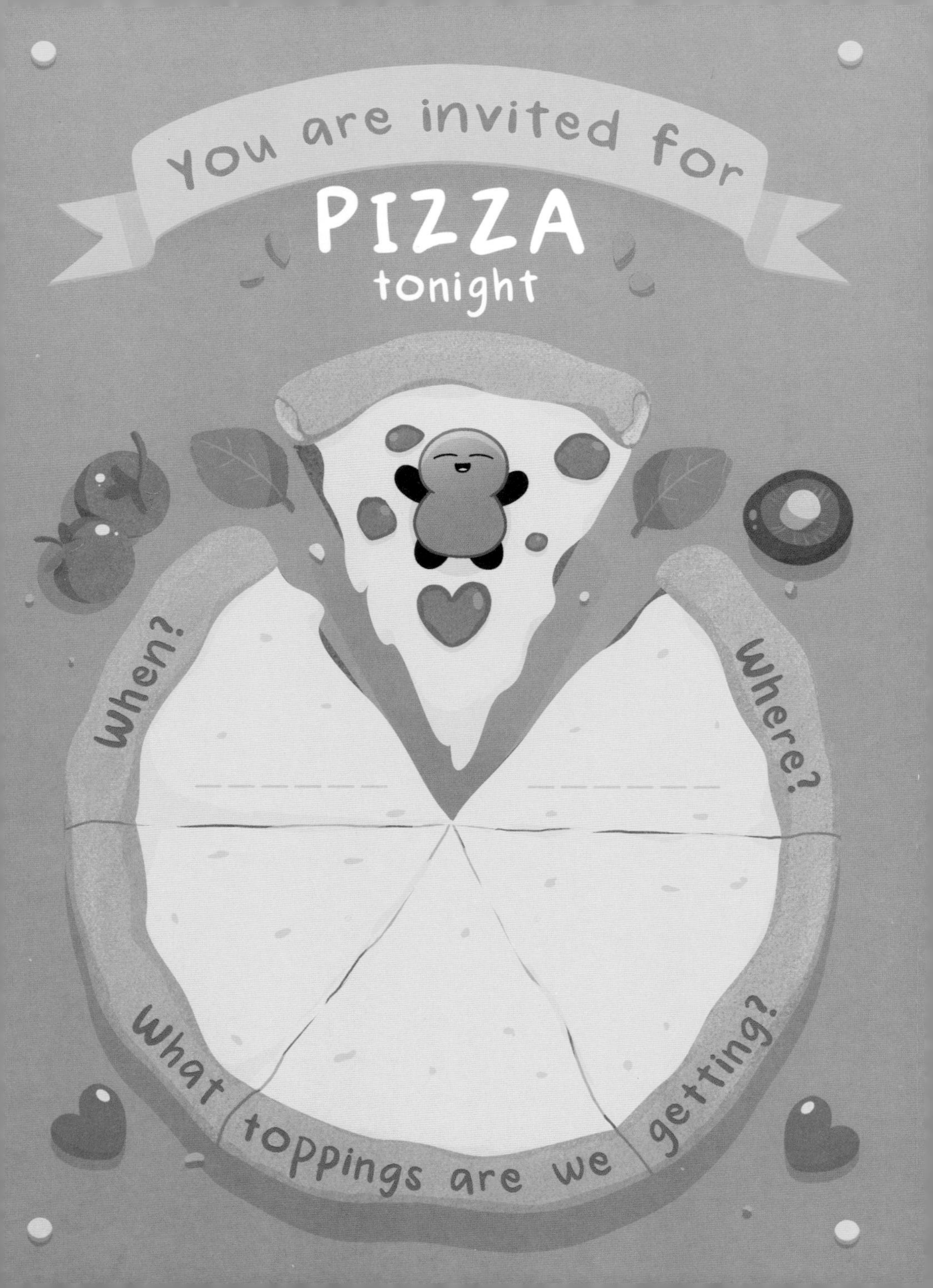
You are invited for
PIZZA
tonight
When?
Where?
What toppings are we getting?

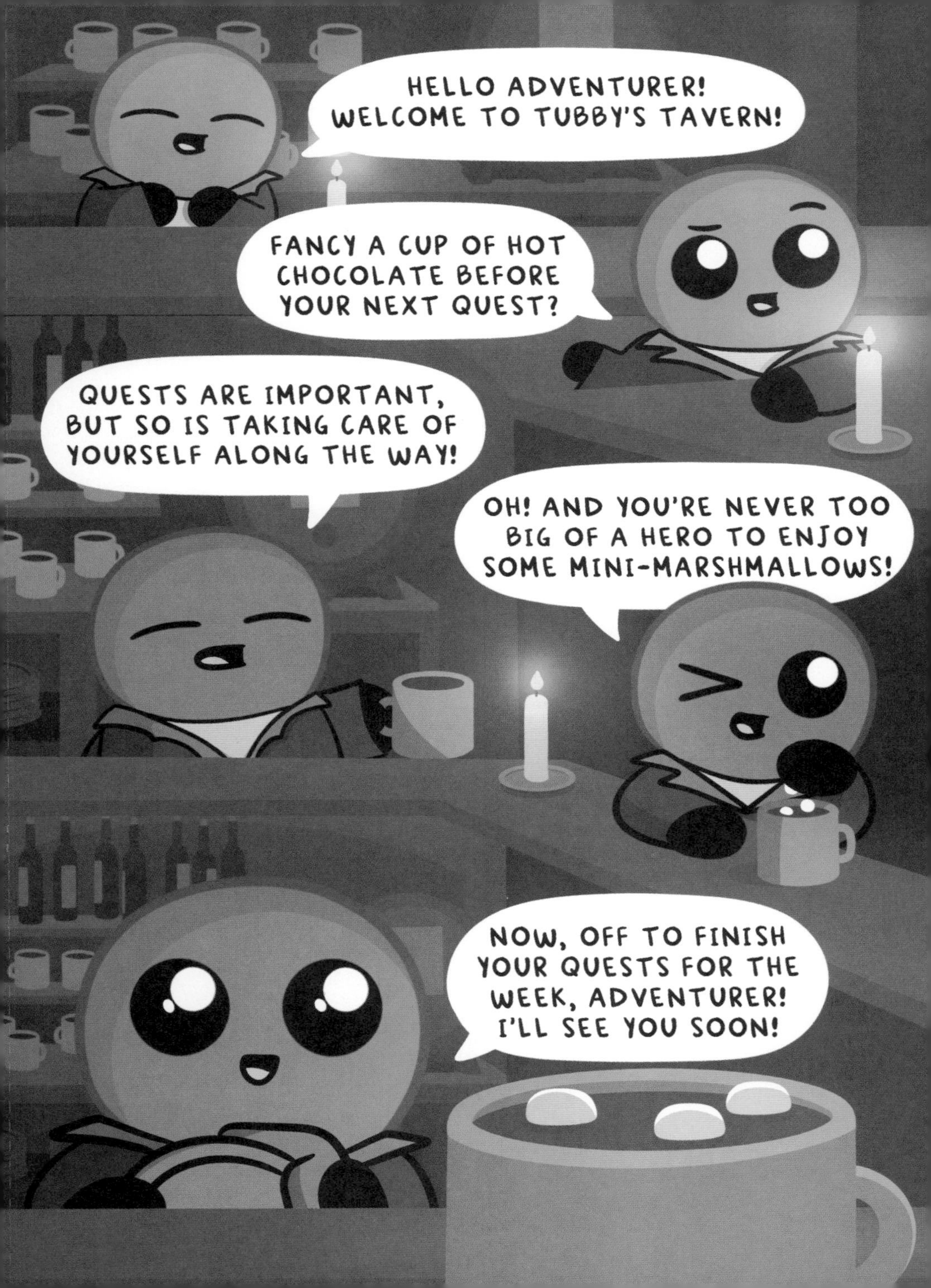
HELLO ADVENTURER! WELCOME TO TUBBY'S TAVERN!
FANCY A CUP OF HOT CHOCOLATE BEFORE YOUR NEXT QUEST?
QUESTS ARE IMPORTANT, BUT SO IS TAKING CARE OF YOURSELF ALONG THE WAY!
OH! AND YOU'RE NEVER TOO BIG OF A HERO TO ENJOY SOME MINI-MARSHMALLOWS!
NOW, OFF TO FINISH YOUR QUESTS FOR THE WEEK, ADVENTURER! I'LL SEE YOU SOON!

FANTASY RACE

CHARACTER CLASS

SPECIAL ABILITIES

BACKSTORY

KNOWN LANGUAGES

PERSONALITY

GO-TO GEAR

LIFE MISSION

A SPECIAL RECIPE FOR US

SERVES: **COOK TIME:**

INGREDIENTS:

DIRECTIONS:

NOTES:

WHY I PICKED THIS RECIPE FOR YOU:

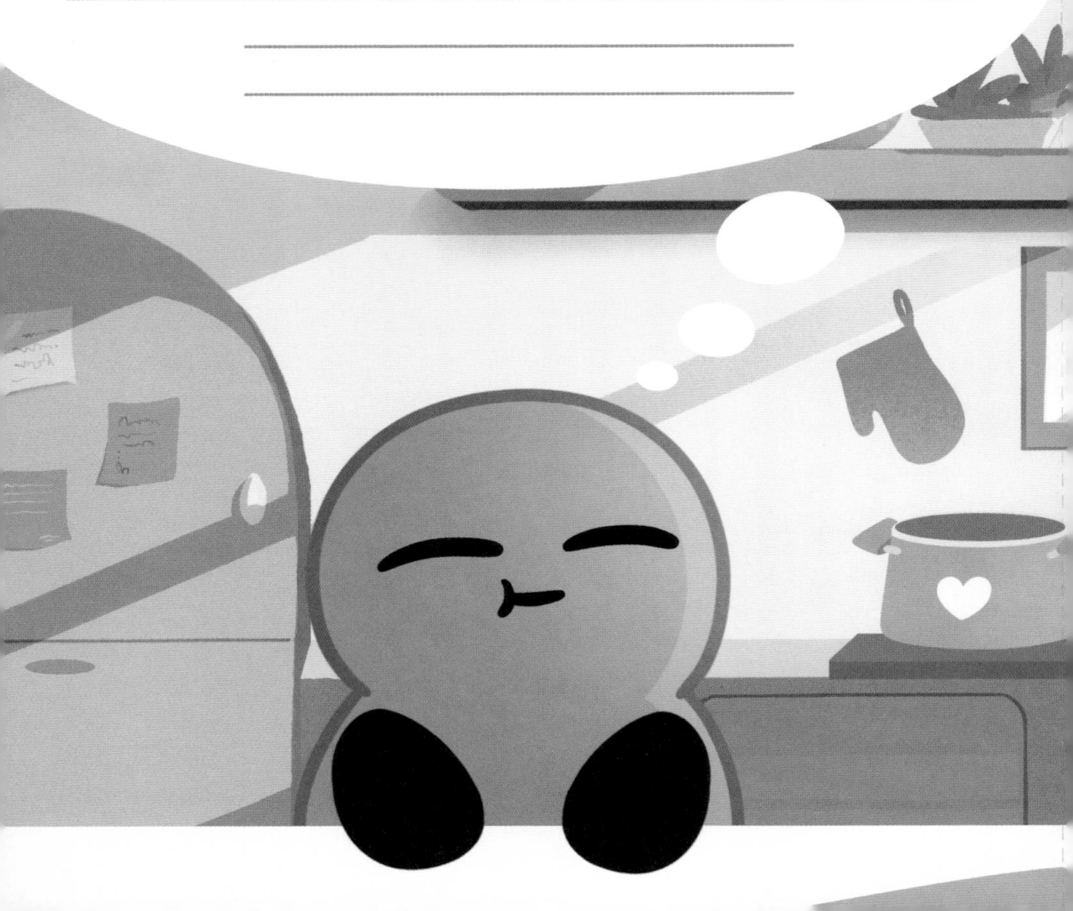

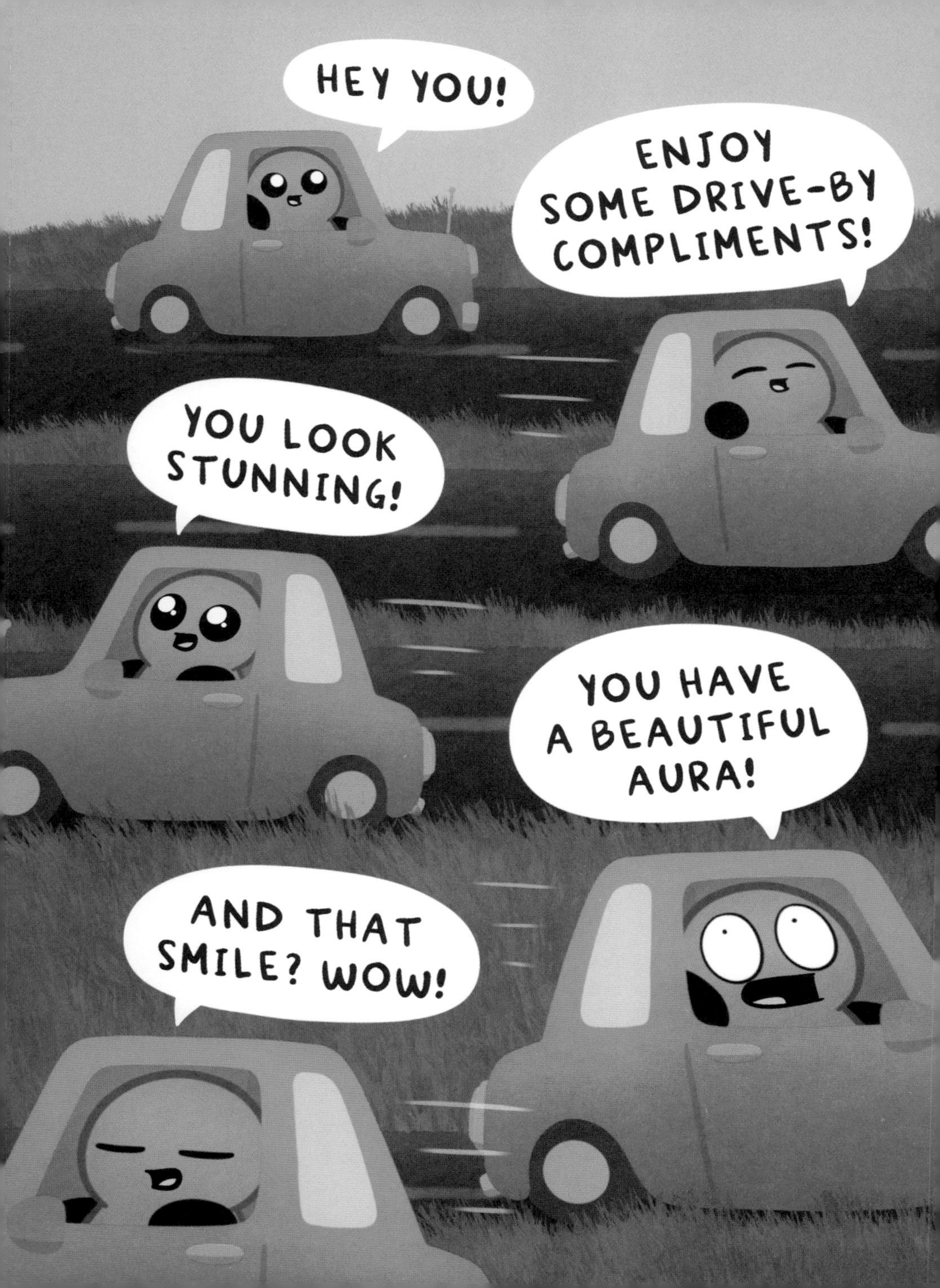
HEY YOU!
ENJOY SOME DRIVE-BY COMPLIMENTS!
YOU LOOK STUNNING!
YOU HAVE A BEAUTIFUL AURA!
AND THAT SMILE? WOW!

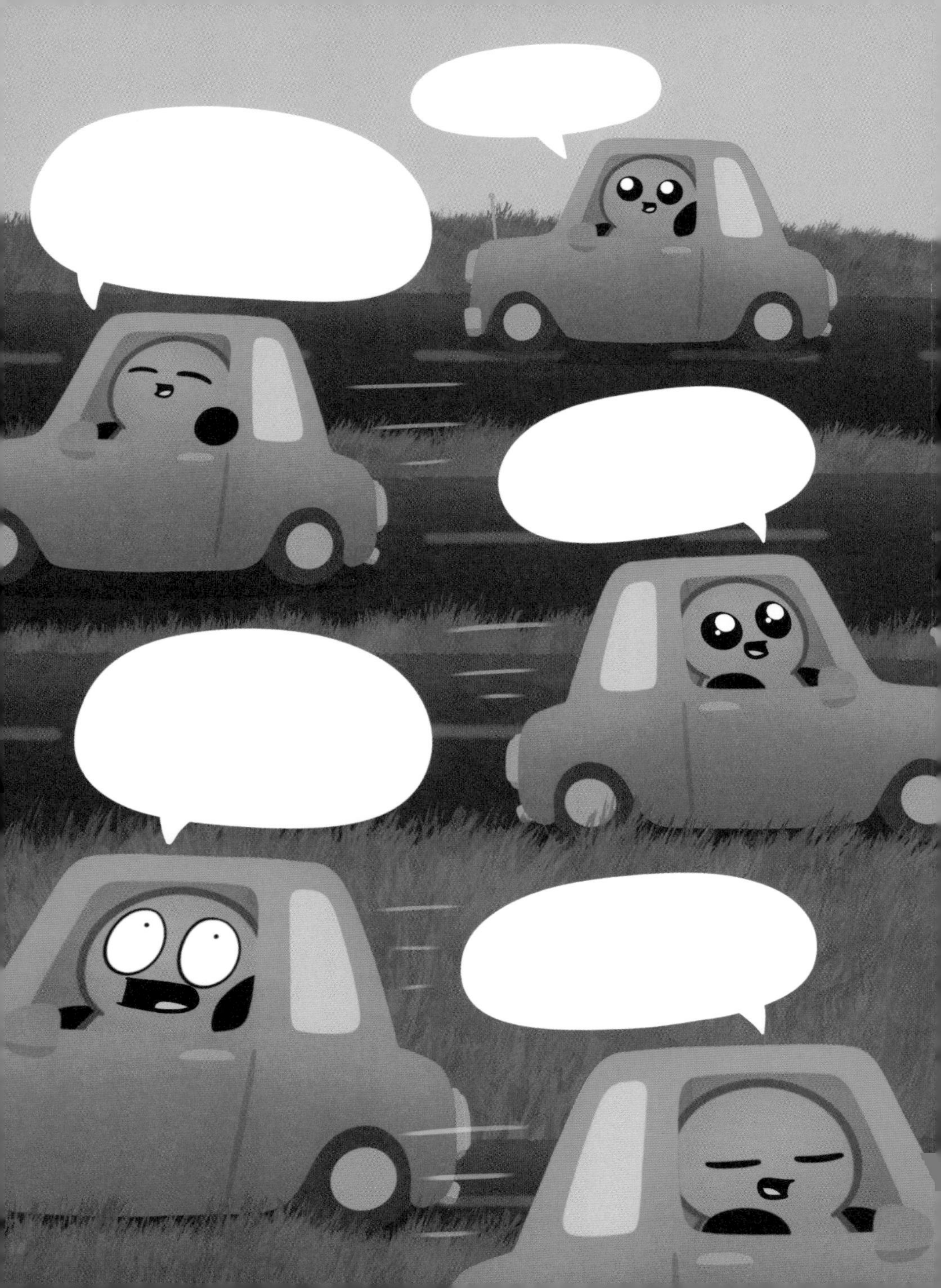

MY BEST FRIEND 101

HERE'S WHAT I THINK PEOPLE SHOULD KNOW ABOUT YOU!

YOUR FAVORITE CONVERSATION TOPIC

YOUR FAVORITE COMFORT FOOD

YOUR FAVORITE COMFY PLACE

YOUR FAVORITE SHOWS TO BINGE

YOUR DREAM VACATION

FROM

TO

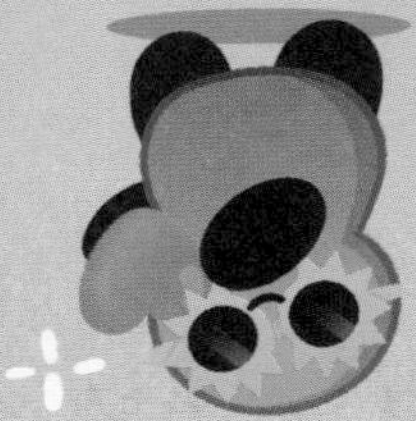

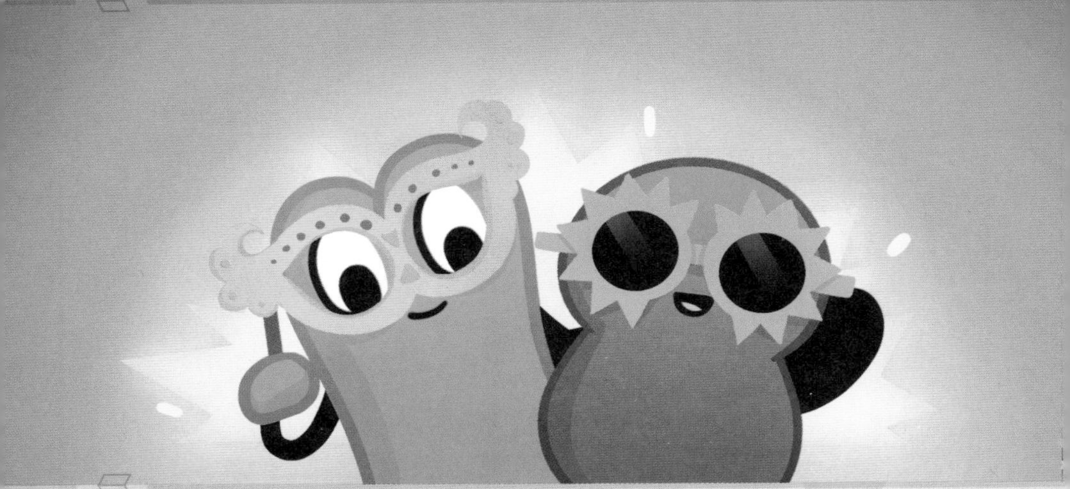

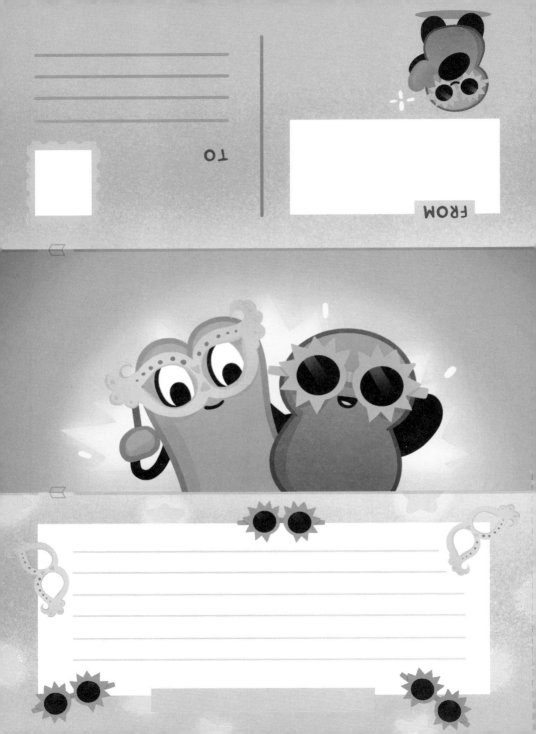

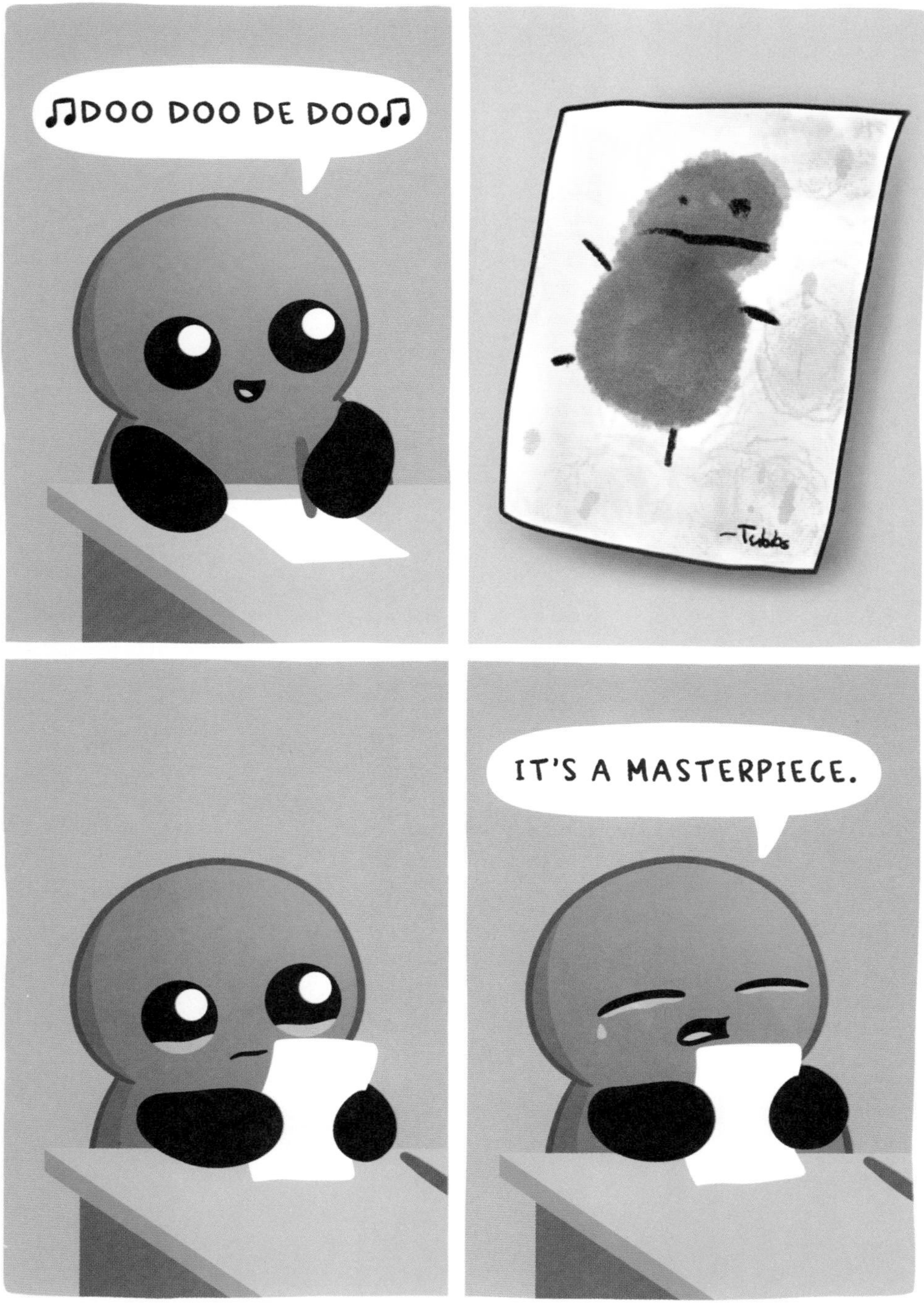
♫DOO DOO DE DOO♫
—Tubbs
IT'S A MASTERPIECE.

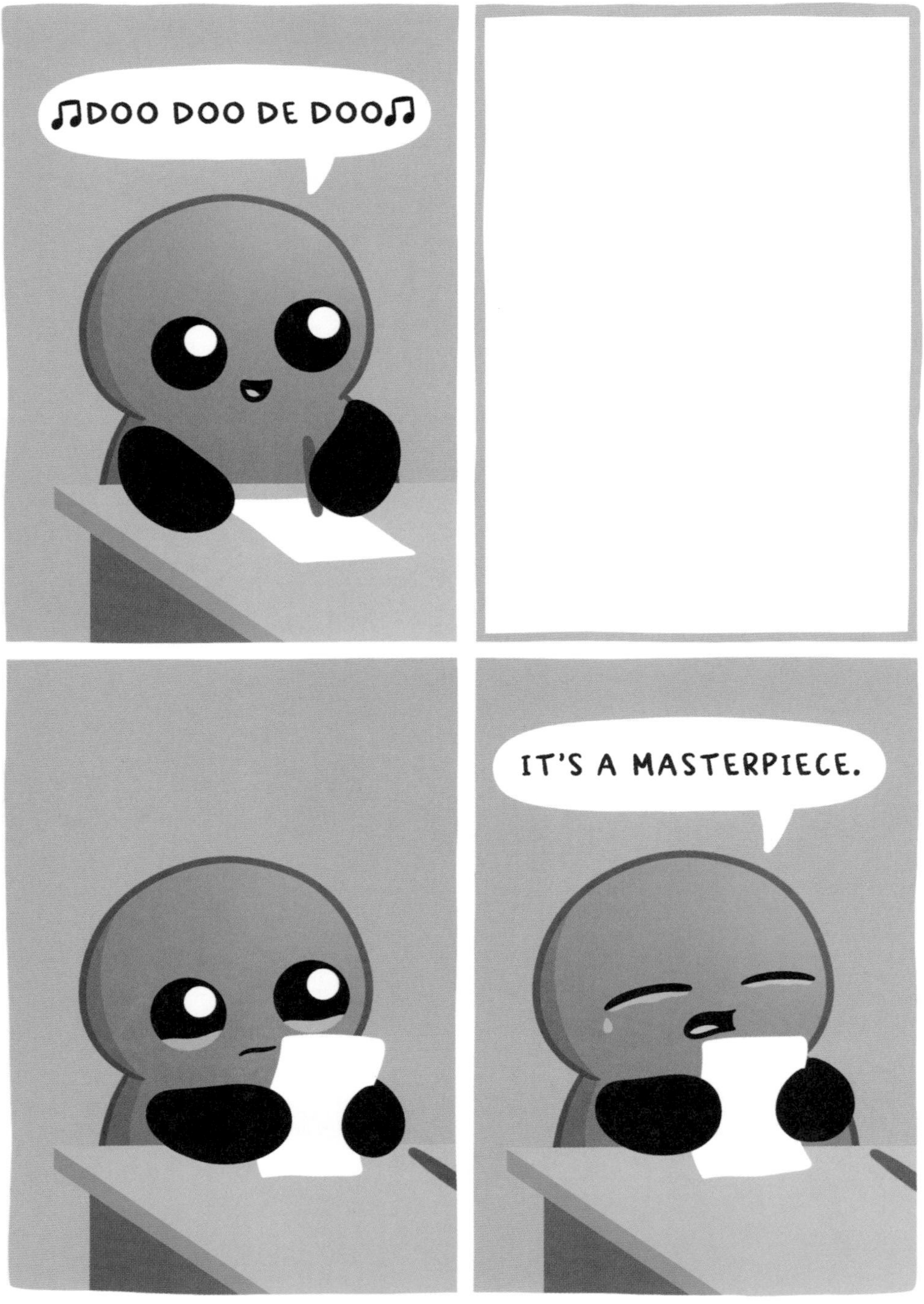
♫DOO DOO DE DOO♫
IT'S A MASTERPIECE.

MY FAVORITE QUOTES & INSIDE JOKES WITH YOU

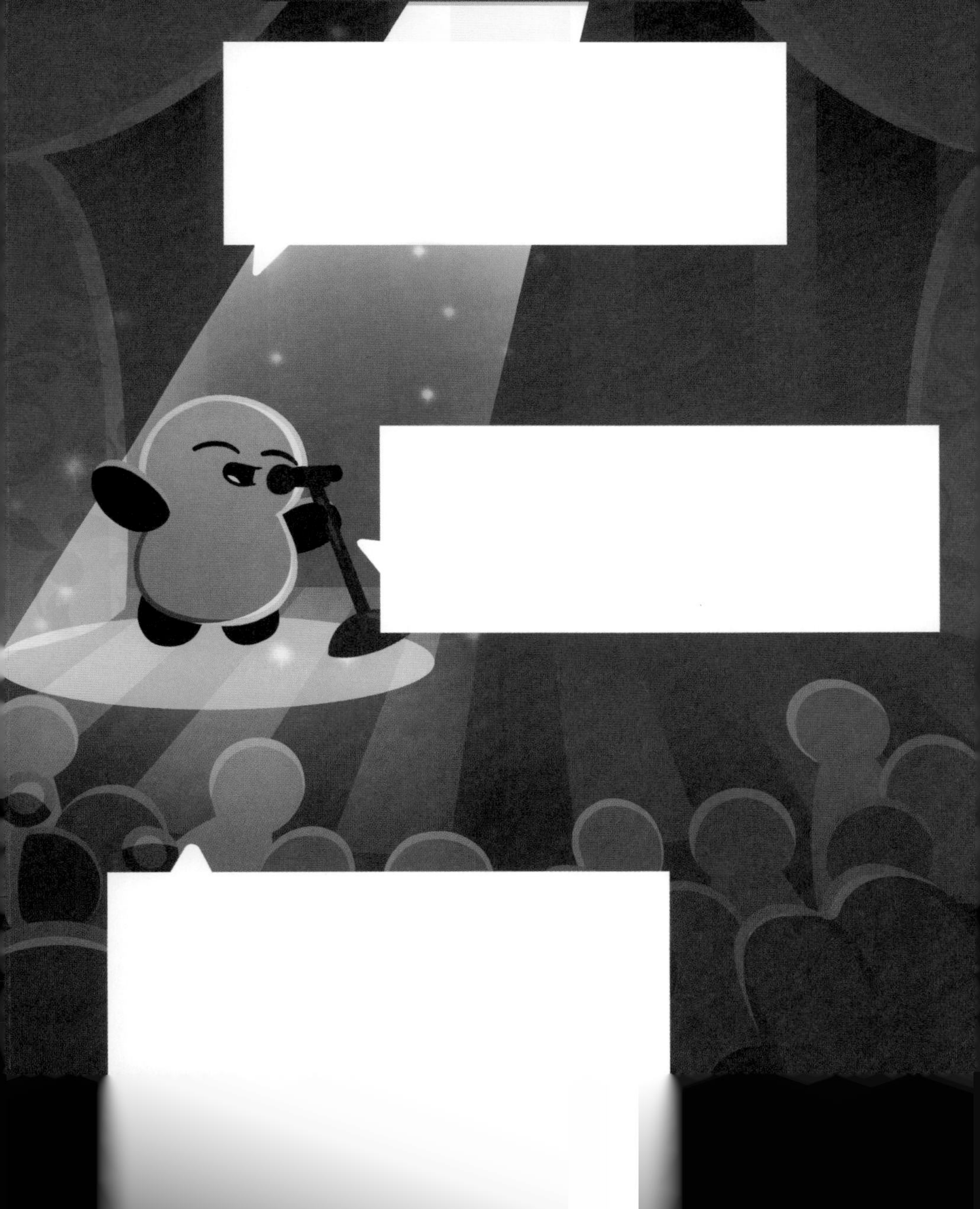

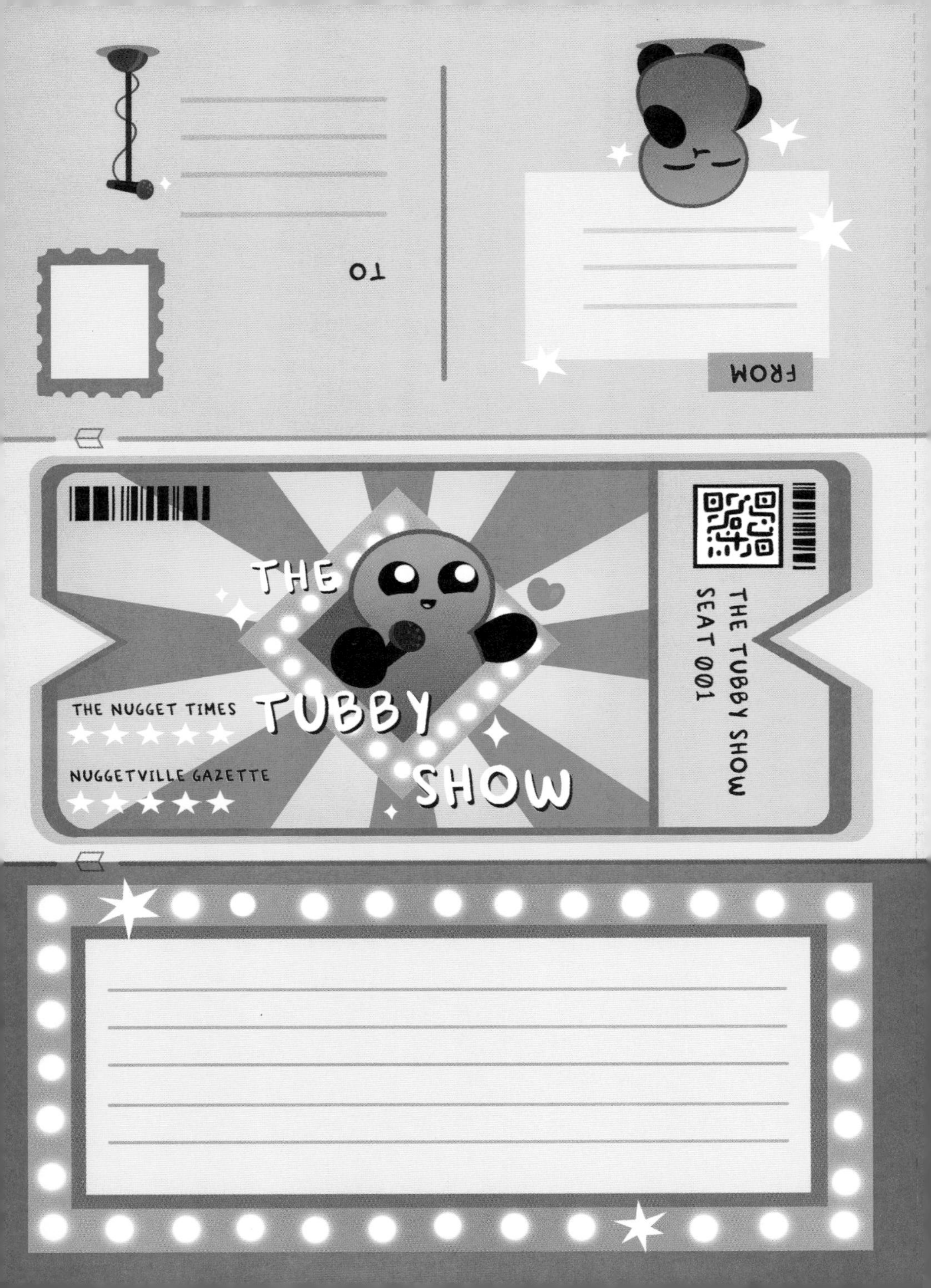
TO
FROM
THE TUBBY SHOW
THE NUGGET TIMES
NUGGETVILLE GAZETTE
THE TUBBY SHOW
SEAT 001

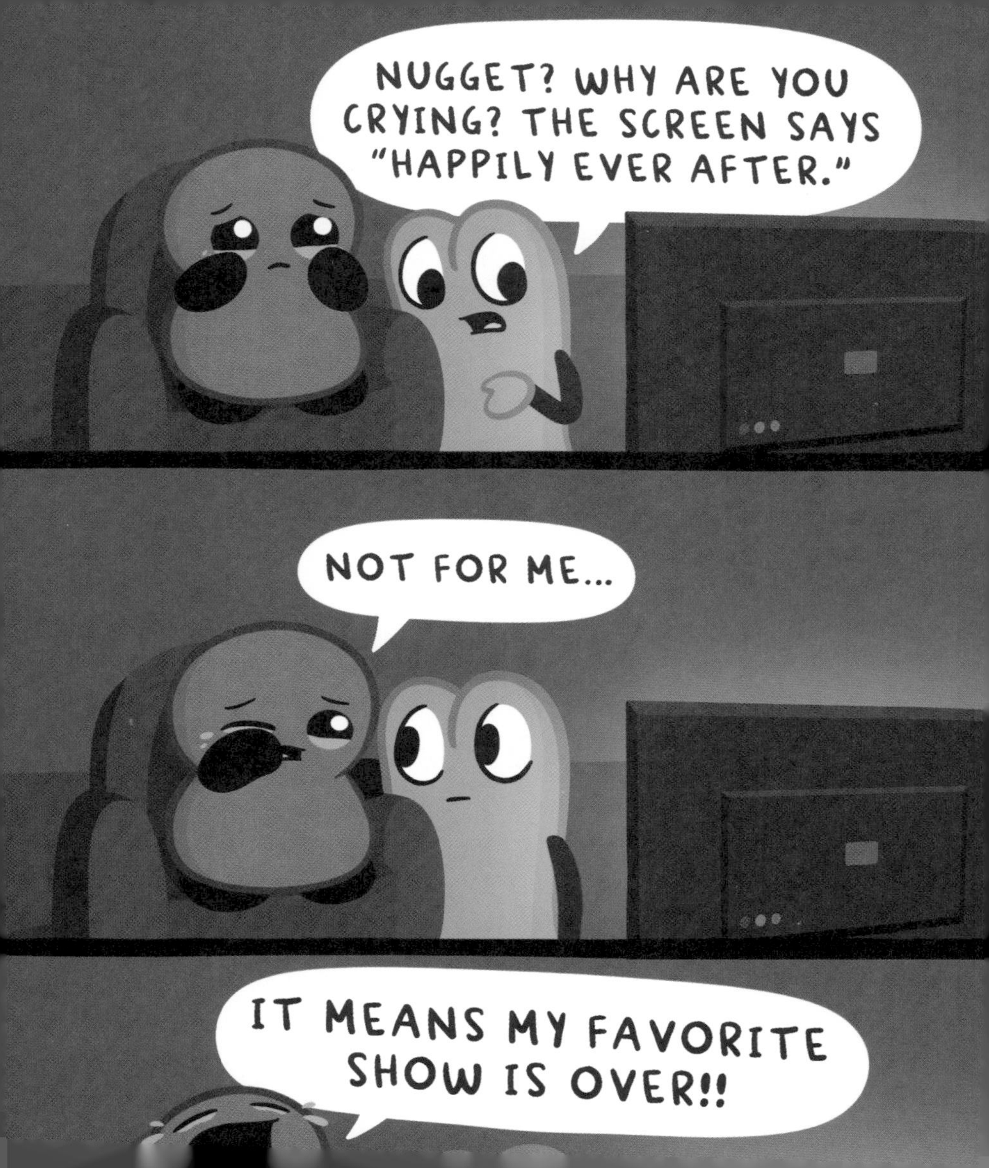
NUGGET? WHY ARE YOU CRYING? THE SCREEN SAYS "HAPPILY EVER AFTER."
NOT FOR ME...
IT MEANS MY FAVORITE SHOW IS OVER!!

SHOWS I THINK YOU'D LOVE

(Now that your favorite one is over)

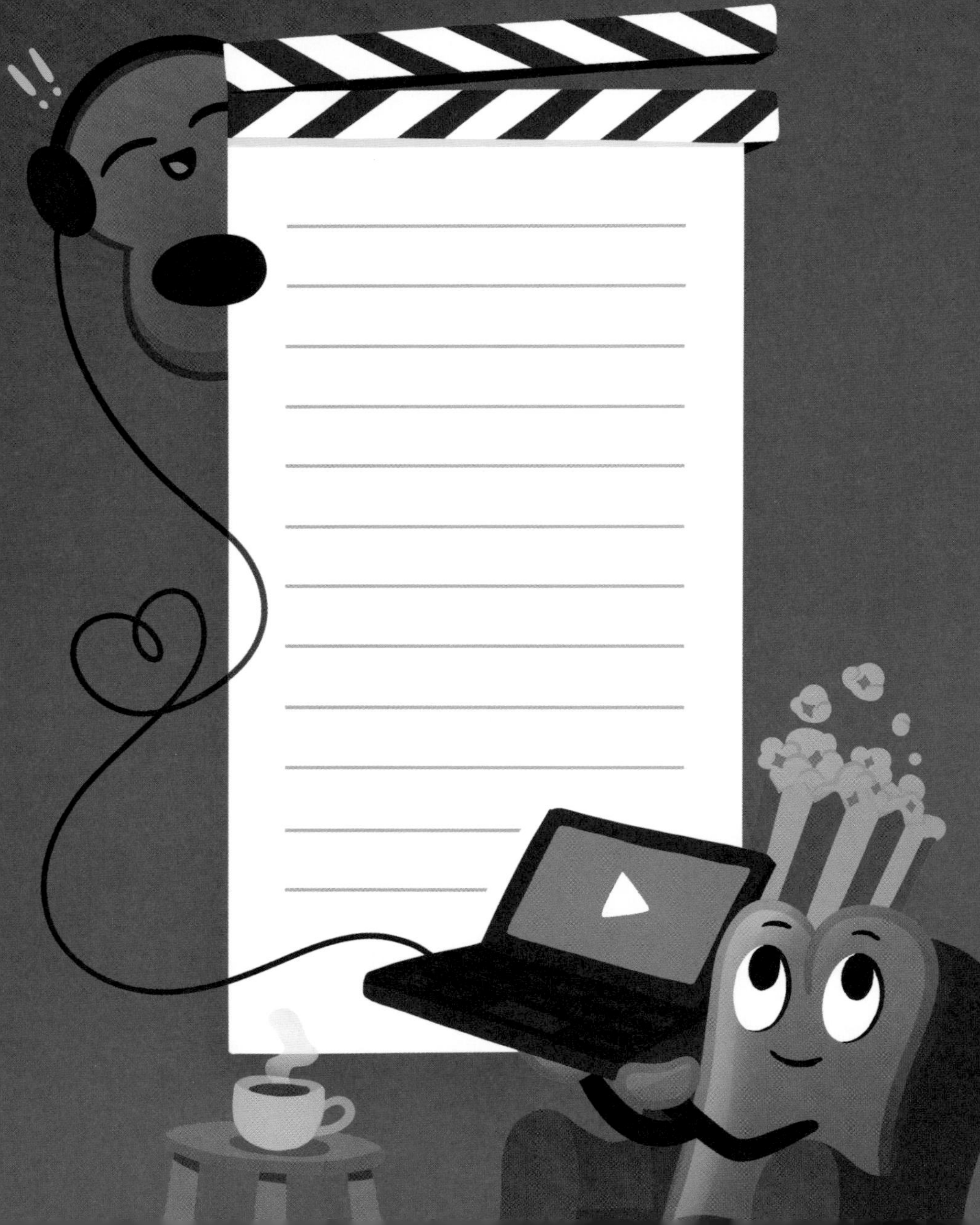

HERE'S WHAT I IMAGINE YOU'D BE LIKE AS A
SUPERHERO!

YOUR SUPERHERO NAME: _____

YOUR SUPERPOWER: _____

YOUR SPECIAL GADGET: _____

YOUR SUPER-ALLIES: _____

YOUR ARCHNEMESIS: _____

YOUR SECRET IDENTITY/DAY JOB: _____

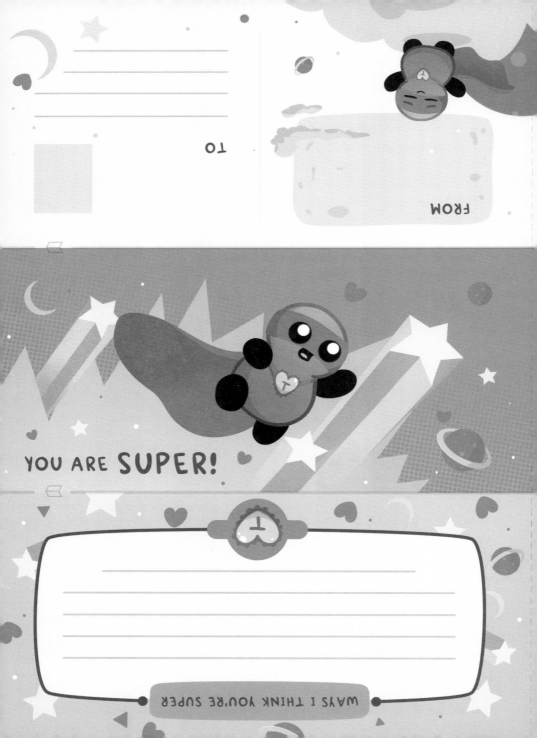

TO

FROM

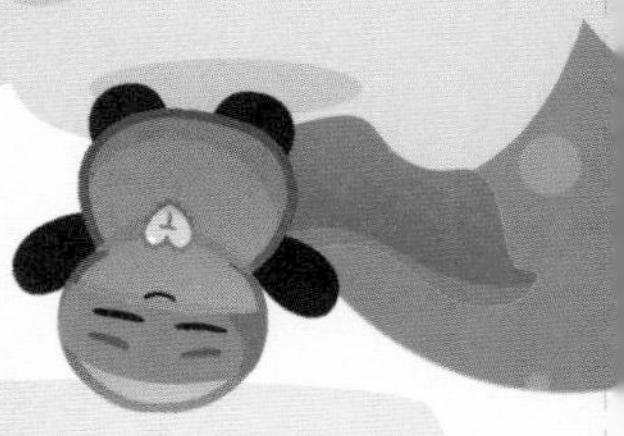

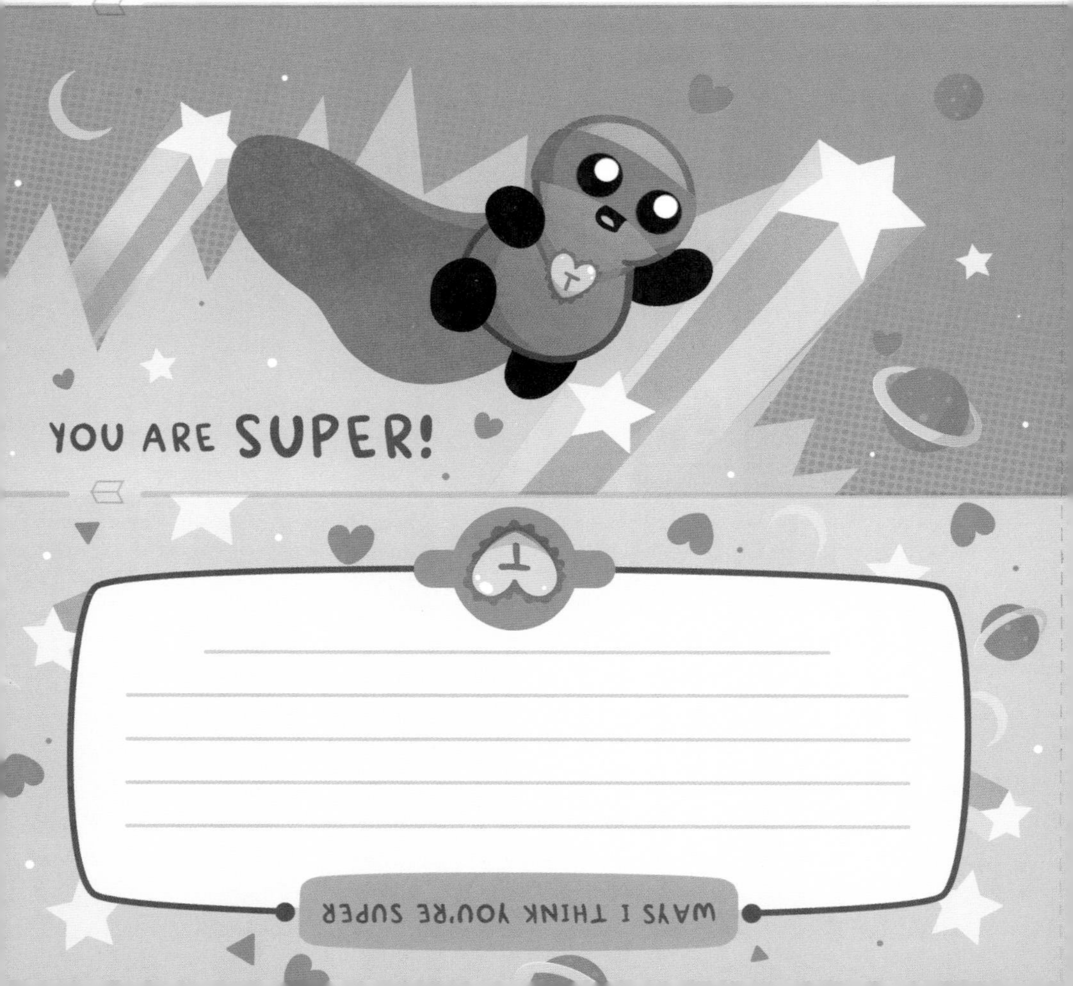
YOU ARE SUPER!

WAYS I THINK YOU'RE SUPER

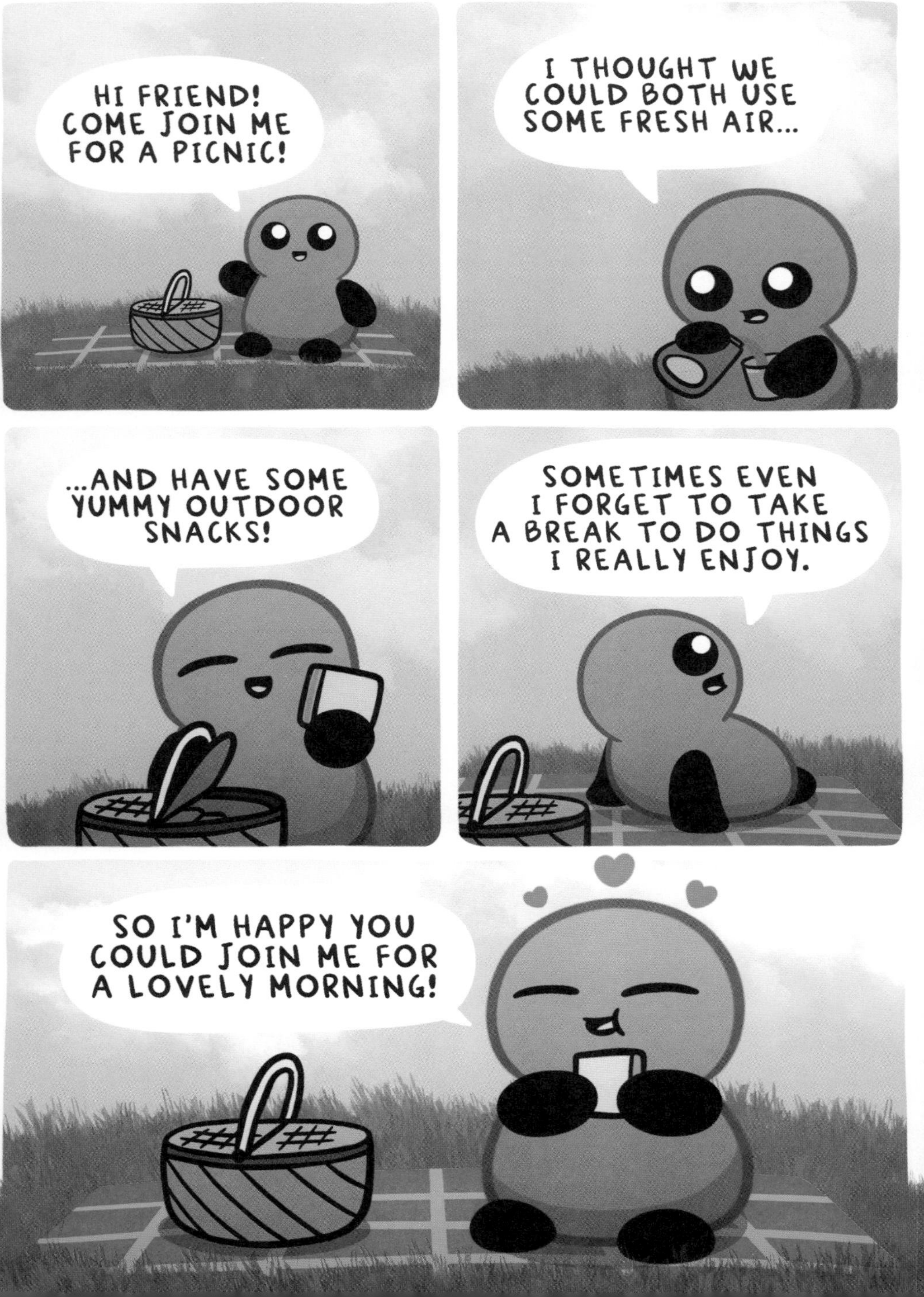
HI FRIEND! COME JOIN ME FOR A PICNIC!
I THOUGHT WE COULD BOTH USE SOME FRESH AIR...
...AND HAVE SOME YUMMY OUTDOOR SNACKS!
SOMETIMES EVEN I FORGET TO TAKE A BREAK TO DO THINGS I REALLY ENJOY.
SO I'M HAPPY YOU COULD JOIN ME FOR A LOVELY MORNING!

I've planned us the perfect picnic!

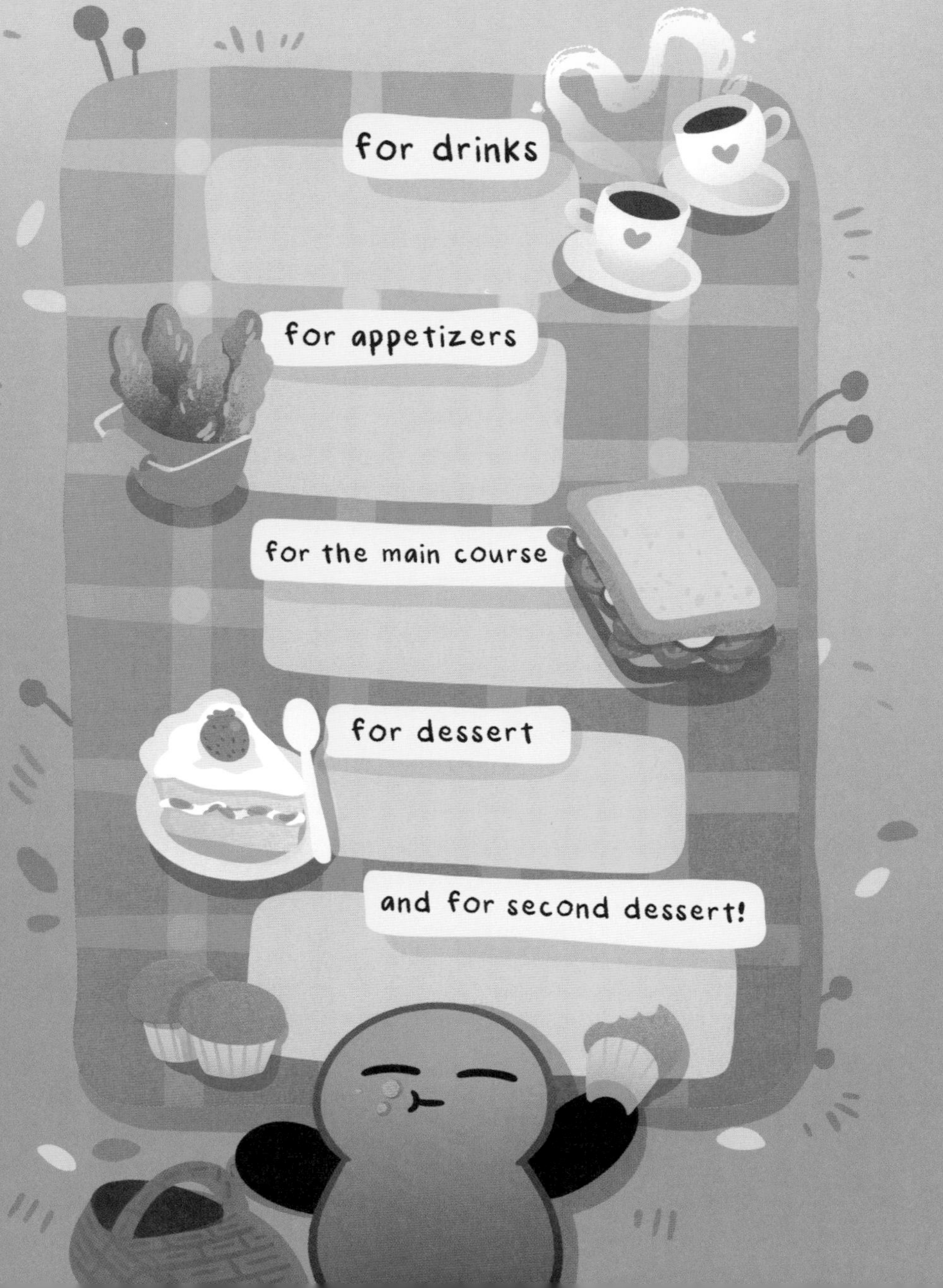
for drinks
for appetizers
for the main course
for dessert
and for second dessert!

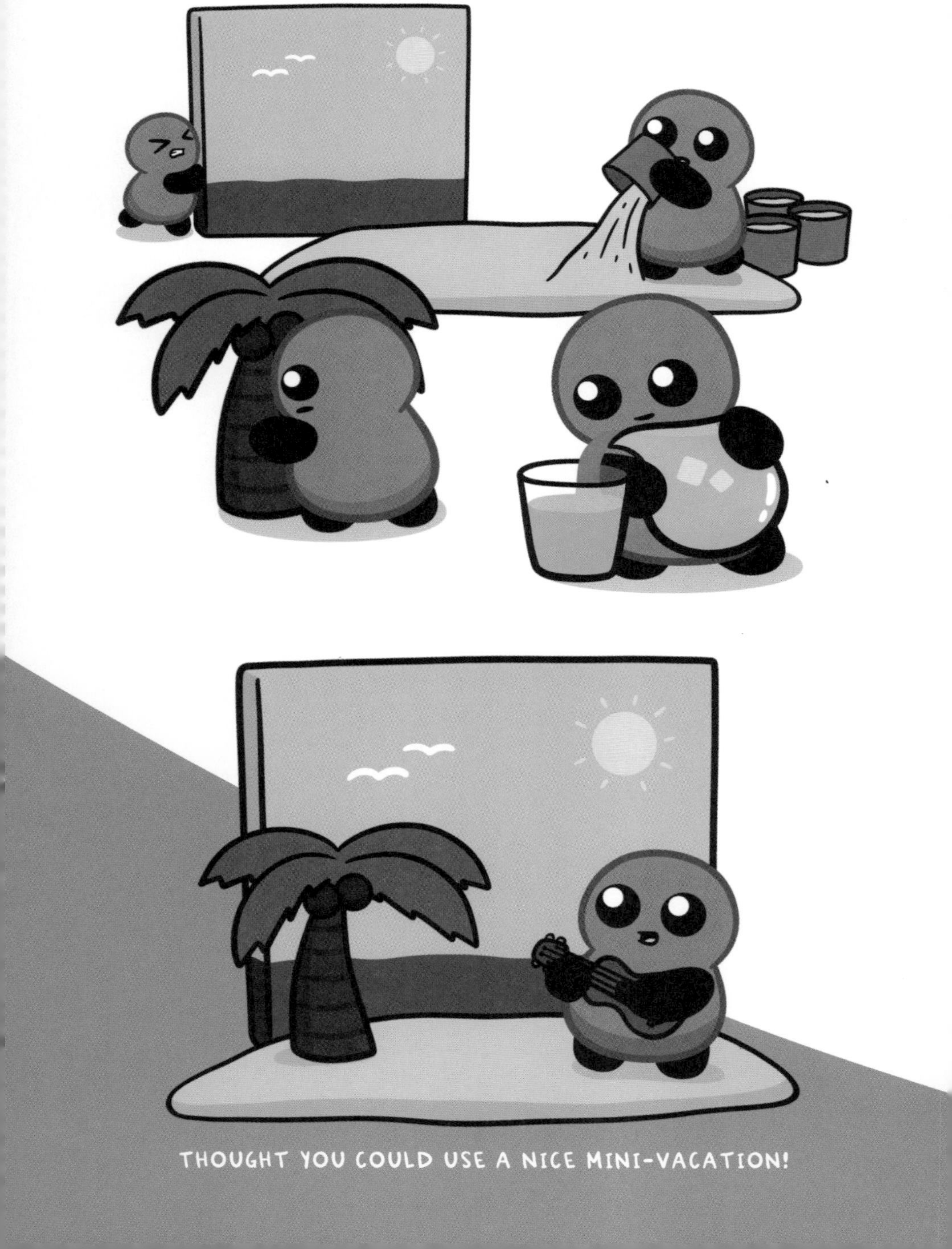

THOUGHT YOU COULD USE A NICE MINI-VACATION!

a mini-vacation we can take at home!

snacks:

_____

_____

_____

_____

activities:

_____

_____

BOOKS
I THINK
YOU
WOULD
LOVE
& WHY

TO

FROM

READY FOR THE NEXT CHAPTER?

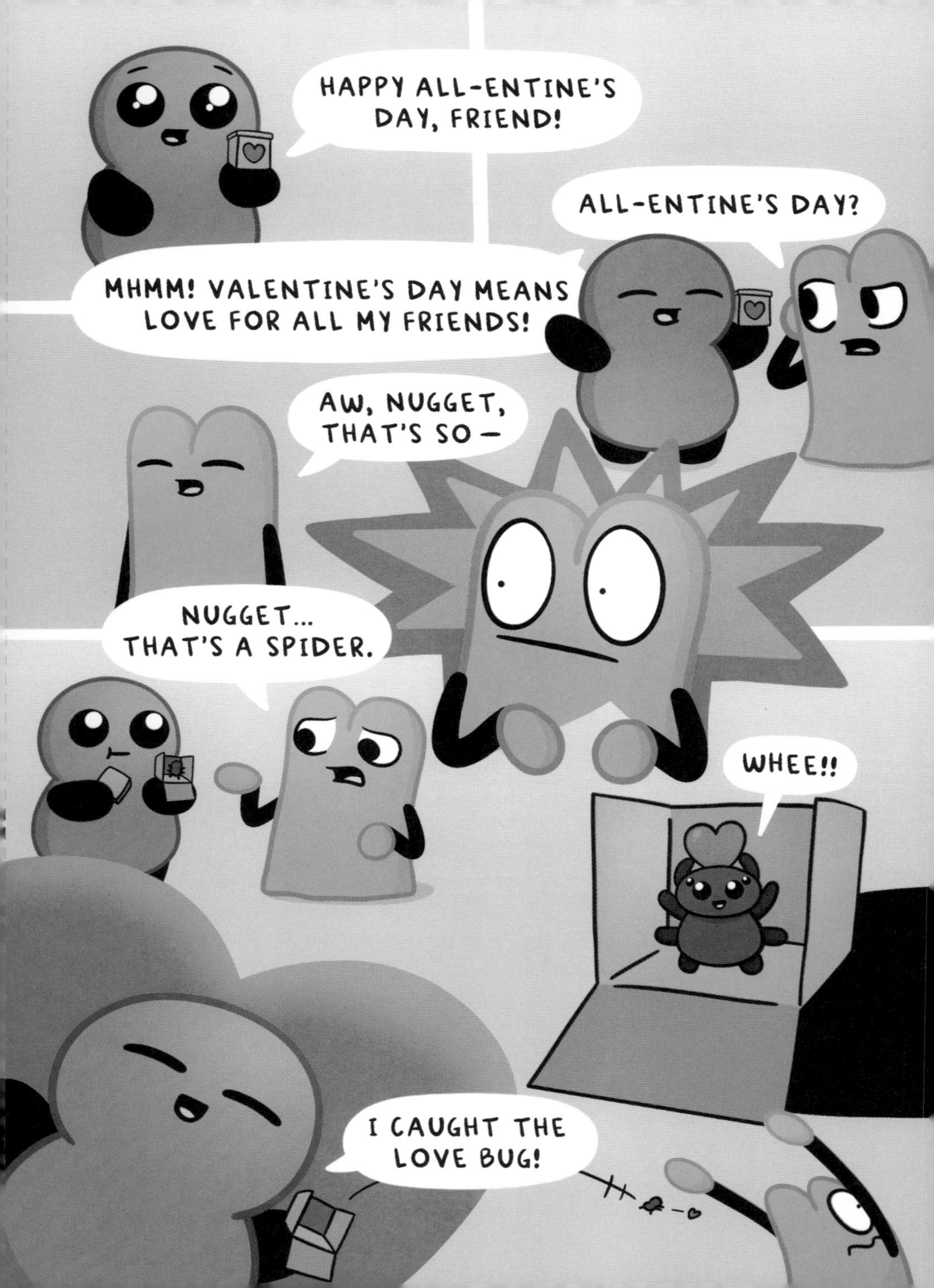
HAPPY ALL-ENTINE'S DAY, FRIEND!
ALL-ENTINE'S DAY?
MHMM! VALENTINE'S DAY MEANS LOVE FOR ALL MY FRIENDS!
AW, NUGGET, THAT'S SO—
NUGGET... THAT'S A SPIDER.
WHEE!!
I CAUGHT THE LOVE BUG!

THE LOVE BUG ACTUALLY HAS A
MESSAGE FOR YOU — FROM ME!

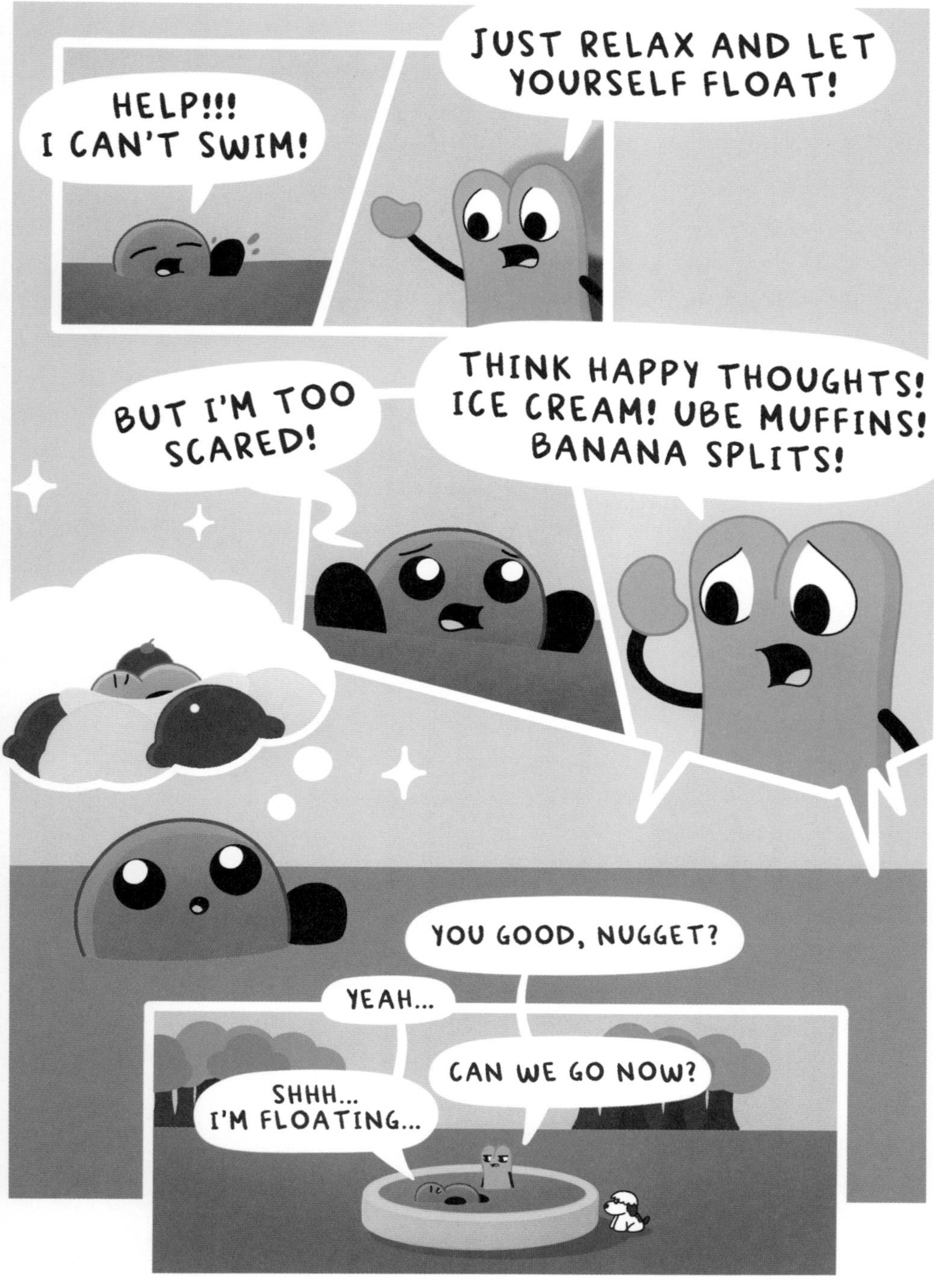
HELP!!! I CAN'T SWIM!
JUST RELAX AND LET YOURSELF FLOAT!
BUT I'M TOO SCARED!
THINK HAPPY THOUGHTS! ICE CREAM! UBE MUFFINS! BANANA SPLITS!
YOU GOOD, NUGGET?
YEAH...
CAN WE GO NOW?
SHHH... I'M FLOATING...

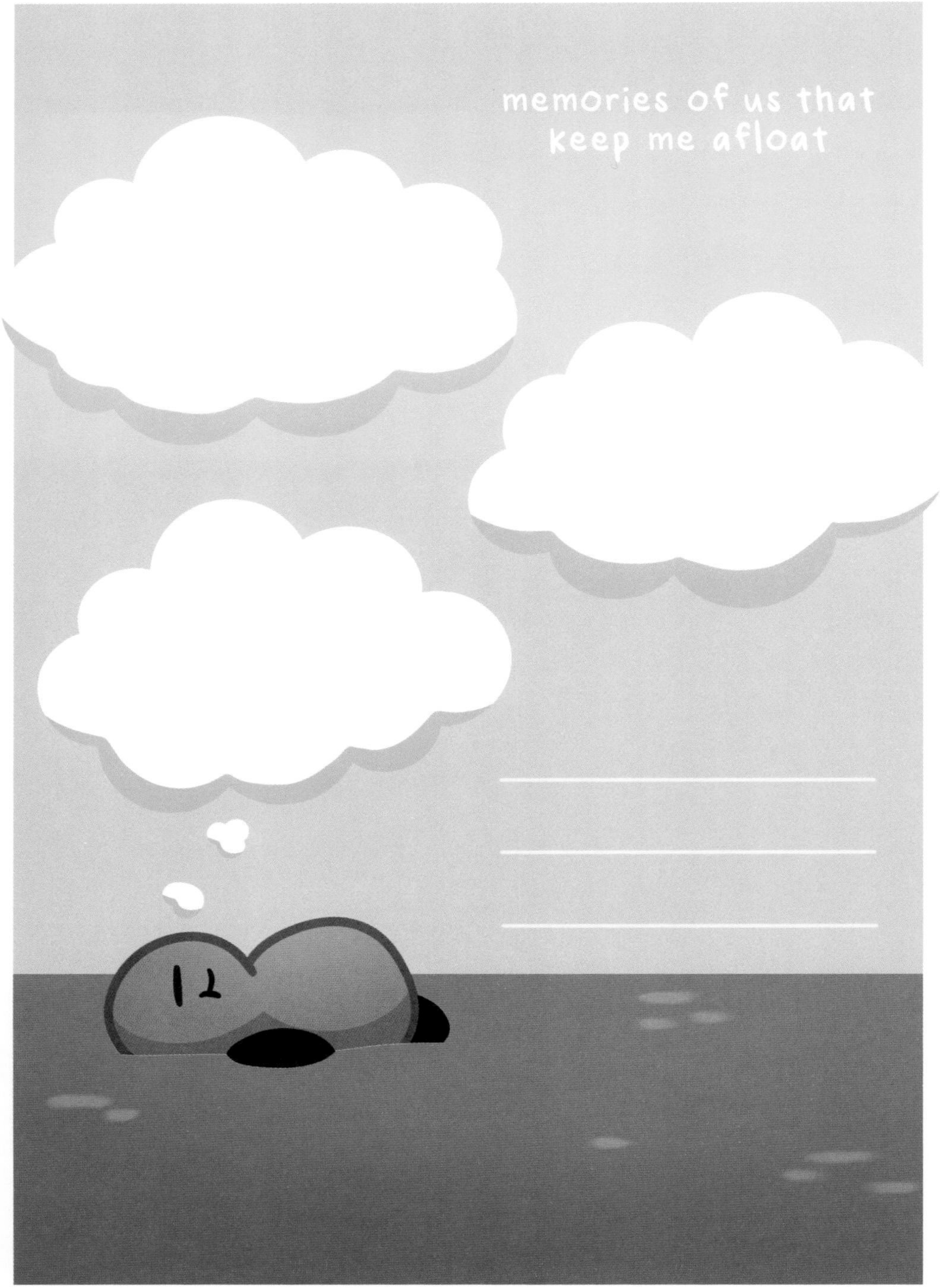
memories of us that keep me afloat

IF WE WERE NUGGETS

OUR FAVORITE...

SNACKS

ACTIVITIES

SPECIAL SKILLS

HI! I'M
_ _ _ _ _ _

AND I'M
_ _ _ _ _ _

TO

FROM

NUGGETS ASSEMBLE!

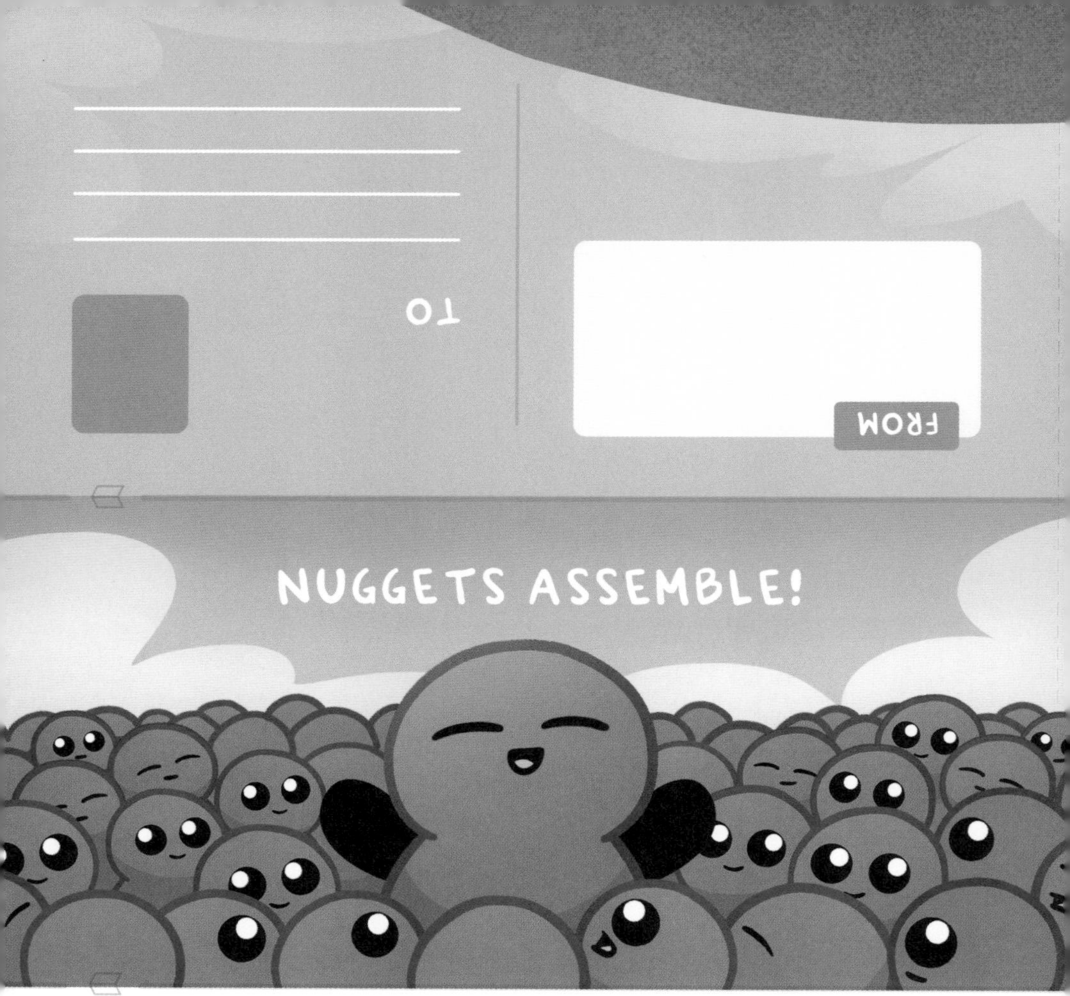

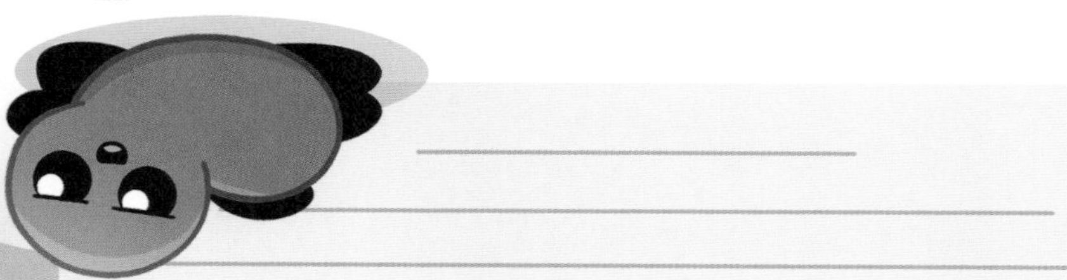

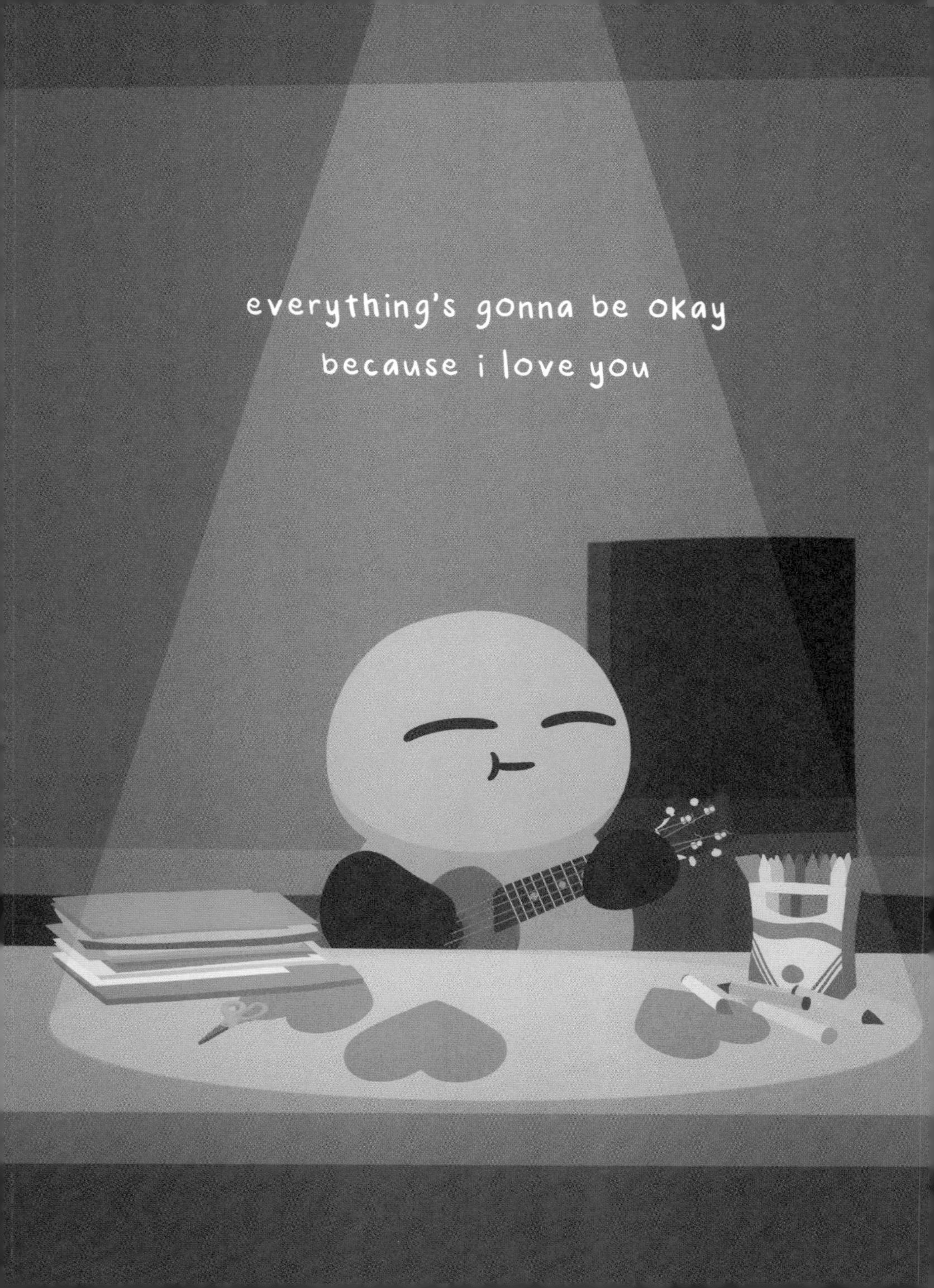
everything's gonna be okay
because i love you

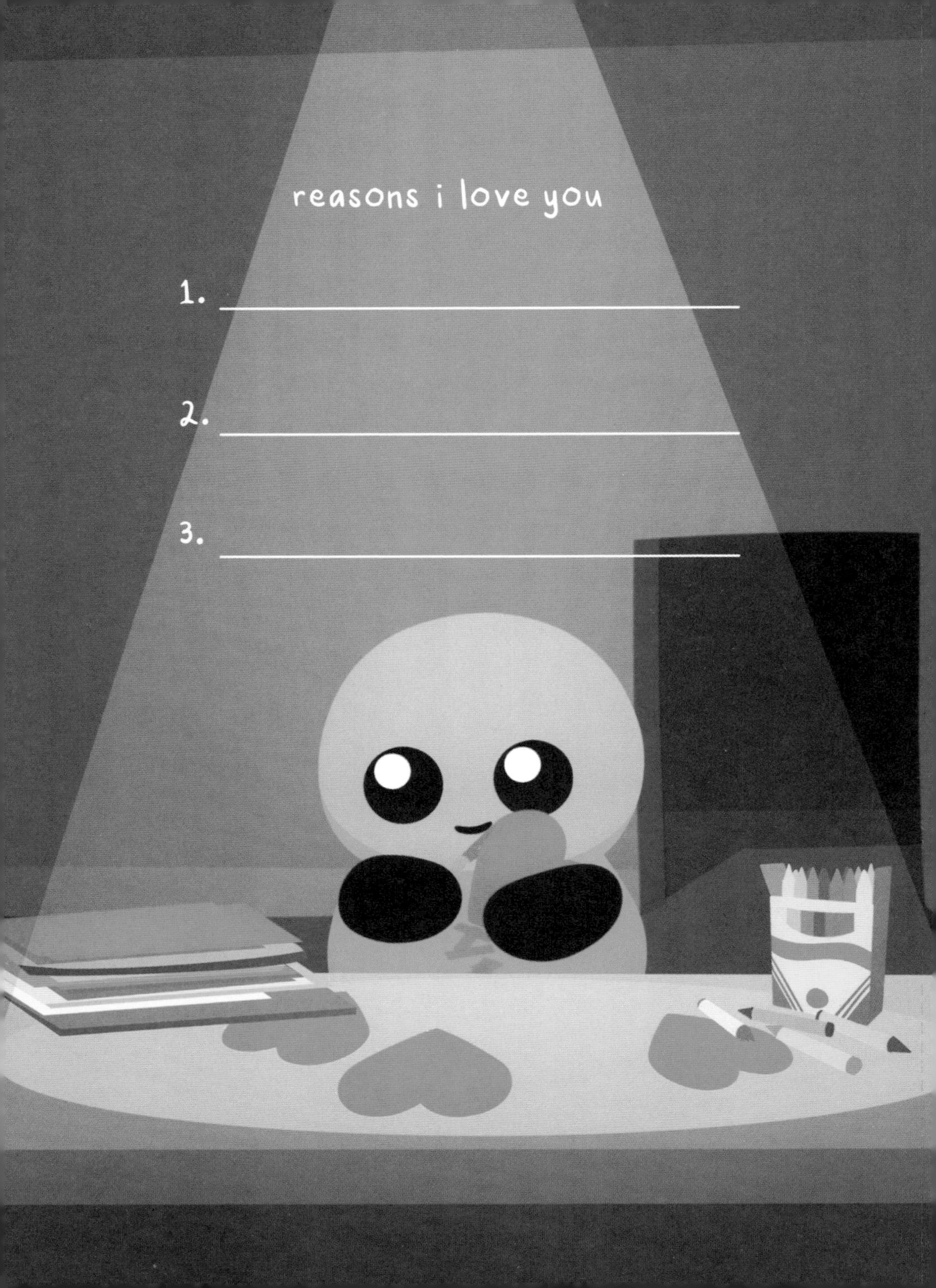
reasons i love you
1.
2.
3.

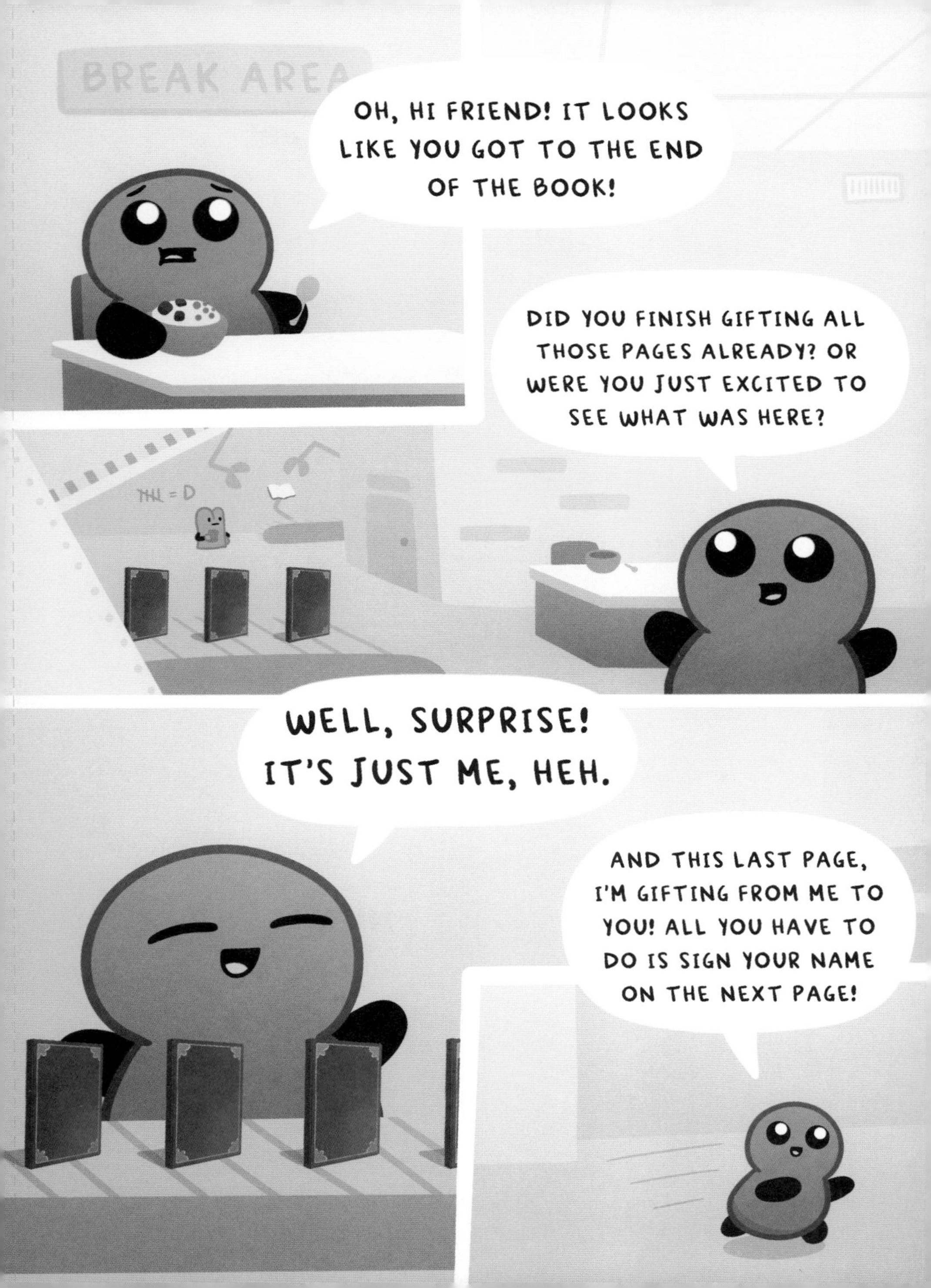
BREAK AREA
OH, HI FRIEND! IT LOOKS LIKE YOU GOT TO THE END OF THE BOOK!
DID YOU FINISH GIFTING ALL THOSE PAGES ALREADY? OR WERE YOU JUST EXCITED TO SEE WHAT WAS HERE?
WELL, SURPRISE! IT'S JUST ME, HEH.
AND THIS LAST PAGE, I'M GIFTING FROM ME TO YOU! ALL YOU HAVE TO DO IS SIGN YOUR NAME ON THE NEXT PAGE!

I, _____, am a beloved friend of Tubby Nugget and did an amazing job of helping Tubby make lots of people's days with these pages.

This page will now be a reminder for me to go save some special days for myself — because I deserve all the love in the world, too!

A MESSAGE FROM JENINE AND JOSH

In 2016, Tubby Nugget was a source of great joy just between the two of us during hard or otherwise busy times. Now, we feel so fortunate that Tubby spreads love to millions of others – the same way he's done for us for years.

Thank you so much for buying this book, and for believing in our little friend. We hope it allows you to spread the same kind of love, laughter, and nuggety moments we've been able to share together online for the last few years.

We can't wait to share more stories with you!

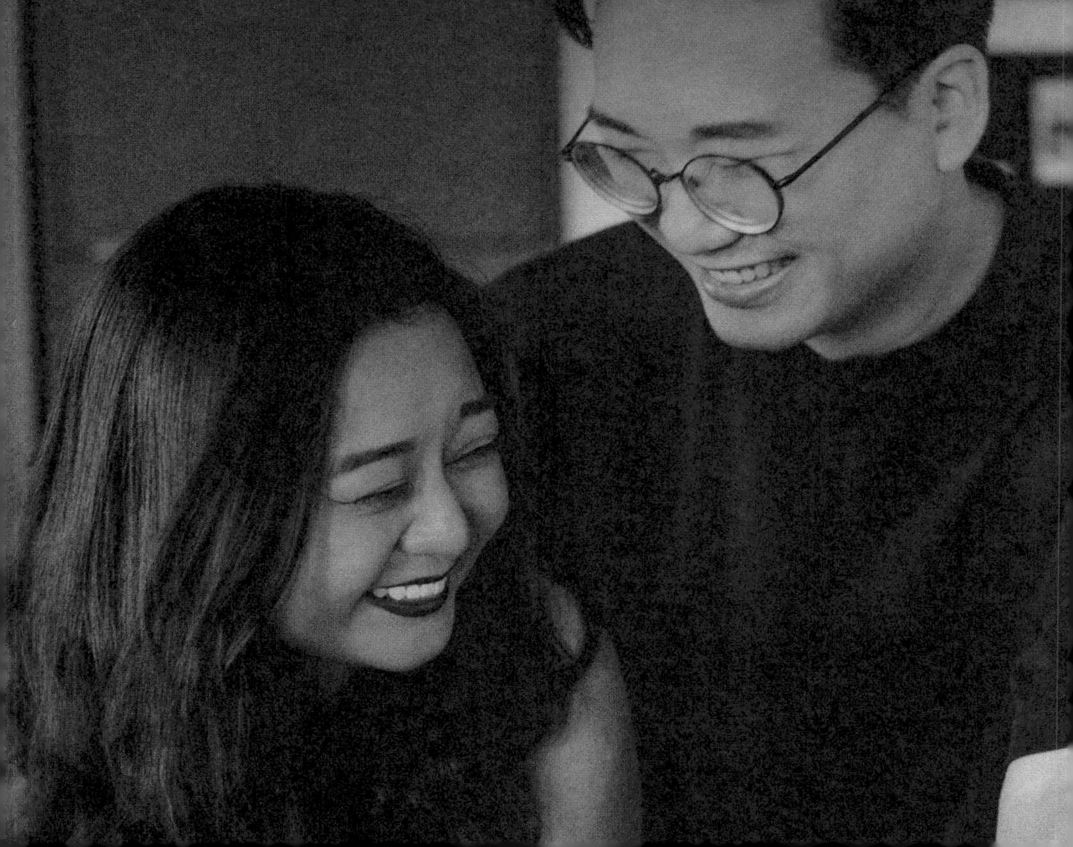

THE NUGGET ALPHABET

HOW TO WRITE IN NUGGET

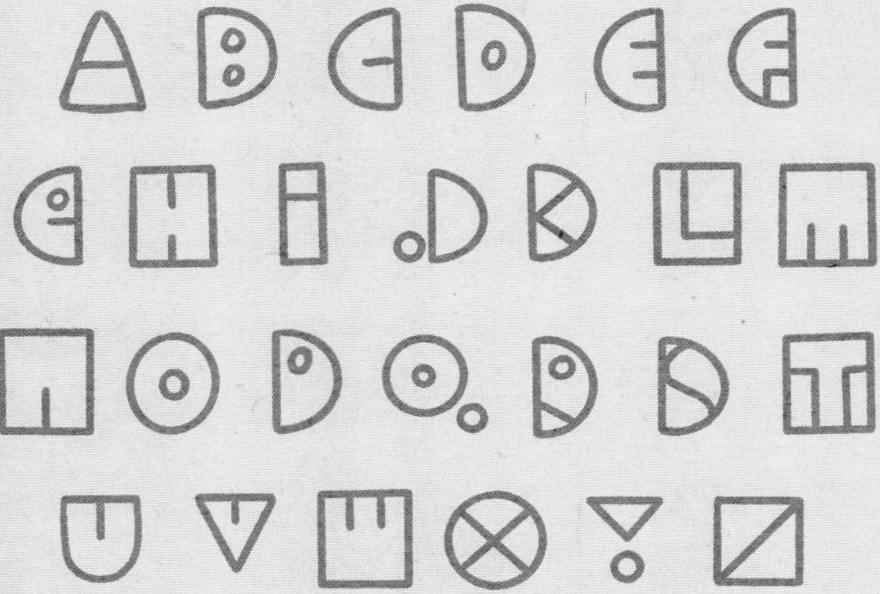

HELLO FRIEND! THANK YOU FOR LETTING ME PLAY SUCH A BIG PART IN SHARING YOUR LOVE FOR OTHERS. IT'S PEOPLE LIKE YOU WHO'VE MADE EARTH FEEL LIKE SUCH A BEAUTIFUL HOME. WITHOUT PEOPLE LIKE YOU SENDING ME SO MUCH LOVE IN RETURN, THIS BOOK WOULDN'T HAVE BEEN POSSIBLE!

I CAN'T WAIT TO TAKE YOU ON SO MANY MORE FUN ADVENTURES. I LOVE YOU!

LOVE, TUBBY NUGGET

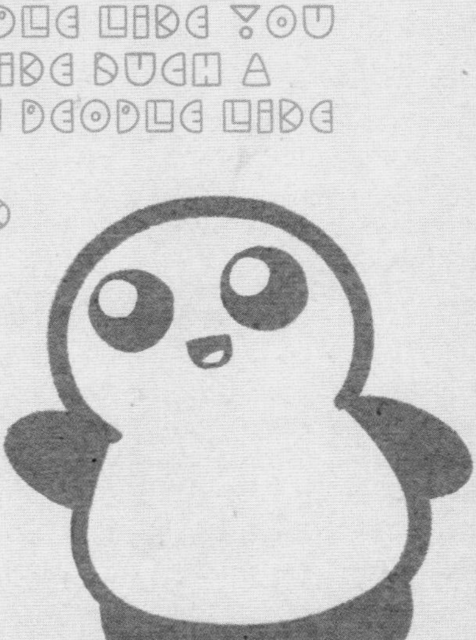